The Nature of School Bullying

The Nature of School Bullying provides a unique worldwide perspective on how different countries have conceptualized the issue of school bullying, how the media have covered the topic, what information has been gathered, and what interventions have been carried out.

Including systematic reports from Scandinavia, England, Scotland and all the major western European countries, the USA and Canada, Japan, Australia and New Zealand, and the developing world, each chapter is written by a leading expert in the country concerned. Each chapter provides a country overview to set the research in context; a discussion of how bullying has been described in that society; the research undertaken; and, where appropriate, the nature and success of anti-bullying interventions.

The book provides an authoritative resource for anyone interested in ways in which this problem is being tackled on a global scale. It allows the reader to make comparisons of the similarities and differences in each country's definitions and approaches, and gives an important historical and cultural context often missing in this area. *The Nature of School Bullying* will be invaluable for teachers, educational policy makers and researchers interested in this vital issue which affects the happiness and well-being of a substantial minority of schoolchildren.

Peter K. Smith is Professor of Psychology at Goldsmiths College, University of London. His previous ten books include *School Bullying: Insights and Perspectives* (edited with Sonia Sharp, 1994) and *Tackling Bullying in Your School* (edited with Sonia Sharp, 1994). **Yohji Morita** is at Osaka City University, Japan; **Josine Junger-Tas** is at the University of Leiden, The Netherlands; **Dan Olweus** is at the Research Centre for Health Promotion in Bergen, Norway; **Richard F. Catalano** is at Developmental Research and Programs, Seattle, USA; and **Phillip Slee** is at Flinders University, Australia.

The Nature of School Bullying

A cross-national perspective

Edited by P. K. Smith, Y. Morita,
J. Junger-Tas, D. Olweus,
R. Catalano and P. Slee

London and New York

First published 1999
by Routledge
11 New Fetter Lane, London EC4P 4EE

Simultaneously published in the USA and Canada
by Routledge
29 West 35th Street, New York, NY 10001

Reprinted 2000

Routledge is a member of the Taylor & Francis Group

Typeset in Goudy by The Florence Group, Stoodleigh, Devon
Printed and bound in Great Britain by TJ International Ltd, Padstow, Cornwall

British Library Cataloguing in Publication Data
A catalogue record for this book is available from the British Library

Library of Congress Cataloging in Publication Data
The nature of school bullying : a cross-national perspective / edited by P. K. Smith ... [et al.].
Includes bibliographical references and index.
1. Bullying–Cross-cultural studies. 2. School discipline–Cross-cultural studies. 3. Aggressiveness (Psychology) in children–Cross-cultural studies. I. Smith, Peter K.
LB3011.5.N38 1998
371.5′8–dc21 98–24527

ISBN 0–415–17984–X (hbk)
ISBN 0–415–17985–8 (pbk)

Contents

Illustrations

Figures

Tables

Contributors

Ana Maria Tomás de Almeida, Instituto de Estudos da Criança, Universidade do Minho, Avenida Central 100, 4700 Braga, Portugal.

Françoise D. Alsaker, University of Berne, Mussmattstrasse 45, 3000 Bern 9, Switzerland.

Dario Bacchini, Dipartimento di Neuroscienze e della Comunicazione Interumana, Universita di Napoli, via Pansini 5, Napoli 80131, Italy.

Kaj Björkqvist, Department of Social Sciences, Åbo Akademi University, Vasa, Finland.

Thomas Bliesener, Department of Psychology, University of Erlangen-Nuremberg, Bismarckstrasse 1, 91054 Erlangen, Germany.

Silvia Bonino, Dipartimento di Psicologia, Universita di Torino, via Lagrange 3, 10123 Torino, Italy.

Andreas Brunner, University of Berne, Mussmattstrasse 45, 3000 Bern 9, Switzerland.

Brendan Byrne, De La Salle College, Churchtown, Dublin 14, Ireland.

Richard F. Catalano, Departmental Research and Programs, 130 Nickerson, Suite 107, Seattle, WA 98109, USA.

Angela Costabile, Dipartimento di Scienze dell'Educazione, Universita della Calabria, 87030 Arcavacata di Rende (CS), Italy.

Niels Dueholm, Undervisnings Ministeriet, Folkeskoleafdelingen, Frederiksholms Kanal 26, 1220 København K, Denmark.

Jean-Claude Emin, Ministère de l'Education Nationale, Direction de l'Enseignement Scolaire, 107 rue de Grenelle, 75007 Paris, France.

Dominique Fabre-Cornali, Ministère de l'Education Nationale, Direction de la Programmation et des Développements, 3–5 Bvd Pasteur, 75015 Paris, France.

Ada Fonzi, Dipartimento di Psicologia, Universita di Firenze, via San Niccolo 93, 50125 Firenze, Italy.

Maria Luisa Genta, Dipartimento di Psicologia, Universita di Bologna, viale Berti-Pichat 5, Bologna 40137, Italy.

Tracy W. Harachi, Social Development Research Group, School of Social Work, University of Washington, Box 359106, Seattle, WA 98195, USA.

J. David Hawkins, Developmental Research and Programs, 130 Nickerson, Suite 107, Seattle, WA 98109, USA.

Andrzej Janowski, Higher School for Special Education, Szczesliwicka 40, 02–353 Warsaw, Poland.

Josine Junger-Tas, Criminological Institute, Hugo de Grootstraat 27, University of Leiden, 2311 XK Leiden, The Netherlands.

Friedrich Lösel, Department of Psychology, University of Erlangen-Nuremberg, Bismarckstrasse 1, 91054 Erlangen, Germany.

Andrew Mellor, Dalry School, St John's Town of Dalry, Castle Douglas DG7 3UZ, Scotland.

Ersilia Menesini, Dipartimento di Psicologia della Sviluppo e della Socializzazione, Universita di Padova, via Venezia 8, Padova 35131, Italy.

Joaquin A. Mora-Merchan, Departamento de Psicologia, EU Trabajo Social, c/o Dr Cantero Cuadrado 6 Universidade de Huelva, 21004 Huelva, Spain.

Yohji Morita, Department of Sociology, Osaka City University, 3–3–138 Sugimoto, Sumiyoshi-ku, Osaka 558–8585, Japan.

Toshio Ohsako, UNESCO Institute for Education, Feldbrunnenstrasse 58, 20148 Hamburg, Germany.

Dan Olweus, Research Center for Health Promotion (HEMIL), Christies gate 13, University of Bergen, N-5015 Bergen, Norway.

Rosario Ortega, Departamento Psicologia Evolutiva y de la Educacion, Universidad de Sevilla, Avenida S. Francisco Javier s/n 41005 Sevilla, Spain.

Karin Österman, Department of Social Sciences, Åbo Akademi University, Vasa, Finland.

Jacques Pain, Université de Paris X, 200 Avenue de la République, Nanterre, 92001 Cedex, France.

Ken Rigby, Faculty of Humanities and Social Science, University of South Australia, Underdale Campus, Holbrooks Road, Underdale, Adelaide 5032, South Australia, Australia.

Phillip T. Slee, Department of Education, Flinders University, GPO Box 2100, Adelaide 5001, Australia.

Peter K. Smith, Department of Psychology, Goldsmiths College, University of London, New Cross, London SE14 6NW, England.

Haruo Soeda, Department of Education, Osaka City University, 3–3–138 Sugimoto, Sumiyoshi-ku, Osaka 558–8585, Japan.

Kumiko Soeda, Department of Education, Osaka City University, 3–3–138 Sugimoto, Sumiyoshi-ku, Osaka 558–8585, Japan.

Keith Sullivan, School of Education, Victoria University of Wellington, Box 600, Wellington, New Zealand.

Mitsuru Taki, National Institute for Educational Research, 6–5–22 Shimomeguro, Meguro-ku, Tokyo 153, Japan.

Nicole Vettenburg, Onderzoeksgroep Jeugdcriminologie, Hooverplein 10, 3000 Leuven, Belgium.

Acknowledgements

We are grateful to the Japanese Ministry of Education, Science, Sports and Culture (Monbusho) for the financial support which led to the production of this book, and to the UNESCO Institute for Education (Hamburg) and UNESCO International Bureau of Education (Geneva) for their contributions to this project. We would like to thank Shu Shu for compiling the indexes.

Introduction

Peter K. Smith and Yohji Morita

Bullying in schools is an international problem; so a book with a cross-national perspective, as this one has, should be useful to educationists, practitioners and researchers across the globe. We feel the time is ripe for such a book, since the research of the last 25 years has revealed much about the nature and extent of the problem, and has begun to show us ways towards if not its solution, at least its amelioration.

Bullying is a subcategory of aggressive behaviour; but a particularly vicious kind of aggressive behaviour, since it is directed, often repeatedly, towards a particular victim who is unable to defend himself or herself effectively. The victimised child may be outnumbered, or younger, less strong, or simply less psychologically confident. The bullying child or children exploit this opportunity to inflict harm, gaining either psychological gratification, status in their peer group, or at times direct financial gain by taking money or possessions.

This abuse of power by the bullying person(s) can happen in any human group. Human groups almost inevitably embody power relationships, and there will always be the temptation to abuse such power for the gains it may bring. Whether bullying does occur is likely to depend on the psychological make-up of the potential bully, the possible support or connivance of others in the group, the response of the potential victim, and the institutional framework which may or may not make bully/victim incidents more likely to happen.

Bullying is particularly likely in groups from which the potential victim cannot readily escape. Schools are such institutions, since schooling is normally compulsory and changing schools or being educated at home are not easy alternatives. Of course, bullying can happen in other settings. There is now much concern about bullying in prisons and of young people in juvenile offenders' institutions, and bullying in the workplace has become a salient topic in a number of countries. Bullying can also happen in the home, although here it tends to be referred to (in English-speaking countries) as abuse.

This book is concerned about bullying in schools; and mainly about peer–peer bullying, although teacher–pupil bullying gets some mention. The research of the last 25 years has shown that pupil bullying in schools is widespread wherever there is institutionalised schooling; moreover, despite some cultural differences, many of the broad features are similar across different countries. For example, there are characteristic sex differences, with boys using and experiencing more physical means of bullying, and girls using and experiencing more indirect or relational means. Another commonly found characteristic is that many victims of bullying do not tell anyone, or seek help; too often, this is seen as despicable by the peer group, even sometimes by adults. Although bullying goes by different names in different languages, these and other common structural features suggest a shared reality and hold some promise of a shared search for solutions.

Although there were isolated studies of bullying before the 1970s (and it is certainly mentioned in novels), the systematic study of the phenomenon dates from the 1970s. Dan Olweus's book *Aggression in the schools: Bullies and whipping boys* (1978; original Swedish version 1973) marks the opening of a stream of research – now certainly a river – which developed first in the Scandinavian countries, especially Sweden, Norway and Finland. It is perhaps not surprising that these countries, with their generally high standard of living, peaceful nature, and concern for human rights and liberties, should have been at the forefront of bringing bullying to the attention of the educational and scientific community, and starting to remove the 'culture of silence' which for too long had cloaked the activities of those who bullied others.

In the 1980s, there was also – and rather independently – considerable interest in Japan, in the topic of *Ijime*, a concept similar (though not identical) to bullying. In the later 1980s this interest declined, but it has resurfaced strongly in the mid-1990s.

Meanwhile, other European countries also took up the issue. In part, this followed a European conference in Stavanger in 1987; and in part, the news of the success of the national intervention campaign against bullying in Norway (as carried out and monitored in Bergen by Olweus). It was perhaps taken up most vigorously in England and Wales, and Scotland, with an intervention project in England modelled in part on the Bergen project and evaluation in the early 1990s. But many other countries have now carried out surveys and started examining interventions. Outside Europe there has been particular interest in Canada and the USA, and in Australia and New Zealand.

The development of this research front would be a topic in itself worthy of study. After a slow beginning, it seems to have been fuelled in part by tragic events – the suicides of children and young people who have been bullied extensively at school and have been unable to cope. Suicides played a major part in inspiring the Norwegian intervention campaign, and a major part in the resurgence of interest in Japan.

Another factor has been media interest. It has been the experience of many researchers that some survey findings on bullying can, especially at certain times, trigger a remarkable spate of newspaper reports and television programmes. This certainly happened in England in 1989, and has happened in other countries. This may occur independently of suicides, although obviously the latter sustain a lot of media coverage, as in Japan in 1994/95. The media, probably quite rightly, judge that school bullying is likely to be a topic of concern to many readers and viewers – particularly parents of school-age children, who will make up a significant proportion of the population.

It appears to be a combination of sound research and media interest (sometimes combined with critical events such as suicides) which leads to governmental response and opportunities for funding and intervention work. Research on its own may just gather dust on library shelves; media interest on its own may just generate temporary concerns lacking a knowledge base for action. But an encouraging phenomenon for us, as researchers, has been how at times this combination of research and concerned publicity (even if at times sensationalised) can lead to resources being devoted to tackle the problem seriously. Furthermore, as several of the contributions in this book show, school-based interventions can make a difference. The combination of knowledge-based and resource-funded interventions can reduce levels of bullying, and improve the lives of many pupils. We still have more to learn about this, but we are undoubtedly making progress in applying our knowledge with success.

This book can be seen as an endeavour in this direction. It brings together 22 chapters; 21 of these represent different country reports. Each author was given a common brief: to first set the scene with an outline of their country and its school system; to discuss the terms used to describe bullying in their language, and the history of interest in the topic; to review the research done on bullying, such as surveys of its nature and extent; and to pay particular attention to any monitored interventions, their nature and their effects. By and large, authors have followed these guidelines. Thus we have a unique and comprehensive view of the development of this research front, and its status in the late 1990s, across the globe. The final chapter summarises some studies from the developing world; here, research is less systematic, and the problems of bullying are often compounded by other socioeconomic and political problems affecting these countries, including sometimes civil violence.

The inspiration for this book came from a cross-national study on bullying, funded by the Japanese Ministry of Education, Science, Sports and Culture and coordinated by Yohji Morita. As a first step, country reports on bullying were gathered across the globe, with the editors of this volume being responsible for particular countries: Peter Smith for England and Wales, Scotland, Italy, Spain and Portugal; Yohji Morita for Japan; Josiane Junger-Tas for France, Belgium, The Netherlands and Switzerland; Dan Olweus for Norway, Sweden, Denmark, Finland, Germany and Ireland; Richard Catalano for the USA and Canada; and Phillip Slee for Australia and New Zealand. In addition, Toshio Ohsako oversaw the contribution from Poland, and produced the report on developing countries.

Yohji Morita coordinated a similarly edited volume to this one (but not totally identical) in Japanese, published as *School Bullying around the World: Challenges and Interventions* by Kaneko Shobou. Peter Smith undertook to oversee the editing of this English-language version.

The cross-national study on bullying is continuing with comparative surveys on bullying in several countries – Japan, England, Norway, The Netherlands and the USA. Many other important developments are taking place, often described in this volume. As we move towards the millennium, we hope that this sharing of global knowledge and experience may play some part in helping to tackle what is clearly a global problem, and help to enhance the safety and rights of school pupils and the well-being and protection of those at risk of being victims of bullying.

London, England
Osaka, Japan
March 1998

Part I

Europe

1 Sweden

Dan Olweus

Geography, social and cultural background

Sweden is an elongated country and measures about 1600 kilometers from north to south. The northern part of the country, in particular the long area bordering on Norway, is mountainous and sparsely populated except for the coastal belt. A majority of the 8.8 million people residing in the country live in the southerly third, which also comprises the three largest cities of the country: Stockholm (about one million inhabitants), Göteborg, and Malmö. Overall, the country is fairly sparsely populated with about 20 inhabitants per square kilometer.

School system

Schooling in Sweden is compulsory from ages 7 (grade 1) through 16 (grade 9). As from 1 July 1997, it is the duty of the municipal authorities to provide places in school for all 6 year olds as well. Compulsory schooling also comprises Lapp nomad schools (for the ethnic minority of Lapp children in the northern part), special schools (for children with impaired vision, hearing, or speech), and compulsory schools for the intellectually handicapped. More than 90 percent of all students attending compulsory basic school go on to upper secondary school. Generally, Sweden's public sector school system is fairly similar to that of Norway, and the country reports on bully/victim problems in Sweden and Norway should be seen as complementary.

The great majority of schools in Sweden are municipal. Most children attend a municipal school near their homes, but students and their parents are entitled to opt for another municipal school or for an independent school. There are about 890,000 students attending compulsory basic schools; about 1 percent of them – some 10,000 students – attend one of the 200 or so independent schools. Teaching in independent schools can be based on a religious creed or on special educational principles, such as Montessori or Waldorf methods. About 15 percent of the students in compulsory basic schools are immigrants, in the sense that they have at least one non-native parent. These students represent more than 90 foreign languages.

Simultaneously with the introduction of a new curriculum and syllabi (in 1994), a new system of grades is being introduced. Under this system, grades are awarded on a three-point scale from the eighth school year. The grades are "Pass," "Pass with distinction," and "Pass with special distinction." The grades relate the students' achievement to the national objective stated in the syllabus for the subject. Students and their parents are to be given regular progress reports all through compulsory school. Starting in the fifth year of school, this information is to be verbal and written.

In compulsory schools, several classes are often joined together to form work units in which the teachers plan work jointly, often together with special teachers. These work units are usually the context in which student welfare activities are discussed, often with the support of special student welfare staff. This latter category may include the school social worker, the school psychologist, and the school nurse, among others.

The school or academic year normally begins at the end of August and ends early the following June, which makes a total of about 40 weeks (minus Christmas and Easter vacations comprising approximately three weeks). The school week is five days long, from Monday through Friday.

The beginning and some terminological distinctions: mobb(n)ing versus bullying

A strong societal interest in the general phenomenon of bully/victim problems was first aroused in Sweden in the late 1960s and early 1970s under the designation "mobbning" or "mobbing" (Heinemann, 1969, 1972; Olweus, 1973a). The term was introduced into the Swedish debate by a school physician, P.-P. Heinemann, in the context of racial discrimination. Heinemann had borrowed the term "mobbing" from the Swedish version of a book on aggression written by the ethologist Konrad Lorenz (1968). In ethology, the word mobbing is used to denote a collective attack by a group of animals on an animal of another species, which is usually larger and a natural enemy of the group. In Lorenz's book (1968), mobbing was also used to characterize the action of a school class or a group of soldiers ganging up against a deviating individual. Incidentally, it has been claimed (Lagerspetz, Björkqvist, Berts and King, 1982) that Lorenz himself never used the word "mobbing" in his German original (1963, 1966) and that the word in fact became introduced into the Swedish debate by Lorenz's Swedish translator Sverre Sjölander, himself an ethologist by profession.

In any case, the English expression "mob" has also been used for quite some time in social psychology, and to some extent by the general public in English-speaking countries, to denote a relatively large group of individuals – a crowd or a mass of people – joined in some kind of common activity or striving. As a rule, the mob has been formed by accident, is loosely organized, and exists only for a short time. In the social psychological literature, distinctions have been made between several types of mob, including the aggressive mob (the lynch mob), the panic-stricken mob (the flight mob), and the acquisitive mob. Finally, the members of the mob experience strong emotions, and the behavior and reactions of the mob are considered to be fairly irrational (see, for example, Lindzey, 1954).

Already at an early stage, I expressed doubts about the suitability of the term mobbing, as used in social psychology/ethology and by Heinemann, to denote the kind of peer harassment that presumably occurred in school settings (Olweus, 1973a, 1978, pp. 4–6). Generally, with my background in aggression research (e.g. Olweus, 1969), I felt that the connotations implied in the concept of mobbing (as described above) could easily lead to inappropriate expectations about the phenomenon and to certain aspects of the problem being overlooked.

One particular point of concern related to the relative importance of the group versus its individual members. The notion that school mobbing is a matter of collective aggression by a relatively homogeneous group did in my view obscure the relative contributions made by individual members. More specifically, the role of particularly active perpetrators or bullies could easily be lost sight of within such a conceptual framework. In this context, I also questioned how often the kind of all-against-one situations implied in mobbing actually occur in school. If harassment by a small group or by a single individual were the more frequent type in our schools, the concept of mobbing might result, for example, in teachers having difficulty noting the phenomenon right in front of their noses. In addition, the concept of mobbing will almost automatically place responsibility for "possible problems" with the recipient of the collective aggression, the victim, who is seen as irritating or provoking the majority of "normal" students in one way or another.

Use of the concept of mobbing might also lead to an overemphasis on temporary and situationally determined circumstances: "The mob, suddenly and unpredictably, seized by the mood of the moment, turns on a single individual, who for some reason or other has attracted the group's irritation and hostility" (Olweus, 1978, p. 5). Although such temporary emotional outbreaks from a group of children may occur, I considered it more important to direct attention to another kind of possible situation, in which an individual student is exposed to aggression systematically and over longer periods of time – whether from another individual, a small group, or a whole class (Olweus, 1973a, 1978, p. 5).

I think it is fair to say that research conducted in the 1970s and later (see, for example, Olweus, 1978, 1993a, 1994a; Farrington, 1993) has shown that these concerns were justified. For example, there is no doubt that students in a class vary markedly in their degree or level of aggressiveness and that these individual differences tend to be quite stable over time, often over several years (Olweus, 1977, 1978, 1979). Similarly, the research clearly shows that a relatively small number of students in a class are usually much more actively engaged in bullying than others, often the great majority of the students in the class, who are not involved in bullying at all or only in marginal roles. Data from our Bergen study (below) indicate that, in the majority of cases, the victim of bullying is harassed by a small group of two or three students, often with a negative leader. A considerable proportion of the victims, some 25–40 percent, report, however, that they are mainly bullied by a single student (Olweus, 1988).

The research-based picture of peer harassment in school is obviously a far cry from what is generally implied in the social psychological or ethological concepts of mobbing. In addition, the actual use of the term mobbing (and derivatives of it) by Scandinavians has certainly come to deviate from both the scientific and the ordinary English "root" meaning of the term. This is particularly evident when we hear a (Scandinavian) student saying "he/she mobbed me today," and also find (above) that about one-fourth or one-third of the students report being mobbed primarily by an individual student. Obviously, the word mobbing has gradually, and in part on the basis of highly publicized research findings, acquired a new meaning in Scandinavian everyday language, loosely implying relatively systematic, repetitive harassment of an individual (or possibly a group) by one or more other individuals (usually but not necessarily by a peer/peers). This new meaning of the word is now well established in Norway, Sweden, and Denmark, and there are of course no grounds for trying to change this usage.

At the same time it was clear at an early stage that, for an English-speaking audience, the terms mob and mobbing are not very useful in denoting the phenomenon of concern; they typically elicit associations in the direction of the social psychological/ethological concepts and the original meaning of the word mob. On the basis of experiences along these lines, I tended to use the term bully/victim (or whipping boy) problems (instead of, or in addition to, mobbing) in my early writings in English (e.g. Olweus, 1978). Nowadays, the terms "bullying," "bully/victim problems," and "victimization" seem to have gained general international acceptance (in English-speaking countries) to denote the kind of peer harassment we Scandinavians, somewhat inappropriately from a linguistic point of view, call mobbing.

Definition of bullying

With this discussion as a background, it is now appropriate to give a more stringent definition of the term bullying. I usually define school bullying or victimization in the following general way: *A student is being bullied or victimized when he or she is exposed, repeatedly and over time, to negative actions on the part of one or more other students*. It is a negative action when someone intentionally inflicts, or attempts to inflict, injury or discomfort upon another – basically what is implied in the definition of aggressive behavior (Olweus, 1973b; Berkowitz, 1993). Negative actions can be carried out by physical contact, by words, or in other ways, such as making faces or mean gestures, and intentional exclusion from a group. Although children or youths who engage in bullying very likely vary in their degree of awareness of how the bullying is perceived by the victim, most or all of them probably realize that their behavior is at least somewhat painful or unpleasant for the victim. (The ways in which this general definition of bullying has been "operationalized" in the Olweus student questionnaire on bully/victim problems are described in the country report on Norway, pp. 30–31, this volume.)

Even if a single instance of more serious harassment can be regarded as bullying under certain circumstances, the definition given above emphasizes negative actions that are carried out "repeatedly and over time." The intent is to exclude occasional non-serious negative actions that are directed against one person at one time and against another on a different occasion.

In order to use the term bullying, there should also be an *imbalance in strength* (an asymmetric power relationship): the student who is exposed to negative actions has difficulty in defending himself or herself and is somewhat helpless against the student or students who harass. The actual and/or perceived imbalance in strength or power may come about in several different ways. The target of bullying may actually be physically weaker, or may simply perceive himself or herself as physically or mentally weaker than the perpetrator(s); or there may be a difference in numbers, with several students ganging up on a single victim. A somewhat different kind of imbalance may be achieved, when the "source" of the negative actions is difficult to identify or confront as in social exclusion from the group, backtalking, or when a student is being sent anonymous mean notes. In line with this reasoning, we do not talk about bullying when there is a conflict or aggressive interchange between two persons of approximately the same physical or mental strength.

In this context, it is also natural to consider briefly the relationship between bullying and teasing. In the everyday social interactions among peers in school, there occurs a good deal of (also recurrent) teasing of a playful and relatively friendly nature – which in most cases cannot be considered bullying. On the other hand, when the repeated teasing is of a degrading and offensive character, and, in particular, is continued in spite of clear signs of distress or opposition on the part of the target, it certainly qualifies as bullying. Here it is thus important to try and distinguish between malignant and more friendly, playful teasing, although the line between them is sometimes blurred and the perception of the situation may to some extent depend on the perspective taken, that of the target or of the perpetrator(s).

In my definition, the phenomenon of bullying is thus characterized by the following three criteria: (1) It is aggressive behavior or intentional "harm doing" (2) which is carried out "repeatedly and over time" (3) in an interpersonal relationship characterized by an imbalance of power. One might add that the bullying behavior often occurs without apparent provocation. This definition makes it clear that bullying may be considered a form of abuse, and sometimes I use the term "peer abuse" as a label of the phenomenon. What sets it apart from other forms of abuse such as child abuse and wife abuse is the context in which it occurs and the relationship characteristics of the interacting parties.

It is useful to distinguish between *direct* bullying/victimization – with relatively open attacks on the victim – and *indirect* bullying/victimization in the form of social isolation and intentional exclusion from a group.

Aggression, violence, and bullying

As defined above, bullying is a subcategory of aggression or aggressive behavior, which in turn is generally defined as "behavior intended to inflict injury or discomfort upon another individual" (Olweus, 1973b; Berkowitz, 1993). Bullying is thus aggressive behavior with certain special characteristics such as repetitiveness and an asymmetric power relationship (the criteria listed above). This makes it clear that there is a good deal of aggressive behavior that is not bullying; for example, when there is conflict and aggressive interchange between two persons of approximately the same physical or mental strength, or when a person in a restaurant line verbally or physically attacks another person whom he has never met.

The terms violence and violent behavior are often used as roughly synonymous with aggressive behavior. In my view, this is unfortunate and "violence/violent behavior" should be defined as aggressive behavior where the actor or perpetrator uses his or her own body or an object (including a weapon) to inflict (relatively serious) injury or discomfort upon another individual. The dictionary meaning of violence is similar, implying use of physical force or power. It is also worth noting that the definition of violent offences in criminal law (including murder, homicide, aggravated assault, assault, robbery, and rape) is based on a closely related understanding. In similarity with bullying, violence is thus a subcategory of aggressive behavior but with its own special characteristics. What is then the relationship between violence and bullying?

The relationships among the three key terms of concern are graphically illustrated in the Venn diagram shown in Figure 1.1. Aggression/aggressive behavior is the general and overarching term (the area delineated by the large, outer circle), whereas both bullying and violence/violent behavior are subcategories of aggressive behavior (covering smaller areas within the large circle). As shown by the shaded area, there is also a certain overlap between violence and bullying. This area denotes situations in which bullying is carried out by physical means or contact (above), or expressed differently, when physical means are used in the context of bullying (e.g. hitting, kicking, shoving, etc. in situations where the general criteria of bullying are met). The diagram also makes it clear that there is a good deal of bullying without violence (e.g. bullying by words, gestures, intentional exclusion from the group, etc.) and, likewise, that there is a good deal of violence that cannot be characterized as bullying (e.g. an occasional fight in the playground, or a row over some trifle between unacquainted, drunk people in a restaurant queue).

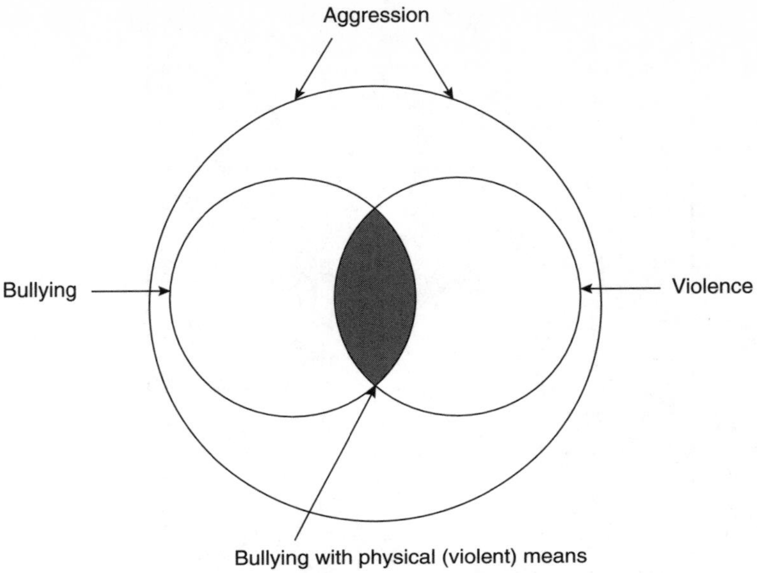

Figure 1.1 Venn diagram showing relationships among concepts of aggression, violence, and bullying.

Research on bullying

Overview of research projects

With this discussion of definitional or terminological issues as a backdrop, it is now natural to give a brief overview of the main empirical research projects on bullying that I have been involved with (so far). In the country report on Norway, I mention a number of results from the large-scale survey of Norwegian schools conducted in 1983 and from the intervention project in the schools of Bergen from 1983 through 1985. Some summary characteristics of these two projects are presented in Table 1.1, along with information on the parallel survey study conducted in Sweden in 1983.

However, my first project on bullying – which is generally regarded as the first systematic research project in the world on this theme – was already initiated in 1970 in Sweden (I am a native Swede, who has lived in Norway since the early 1970s; Olweus, 1973a, 1978). This longitudinal study, which is still continuing, comprises some 900 boys from Greater Stockholm. At the start of the project, the participants were in grades 6 through 8, but through registers and retrospective interviews with parents, a lot of information has been collected about the participants' childhood years as well

Table 1.1 An overview of research projects by Olweus

	Nationwide study in Norway (1983)	*Large-scale study in Sweden (1983–1984)*	*Intensive study in Bergen, Norway (1983–1985)*	*Study in Greater Stockholm, Sweden (1970–)*
Units of study	715 schools, grades 2–9 (130,000 boys and girls)	60 schools, grades 3–9 (17,000 boys and girls)	Four cohorts of 2500 boys and girls in grades 4–7 (1983); 300–400 teachers; 1000 parents	Three cohorts of boys (900 boys in all), originally in grades 6–8 (1973)
Number of measurement occasions	One	One	Several	Several
Measures include	Questionnaire on bully/victim problems (aggregated to grade and school level). Recruitment area of the school: population density; socioeconomic conditions; percentage of immigrants; school size; average class size; composition of staff	Questionnaire on bully/victim problems School size, average class size	Self-reports on bully/victim problems, aggression, antisocial behavior, anxiety, self-esteem, attachment to parents and peers, etc., grades, some peer ratings. Teacher data on characteristics of class, group climate, staff relations, etc.	Self-reports and reports by mothers on a number of dimensions. Peer ratings, teacher nominations, official records on criminal offences, drug abuse for subgroups; interviews on early child-rearing, hormonal data, psycho-physiological data

(for all students or certain subgroups). All participants have also been followed in the official crime registers, so far up to age 24. A number of different methods have been used in the study of these boys/young men.

Characteristics of typical victims

A good deal of information about the prevalence of bully/victim problems under various conditions is presented in the country report from Norway. These results were derived chiefly from the large-scale questionnaire surveys conducted in Norway and Sweden, and will not be duplicated here. However, the report on Norway does not provide much information on the characteristics of typical victims and bullies; this is done in the present context, since the first outline of the characteristics of (young male) bullies and victims was drawn on the basis of findings from the longitudinal Swedish project (Olweus, 1973a, 1978). The main results from this early study have been largely corroborated and extended by later research, either within our own projects or by other independent researchers.

A relatively clear picture of both the typical victims and the typical bullies has emerged from research (e.g. Björkqvist, Ekman and Lagerspetz, 1982; Boulton and Smith, 1994; Farrington, 1993; Lagerspetz, Björkqvist, Berts and King, 1982; Olweus, 1973a, 1978, 1981a, 1984, 1993a; Perry, Kusel and Perry, 1988). By and large, this picture seems to apply to both boys and girls, although it must be emphasized that less research has so far been done on bullying among girls.

The typical victims are more anxious and insecure than students in general. Further, they are often cautious, sensitive, and quiet. When attacked by other students, they commonly react by crying (at least in the lower grades) and withdrawal. In addition, victims suffer from low self-esteem, and they have a negative view of themselves and their situation. They often look upon themselves as failures and feel stupid, ashamed, and unattractive.

The victims are lonely and abandoned at school. As a rule, they do not have a single good friend in their class. They are not aggressive or teasing in their behavior, however, and accordingly, one cannot explain the bullying as a consequence of the victims themselves being provocative to their peers (see below). These children often have a negative attitude toward violence and use of violent means. If they are boys, they are likely to be physically weaker than boys in general (Olweus, 1978).

I have labeled this type of victim the *passive or submissive victim*, as opposed to the far less common type described below. In summary, it seems that the behavior and attitude of the passive/submissive victims signal to others that they are insecure and worthless individuals who will not retaliate if they are attacked or insulted. A slightly different way of describing the passive/submissive victims is to say that they are characterized by an anxious or submissive reaction pattern combined (in the case of boys) with physical weakness.

In-depth interviews with parents of victimized boys indicate that these boys were characterized by a certain cautiousness and sensitivity from an early age (Olweus, 1993b). Boys displaying such characteristics (perhaps combined with physical weakness) are likely to have had difficulty in asserting themselves in the peer group and may have been somewhat disliked by their age mates. There are thus good reasons to believe that these characteristics contributed to making them victims of bullying (see also Schwartz, Dodge and Coie, 1993). At the same time, it is obvious that the repeated harassment by peers must have considerably increased their anxiety, insecurity, and generally negative evaluation of themselves. In sum, the typical reaction patterns or personality traits characterizing children who have been identified as victims (and who, by definition, have been exposed to bullying for some time) are likely to be both a cause, and a consequence, of the bullying.

As mentioned earlier, there is also another, clearly smaller group of victims, the *provocative victims*, who are characterized by a combination of both anxious and aggressive reaction patterns. These students often have problems with concentration, and behave in ways that may cause irritation and tension for those around them. Some of these students may be characterized as hyperactive. It is not uncommon that their behavior provokes many students in the class, thus resulting in negative reactions from a large part of, or even the entire class. The dynamics of bully/victim problems in a class with provocative victims differ in part from problems in a class with passive victims (Olweus, 1978).

A follow-up study of two groups of boys (Olweus, 1993b) who had or had not been victimized by their peers in school (from grades 6 through 9) shows that the former victims had 'normalized' in many ways as young adults at age 23. This was seen as a consequence of the fact that the boys, after having left school, had considerably greater freedom to choose their own social and physical environments. In two respects, however, the former victims had fared much worse than their non-victimized peers: they were more likely to be depressed and had poorer self-esteem. The pattern of findings clearly suggested that this was a consequence of the earlier, persistent victimization which had left its mental scars on their minds.

Characteristics of typical bullies

A distinctive characteristic of typical bullies is their aggression toward peers – this is implied in the definition of a bully. But bullies are often aggressive toward adults as well, both teachers and parents. Generally, bullies have a more positive attitude toward violence than students in general. Further, they are often characterized by impulsivity and a strong need to dominate others. They have little empathy with victims of bullying. If they are boys, they are likely to be physically stronger than boys in general, and the victims in particular (Olweus, 1978).

A commonly held view among psychologists and psychiatrists is that individuals with an aggressive and tough behavior pattern are actually anxious and insecure "under the surface." The assumption that the bullies have an underlying insecurity has been tested in several of my own studies, also using "indirect" methods such as stress hormones (adrenaline and noradrenaline) and projective techniques. There was nothing in the results to support the common view, but rather pointed in the opposite direction: the bullies had unusually little anxiety and insecurity, or were roughly average on such dimensions (Olweus, 1981a, 1984, 1986; see also Pulkkinen and Tremblay, 1992). They did not suffer from poor self-esteem.

These conclusions apply to the bullies as a group (as compared with groups of control boys and victims). The results do not imply that there cannot be individual bullies who are both aggressive and anxious.

It should also be emphasized that there are students who participate in bullying but who do not usually take the initiative – these may be labeled *passive bullies*, *followers*, or *henchmen*. A group of passive bullies is likely to be fairly mixed and may also contain insecure and anxious students (Olweus, 1973a, 1978).

Several studies have found bullies to be of average or slightly below average popularity (Björkqvist, Ekman and Lagerspetz, 1982; Lagerspetz, Björkqvist, Berts and King, 1982; Olweus, 1973a, 1978; Pulkkinen and Tremblay, 1992). Bullies are often surrounded by a small group of two or three peers who support them and seem to like them (Cairns, Cairns, Neckerman, Gest and Gariépy, 1988). The popularity of the bullies decreases, however, in the higher grades and is considerably less than average in grade 9 (around age 16). Nevertheless, the bullies do not seem to reach the low level of popularity that characterizes the victims.

In summary, typical bullies can be described as having an aggressive reaction pattern combined (in the case of boys) with physical strength.

It should be noted that not all highly aggressive children or youths can be classified as bullies. In an as yet unpublished study of one of the Swedish cohorts, the boys belonging to the upper 15–20 percent of the distribution of peer ratings of aggressive behavior ('Start Fights' and 'Verbal Hurt' in grades 6–9; see Olweus, 1980) were examined as to whether they had been identified as bullies by their teachers (Olweus, 1978). Depending upon the cut-off point chosen, between 40 and 60 percent of the boys rated as "highly aggressive" were nominated as bullies by their teachers. Exploratory comparisons between the teacher-nominated bullies and the aggressive non-bullies suggested interesting differences. Because of their preliminary nature they will not be reported on here, but they clearly indicate the need for more detailed analyses of possible differences between students who are identified as bullies and other aggressive youngsters.

As regards the possible psychological sources underlying bullying behavior, the pattern of empirical findings suggests at least three, partly interrelated motives (in particular for male bullies who have so far been studied more extensively). First, the bullies have a strong need for power and dominance;

they seem to enjoy being "in control" and to subdue others. Second, considering the family conditions under which many of them have been reared (see below), it is natural to assume that they have developed a certain degree of hostility toward the environment; such feelings and impulses may make them derive satisfaction from inflicting injury and suffering upon other individuals. Finally, there is an "instrumental component" to their behavior. The bullies often coerce their victims to provide them with money, cigarettes, beer, and other things of value (see also Patterson, Littman and Bricker, 1967). In addition, it is obvious that aggressive behavior is in many situations rewarded with prestige (e.g. Bandura, 1973).

Bullying can also be viewed as a component of a more generally antisocial and rule-breaking ("conduct-disordered") behavior pattern. From this perspective, it is natural to predict that youngsters who are aggressive and bully others run a clearly increased risk of later engaging in other problem behaviors such as criminality and alcohol abuse. A number of studies confirm this general prediction (e.g. Loeber and Dishion, 1983; Magnusson, Stattin and Dunér, 1983).

My Swedish follow-up studies have also found strong support for this view. Approximately 60 percent of boys who were characterized as bullies in grades 6–9 (on the basis of a combination of teacher nominations and peer ratings) had been convicted of at least one officially registered crime by the age of 24. Even more dramatically, as many as 35–40 percent of the former bullies had three or more convictions by this age, while this was true of only 10 percent of the control boys (those who were neither bullies nor victims in grades 6–9). Thus, as young adults, the former school bullies had a fourfold increase in the level of relatively serious, recidivist criminality as documented in official crime records (Olweus, 1993a). It may be mentioned that the former victims had an average or somewhat below average level of criminality in young adulthood.

Development of an aggressive reaction pattern

In light of the characterization of the bullies as having an aggressive reaction pattern – that is, they display aggressive behavior in many situations – it becomes important to examine the question: What kind of rearing and other conditions during childhood are conducive to the development of an aggressive reaction pattern? Very briefly, the following four factors have been found to be particularly important (based chiefly on research with boys; for details, see Olweus, 1980; see also Loeber and Stouthamer-Loeber, 1986):

- The basic emotional attitude of the primary caretaker(s) toward the child during early years (usually the mother). A negative emotional attitude, characterized by lack of warmth and involvement, increases the risk that the child will later become aggressive and hostile toward others.

- Permissiveness for aggressive behavior by the child. If the primary caretaker is generally permissive and 'tolerant' without setting clear limits on aggressive behavior toward peers, siblings, and adults, the child's aggression level is likely to increase.
- Use of power-assertive child-rearing methods such as physical punishment and violent emotional outbursts. Children of parents who make frequent use of these methods are likely to become more aggressive than the average child. "Violence begets violence." We can summarize these results by stating that too little love and care and too much "freedom" in childhood are conditions that contribute strongly to the development of an aggressive reaction pattern.
- Finally, the temperament of the child. A child with an active and hotheaded temperament is more likely to develop into an aggressive youngster than a child with a quieter temperament. The effect of this factor is less powerful than those of the two first-mentioned conditions.

These are main trends. In individual cases, other factors such as the presence of an alcoholic and brutal father may have been of crucial importance, and the causal pattern may appear partly different.

The factors listed above can be assumed to be important for both younger and somewhat older children. For adolescents, it is also of great significance whether the parents supervise the children's activities outside the school reasonably well (Patterson, 1986; Patterson and Stouthamer-Loeber, 1984) and check on what they are doing and with whom.

It should also be pointed out that the aggression levels of the boys participating in the analyses above (Olweus, 1980) were not related to the socioeconomic conditions of their families such as parental income level, length of education, and social class. Similarly, there were no (or only very weak) relations between the four childhood factors discussed and the socioeconomic conditions of the family (Olweus, 1981a).

Some group mechanisms

In order to understand bullying, it is necessary to know the characteristics of students who are bullies and victims, respectively. We have already discussed several such characteristics that have been found to be important. But because bullying is often a group phenomenon, we will touch briefly on some mechanisms that may be assumed to be at work when several individuals take part in the bullying (see Olweus (1973a, 1978) for a more detailed discussion).

Many studies have shown that both children and adults may behave more aggressively after having observed someone else, a "model," acting aggressively. The effect will be stronger if the observer has a positive evaluation of the model, for example, perceives him/her as tough, fearless, and strong. These results can of course apply to a bully/victim situation – with the bully/bullies acting as the model. Those who are most strongly influenced by such model effects are probably students who are themselves somewhat insecure and dependent (passive bullies, henchmen), who do not have a natural status among their peers, and who would like to assert themselves. The term "social contagion" has been used for this type of effect.

Another and closely related mechanism is the weakening of the control or inhibitions against aggressive tendencies. The main principle here is that seeing a model getting "rewarded" for aggressive behavior tends to decrease the observer's own "inhibitions" (i.e. ordinary blocks and controls) against being aggressive. Conversely, negative consequences for the model often activate and strengthen inhibitory tendencies in the observer.

In a bully/victim situation, this mechanism can operate in the following way. The model (i.e. the bully, or the bullies) will usually be rewarded through his or her "victory" over the victim. In addition, as evident from the research presented earlier, there will only to a very limited degree be negative consequences for such behavior from teachers, parents, and peers. All of these factors combine to weaken the controls against aggressive tendencies in "neutral" students/observers and may contribute to their participation in bullying.

There is also a third factor that can contribute to an explanation of why certain students who are usually nice and non-aggressive sometimes participate in bullying without great misgivings: a decreased sense of individual responsibility. It is well known from social psychology that a person's sense of individual responsibility for a negative action such as bullying may be considerably reduced when several people participate. This "diffusion" or "dilution" of responsibility also results in fewer guilt feelings after the incident.

Finally, there may occur changes in fellow-students' perception of the victim over time. As a result of repeated attacks and degrading comments, the victim will gradually be perceived as a fairly worthless person who almost "begs to be beaten up" and who deserves to be harassed. Such changes in perception also contribute to a weakening of possible guilt feelings in the bullies.

A wider perspective on bully/victim problems

In the nationwide survey we have found broad differences in the extent of bully/victim problems among schools. In some schools the risk of being bullied was up to four or five times greater than in other schools within the same community.

More generally, such differences between schools or areas in the extent of bully/victim problems may be viewed as a reflection of the interplay between two sets of countervailing factors: some conditions tend to create or enhance bully/victim problems, whereas other factors have controlling or mitigating effects.

Among the bullying- or aggression-generating factors, poor childhood conditions in general and certain forms of child-rearing and family problems in particular are important. It is natural to postulate that schools with high levels of bullying are situated in areas where a relatively large proportion of children receive a less "satisfactory upbringing" and there are many family problems. A less satisfactory upbringing implies among other things that the child gets too little love, care, and supervision, and that the caretakers do not set clear limits to the child's behavior (above). Family problems can be conflict-filled interpersonal relationships between the parents, divorce, psychiatric illness, alcohol problems, etc.

The degree to which a school will manifest bully/victim problems is not only dependent on the amount of aggression-generating factors in the area, however; it is also largely contingent on the strength of the countervailing forces. The attitudes, routines, and behaviors of the school personnel, in particular the teachers, are certainly decisive factors in preventing and controlling bullying activities and in redirecting such behaviors into more socially acceptable channels. This generalization is supported, for example, by the finding of a clear negative correlation between teacher density during recess and amount of bully/victim problems in the Bergen study. In addition, the attitudes and behaviors of the students themselves, as well as of their parents, can in important ways reduce the probability or extent of bully/victim problems in the school. And in a situation where bullying problems already exist, it is obvious that the reactions of students who do not participate in bullying can have a major influence both on the short-term and long-term outcome of the situation (see more on appropriate countermeasures in the country report on Norway).

A question of fundamental democratic rights

The victims of bullying form a large group of students who have been to a great extent neglected by the school. We have shown that many of these youngsters are the targets of harassment for long periods of time, often for many years (Olweus, 1977, 1978). It does not require much imagination to understand what it is to go through the school years in a state of more or less permanent anxiety and insecurity and with poor self-esteem. It is not surprising that the victims' devaluation of themselves sometimes becomes so overwhelming that they see suicide as the only possible solution.

Bully/victim problems in school really concern some of our basic values and principles. For a long time, I have argued that it is *a fundamental democratic right for a child to feel safe in school and to be spared the oppression and repeated, intentional humiliation implied in bullying.* No student should be afraid of going to school for fear of being harassed or degraded, and no parent should need to worry about such things happening to his or her child.

As early as 1981, I proposed the introduction of a law against bullying at school (Olweus, 1981b). At that time, there was little political support for the idea. In 1994, however, this suggestion was followed up by the Swedish Parliament with a new school law article, including formulations that are very similar to those expressed above. In addition, the associated regulations place responsibility for realization of these goals, including development of an intervention program against bullying for the individual school, with the principal. As will be seen (below), the Children's Ombudsman has recently (1997) proposed that the legislation against bullying in school should be extended and sharpened.

Action, initiatives, and resource materials

General guidelines and strategies for dealing with bully/victim problems in school were discussed already in *Hackkycklingar och översittare* (Olweus, 1973a; Olweus, 1978). However, no systematic scientific evaluation of use of the Olweus core intervention program (Olweus, 1992, 1993), similar to that done in Norway (see country report on Norway, this volume), has been carried out in Sweden. It is well documented, however, that many Swedish schools and even whole communities have followed the general approach proposed by Olweus (1992, 1993a), with use of the (Swedish version of the) Olweus Bully/Victim Questionnaire (see pp. 30–31 and p. 40 in the country report on Norway, this volume) for registration of the level of problems in the school/community, arrangement of a school conference day on bullying, and subsequent intervention work at the school, class, and individual levels.

Another method for dealing with bully/victim problems has been proposed by Anatol Pikas (1975). It is differentiated into two variants, one called the Method of Suggestive Command and the other the Method of Shared Concern (1989). A slightly modified version of the Pikas methods, named the Farsta method, was proposed in the latter half of the 1980s by the teacher K. Ljungström (1989). Two central aspects of this method are that a special 'treatment team' or anti-bullying group consisting of between two and five adults (mostly teachers) is established at the individual school, and that the parents of the children/youths concerned are usually not informed of the problems, nor involved in the intervention work. The latter characteristic, which is also central to the work of Pikas, has turned out to be quite controversial – it may in fact be considered to conflict with the Swedish school law (Olweus, 1994b). No rigorous scientific evaluation of the effectiveness of these methods, as commonly used, has been undertaken so far.

The Pikas method was used with reportedly positive results in some schools in the recent Sheffield project in England (Smith and Sharp, 1994). It should be emphasized, however, that the use of the Pikas method in these schools was quite atypical in that it was part of an explicit whole-school policy against bullying, and that the parents of involved students were not barred from information or participation in the intervention work. In addition, the anti-bullying work in these schools comprised several other strategies, and, as evaluated, it is difficult to know to what extent the results were a consequence of the (modified) Pikas method or some other component or combination of components.

An extensive critique of the Farsta method, and thereby also the Pikas approach on which it is based, was presented in the Swedish *Lärartidningen* (The Teacher's Journal; Olweus, 1994b, 1994c) with a rebuttal by Ljungström (1994). In spite of these controversies and the lack of scientific evidence of their effectiveness, these methods have been used in many Swedish schools – often in a somewhat modified form.

From 1993 through 1996, the National Agency for Education (Skolverket), which has a supervisory role in regard to Swedish schools, has financially supported a number of local school projects aimed at preventing and counteracting bullying at school. The main object of this work has been to stimulate local initiatives in this area. The National Agency has published two documents on this work: "*Kränk mig inte . . .* " ("Do not abuse me . . . "; Skolverket, 1995), and *Perspektiv på mobbning* (Perspectives on bullying; Hägglund, 1996).

Several different perspectives on violence among youth are presented in a collection of relatively popular articles/chapters published under the title *Det obegripliga våldet* (The incomprehensible violence; Forskningsrådsnämnden, 1995). One of the articles (Stattin, 1995) reported on the relationship between bullying behavior and acts of street and other public violence among a large group of 8th graders (approximately 15 years old) in a medium-sized Swedish town. A substantial relationship was found between these two behavior categories, thereby confirming the previously reported finding of a close connection between bullying of peers and other antisocial and criminal behavior (Olweus, 1993a, and this volume, p. 18).

In the last few years, two extensive theses on bullying have also been published (Björk, 1995; Fors, 1994). Both reports are based on detailed analyses of a small number of case studies, and both apply a power perspective in attempting to describe and understand bullying behavior and bully/victim situations.

In recent years, several non-profit, parent associations working against bullying have been established. Their aim is generally to disseminate information about bully/victim problems and how to counteract them, and to support students and their families in situations involving such problems. An example of such an association is *Föreningen mot mobbning* (The Association Against Bullying – FMM).

Since the beginning of 1995, the Children's Ombudsman has had main responsibility for stimulating and coordinating efforts to counteract bullying among children and youth on the part of various authorities, and for raising public awareness of the problem. In order to elicit the reactions and viewpoints of the students themselves, in 1995 the Ombudsman invited some 50 percent of all 13 year olds in the country to write letters to the Ombudsman expressing their views of the problem and suggestions about how to work against it. More than 6000 letters were received, with over 200 suggestions of ways of counteracting bullying (Barnombudsmannen, 1996a). A major message in the letters (as interpreted by the Ombudsman) was that the adults at school do not see, or do not want to see, the bullying that goes on among the students. Another related message was that the students would like to have more involved adults at school, adults who care and dare see and interfere in bullying situations.

The Children's Ombudsman recently (1997) submitted a report to the government – *Blunda inte för mobbningen* (Don't shut your eyes to the bullying; Barnombudsmannen, 1997) – on its work and made a number of proposals to improve the situation. One of the key suggestions is that the obligations of the teachers and other school staff to counteract bullying at school should be made more stringent and imperative than what is stated in the formulations used in the school law (Education Act) and associated regulations of 1994 (SFS, 1994; Lpo94). Among other things, it is proposed that teachers and other staff have an obligation to actively try to prevent/counteract any attempt to inflict violence and abusive treatment. It is also proposed that those who work in school have a duty to report to the head teacher/principal all possible or suspected instances of bullying and violence, regardless of whether they do or do not have detailed knowledge of who is involved.

Another major proposal by the Children's Ombudsman concerns the training of teachers, both the basic training and further training of those who already work as teachers. It is strongly emphasized that knowledge of bully/victim problems and how to counteract and prevent such problems should be a required part of the curriculum of basic teacher training. It is also proposed that the government provide funds during a three-year period for intensive in-service training of teachers with the aim of enhancing their competence to detect, counteract, and prevent bully/victim problems.

Generally, the Children's Ombudsman emphasizes the importance of a closer cooperation among central and local authorities in their anti-bullying work in order to achieve effective and lasting results in school and elsewhere, including leisure centers and sports clubs. The Ombudsman has also compiled a useful booklet on available resource materials and possible lecturers (Barnombudsmannen, 1996b).

Conclusion

As in Norway, relevant authorities and departments in Sweden have taken bully/victim problems among children and youth seriously and engaged themselves, at least to some degree, in efforts to tackle the problem. A marked problem with the intervention efforts in Sweden, however, has been that they have not been systematic enough and that they typically have not been exposed to rigorous scientific evaluation, or any systematic evaluation at all. This has resulted in a proliferation of "approaches/methods" for dealing with bully/victim problems, often with grandiose claims about effectiveness but basically no scientific evidence to support the claims.

In my view, future work against bullying among children and youth would benefit susbstantially from having several of the Ombudsman's proposals realized – in particular those concerning a more stringent legislation and more effective training of teachers – and from more systematic use of research-based knowledge about the problems and how to counteract them.

Acknowledgments

The research program reported on in this chapter was supported by grants from the Research Council of Norway (NFR, NAVF), the Ministry of Children and Family Affairs (BFD), the William T. Grant Foundation, USA, the Johann Jacobs Foundation, Switzerland, and, in earlier phases, from the Swedish Delegation for Social Research (DSF), and the Norwegian Ministry of Education (KUD), which is gratefully acknowledged.

References

Bandura, A. (1973) *Aggression: A social learning analysis*. Englewood Cliffs, NJ: Prentice-Hall.

Barnombudsmannen (1996a) *Blunda inte för mobbningen – ungdommars idéer och förslag*.

Barnombudsmannen (1996b) *Blunda inte för mobbningen – tips på material och föreläsare*.

Barnombudsmannen (1997) *Blunda inte för mobbningen. BO:s rapport och förslag mot mobbning*.

Berkowitz, L. (1993) *Aggression: Its causes, consequences, and control*. New York: McGraw-Hill.

Björk, G. (1995) *Mobbning – ett spel om makt. Fyra fallstudier av mobbning i skolmiljö*. Göteborgs universitet, Institutionen för social arbete, Skriftserien 1995:5.

Björkqvist, K., Ekman, K. and Lagerspetz, K. (1982) Bullies and victims: Their ego picture, ideal ego picture and normative ego picture. *Scandinavian Journal of Psychology*, 23, 307–313.

Boulton, M.J. and Smith, P.K. (1994) Bully/victim problems among middle school children: Stability, self-perceived competence, and peer acceptance. *British Journal of Developmental Psychology*, 12, 315–329.

Cairns, R.B., Cairns, B.D., Neckerman, H.J., Gest, S.D. and Gariépy, J.L. (1988) Social networks and aggressive behavior: Peer support or peer rejection? *Developmental Psychology*, 24, 815–823.

Farrington, D. (1993) Understanding and preventing bullying. In M. Tonry (ed.), *Crime and justice: A review of research*, Vol. 17 (pp. 348–458). Chicago, Ill.: University of Chicago Press.

Fors, Z. (1994) *Makt, maktlöshet och mobbning*. Göteborg: Psykologiska institutionen, Göteborgs universitet.

Hägglund, S. (1996) *Perspektiv på mobbning*. Göteborg: Institutionen för pedagogik, Göteborgs universitet, rapport nr. 14.

Heinemann, P.-P. (1969) Apartheid. *Liberal Debatt*, 3–14.

Heinemann, P.-P. (1972) *Gruppvåld bland barn och vuxna*. Stockholm: Natur och kultur.

Lagerspetz, K.M., Björkqvist, K., Berts, M. and King, E. (1982) Group aggression among school children in three schools. *Scandinavian Journal of Psychology*, 23, 45–52.

Lindzey, G. (ed.) (1954) *Handbook of social psychology*, Vol. 1. Cambridge, MA: Addison-Wesley.

Ljungström, K. (1989) *Handledning till utbildningsprogrammet "Mobbing i skolan"*. Stockholm: Elevvårdsbyrån, Stockholms skolor.

Ljungström, K. (1994) Till försvar för Farstametoden. *Lärartidningen* (The Teacher's Journal), 14, 27.

Loeber, R. and Dishion, T. (1983) Early predictors of male delinquency: A review. *Psychological Bulletin*, 94, 69–99.

Loeber, R. and Stouthamer-Loeber, M. (1986) Family factors as correlates and predictors of conduct problems and juvenile delinquency. In M. Tonry and N. Morris (eds), *Crime and justice*, Vol. 7 (pp. 29–149). Chicago, Ill.: University of Chicago Press.

Lorenz, K. (1963) *Das sogenannte Böse*. Wien: Borotha-Schoeler.

Lorenz, K. (1966) *On aggression*. London: Methuen.

Lorenz, K. (1968) *Aggression: Dess bakgrund och natur*. Stockholm: Norstedt & söner.

Lpo94 (1994) *Läroplan för den obligatoriska skolan.*

Magnusson, D., Stattin, H. and Dunér, A. (1983) Aggression and criminality in a longitudinal perspective. In K.T. Van Dusen and S.A. Mednick (eds), *Prospective studies of crime and deliquency* (pp. 227–301). Boston, MA: Kluwer-Nijhoff.

Olweus, D. (1969) *Prediction of aggression*. Stockholm: Skandinaviska testförlaget.

Olweus, D. (1973a) *Hackkycklingar och översittare. Forskning om skolmobbning.* Stockholm: Almqvist & Wicksell.

Olweus, D. (1973b) Personality and aggression. In J.K. Cole and D.D. Jensen (eds), *Nebraska Symposium on Motivation 1972* (pp. 261–321). Lincoln: University of Nebraska Press.

Olweus, D. (1977) Aggression and peer acceptance in adolescent boys: Two short-term longitudinal studies of ratings. *Child Development*, 48, 1301–1313.

Olweus, D. (1978) *Aggression in the schools. Bullies and whipping boys*. Washington, DC: Hemisphere Press (Wiley).

Olweus, D. (1979) Stability of aggressive reaction patterns in males: A review. *Psychological Bulletin*, 86, 852–875.

Olweus, D. (1980) Familial and temperamental determinants of aggressive behavior in adolescent boys: A causal analysis. *Developmental Psychology*, 16, 644–660.

Olweus, D. (1981a) Bullying among school-boys. In N. Cantwell (ed.), *Children and violence* (pp. 97–131). Stockholm: Akademilitteratur.

Olweus, D. (1981b) Vad skapar aggressiva barn? In A.O. Telhaug and S.E. Vestre (eds), *Normkrise og oppdragelse* (pp. 67–82). Oslo: Didakta.

Olweus, D. (1984) Aggressors and their victims: Bullying at school. In N. Frude and H. Gault (eds), *Disruptive behavior in schools* (pp. 57–76). New York: Wiley.

Olweus, D. (1986) Aggression and hormones: Behavioral relationship with testosterone and adrenaline. In D. Olweus, J. Block and M. Radke-Yarrow (eds), *Development of antisocial and prosocial behavior* (pp. 51–72). New York: Academic Press.

Olweus, D. (1988) Vad menar man med termen mobbning? *Psykologtidningen*, 7, 9–10.

Olweus, D. (1992) *Mobbning i skolan: Vad vi vet och vad vi kan göra*. Stockholm: Almqvist &Wiksell.

Olweus, D. (1993a) *Bullying at school: What we know and what we can do*. Oxford, and Cambridge, MA: Blackwell Publishers. (This book has also been published in a number of other languages.)

Olweus, D. (1993b) Victimization by peers: Antecedents and long-term outcomes. In K.H. Rubin and J.B. Asendorf (eds), *Social withdrawal, inhibition, and shyness in childhood* (pp. 315–342). Hillsdale, NJ: Erlbaum.

Olweus, D. (1994a) Annotation: Bullying at school: Basic facts and effects of a school based intervention program. *Journal of Child Psychology and Psychiatry*, 35, 1171–1190.

Olweus, D. (1994b) Farstametoden – en olycka för svensk skola. *Lärartidningen* (The Teacher's Journal), 13, 22–23.

Olweus, D. (1994c) Farstametoden är otillräcklig. *Lärartidningen* (The Teacher's Journal), 16, 22.

Patterson, G.R. (1986) Performance models for antisocial boys. *American Psychologist*, 41, 432–444.

Patterson, G.R., Littman, R.A. and Bricker, W. (1967) Assertive behavior in children: A step toward a theory of aggression. *Monographs of the Society for Research in Child Development*, 32, 1–43.

Patterson, G.R. and Stouthamer-Loeber, M. (1984) The correlation of family management practices and delinquency. *Child Development*, 55, 1299–1307.

Perry, D.G., Kusel, S.J. and Perry, L.C. (1988) Victims of peer aggression. *Developmental Psychology*, 24, 807–814.

Pikas, A. (1975) *Så stoppar vi mobbning*. Stockholm: Prisma.

Pikas, A. (1989) A pure concept of mobbing gives the best results for treatment. *School Psychology International*, 10, 95–104.

Pulkkinen, L. and Tremblay, R.E. (1992) Patterns of boys' social adjustment in two cultures and at different ages: A longitudinal perspective. *International Journal of Behavioral Development*, 15, 527–553.

Schwartz, D., Dodge, K. and Coie, J. (1993) The emergence of chronic peer victimization in boys' play groups. *Child Development*, 64, 1755–1772.

SFS (1994) *Svensk forfattningssam king.*

Skolverket (1995) *"Kränk mig inte . . . ". Att förebygga, upptäcka och åtgärda mobbning.* Värnamo: Fälths Tryckeri AB.

Smith, P.K. and Sharp, S. (eds) (1994) *School bullying: Insights and perspectives*. London: Routledge.

Stattin, H. (1995) Våld bland 15-åringar i en svensk stad. In Forskningsrådsnämnden (ed.), *Det obegripliga våldet* (pp. 29–39). Stockholm: Forskningsrådsnämnden, Källa 46.

2 Norway

Dan Olweus

Geographic, social, and cultural background

Mainland Norway measures about 1800 kilometers from north to south. Thousands of islands are scattered along the coast, which is deeply indented by fjords. Most of the interior is covered by mountains and plateaus. The country is sparsely populated with about 4.3 million inhabitants, corresponding to an average of thirteen people per square kilometer. The country is usually regarded as a "welfare state" and, in comparison with many other western countries, the socioeconomic differences in the population are relatively limited.

The school system

Schooling is compulsory from 7 years (grade 1) to 16 years (grade 9), comprising the primary (grades 1 through 6) and the lower secondary school grades (grades 7 through 9). From the academic year 1997–1998, 6 year olds will also be part of the primary school system and the grade notation will change correspondingly (grades 1 through 10). After age 16, a large proportion of the students – some 95 percent – continue with a three-year upper secondary education, either in the form of general education or vocational training. The educational level of the Norwegian population has risen considerably in recent years. In 1970, 30 percent had upper secondary or higher education; in 1992, this figure was more than 60 percent.

There are about 480,000 students at the primary and lower secondary school levels. Some 1500 of these belong to the Sami culture (in the northern part of the country), an ethnic minority with its own language and culture. In addition, there is a relatively small group of some 21,000 immigrant children, representing about 75 different language groups but less than 5 percent of the total school population. The majority of immigrant children are to be found in the three largest cities of the country: Oslo (about 500,000 inhabitants), Bergen, and Trondheim.

The overwhelming majority of the schools in Norway are state schools. Only 1.5 percent of primary and lower secondary students attend private schools which are usually seen as a supplement to state schools rather than as competitors.

Since Norway has a scattered population, many of the primary and even lower secondary schools are quite small, with fewer than 100 students. In fact, almost half of the primary schools have so few students that children from different grades are taught together in the same classroom ("one-room schools"). The maximum number of students in one class is 28 at primary level and 30 at lower secondary level. However, due to the large number of small schools, the actual number of students per class is often much smaller. In 1990–1991, the average number of students per class was eighteen for primary schools and 22 for the lower secondary level.

The buildings for primary and lower secondary schools are usually separate, but some 15 percent of the schools are "combined" schools covering all grades from 1 through 9.

In primary school there are no examinations and no marks, but the school is obliged to inform the parents at least twice a year about a child's progress. At the end of grade 9, there is a school leaving examination. Generally, the aim of compulsory education is not only to impart knowledge and academic skills, but also to promote personal and social development (see also Kallestad and Olweus, in press).

The school year is 38 weeks, or 190 days. The school week is five days long and each lesson typically lasts for 45 minutes. Between the lessons there is a ten-minute break. However, the lunch break in the middle of the day is 30 minutes (the students bring their own food, usually consisting of sandwiches). The teachers are supposed to supervise the students during break periods.

The early phase in Norway

As described in the country report for Sweden (Olweus, Chapter 1, this volume), a strong societal interest in bully/victim problems was first aroused in Sweden in the late 1960s and early 1970s. The interest quickly spread to the other Scandinavian countries, Norway and Denmark. In the 1970s and early 1980s, bully/victim problems were an issue of general concern in Norwegian mass media and among teachers and parents, but the school authorities did not engage themselves officially with the phenomenon. In 1982–1983 a marked change took place.

In late 1982, a newspaper reported that three 10–14-year-old boys from the northern part of Norway had committed suicide, in all probability as a consequence of severe bullying by peers. This event aroused considerable uneasiness and tension in the mass media and the general public. It triggered a chain of reactions, the end result of which was a nationwide campaign against bully/victim problems in Norwegian primary and lower secondary schools (grades 1–9), launched by the Ministry of Education in the fall of 1983.

The public interest in bullying decreased somewhat in the late 1980s, but in the 1990s the topic has again become a high-priority area. This will become evident when I briefly describe some recent initiatives and developments later in the chapter.

"Questionnaire definition" of bullying

Being a member of a small committee appointed by the Ministry of Education to plan for and organize the nationwide campaign against bullying, I was fortunate in being able to persuade the political leadership of the Ministry that they should also provide financial support for research in connection with the campaign. Among other things, I was given responsibility for conducting a nationwide questionnaire survey of bully/victim problems in a large sample of schools.

Although some questionnaire studies had been carried out in the 1970s in both Sweden and Norway, these were of a very preliminary nature, usually with small sample sizes and no clear definition of what was meant by bullying. In addition, they were often conducted by undergraduate students with little supervision from more experienced researchers. Accordingly, a key step in carrying out the survey involved the development of a new questionnaire for the measurement of various aspects of bully/victim problems. (In my Swedish study from the early 1970s, bully/victim problems were identified through teacher assessments, peer ratings, or a combination of both; although a number of questionnaires were included in the project, they were mainly used as "dependent variables" or correlates of bully/victim problems; see Olweus, 1973, 1978.)

The resulting questionnaire, which was filled out anonymously by the students and could be administered by teachers, differed from previous questionnaires in this area in a number of respects, including the following:

- It provided a "definition" of bullying so as to give the students a clear understanding of what they were to respond to.
- It referred to a specific time period (a "reference period").
- Several of the response alternatives were fairly specific, such as "about once a week" and "several times a week," in contrast to alternatives like "often" and "very often" which lend themselves to more subjective interpretation.
- It included questions about the others' reactions to bullying, as perceived by the respondents; that is, the reactions and attitudes of peers, teachers, and parents.

One important step was to develop a "definition" that could be easily understood by the students, while at the same time being true to a scientific definition of bullying. The formulation presented in the student questionnaire was the following:

> We say a student is *being bullied* when another student, or a group of students, say nasty and unpleasant things to him or her. It is also bullying when a student is hit, kicked, threatened, locked inside a room, and things like that. These things may take place frequently and it is difficult for the student being bullied to defend himself or herself. It is also bullying when a student is teased repeatedly in a negative way. But it is *not bullying* when two students of about the same strength quarrel or fight.

As can be seen, this formulation tries to capture the three basic criteria of bullying, as spelled out in the country report from Sweden and elsewhere (Olweus, this volume; Olweus, 1993, 1994a): (a) It is aggressive behavior or intentional "harm doing" (b) which is carried out "repeatedly and over time" (c) in an interpersonal relationship characterized by an imbalance of power.

In the recently revised version of the Olweus Bully/Victim Questionnaire, the definition has been slightly expanded to include more explicit forms of bullying or aggression that are used particularly by girls (cf., for example, Björkqvist, 1994; Björkqvist, Lagerspetz and Kaukiainen, 1992; Crick and Grotpeter, 1995). I also believed it was important to clarify further when *teasing* could be considered bullying or not. The resulting definition and many of the questions in the revised Olweus questionnaire are used in the cross-national research project on bullying of which the present country reports form a part. The somewhat expanded definition, which is presented to the students in a slightly different format, reads as follows:

> We say *a student is being bullied when another student, or a group of students*
>
> - say mean and unpleasant things or make fun of him or her or call him or her mean and hurtful names
> - completely ignore or exclude him or her from their group of friends or leave him or her out of things on purpose
> - hit, kick, push and shove around, or threaten him or her
> - tell lies or false rumors about him or her or send mean notes and try to make other students dislike him or her
> - and things like that.
>
> These things may take place frequently and it is *difficult for the student being bullied to defend himself or herself*. It is also bullying when a student is teased repeatedly in a negative and hurtful way.
>
> But we *don't call it bullying* when the teasing is made in a friendly and playful way. Also, it is *not bullying* when two students of about the same strength or power argue or fight.

Research on prevalence and characteristics

Some findings from the nationwide survey

In connection with the nationwide campaign, all primary and junior high schools in Norway were invited to take the Olweus Bully/Victim Questionnaire (1983 version). We estimate that approximately 85 percent actually participated. For closer analyses I selected representative samples of some 830 schools and obtained valid data from 715 of them, comprising approximately 130,000 students from all over Norway. These samples constitute almost a quarter of the whole student population in the relevant age range (approximately 8 to 16; first-grade students did not participate, since they did not have sufficient reading and writing ability to answer the questionnaire). This set of data gives good estimates of the frequency of bully/victim problems in different school forms, in different grades, in boys as compared with girls, etc.

On the basis of this large-scale survey, one can estimate that some 15 percent of the students in primary and lower secondary (junior high) schools (grades 1–9, roughly corresponding to ages 7 through 16) in Norway were involved in bully/victim problems with some regularity – either as bullies or victims (Olweus, 1985, 1987, 1991, 1992a, 1993). This figure corresponds to 84,000 students (fall 1983). Approximately 9 percent, or 52,000 students, were victims, and 7 percent, or 41,000, bullied other students regularly. Some 9000 students were both victim and bully (1.6 percent of the total of 568,000 students or 17 percent of the victims). A total of some 5 percent of the students were involved in more serious bullying problems (as bullies or victims or bully/victim), occurring "about once a week" or more frequently.

With regard to the validity of self-reports on variables related to bully/victim problems, in the early Swedish studies (Olweus, 1978) composites of three to five self-report items on being bullied or bullying and attacking others, respectively, correlated in the .40–.60 range (Pearson correlations) with reliable peer ratings on related dimensions (Olweus, 1977). Similarly, Perry, Kusel and Perry (1988) reported a correlation of .42 between a self-report scale of three victimization items and a reliable measure of peer nominations of victimization in elementary schoolchildren. In the intervention study (below), we also found class-aggregated student rating estimates of the number of students in the class who were bullied or who bullied others during the reference period to be highly correlated with class-aggregated estimates derived from the students' own reports of being bullied or bullying others: correlations were in the .60–.70 range (see Olweus, 1991, for details).

Analyses of parallel teacher nominations in approximately 90 classes (Olweus, 1987) also suggest that these results do not give an exaggerated picture of the prevalence of bully/victim problems. Indeed, as both the student and the teacher questionnaires refer only to part of the fall term, there is little doubt that the figures actually underestimate the number of students who are involved in such problems during a whole year.

It is apparent, then, that bullying was (and still is, according to more recent and less comprehensive surveys) a considerable problem in Norwegian schools and affects a very large number of students. Data from other countries (in large measure collected with the Olweus Bully/Victim Questionnaire) such as Sweden (Olweus, 1992b), Finland (Lagerspetz, Björkqvist, Berts and King, 1982), the UK (Smith, 1991; Whitney and Smith, 1993), USA (Perry, Kusel and Perry, 1988), Canada (Ziegler and Rosenstein-Manner, 1991), The Netherlands (Haeselager and van Lieshout, 1992; Junger, 1990), Japan (Hirano, 1992), Ireland (O'Moore and Brendan, 1989), Spain (Ruiz, 1992), and Australia (Rigby and Slee, 1990), have convincingly shown that the problem certainly also exists outside Norway and with similar or higher prevalence rates. It should be emphasized in this context that national differences in level must be interpreted with great caution, since student responses may be affected by such factors as the availability in the foreign language of appropriate words for the key terms, familiarity with the concept of bullying in the relevant culture, degree of public attention to the phenomenon, etc.

Bully/victim problems in different grades

As seen in Figure 2.1, the percentage of students who reported being bullied decreased with higher grades. It was the younger and weaker students who were most exposed. With regard to the ways in which the bullying was carried out, there was a clear trend toward less use of physical means (physical violence) in the higher grades. It was also found that a considerable amount

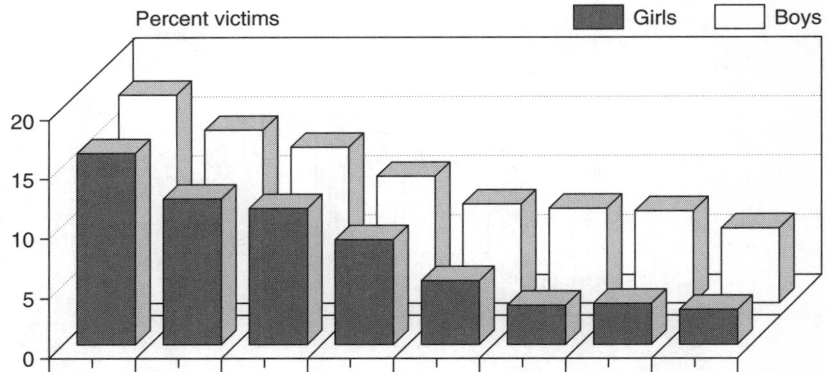

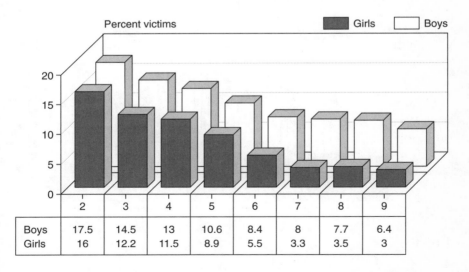

	2	3	4	5	6	7	8	9
Boys	17.5	14.5	13	10.6	8.4	8	7.7	6.4
Girls	16	12.2	11.5	8.9	5.5	3.3	3.5	3

Figure 2.1 Percentage of students in different grades who reported being bullied (being exposed to direct bullying) (n for boys = 42,390; n for girls = 40,940).

of the bullying was carried out by older students. This was particularly marked in the lower grades: more than 50 percent of the bullied children in the lowest grades (2 and 3, correponding to ages 8 and 9 in this survey) reported that they were bullied by older students.

It is natural to invoke the latter finding at least as a partial explanation of the form of the curves in Figure 2.1. The younger the students are, the more potential bullies they have above them; accordingly, an inverse relationship between percentage of victims and grade level seems reasonable. It may also be the case that the form of the curves reflects the possibility that a certain proportion of the victims are able gradually to develop strategies for escaping bullying as they grow older. In a similar vein, it may be argued that a certain proportion of the students may become less vulnerable with increasing age and, accordingly, will report being less bullied. All of these explanations (and perhaps additional ones) may be partly correct, and more detailed analyses of the factors affecting the shape of the curves are to be undertaken in future research.

As regards the tendency to bully other students, depicted in Figure 2.2, the changes with grades are not so clear and systematic as shown in Figure 2.1. The relatively marked drop in the curves for grade 7 (around age 13), in particular for boys, may partly reflect the fact that these students were the youngest in their schools and accordingly did not have "access to suitable victims" in lower grades to the same extent. (As mentioned in the description of the Norwegian school system at the beginning of the chapter, the majority of Norwegian students make a transfer from primary school to separate lower secondary/junior high school at the start of grade 7.)

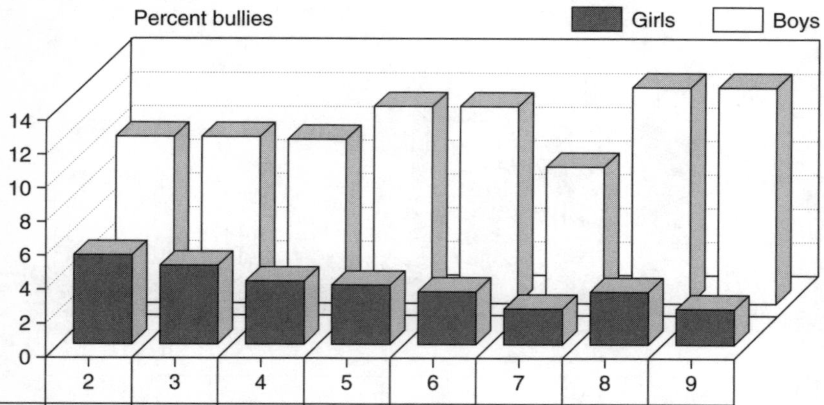

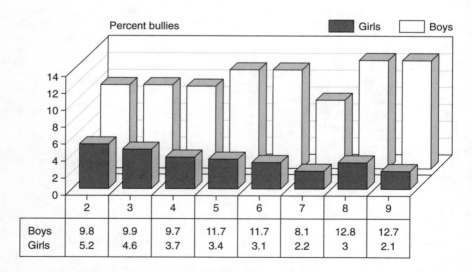

	2	3	4	5	6	7	8	9
Boys	9.8	9.9	9.7	11.7	11.7	8.1	12.8	12.7
Girls	5.2	4.6	3.7	3.4	3.1	2.2	3	2.1

Figure 2.2 Percentage of students in different grades who reported having bullied other students (n for boys = 42,324; n for girls = 40,877).

Bullying among boys and girls

As is evident from Figure 2.1, there is a trend for boys to be more exposed to bullying than girls. This tendency is particularly marked in the lower secondary/junior high school grades.

These results concern what is called direct bullying, with relatively open attacks on the victim. It is natural to ask whether girls were more often exposed to indirect bullying in the form of social isolation and intentional exclusion from the peer group. Analyses of the questionnaire data confirm that girls were more exposed to indirect and more subtle forms of bullying than to bullying with open attacks. At the same time, however, the percentage of boys who were bullied in this indirect way was approximately the same as that for girls. In addition, a somewhat larger percentage of boys were exposed to direct bullying, as mentioned above.

An additional result was that boys carried out a large part of the bullying to which girls were subjected. More than 60 percent of bullied girls (in grades 5–7) reported being bullied mainly by boys. An additional 15–20 percent said they were bullied by both boys and girls. The great majority of boys, on the other hand – more than 80 percent – were bullied chiefly by boys.

Figure 2.2 shows the percentage of students who had taken part in bullying other students with some regularity. It is evident here that a considerably larger percentage of boys than girls had participated in bullying. In lower secondary/junior high school, more than four times as many boys as girls reported having bullied other students.

Bullying by physical means was more common among boys than girls. In contrast, girls often used more subtle and indirect ways of harassment such as slander, spreading of rumors, and manipulation of friendship relationships (for example, depriving a girl of her "best friend"). None the less, harassment by non-physical means (words, gestures, etc.) was the most common form of bullying also among boys.

In summary, boys were more often victims and in particular perpetrators of direct bullying. This conclusion is in agreement with what can be expected from research on sex differences in aggressive behavior (Ekblad and Olweus, 1986; Maccoby and Jacklin, 1974, 1980). It is well documented that relationships among boys are by and large harder, tougher, and more aggressive than among girls (Maccoby, 1986). These differences certainly have both biological and social/environmental roots.

The results presented here should by no means be construed to imply that we do not need to pay attention to bullying problems among girls. As a matter of course, such problems must be acknowledged and counteracted, whether girls are the victims of bullying or they themselves perpetrate such behavior.

The pattern of results found in the Norwegian data has been replicated in all essentials in the corresponding analyses with Swedish students (Olweus, 1992b), and with students in the Sheffield area in England (although the reported levels of problems were somewhat higher for these students; see Whitney and Smith, 1993). For a number of other research findings on bullying, concerning, for example, teacher and parent awareness of the problems, bullying on the way to and from school, and levels of problems in "big-city" versus small-town schools, see Olweus, 1993.

Three common "myths" about bullying

School/class size

A common view holds that bully/victim problems are a consequence of large classes and/or schools: the larger the class or the school, the higher the level of bully/victim problems. Closer analysis of this hypothesis, making use of the Norwegian survey data from more than 700 schools and several thousand classes (with wide variations in size), gave clear-cut results: there were no positive associations between level of bully/victim problems (the percentage of bullied and/or bullying students) and school or class size. Thus, the size of the class or school appears to be of negligible importance for the relative frequency or level of bully/victim problems (Olweus, 1993). It is nevertheless a fact that the absolute number of bullied and bullying students is greater on average in big schools and in big classes. One might therefore think that it would be somewhat easier to do something with the problems in a small school or a small class. However, analyses of data from our intervention study (below) do not support this assumption either. (It may be added that international research on the "effects" of class and school size agrees in suggesting that, in general, these factors are of no great significance, at least within the ranges of size variation typically found; e.g. Rutter, 1983.)

Competition for grades

In the general debate in Scandinavia (and probably elsewhere) it has been commonly maintained that bullying is a consequence of competition and striving for grades in school. More specifically, it has been argued that the aggressive behavior of bullies toward their environment can be explained as a reaction to failures and frustrations in school. Such ideas are in fact central elements in many criminological theories. A detailed causal–analytic analysis of data on 444 boys in the Swedish study (Olweus, 1983), who were followed from grade 6 through grade 9 (from ages 13 to 16), gave no support at all to these ideas. Though there was a moderate association (r around .30) between poor grades in school and aggressive behavior both in grade 6 and in grade 9, there was nothing in the results to suggest that the behavior of the aggressive boys was a consequence of poor grades and failure in school. A similar finding, but more specifically concerned with delinquent behavior, has recently been reported by a Canadian research group (Tremblay, Masse, Perron, Leblanc, Schwartzman and Ledigham, 1992).

External deviations

A widely held view explains victimization as caused by external deviations. It is argued that students who are fat, red-haired, wear glasses, or speak with an unusual dialect, etc. are particularly likely to become victims of bullying. Again, this hypothesis received no support from empirical data. In two samples of boys, victims of bullying were by and large found to be no more externally deviant (with regard to fourteen external characteristics assessed by means of teacher ratings) than a control group of boys who were not exposed to bullying (Olweus, 1973, 1978). It was concluded that external deviations play a much smaller role in the origin of bully/victim problems than generally assumed (see also Junger, 1990). In spite of the lack of empirical support for this hypothesis, it seems still to enjoy considerable popularity. Some probable reasons why this is so have been advanced, and the interested reader is referred to this discussion (Olweus, 1978, 1993).

All of these hypotheses have thus failed to receive support from empirical data. Accordingly, one must look for other factors to find the origins of these problems. The research evidence collected so far and presented in my book *Bullying at school: What we know and what we can do* (1993) clearly suggests that personality characteristics/typical reaction patterns, in combination with physical strength or weakness in the case of boys, are important for the development of these problems *in individual students*. At the same time, environmental factors such as the teachers' attitudes, routines, and behavior play a major role in the extent to which the problems will manifest themselves in a larger unit such as a classroom or a school (see Olweus, 1993).

Characteristics of typical victims and bullies

Since characteristics of victims and bullies are presented in some detail in the country report on Sweden, I will limit myself here to mentioning that two main groups of victims have been identified: the *passive or submissive victim* and the less frequent *provocative victim* (see Olweus, Chapter 1, this volume, for details; Olweus, 1978, 1993). In summary, typical victims are characterized by an anxious or submissive reaction pattern combined, in the case of boys, with physical weakness. The typical bullies, on the other hand, can be described as having an aggressive reaction pattern combined, in the case of boys, with physical strength.

The main characteristics of typical victims and bullies were evident already in my early Swedish research (Olweus, 1973, 1978). The general picture has later been largely confirmed by other researchers (see Olweus, this volume, for references). It is also worth emphasizing that many of these findings have been replicated in the data from the Bergen intervention project (below), although these results have not generally been reported in separate articles.

Research on a school-based intervention program

Against this general background, it is appropriate to describe briefly the effects of the intervention program that I took part in developing and scientifically evaluated in connection with the nationwide campaign against bully/victim problems in Norwegian schools (above).

Evaluation of the effects of the intervention program was based on data from approximately 2500 students originally belonging to 112 grade 4–7 classes (modal ages were 11–14 years at the start of the project) in 42 primary and lower secondary/junior high schools in Bergen, Norway. The students in the study were followed over a period of 2.5 years, from 1983 to 1985 (see, for example, Olweus, 1991, for details).

The major goals of the program were to reduce as much as possible existing bully/victim problems and to prevent the development of new problems.

The main findings of the analyses can be summarized as follows:

- There were marked reductions – by 50 percent or more – in bully/victim problems for the periods studied, with eight and 20 months of intervention, respectively. By and large, these reductions were obtained for "direct bullying" (where the victim is exposed to relatively open attacks), for "indirect bullying" (where the victim is isolated and excluded from the group, involuntary loneliness), and for "bullying others." The results generally applied to both boys and girls and to students from all grades studied.
- There was no "displacement" of bullying from the school to the way to and from school. There were reductions or no change with regard to bully/victim problems on the way to and from school.
- There were also clear reductions in general antisocial behavior such as vandalism, fighting, pilfering, drunkenness, and truancy.
- In addition, we could register a marked improvement as regards various aspects of the "social climate" of the class: improved order and discipline, more positive social relationships, and a more positive attitude to schoolwork and the school in general. At the same time, there was an increase in student satisfaction with school life.
- The intervention program not only affected already existing victimization problems; it also reduced considerably the number (and percentage) of new victims (Olweus, 1992c). The program had thus both primary and secondary prevention effects (Cowen, 1984).

In the majority of comparisons for which reductions were reported above, the differences between baseline and intervention groups were significant/highly significant and with medium, large, or even very large effect sizes (*d*-values at the classroom level of more than 1.0 for several variables).

Detailed analyses of the quality of the data and the possibility of alternative interpretations of the findings led to the following general statements

(Olweus, 1991, 1994a). It is very difficult to explain the results obtained as a consequence of (1) under-reporting by the students, (2) gradual changes in the students' attitudes to bully/victim problems, (3) repeated measurement, and (4) concomitant changes in other factors, including general time trends.

In addition, a clear "dosage–response" relationship has been established in preliminary analyses at the class level (which is the natural unit of analysis in this case). Those classes that showed larger reductions in bully/victim problems had implemented three presumably essential components of the intervention program (including establishment of class rules against bullying and use of regular class meetings) to a greater extent than those with smaller changes (Olweus and Alsaker, 1991). This finding provides corroborating evidence for the hypothesis that the changes observed were due to the intervention program.

All in all, it was concluded that the changes in bully/victim problems and related behavior patterns were likely to be mainly a consequence of the intervention program and not of some other "irrelevant" factor. It was also noted that self-reports, which were implicated in most of these analyses, are probably the best data source for the purposes of this study. At the same time, largely parallel results were obtained for two peer rating variables and for teacher ratings of bully/victim problems at the class level; for the teacher data, however, the effects were somewhat weaker.

In a relatively recent publication (Roland, 1989, p. 28), it has been claimed that an intervention study parallel to the one in Bergen was conducted in the county of Rogaland (by Roland) with partly negative results when outcome data were collected after three years, in 1986. In several respects, this account is grossly misleading. Owing to space limitations, it is not possible to present in detail the reasons for my critique of Roland's presentation. However, in summary, it can be shown that the studies in Bergen and Rogaland were two completely different projects in terms of planning, data quality, times of measurement, and contact with the schools, and accordingly, also in terms of expected results. In line with these arguments, I am anxious to emphasize that the positive and extensive changes registered in the Bergen project were a consequence of the intervention program *as it was introduced and developed in Bergen*.

Basic principles

The intervention program is built on a set of four key principles derived chiefly from research on the development and modification of the problem behaviors concerned, in particular aggressive behavior. It is thus important to try to create a school (and ideally also a home) environment characterized by (1) warmth, positive interest, and involvement from adults, on the one hand, and (2) firm limits to unacceptable behavior, on the other. Third (3), in cases of violations of limits and rules, non-hostile, non-physical sanctions should be consistently applied. Implied in the latter two principles is also a certain degree of monitoring and surveillance of the students' activities in and out of school (Patterson, 1982, 1986). Finally (4), adults both at school and home are supposed to act as authorities at least in some respects.

As regards the role of adults, the intervention program is based on an authoritative (*not* authoritarian) adult–child interaction or child-rearing model (cf. Baumrind, 1967) in which the adults are encouraged to take responsibility for the children's total situation – not only their learning, but also their social relationships.

These principles were translated into a number of specific measures to be used at the *school*, *class*, and *individual* levels. It is considered important to work on all of these levels if possible. Space limitations prevent a description of the various measures but such an account can be found in *Bullying at school: What we know and what we can do* (Olweus, 1993). The updated "package" relating to the intervention program consists of the Bully/Victim Questionnaire (a manual will be published; the questionnaire with instructions may meanwhile be ordered from the author at HEMIL, Christies gate 13, N-5015 Bergen, Norway), a 20-minute video cassette showing scenes from the everyday lives of two bullied children (with English subtitles; this video can also be ordered from the author), and a copy of the book (Olweus, 1993) which describes in some detail the program and its implementation.

Table 2.1 lists a set of core components which are considered, on the basis of statistical analyses and our experience with the program, to be particularly important in any implementation of the program. With regard to implementation and execution, the program is mainly based on a utilization of the existing social environment: teachers and other school personnel,

Table 2.1 An overview of Olweus' core program

General prerequisites	
+ +	Awareness and involvement on the part of adults
Measures at the school level	
+ +	Questionnaire survey
+ +	School conference day
+ +	Better supervision during break periods
+	Formation of coordinating group
Measures at the class level	
+ +	Class rules against bullying
+ +	Regular class meetings with students
+	Class PTA meetings
Measures at the individual level	
+ +	Serious talks with bullies and victims
+ +	Serious talks with parents of involved students
+	Teacher and parent use of imagination

Notes: + + core component; + highly desirable component

students, and parents. Non-mental health professionals thus play a major role in the desired "*restructuring of the social environment.*" "Experts" such as school psychologists, counsellors, and social workers serve important functions as planners and coordinators, in counselling teachers and parents (groups), and in handling more serious cases.

Additional comments

Possible reasons for the effectiveness of this non-traditional intervention approach have been discussed in some detail (Olweus, 1992c). They include a change of the "opportunity" and "reward structures" for bullying behavior (resulting in fewer opportunities and rewards for bullying). It is also generally emphasized that bully/victim problems can be seen as an excellent entry point for dealing with a variety of problems that plague today's schools. Furthermore, one can view the program from the perspective of planned organizational change (with quite specific goals) and in this way link it with the work on school effectiveness and school improvement. It may also be pointed out that the program in many ways represents what is sometimes called "a whole-school policy approach to bullying" in the English literature. It consists of a set of routines, rules, and strategies of communication and action for dealing with existing and future bullying problems in the school.

This anti-bullying program is now in use or in the process of being implemented in a considerable number of schools in Europe and North America. Though there have so far been few research-based attempts to evaluate the effects of the program beyond the study in Bergen, unsystematic information and reports indicate that the general approach is well received by the adults in the school community and that the program (with or without cultural adaptations or addition of culture-specific components) works well under varying cultural conditions including ethnic diversity. There has, however, recently been one additional large-scale evaluation of the basic approach, containing most of the core elements of the program and with a research design similar to that of our study (Smith and Sharp, 1994). Also in this project, comprising 23 schools (with a good deal of ethnic diversity) in Sheffield, England, the results were quite positive (though fewer behavioral aspects were studied; see Smith, Chapter 5, this volume). It can be argued that the robustness and possible generalizability of the program is not really surprising, since the existing evidence seems to indicate that the factors and principles affecting the development and modification of aggressive, antisocial behaviour are fairly similar across cultural contexts, at least within the western industrialized part of the world.

Bullying of students by teachers

As part of the Bergen study in the 1980s, a special questionnaire was used to explore the possibility that students were bullied by teachers. The questionnaire, which included only six items in addition to a "definition" of teacher bullying, was to be answered anonymously by the students. Although the study was actually conducted in 1985, the data, for various reasons, were not analysed and reported until 1996 (Olweus, 1996). So far as is known, it is the first scientific investigation of this sensitive topic.

The study comprised some 2400 students in 102 grade 6 through 9 classes coming from 31 primary and lower secondary/junior high schools. To avoid non-serious or erratic responses by students influencing the results, fairly strict criteria were used to identify whether or not teacher bullying occurred in the various classrooms. Care was also taken to avoid "double-counting" of teachers who taught in more than one of the participating classes. Our analyses clearly suggested that it is possible to measure bullying of students by teachers in a reasonably objective and sensible way through the use of an anonymous student questionnaire.

Some 40 of the 2400 students, or slightly less than 2 percent, could be identified as having been bullied by one or (in a minority of cases) several teachers during the "reference period" of about five months. Conversely, as many as 10 percent of the teachers were identified as having bullied one or (concerning 30 percent of the bullying teachers) more students. Approaching the problem from a slightly different angle, there were eleven out of 21 classes in which "only" one student was bullied by a teacher. It is reasonable to assume that it is a particularly difficult situation for a student to be the only one in the class to be bullied by a teacher. This thus occurred in about 50 percent of the classes.

The results from this study showed clearly that bullying of students by teachers occurs at a much higher rate than expected in Norwegian primary and lower secondary/junior high schools. (Strictly speaking, the preceding conclusion should have been stated in the past tense, but there is little reason to suppose that the situation is any better today than a decade ago.) As emphasized in the report, these findings make it mandatory that schools become more open to "public control" and that potential problems in teacher–student relations be taken more seriously by the schools.

In the report, I proposed that special complaint authorities or committees be established, possibly in each community, for the handling of these and related problems. Although the issue was not empirically investigated in this study, some hypotheses were also considered concerning the possible kinds of teachers who might be involved in bullying students (Olweus, 1996).

Generally, the problem of teacher bullying of students seems to deserve considerably more attention than it has received so far, primarily because of the seriousness of the problem in and of itself for the students concerned. In addition, it is obvious that a teacher who bullies students is not likely to be good at solving or preventing bullying among students. He or she may actually contribute to the development of such problems by (more or less inadvertently) "pointing out suitable victims" who can be harassed by the students without any expected interference on the part of the teacher. It is also possible that a certain proportion of teacher-bullied students may develop a generally hostile and rebellious attitude to the school and the teachers, thereby increasing their readiness to engage in aggressive behavior, including the bullying of peers.

Initiatives and resource materials

As mentioned in the introductory part of this chapter, the interest in bullying as a societal phenomenon spread in a short period of time from Sweden to the other Scandinavian countries. As one indicator of this development, the first two books on the topic – that by the school physician Peter-Paul Heinemann (1972) which was based on everyday observations and personal reflections, and my own research-based treatise (Olweus, 1973) – were quickly translated from Swedish and published in Norway and Denmark (a modified version of the latter book was also published in English: Olweus, 1978). A number of books written for children and youth dealing with the theme of bullying have also been published in the last two decades.

As also mentioned, a nationwide campaign against bullying was launched by the Ministry of Education in the autumn of 1983. In that context, the following resource materials were developed:

1 A 32-page booklet for school personnel describing what is known about bully/victim problems (or rather what was known in 1983) and giving suggestions about what teachers and the school can do to counteract and prevent the problems (Olweus and Roland, 1983). Efforts were also made to dispel some common myths about the nature and causes of bully/victim problems which might interfere with an adequate handling of them. This booklet was distributed free of charge to all primary and lower secondary/junior high schools in Norway.
2 A four-page folder with information and advice to parents of victims and bullies as well as "ordinary" children. This folder was distributed by the schools to all families in Norway with school-age children.
3 A 20-minute video cassette showing episodes from the everyday lives of two bullied children, a 10-year-old boy and a 14-year-old girl. This cassette could be bought or rented at a highly subsidized price.
4 A short questionnaire designed to obtain information about different aspects of bully/victim problems in the school, including frequency and the readiness of teachers and students to interfere with the problems. A number of the results presented earlier in this chapter were based on information collected with the aid of this questionnaire.

In 1987, Roland arranged, with the support of the Ministry of Education and the Council of Europe, a European conference on "Bullying in School" at Stavanger. Participants came from twelve different countries and most were teachers or school principals. In part, the publication of the edited book

Bullying: An international perspective (Roland and Munthe, 1989) was the result of this conference. Roland himself had earlier written a book on bullying in Norwegian, published in 1983 (Roland, 1983).

In 1986, I published a small book, *Mobbning: Vad vi vet och vad vi kan göra*, in Swedish. This book was later expanded to include the scientific evaluation of the effects of the intervention program as it was developed in the Bergen project (above). The expanded version, which also describes in some detail the Olweus core program, was published almost simultaneously in Norway and Sweden under the title (translated) "Bullying at school: What we know and what we can do" (Olweus, 1992a, 1992b). Subsequently, this book has been published in thirteen different languages including English (Olweus, 1993), German (Olweus, 1994c), French (in press), Spanish (1998), and Japanese (1995).

To meet the frequent demands for a more thorough introduction to and training in the Olweus core intervention program, I arranged a three-day conference on that topic in 1994 (financially supported by the Swiss Johann Jacobs Foundation); this attracted participants from sixteen different, largely European countries.

In the 1990s, there has been growing interest and concern about bullying at school. This has manifested itself in several different ways. For example, both the Ombudsman for Children and a mental health organization for children (*Mental barnehjelp*) have opened Childline telephone services which have received a lot of calls related to the theme of bullying. There have also been public discussions involving top political figures about a possible law against bullying in school, similar to the one introduced in Sweden (see Olweus, Chapter 1, this volume; Olweus, 1994b). A proposal to that effect has also been recently submitted by an expert committee appointed by Parliament (Norwegian Official Reports, NOU, 1995:18, Chapter 25.4).

Recent official initiatives have involved activities on the part of two different governmental departments, the Ministry of Church, Education, and Research (Ministry of Education) and the Ministry of Children and Family Affairs. As part of the first of these initiatives, a new teacher booklet with guidelines has been written by Roland and Sørensen Vaaland (1996). In addition, materials designed for various student activities against bullying have been produced and disseminated to student councils all over Norway and some 350 "resource persons" have been trained in two-day seminars (with later follow-up meetings) with Roland and his associates from the Center for Research on Behavior Problems at Stavanger. These resource persons are distributed across the various counties in Norway.

Although the goals of this initiative are certainly ambitious, there are some doubts about the usefulness of the loose "organizational model" chosen. At present, it is unclear to what extent the resource persons will be actually used by the schools and thereby have a possible effect on the work against bullying. There is also uncertainty as to how much the student material will be employed in actual classroom work, since it has been channeled through the student councils and not through the teachers. There seem to be no plans for a scientific evaluation of the possible effects of this initiative.

In 1996, the University of Bergen established a Group for the Prevention of Bullying and Antisocial Behavior with myself as leader. At present, the group consists of six researchers and is funded by the Ministry of Children and Family Affairs and the Norwegian Council for Research, among others. This group has now initiated a new large-scale project on bullying in the schools of Bergen, beginning with a survey on the theme of bullying and related problems in a large number of schools in the spring of 1997. This survey forms part of the international project referred to above in connection with the discussion about the definition of bullying. An intervention part, based on a slightly revised version of the Olweus core program (above), and involving close cooperation with the school psychology services in Bergen (the so-called PPT) has been initiated in the academic year 1997/8.

The Ministry of Children and Family Affairs has also begun a large-scale parent guidance program involving, among other things, the production of a number of high-quality booklets on themes related to parenthood, the rearing of children and youth, and associated problems. As part of this program, I, together with a co-author, have recently written a 25-page booklet for parents on bullying at school (Olweus and Solberg, 1997). A central message of the booklet is that parents of children/youths who are bullied should not accept the situation as a natural part of children's school life and must not give up in the face of possible indifference, reluctance, or even rejection on the part of the school. This booklet is being distributed free of charge all over Norway to a very large number of institutions and resource persons having frequent contact with parents.

Epilogue

There is no doubt that public awareness of, and knowledge about, the problem of bullying in schools has increased markedly over the last two decades in Norway. Both local and national politicians have engaged themselves officially with the theme. As just one example, both the prime minister and the king mentioned, independently of each other, active work against bullying in schools as an important societal task for the coming year (1997) in their New Year speeches on the national radio and television.

We have also seen a marked change in schools' attitude to bullying over the years. While a defensive and denying attitude was quite common in the 1970s and early 1980s, nowadays many schools reach out for help, being eager to learn about good ways of counteracting and preventing the problem. A large number of communities have also arranged conferences and in-service training courses about bullying for their teachers and other school personnel.

However, courses about bullying and its treatment/prevention are still not required but elective courses at most teacher training colleges. It is reasonable to expect that this will change in the near future. From the academic year of 1997–1998, a new National Curriculum (Læroplan for den 10-årige grunskole, 1996) has been introduced, and the topic of bullying is mentioned in a number of places, both at the primary and lower secondary/junior high school levels, as a theme to be taught by the teachers and discussed with the students. In addition, the schools are strongly encouraged/obliged to prevent and counteract the problem of bullying among their students as much as possible. Accordingly, future textbooks for both students and teachers will very likely include chapters on bullying, and we may expect that the training of future teachers will contain a required course on the "basics of bullying."

Acknowledgments

The research program reported on in this chapter was supported by grants from the Research Council of Norway (NFR, NAVF), the William T. Grant Foundation, USA, the Johann Jacobs Foundation, Switzerland, the Ministry of Children and Family Affairs (BFD), and in earlier phases, from the Swedish Delegation for Social Research (DSF), and the Norwegian Ministry of Education (KUD), which is gratefully acknowledged.

References

Baumrind, D. (1967) Child care practices anteceding three patterns of preschool behavior. *Genetic Psychology Monographs*, 75, 43–88.

Björkqvist, K. (1994) Sex differences in physical, verbal, and indirect aggression: A review of recent research. *Sex Roles*, 30, 177–188.

Björkqvist, K., Lagerspetz, K.M.J. and Kaukiainen, A. (1992) Do girls manipulate and boys fight? Developmental trends regarding direct and indirect aggression. *Aggressive Behavior*, 18, 117–127.

Cowen, E.L. (1984) A general structural model for primary program development in mental health. *Personnel and Guidance Journal*, 62, 485–490.

Crick, N.R. and Grotpeter, J.K. (1995) Relational aggression, gender, and social-psychological adjustment. *Child Development*, 66, 710–722.

Ekblad, S. and Olweus, D. (1986) Applicability of Olweus's aggression inventory in a sample of Chinese primary schoolchildren. *Aggressive Behavior*, 12, 315–325.

Haeselager, G.J.T. and van Lieshout, C.F.M. (1992) Social and affective adjustment of self- and peer-reported victims and bullies. Paper presented at the European Conference on Developmental Psychology, Seville, Spain, September.

Heinemann, P.P. (1972) *Mobbning-gruppvåld bland barn och vuxna*. Stockholm, Sweden: Natur och Kultur.

Hirano, K. (1992) Bullying and victimization in Japanese classrooms. Paper presented at the European Conference on Developmental Psychology, Seville, Spain, September.

Junger, M. (1990) Intergroup bullying and racial harassment in the Netherlands. *Sociology and Social Research*, 74, 65–72.

Kallestad, J.H. and Olweus, D. (in press) Teachers' emphasis on general educational goals: A study of Norwegian teachers. *Scandinavian Journal of Educational Research.*

Læroplan for den 10-årige grunskole (1996) (National Curriculum for the 10-year comprehensive school.) Oslo, Norway.

Lagerspetz, K.M., Björkqvist, K., Berts, M. and King, E. (1982) Group aggression among schoolchildren in three schools. *Scandinavian Journal of Psychology*, 23, 45–52.

Maccoby, E.E. (1986) Social groupings in childhood: Their relationship to prosocial and antisocial behavior in boys and girls. In D. Olweus, J. Block and M. Radke-Yarrow (eds), *Development of antisocial and prosocial behavior*. New York: Academic Press.

Maccoby, E.E. and Jacklin, C.N. (1974) *The psychology of sex differences*. Stanford, CA: Stanford University Press.

Maccoby, E.E. and Jacklin, C.N. (1980) Sex differences in aggression. A rejoinder and replies. *Child Development*, 51, 964–980.

NOU (1995) 18 "Ny lovgivning om opplæring," kap. 25.4.

Olweus, D. (1973) *Hackkycklingar och översittare: Forskning om skol-mobbning.* Stockholm, Sweden: Almqvist & Wiksell.

Olweus, D. (1977) Aggression and peer acceptance in adolescent boys: Two short-term longitudinal studies on ratings. *Child Development*, 48, 1301–1313.

Olweus, D. (1978) *Aggression in the schools. Bullies and whipping boys*. Washington, DC: Hemisphere Press (Wiley).

Olweus, D. (1983) Low school achievement and agressive behavior in adolescent boys. In D. Magnusson and V. Allen (eds), *Human development. An interactional perspective* (pp. 353–365). New York: Academic Press.

Olweus, D. (1985) 80.000 barn er innblandet i mobbing. *Norsk skoleblad* (Oslo, Norway), 2, 18–23.

Olweus, D. (1986) *Mobbning: Vad vi vet och vad vi kan göra*. Stockholm, Sweden: Liber.

Olweus, D. (1987) Bully/victim problems among schoolchildren. In J.P. Myklebust and R. Ommundsen (eds), *Psykologprofesjonen mot år 2000* (pp. 395–413). Oslo, Norway: Universitetsforlaget.

Olweus, D. (1991) Bully/victim problems among schoolchildren: Basic facts and effects of a school based intervention program. In D. Pepler and K. Rubin (eds), *The development and treatment of childhood aggression* (pp. 411–448). Hillsdale, NJ: Erlbaum.

Olweus, D. (1992a) *Mobbing i skolen – hva vi vet og hva vi kan gjøre*. Oslo, Norway: Universitetsforlaget.

Olweus, D. (1992b) *Mobbning i skolan. Vad vi vet og vad vi kan göra.* Stockholm, Sweden: Almqvist & Wiksell.

Olweus, D. (1992c) Bullying among schoolchildren: Intervention and prevention. In R.D. Peters, R.J. McMahon and V.L.Quincy (eds), *Aggression and violence throughout the lifespan* (pp. 100–125). Newbury Park, CA: Sage.

Olweus, D. (1993) *Bullying at school: What we know and what we can do*. Oxford: Blackwell Publishers. (Available through bookstores or direct from Blackwell, 108 Cowley Road, Oxford OX4 1JF, UK, or Blackwell, 238 Main Street, Cambridge, MA 02142, USA.)

Olweus, D. (1994a) Annotation: Bullying at school: Basic facts and effects of a school based intervention program. *Journal of Child Psychology and Psychiatry*, 35, 1171–1190.

Olweus, D. (1994b) Derfor trenger vi mobbeloven. *Dagbladet*, 18 January.

Olweus, D. (1994c) *Gewalt in der Schule*. Bern, Switzerland: Huber Verlag.

Olweus, D. (1996) *Mobbing av elever fra lærere* (Bullying of students by teachers). Bergen, Norway: Alma Mater Forlag.

Olweus, D. and Alsaker, F.D. (1991) Assessing change in a cohort longitudinal study with hierarchical data. In D. Magnusson, L. Bergman, G. Rudinger and B. Torestad (eds), *Problems and methods in longitudinal research* (pp. 107–132). New York: Cambridge University Press.

Olweus, D. and Roland, E. (1983) *Mobbing – bakgrunn og tiltak*. Oslo, Norway: Kirke- og undervisningdepartementet.

Olweus, D. and Solberg, C. (1997) *Mobbing blant barn og unge. Informasjon og veiledning til foreldre* (Bullying among children and youth. Information and guidance for parents). Oslo, Norway: Ministry of Children and Family Affairs.

O'Moore, M. and Brendan, H. (1989) Bullying in Dublin schools. *Irish Journal of Psychology*, 10, 426–441.

Patterson, G.R. (1982) *Coercive family process*. Eugene, Oregon: Castalia Publishing Co.

Patterson, G.R. (1986) Performance models for antisocial boys. *American Psychologist*, 41, 432–444.

Perry, D.G., Kusel, S.J. and Perry, L.C. (1988) Victims of peer aggression. *Developmental Psychology*, 24, 807–814.

Rigby, K. and Slee, P. (1990) Victims in school communities. *Journal of the Australasian Society of Victimology*, 1(2), 25–31.

Roland, E. (1983) *Strategi mot mobbing*. Oslo, Norway: Universitetsforlaget.

Roland, E. (1989) Bullying: The Scandinavian research tradition. In D.P. Tattum and D.A.Lane (eds), *Bullying in schools* (pp. 21–32). Stoke-on-Trent: Trentham Books.

Roland, E. and Munthe, E. (eds) (1989) *Bullying: An international perspective*. London: Fulton Publishers.

Roland, E. and Sørensen Vaaland, G. (1996) *Mobbing i skolen. En lærerveiledning*. Oslo, Norway: Kirke-, utdannings- og forskningsdepartementet.

Ruiz, R.O. (1992) Violence in schools. Problems of bullying and victimization in Spain. Paper presented at the European Conference on Developmental Psychology, Seville, Spain, September.

Rutter, M. (1983) School effect on pupil progress: Research findings and policy implications. *Child Development*, 54, 1–19.

Smith, P.K. (1991) The silent nightmare: Bullying and victimization in school peer groups. *The Psychologist*, 4, 243–248.

Smith, P.K. and Sharp, S. (eds) (1994) *School bullying: Insights and perspectives*. London: Routledge.

Tremblay, R.E., Masse, B., Perron, D., Leblanc, M., Schwartzman, A.E. and Ledigham, J.E. (1992) Early disruptive behavior, poor school achievement, delinquent behavior, and delinquent personality: Longitudinal analysis. *Journal of Consulting and Clinical Psychology*, 60, 64–72.

Whitney, I. and Smith, P.K. (1993) A survey of the nature and extent of bully/victim problems in junior/middle and secondary schools. *Educational Research*, 35, 3–35.

Ziegler, S. and Rosenstein-Manner, M. (1991) *Bullying at school: Toronto in an international context* (Report No. 196). Toronto: Toronto Board of Education, Research Services.

3 Denmark

Niels Dueholm

Overview

This chapter gives a short description of demographic figures and developments in recent history in Denmark of relevance to the topic of bullying. It is argued that during the last half century Danish society has undergone a marked development almost amounting to a revolution. This goes for public administration, industrial development and demographic figures. The immigration rate has developed markedly since the 1960s, and this contributes naturally to a period of dissonance – especially in the areas of larger cities where the concentration of population is greater. It is argued, however, that despite the many problems of tolerance, understanding and integration between ethnic groups, this issue of immigration is not strongly associated with bullying.

There has been no specific scientific effort in Denmark to unfold the subtleties concerned with bullying behaviour (except for the WHO study described below), but more examples of related investigation projects are mentioned. On the other hand, more projects to improve social development in the schools have been implemented. These projects are characterized by their inclusion of pupils themselves in project management.

As for the future, it is argued that the evidence points clearly to the need for the Danish authorities to deal with the area of pupils' well-being in schools in a more serious manner.

Country summary

Denmark is a Scandinavian country, adjoining Germany but with strong links to Norway and Sweden. The capital, Copenhagen, is on the island of Sjaelland; the largest land area is Jutland, adjoining Schleswig-Holstein in Germany; and there are other islands including Fyn, with the city of Odense. Altogether, there are fourteen administrative counties in Denmark. The population in Denmark is just over five million inhabitants. This number has shown a marked stability over time – at least since the beginning of the century. During this period Danish society has undergone a development from a typically agricultural country through industrialization to what has been called a 'society of service'.

This general development in society has increased over the years – especially the demographic changes and movements following the transfer from a predominantly agricultural culture up to the 1950s, to industrialization, the consequent depopulating of agricultural areas and a marked growth in towns and cities: the so-called 'syndrome of urbanization'.

The employment rate in Denmark is now growing following a period of unemployment amounting to about 12–13 per cent. Since the 1950s the employment of women has grown rapidly. General unemployment has now decreased to about 200,000 persons. The employment rate of women in Denmark is one of the highest in the western world.

These changes have of course had a great impact on children's upbringing – where do they spend their leisure time when parents are at work? Denmark is one of the countries in the western world to have the highest rate of public day care facilities. This is true both in the preschool period and for leisure time after the school day. In a socioeconomic sense Danish society may be labelled as one where 'few have too much and less have too little'.

Since the 1960s there has been a rather marked increase in immigration from different ethnic groups. In fact, the general proportion of people coming from other countries is about 3 per cent of the total population; this approximately divides into a 50/50 proportion of immigrants coming from western countries, and from more distant cultures such as Turkey. The percentage of immigrant children in Danish schools is slowly but steadily growing, having reached some 7 to 8 per cent in 1997 with a projected number of about 10 per cent by the end of the decade. Denmark has gone through a period of a decreasing birth rate but since the beginning of the 1990s this has started to grow.

The school system

Denmark has some 2000 schools: 1734 of the schools are 'folkeskoler'. These are under the school authorities in the municipalities; the schools are guided – not actually governed – by a board, where parents have the majority of influence within certain topics. The rest of the schools are private schools where parents – with 85 per cent economic support from the state – are in charge of the school. Eighty-eight per cent of all Danish children attend the local public schools and 12 per cent attend the private schools. The total number of Danish pupils is about 800,000.

Education at primary and lower secondary level is compulsory. Schoolchildren in Denmark start school at or just before 7 years of age. The 'folkeskole' covers primary and lower secondary education, starting with a non-obligatory kindergarten class (in which about 90 per cent of all school beginners participate) and a schedule of class/grade 1 until (and inclusive) grade 9 – this period being mandatory. A tenth grade must be offered, and a large proportion of pupils also continue into this grade. Some pupils transfer after the ninth grade and participate in secondary education (gymnasium, high school and vocational education); some do so after the tenth grade.

Special education must be offered, according to the regulations concerning the 'folkeskole', if the pedagogical-psychological counselling office, in agreement with the parents and headteacher of the school, finds evidence of a special educational need in a pupil. Some 13 per cent of all pupils receive some kind of special education during a school year. This percentage has been stable for a period of at least fifteen years. However, this number does not reflect the expenditure or resources devoted to special education; it only covers the fact that some kind of special education is offered and indicates nothing about, for instance, how many lessons are given, etc.

Special education in Denmark is administratively and economically differentiated into two forms. The 'common' special education, mentioned above, is under the responsibility of the local municipality; the 'advanced special education' is under the responsibility of the regional counties. One per cent of all pupils are assigned to the advanced special education level (typically severely handicapped pupils with intellectual, physical and motor impairments).

Bullying in schools – concepts and opinions

In Denmark, bullying in more academic surroundings is normally defined in a way similar to that of Dan Olweus: 'A student is being bullied or victimized when he or she is exposed, repeatedly and over time, to negative actions on the part of one or more other students.'

In common speech this definition is considerably broadened, so that the term 'bullying' covers all kinds of negative actions between individuals. In the common language of pupils, this sense of the term is the one practised. The Danish word for bullying is 'mobbe' which in fact is a rather new term in Denmark. I believe the term 'mobbe' was first used widely among pupils in the 1980s. Before then the words 'teasing' or 'violence' or 'aggressive behaviour' were used, depending on the kind and degree of offensive behaviour.

Over time there have been quite different and varying opinions and interest in the subject of bullying. The Ministry of Education first became aware of the topic in the late 1980s, when the term 'mobbe' was used more in public, and the first newspaper articles and television features on the topic appeared. In the 1990s there was at first a decline of interest in the topic – in the public, in research areas and from the central authorities. But in 1995–1996 interest grew again, stimulated by a number of rather sensational newspaper articles. In a few instances, suicides have been mentioned in some newspapers as caused by bullying. There have been no court cases to the best of my knowledge.

In the Ministry of Education we are aware that a number of parents are asking for initiatives and information on how to avoid and overcome bullying behaviour. However, generally speaking, bullying behaviour is not seen as a major social problem in Denmark. In the public as well as in more academic environments, I believe that the understanding of bullying behaviour might be summarized as follows:

- it is a 'normal' developmental risk while learning and mastering social behaviour;
- it is behaviour caused by malfunctioning, low self-esteem and poorly developed group behaviour skills;
- it is a symptom on a more general level of non-specific problems of vigorous development (failure to thrive);
- in severe (and rare) cases it is a symptom of antisocial behaviour caused by deviant psychosocial development.

Research studies and projects

There has been little systematic research on the specific topic of bullying in Denmark, and no study – except one by WHO – to which I can refer as an example of genuine research on bullying. There have been several examples of local development projects including questionnaires on bullying, most of which lack sufficient basis for generalization.

In 1996 WHO published *The health of youth – a cross-national survey* in which bullying behaviour is one of the topics covered. According to this study, Denmark has a rather high score on students' bullying behaviour, coming in the top three for 'taking part in bullying others' out of the 24 countries, and in the top half for students who reported being bullied. One of the researchers behind the Danish figures remarked that the extent of bullying behaviour corresponds with the general sense of well-being (thriving, or vigorous behavior) among pupils in Denmark; he stresses that from his research, the degree of well-being among pupils has decreased markedly in Denmark over the last ten years.

The term 'mobbe' is not used to describe racial offences, or offensive behaviour to other ethnic groups, and it is generally not regarded (or used) as an appropriate word where ethnic or racial elements are in the foreground.

Intervention, initiatives and projects to combat or prevent bullying behaviour

In 1988 the former Danish minister of the Ministry of Education and Research took an initiative to deal with the topic of bullying as seen from the pupils' point of view. He sent a letter to all pupil boards in the country and asked them to help in preventing antisocial behaviour such as bullying, and improving social behaviour. (It should be mentioned at this point that all schools have a board of pupils, some of whom are the pupils' representatives on the general school board.) He also asked for information on how the pupils regarded bullying, how much bullying behaviour took place, what kind of bullying was most prominent, and finally what had been done and what could possibly be done to avoid bullying behaviour in future. Some 10 per cent of all schools responded to this letter by including a lot of material on the above-mentioned questions. According to this 'pilot study' it was estimated that some 10 per cent of all pupils in schools were victims of bullying. At the local level there are some – but to the best of my knowledge not many – initiatives and projects to avoid bullying behaviour and improve social functioning.

In 1994 the Inter-Ministerial Committee (which consists of fifteen representatives from the different ministries in the central administration) suggested a focus of initiatives for children at risk in Danish society. (This committee corresponds to a board at the political level: the Governmental Board for Children. The underlying idea is that in a highly developed and organized society like Denmark, it is necessary to develop cooperation between different ministries, all of which have something to do with children.) As far as the schools were concerned, there was agreement on the need to develop and strengthen pupils' social relationships in school in order to reach the above-mentioned goals.

This 'intervention' was implemented in two ways:

1 A project to obtain pupils' own opinions, participation and ideas about 'well-being' in school (the Danish title 'Ha' det godt i skolen' is difficult to translate into English).

   This project developed in cooperation with seven schools, and resulted in a newspaper to be distributed to every single pupil (800,000) in Denmark. There were three editions of the newspaper, each covering the same topics but adapted to three different age groups. The papers described how these seven schools – and especially the pupils – worked and collaborated to develop social relationships and to avoid segregation, loneliness and maladjustment. Finally the papers asked the pupils, teachers and parents to contribute to the project by sending ideas, comments and experiences to the Ministry of Education to develop further actions and initiatives following the target.

   This phase was implemented through 1997, and it is planned to publish a catalogue aimed at teachers containing ideas and descriptions of how to develop a school for all: a school where there exists a minimum of antisocial behaviour and a maximum of developmental power.

2 A project utilizing the pedagogical-psychological counselling services (PPC; this is a service provided in each of the 275 municipalities in Denmark, each employing between ten and fifteen psychologists and consultants within different pedagogical and psychological areas); in principle, every parent, pupil, teacher, etc. is in a position to receive information and guidance concerning pedagogical-psychological questions and problems; this should investigate such problems and develop answers and ideas as to how to cope with bullying situations.

The project has now gone beyond the investigation and inspiration phase and presents some observations to the minister. Of interest to the theme of bullying are:

- PPC is often called upon to solve problems in classes where the social and collaborative climate is very low or even destructive. It is easy to label negative behaviour as bullying in most of these classes. It is therefore recommended that the PPC personnel should receive further education and practice to deal adequately with these problems; for example, using classroom-based interventions, or even 'classroom therapy'.
- PPC is often called upon by parents and also by pupils having problems or at least essential questions concerning general behaviour, upbringing, school achievement, etc. It is recommended that PPC invests more energy, time and effort into coping with these problems.

In a separate development, at the beginning of 1996 there was a discussion in the Danish Parliament, raised by a politician who held the opinion that the Danish school was characterized by loose and weak discipline and that the pupils suffered from poor social adjustment evidenced in antisocial behaviour; and that there was no response to these problems at the 'system level'.

This discussion resulted in a major investigation in which pupil behaviour was in the foreground. It focused on what characterizes the typical Danish school so far as the pupils' general behaviour, ability to work together and to be constructive (according to the aims or policy of the school) was concerned. This project includes questionnaires covering some 120,000 pupils and 12,000 teachers as well as many parents, and is currently underway, with the results being delivered to Parliament in late 1997.

Future directions and initiatives

There have not been any other initiatives planned on the central level so far. The WHO research may eventually contribute to a renewed debate about matters of importance in development in Danish schools, and thus contribute to a higher priority for dealing with bullying behaviour in the future.

References

World Health Organisation (1996) *The health of youth – a cross-national survey*. WHO.

Government reports

(Available from Undervisningsministeriet Forlag, Frederiksholms Kanal 25 F, 1220 Kobenhavn K, Denmark)

Fra Skolepsykologi til Paedagogisk-Psykologisk Rådgivning (1996) Undervisningsministeriet Folkeskoleafdelingen.
Paedagogisk-Psykologisk Rådgivning I Danmark (1995) Undervisningsministeriet Folkeskoleafdelingen.
Paedagogisk-Psykologisk Rådgivning I Danmark: Udviklingstendenser I arbejdet (1996) Undervisningsministeriet Folkeskoleafdelingen.
Paedagogisk-Psykologisk Rådgivning I Danmark: Afsluttende rapport og handlinsplan (1997) Undervisningsministeriet Folkeskoleafdelingen.
Urolige elever i folkeskolens almindelige klasse: En kvantitativ og kvalitativ undersøgelse af urolige elever i folkeskolens almindelige klasse (1997) Undervisningsministeriet Folkeskoleafdelingen.

4 Finland

Kaj Björkqvist and Karin Österman

Overview

In this chapter, research on bullying in Finnish schools and measures taken in order to counter bullying in our nation are presented. Finland is a Nordic country, located on the eastern side of the Baltic and bordering Sweden and Russia. Finland has two official languages: Finnish (spoken by the majority of the inhabitants) and Swedish (spoken by a minority). The social and educational systems are similar to those of other Nordic countries. Due to historical and geographical circumstances, Finland has had especially close ties to Sweden, and, accordingly, the cultural climate is similar in both countries. As an example, corporal punishment of children by parents is prohibited by law in both Sweden and Finland.

The Finnish school system

In Finland, children attend compulsory comprehensive school from ages 7 to 16. Comprehensive school, in turn, is divided into two parts: primary school (grades 1 to 6), and junior secondary school (grades 7 to 9). After age 16, those who wish may continue at senior secondary school (grades 10 to 12). After that, they either pass or do not pass a matriculation examination, giving them the right to apply for university.

Bullying is a relatively frequent phenomenon at comprehensive school, especially as pupils usually have the same class-mates all through the grades. At senior secondary school, bullying is much less frequent: pupils at that level are more motivated, and also more mature, than at the junior secondary level.

School is free of charge at all levels, and government funded. Private schools are not prohibited, but almost non-existent. In major cities, private Waldorf schools may be found, based on Rudolf Steiner's educational philosophy (for example, no marks are awarded and pupils compile their own textbooks), but these are exceptions.

The Ministry of Education makes decisions pertaining to nationwide requirements about curricula and teacher education. In order to become a teacher at any level within the Finnish school system, one must earn the degree of

Master of Education, which requires between five and six years of university level study.

The beginning: bullying is acknowledged and given a name

Bullying has probably occurred as long as there have been schools; the phenomenon became known to the general public and was recognized as a societal problem, however, through a book by the Swedish author/physician Heinemann (1972). Prior to that, bullying was more or less a taboo subject, which teachers and teacher organizations avoided. In his book, Heinemann used the term 'mobbing', which rapidly became the generally accepted word for bullying in Scandinavian languages.

In his attempts to understand the phenomenon, Heinemann felt that he had found an answer in the book *On aggression* (Lorenz, 1966; German original, 1963; Swedish translation, 1968). In this book, Konrad Lorenz describes a phenomenon referred to in the German original as 'ausstiessen', or 'die soziale Verteidigungsreaktion' (Lorenz, 1963, pp. 69, 114). By these terms, Lorenz referred to a collective group attack by one group of animals on an animal of another species, or on an individual who is, in one way or another, deviant from the rest of the group. The translator of Lorenz's book into Swedish selected an English word, 'mobbing', for the phenomenon; Heinemann picked it up and used it to denote bullying in schools, and it became the standard term used in Scandinavia.

The questionable credit for coining the term mobbing thus goes to translator Sjölander, not to Lorenz, as has been thought mistakenly in Scandinavia; Björkqvist has pointed out this fact in another article (Lagerspetz, Björkqvist, Berts and King, 1982). The fact that Heinemann chose Lorenz's description as his starting point had detrimental consequences for the general views on bullying in Scandinavia, however, since mobbing was regarded as (1) a group phenomenon of collective aggression, and (2) victims of bullying were regarded as deviant. Both of these rather prejudiced views have been questioned already in the early works by Olweus (1973).

Research: early studies

Since Swedish is spoken in Finland, Heinemann's works (1969, 1972) are read and familiar to school psychologists. The book by Dan Olweus (1973), however, became a milestone: this was the first serious empirical study on bullying in schools. Kirsti Lagerspetz, who had founded a research group focusing on aggression at the Åbo Akademi University in Turku, Finland, decided to replicate Olweus' research in Finnish schools. Two studies were conducted in the late 1970s and published in the early 1980s (Lagerspetz *et al.*, 1982; Björkqvist, Ekman and Lagerspetz, 1982). The Lagerspetz *et al.* (1982) study was a close replication, following Olweus' methodology. Bullying (or mobbing, as it was referred to, although we were unhappy with the term) was measured by a peer nomination technique; mobbing was defined and explained to the participants in the study, and pupils were to assess who in the class, if any, were bullies and/or victims.

The replication corroborated Olweus' findings: frequencies of bullying were similar. In the Lagerspetz *et al.* (1982) study, bullies among 12- to 16-year-old children amounted to 5.5 per cent of the samples, and victims to 3.9 per cent. Bullying was somewhat more frequent among boys than among girls. We found no difference between city and country schools as far as frequency was concerned. As in the study by Olweus, deviance in the form of handicap was no more common among victims than among controls. Bullies were found to be physically stronger than their victims.

In the second study (Björkqvist *et al.*, 1982), it was investigated how bullies, victims and controls viewed themselves. Their ego picture (their image of their own personality), ideal ego picture (their image of how they would like to be), and normative ego picture (their image of general norms of various personality traits) were investigated by use of a semantic differential technique. The difference between the ego picture and the ideal ego picture was regarded as a measure of self-esteem (a small difference being a sign of good self-esteem), and the difference between the ego picture and the normative ego picture as a measure of subjective social success (a small difference being a sign of good subjective social success).

As might be expected, victims had extremely poor self-esteem and felt themselves to be social failures. On items related to their ego picture, they scored high on depression and low on impulsiveness and on personal attractiveness. It is worth noting that female victims were even more depressed than male victims, and likewise felt themselves to be less attractive and less impulsive.

The most typical personality feature of the bullies was that they scored extremely high on dominance; in fact, male bullies wanted to be even more domineering than they felt they were. This finding was exceptional, since scores of the ideal ego picture usually did not exceed scores of the individual ego picture on personality traits regarded as negative. The result indicated that male bullies did not consider dominance to be a negative trait, but quite the opposite. Female bullies also scored very high on dominance, on items pertaining to their ego picture as well as on items pertaining to their ideal ego picture. Bullies of both sexes not only considered themselves to be dominant, they also idealized dominant behaviour.

Bullies further scored high on impulsiveness, and on a variable defined as 'dominated by feelings'. That is, they obviously felt they had poor control over their emotions and impulses, a fact that was likely to get them into trouble.

Research on sex differences

In the second half of the 1980s, our research group became convinced that the traditional view on sex differences in aggressive behaviour, suggesting that females display very little aggressiveness, was basically incorrect. Rather than being a quantitative difference, we felt it might be a question of a difference in quality; girls perhaps display their aggressiveness in different ways from boys. Aggressive behaviour – including bullying – occurs more between opponents of the same sex than between opponents of different sexes. In a series of studies targeting adolescent aggressive behaviour in the school environment (Lagerspetz, Björkqvist and Peltonen, 1988; Björkqvist, Lagerspetz and Kaukiainen, 1992; Björkqvist and Niemelä, 1992; Björkqvist, Österman and Kaukiainen, 1992; Österman *et al.*, 1994), it was shown that indirect aggression was more typical of females. A specific instrument, the Direct and Indirect Aggression Scales (DIAS), based on peer estimations, was developed, by which three types of aggression – physical, direct verbal and indirect – may be measured. This research on sex differences was reviewed in Björkqvist (1994).

Similar findings were later presented in other countries (e.g. Crick and Grotpeter, 1995, in the USA; Owen, 1996, in Australia), and we have collected data from several countries by the use of DIAS, suggesting that the female preference for indirect aggression during adolescence indeed seems to appear in at least Finland, Poland, Israel and Italy (Österman *et al.*, 1998). Whitney and Smith (1993) adapted the concept of indirect aggression specifically to research on bullying, and they found that girls, in their British sample, bully in more indirect ways than do boys. This by no means implies that indirect bullying, aimed at causing psychological harm and mental rather than physical pain, is less damaging for the victim than direct bullying. In fact, in our research we have consistently found that girls experience victimization to indirect bullying as extremely painful. As mentioned above, in the early Björkqvist *et al.* (1982) study, we found female victims to be more depressed than male victims.

Research on participant roles

Christina Salmivalli, of our research group, has focused her interest on the participant roles of the pupils of a class in which bullying occurs: as studies tend to show (Olweus, 1973, 1978; Björkqvist *et al.*, 1982; Lagerspetz *et al.*, 1982), 70 per cent of the pupils in school classes do not actively participate in bullying, and the Heinemann (1972) concept of collective aggression – the whole group against the lonely victim – is incorrect. In Salmivalli, Lagerspetz, Björkqvist, Österman and Kaukiainen (1996), six participant roles were identified: besides the bully and the victim, there were the assistant of the bully, the reinforcer of the bully, the defender of the victim, and the outsider. Children were moderately aware of their participant roles, and they tended to underestimate their participation in active bullying, overemphasizing tendencies to defend the victim, or being outsiders. Their roles were further related to five sociometric status groups: popular, rejected, neglected, controversial and average (cf. Coie, Dodge and Coppotelli, 1982; Coie, Dodge and Kupersmidt, 1990). Defenders were the most popular children. Bullies, their assistants and their reinforcers were rejected pupils. Neglected children tended not to have a clear participant role in the bullying process, while controversial children typically scored above average on all scales measuring participant roles.

In another study, Salmivalli, Karhunen and Lagerspetz (1996) found (a) sex differences in the behaviour of victims, and (b) that the type of behaviour displayed by the victim may be crucial for the outcome of the bullying process. Three different response types to bullying were identified: being counter-aggressive, helpless or nonchalant. Female victims tended to be either helpless or nonchalant, while male victims responded more with either counter-aggressiveness or nonchalance. Nonchalance appeared to be the best strategy to stop bullying, while helplessness and counter-aggressiveness resulted in continuation of the vicious bullying/victimization circle.

In a third study (Salmivalli, Huttunen and Lagerspetz, 1997) participant roles were shown to be related to social networks within the class. Children who had or took similar roles formed friendship networks with each other, and how a child behaved was largely related to the behaviour of his or her friends. Bullies, their assistants and reinforcers in general belonged to larger networks than did defenders, outsiders and victims.

Prevention and intervention

Although prevention and intervention here are mentioned as two separate categories – which they logically are – in practice, preventive and intervention techniques are commonly interwoven with each other. Both types of countermeasures have been taken in Finnish schools, but in our opinion to a far too limited extent. In the following, we will review some of the measures that have been taken.

Implementation of Olweus' principles

Initiatives to stop bullying in Finnish schools were taken in the early 1980s, as soon as the research findings were commonly known. Journalists described horrifying cases of bullying in daily newspapers, and spontaneous initiatives – by private individuals as often as by organizations – appeared all over the country. An organization named Hem och Skola (Home and School) was particularly active in schools with Swedish as the teaching language. Small courses, based usually on Olweus' (1973, 1978, 1986) principles of prevention and intervention, were organized. Hem och Skola includes both parents and teachers as members. All activities arranged are on a voluntary basis. Accordingly, schools varied greatly in their attempts to stop bullying and in success.

One of the present authors (Björkqvist) lectured and informed on countermeasures against bullying in a wide variety of schools, invited by Hem och Skola, during the 1980s. He also gave practical advice in a number of individual cases.

The principles outlined in the book *Mobbning – vad vi vet och vad vi kan göra* (Olweus, 1986) proved especially useful, and together they form probably the most commonly applied system in programmes aimed at countering bullying in Finnish schools. Since these principles are available for English readers, we will not discuss them further in this context.

The book was published in Finnish in 1992. In 1993, three nationwide organisations – Mannerheimin Lastensuojeluliitto (Mannerheim's Association for the Protection of Children), The Red Cross of Finland, and Folkhälsan (People's Health) – cooperated in a large nationwide project aimed at teaching prevention and intervention principles in Finnish schools. The programme was, to a large extent, based upon Olweus' principles, but it also suggested ideas on how victims of bullying could be supported. Regrettably, the effects of this project were not evaluated.

Pikas' method

As mentioned above, Olweus' principles are the best known and most applied intervention and prevention techniques in Finland. The intervention principles offered by Pikas (1975a, b), also known as the Farsta method, have, however, also received supporters. On the Åland Islands, located between Finland and Sweden, Pikas' system is especially much in use.

There is one fundamental difference between Olweus' and Pikas' techniques, making them difficult to combine. While Olweus stresses the importance of informing and activating parents in the intervention process, Pikas suggests that parents of bullies should not be informed, but teachers should agree a kind of 'pact' with the bullies: if they stop bullying, their parents will not be informed.

Our personal opinion is that the help of parents is extremely valuable. If parents of bullies do take an active stand they are quite often able to stop the bullying altogether.

Nuutinen's victim slide show

Timo Nuutinen, who worked for years in a department at a polyclinic, was shocked to find how frequently young victims of other adolescents' violent bullying were admitted, and how easily severe injuries were inflicted: tripping a victim in the school yard, a snowball aimed at the eyes, or a single blow to the nose. Seemingly harmless bullying often caused broken teeth, damaged eyes, broken noses, concussion of the brain or even irreversible brain damage.

Nuutinen compiled a slide show, presenting photographs and X-rays of real-life cases of injured young victims. The slides were quite shocking. He presented this slide show to pupils in schools, accompanied by lively descriptions of how the injuries were produced.

Nuutinen's victim slide show became very popular – in fact so popular that during the 1980s it was presented in practically every school in Finland. Everywhere he went, the pupils appeared impressed by the pictures and his vivid descriptions. The slide show seemed to have an almost shocking effect.

To our understanding, Nuutinen's slide-show shock might have an effect in two ways: (a) schoolchildren gain information about the consequences of violence. Since young people watch so many movies in which violence is glorified, and the consequences of violence – to a large extent – are understated or totally ignored, they do not have a proper understanding of the dangers of violence; (b) watching the slides, the pupils also feel increased empathy towards victims. Accordingly, it combined information with empathy training.

We measured 12- to 16-year-old pupils' attitudes to the behaviour described by Nuutinen in his lecture and slide show. These attitudes were measured on three occasions: before they were exposed to the slide show and lecture; four days after; and five months later. The results are presented graphically in Figures 4.1 and 4.2.

As the figures reveal, even a short shock treatment of this kind has some effect, at least on attitude. We did not really expect any long-term effects, but there were significant long-term effects on the presumed danger of violent

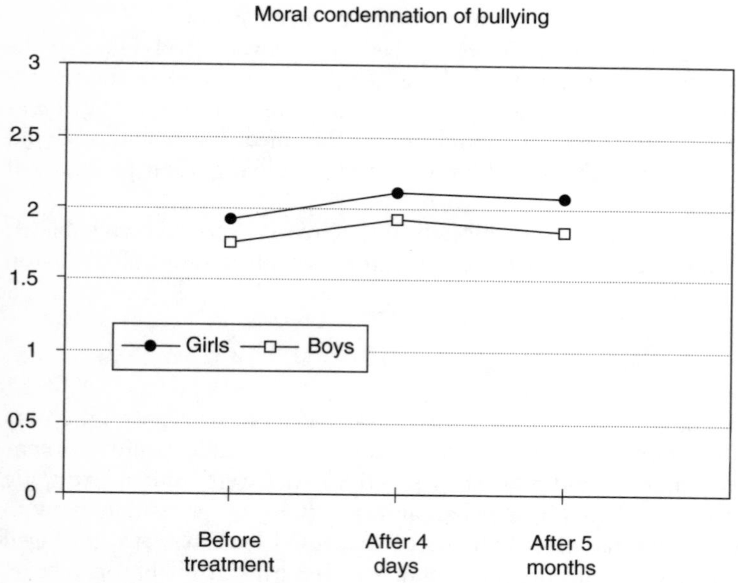

Figure 4.1 The level of moral condemnation of bullying among 12- to 16-year-old pupils, before exposure to the victim slide show, four days after, and five months later. Moral condemnation was measured by use of a ten-item scale ($\alpha = 0.85$).

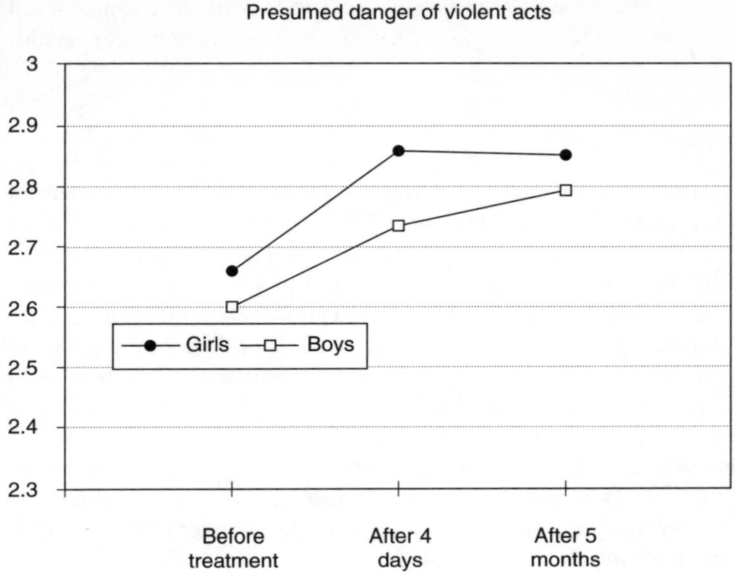

Figure 4.2 The level of presumed danger of violent acts among 12- to 16-year-old pupils, before exposure to the victim slide show, four days after, and five months later. The presumed danger of violent acts was measured by use of a five-item scale ($\alpha = 0.92$).

acts, and significant short-term effects on moral condemnation of bullying. Although this study was limited and we did not measure changes in actual behaviour, only in attitude, the results were still encouraging.

Support of victims

In the early 1990s, Kiusattujen Tuki r.y. (Victims' Support Organization) was founded by Esko Leipälä. A private initiative, the organization's active members are, to a large extent, parents of victims of bullying. Its influence has been important: besides spreading information about bullying and arranging training in prevention and intervention, it has focused especially on the victims and their need of support.

It is well known that victims suffer especially from a loss of self-esteem (e.g. Björkqvist *et al.*, 1982), and clinical (unpublished) data suggest that victims of severe bullying frequently foster suicidal thoughts; it appears that adolescents who commit suicide often have a history of being victimized by bullying. This is an issue which deserves empirical study.

Training programmes aimed at supporting victims of bullying have recently been provided by several independent therapists in Finland. Such training usually focuses on two aspects: (a) training in how to defend oneself against further bullying, and (b) various activities with the purpose of increasing self-esteem. The effect of these programmes has not been evaluated however.

Legal measures

Bullying may now be prosecuted according to Finnish law. In a precedential case in the city of Raahe in September 1995, two 15-year-old pupils were fined for systematic bullying of a same-aged peer over an extended period of time. The bullying consisted of both physical and psychological harassment. Interestingly, fines for inducing mental pain were greater than fines for physical abuse of the victim: one of the bullies was fined 10,000 FIM for psychological harassment, but only 1000 FIM for physical bullying; the other was fined 600 FIM for physical abuse, but 5000 FIM for psychological harassment (1000 FIM equals approximately US$180; £110) (Simonen, 1995).

By making bullying a penal offence, it was hoped it would serve as an exemplary deterrent. Whether it has had a deterring effect is not known so far, but it has certainly contributed to an attitude change within Finnish society, making bullying more condemnable.

Bullying of and by teachers

Bullying in schools is not only a case of pupils bullying peers: teachers are also involved, in some cases as victims, in others as bullies. During the 1980s, several cases of severe bullying of teachers became known in Finland. In one case, a teacher in the city of Turku was brutally killed by a pupil using a shovel as a weapon.

During the 1990s, a growing awareness of the fact that teachers bully and harass pupils has surfaced. Journalist Udd-Ståhl (1993) documented several cases of teacher bullying. In a scandalous case a headmaster was fined for sexual harassment of pupils, but was still allowed to keep his job. In another school, where pupils required special education, several teachers harassed pupils systematically; one teacher who objected to these practices was harassed in turn, and forced to leave her job.

The lack of obligatory measures against bullying within the educational system

One would expect that in a highly developed society such as Finland, the teacher training in faculties of education at Finnish universities would provide compulsory training in prevention and intervention of bullying. Regrettably, this is not the case. In 1995, Kaj Björkqvist provided a course on countermeasures against bullying at the Faculty of Education of Åbo Akademi University, which educates all Swedish-speaking teachers in Finland; this was by special request of the teachers-to-be, and not an initiative on behalf of the faculty. Otherwise, such training has not been provided to our knowledge.

We have, on several occasions and in various circumstances, suggested that the school curriculum should include a subject called 'human relations', starting from the very first year of school. The object of this subject would be to provide pupils with training in how to deal with relational problems, such as conflicts between themselves and their peers and conflicts with adults; to teach them how to intervene when they witness bullying; and to assist pupils in increasing their awareness of their own emotional life. Role play, films and discussions could be applied as teaching methods, besides regular didactics. To understand and be able to deal with human relations, we argue, is far more important than history and geography (although these are important subjects, too). It is somewhat strange that society provides education in a large variety of subjects of a scholarly nature, but when it comes to human relations, which is the source of both the greatest misery and the greatest joy in life, we do not consider it worth covering in our educational system.

Conclusions

To sum up, there has been a fair amount of research on bullying in Finnish schools; preventive and intervening measures have also been taken. However, training in countermeasures has been left completely to voluntary initiative from individuals and organizations, and the educational system has in this respect neglected its moral obligations. Even so, the awareness of bullying problems is probably high in Finland in comparison with most nations of the world.

References

Björkqvist, K. (1994) Sex differences in physical, verbal, and indirect aggression: A review of recent research. *Sex Roles*, 30, 177–188.

Björkqvist, K., Ekman, K. and Lagerspetz, K. M. J. (1982) Bullies and victims: Their ego picture, ideal ego picture and normative ego picture. *Scandinavian Journal of Psychology*, 23, 307–313.

Björkqvist, K., Lagerspetz, K. M. J. and Kaukiainen, A. (1992) Do girls manipulate and boys fight? Developmental trends regarding direct and indirect aggression. *Aggressive Behavior*, 18, 117–127.

Björkqvist, K. and Niemelä, P. (1992) New trends in the study of female aggression. In K. Björkqvist and P. Niemelä (eds), *Of mice and women: Aspects of female aggression* (pp. 3–16). San Diego, CA: Academic Press.

Björkqvist, K. and Österman, K. (unpublished) Short-term and long-term effects on attitudes towards aggression and bullying in schools by a slide show showing injured victims of violent bullying.

Björkqvist, K., Österman, K. and Kaukiainen, A. (1992) The development of direct and indirect aggressive strategies in males and females. In K. Björkqvist and

P. Niemelä (eds), *Of mice and women: Aspects of female aggression* (pp. 51–64). San Diego, CA: Academic Press.

Coie, J. D., Dodge, K. A. and Coppotelli, H. (1982) Dimensions and types of social status: A cross-age perspective. *Developmental Psychology*, 18, 557–570.

Coie, J. D., Dodge, K. A. and Kupersmidt, J. B. (1990) Peer group behavior and social status. In S. R. Asher and J. D. Coie (eds), *Peer rejection in childhood*. Cambridge: Cambridge University Press.

Crick, N. R. and Grotpeter, J. K. (1995) Relational aggression, gender, and social-psychological adjustment. *Child Development*, 66, 710–722.

Heinemann, P.-P. (1969) Apartheid. *Liberal Debatt*, 3, 3–14.

Heinemann, P.-P. (1972) *Gruppvåld bland barn och vuxna*. Stockholm, Sweden: Natur och Kultur.

Lagerspetz, K. M. J., Björkqvist, K., Berts, M. and King, E. (1982) Group aggression among school children in three schools. *Scandinavian Journal of Psychology*, 23, 45–52.

Lagerspetz, K. M. J., Björkqvist, K. and Peltonen, T. (1988) Is indirect aggression typical of females? Gender differences in 11- to 12-year-old children. *Aggressive Behavior*, 14, 403–414.

Lorenz, K. (1963) *Das Sogenannte Böse*. Vienna, Austria: Borotha-Schoeler.

Lorenz, K. (1966) *On aggression*. London: Methuen.

Lorenz, K. (1968) *Aggression: Dess bakgrund och natur*. Stockholm, Sweden: Norstedt & Söner.

Olweus, D. (1973) *Hackkycklingar och översittare*. Kungälv, Sweden: Almqvist & Wiksell.

Olweus, D. (1978) *Aggression in the schools: Bullies and whipping boys*. New York: John Wiley.

Olweus, D. (1986) *Mobbning – vad vi vet och vad vi kan göra*. Stockholm, Sweden: Liber.

Olweus, D. (1992) *Kiusaaminen koulussa*. Helsinki, Finland: Otava.

Österman, K., Björkqvist, K., Lagerspetz, K. M. J., Kaukiainen, K., Huesmann, L. R. and Frazcek, A. (1994) Peer- and self-estimated aggression and victimization in 8-year-old children from five ethnic groups. *Aggressive Behavior*, 20, 411–428.

Österman, K., Björkqvist, K. and Lagerspetz, K. M. J., with Kaukiainen, K., Landau, S. F., Frazcek, A. and Caprara, G. V. (1998) Cross-cultural evidence of female indirect aggression. *Aggressive Behavior*, 24, 1–8.

Owen, L. (1996) Sticks and stones and sugar and spice: Girls' and boys' aggression in schools. *Australian Journal of Guidance and Counselling*, 6, 45–55.

Pikas, A. (1975a) *Så stoppar vi mobbning!* Lund, Sweden: Berlingska Boktryckeriet.

Pikas, A. (1975b) Treatment of mobbing in school: Principles for and the results of the work of an anti-mobbing group. *Scandinavian Journal of Educational Research*, 19, 1–12.

Salmivalli, C., Huttunen, A. and Lagerspetz, K. M. J. (1997) Peer networks and bullying in schools. *Scandinavian Journal of Psychology*, 38, 305–312.

Salmivalli, C., Karhunen, J. and Lagerspetz, K. M. J. (1996) How do the victims respond to bullying? *Aggressive Behavior*, 22, 99–109.

Salmivalli, C., Lagerspetz, K. M. J., Björkqvist, K., Österman, K. and Kaukiainen, A. (1996) Bullying as a group process. Participant roles and their relations to social status within the group. *Aggressive Behavior*, 22, 1–15.

Simonen, M. (1995) Kahdelle pojalle sakkoja koulukiusaamisesta. *Iltalehti*, 21 September, p. 9.

Udd-Ståhl, H. (1993) *Varning för skolan*. Jakobstad: Sahlberg.

Whitney, I. and Smith, P.K. (1993) A survey of the nature and extent of bullying in junior/middle and secondary schools. *Educational Research*, 35, 3–25.

5 England and Wales

Peter K. Smith

Overview

School bullying has been of concern in England and Wales since 1989, when the government's Elton Report on discipline appeared and three books on the topic were published. Survey results suggested bullying was widespread, with around one child in five being involved in bullying during a school term. This generated media interest, which has continued to the present day. The Gulbenkian Foundation supported a number of initiatives to tackle bullying, including a booklet, a telephone helpline, drama work, and a bibliography (recently into a second edition). It also supported the first large-scale survey of school bullying, of nearly 7000 pupils in 24 Sheffield schools.

Subsequent surveys have substantiated the seriousness of the problem. Pupils with special educational needs or disabilities are particularly at risk of being bullied. Those bullied tend to have fewer friends, lower self-esteem, and are at risk of various academic and health-related problems. Every year, several young people commit suicide, in part because of school bullying.

In 1991, the Department for Education supported an intervention project, based in 23 of the 24 schools in the Sheffield survey. Interventions comprised a whole-school policy, curriculum work, work in playgrounds, and work with individual pupils and small groups involved in bullying situations. Using anonymous self-report questionnaires, together with other assessment measures, the effects of the interventions were monitored over four school terms. Significant reductions in bullying were obtained; these were larger in primary schools, and largest in those schools which had put most effort into interventions and consulted widely on policy development. In secondary schools there were large increases in willingness to seek help when bullied.

Two smaller intervention projects also took place during this period, one in Wolverhampton, and one funded by the Home Office, in London and Liverpool.

In 1994 the Department for Education and Employment produced a pack, *Don't suffer in silence*, based on the findings from the Sheffield intervention project, with a video from the Wolverhampton project. This was offered free to state schools and has been requested to date by 19,000 schools. Bullying is now a topic considered during regular inspections of schools. The climate of opinion on the matter has shifted significantly over the last eight years; bullying is discussed much more openly, and many schools now have anti-bullying policies.

England and Wales: social and cultural background

The United Kingdom consists of England and Wales, Scotland, and Northern Ireland. The latter two countries have a somewhat separate educational system, and the situation regarding school bullying in Scotland is described by Andrew Mellor in Chapter 6; but the broad features are similar in all parts of the UK. Concern about school bullying is also nationwide; a good summary of work up to 1993 is provided by Farrington (1993).

Schooling is compulsory from 5 years to 16 years of age. Children enter primary school as 'rising fives'; the primary sector covers infant schools (5 to 7 years) and junior schools (8 to 10 years), infant and junior schools often being on the same site. Such schools typically have classes of between 25 and 35 pupils, with one or two classes in each year group, school sizes being between 100 and 400 pupils. From 11 to 16 years pupils are in secondary schools, with several classes in each year group and around 1000 pupils in total. After age 16, some pupils will continue into further education (FE), either at school or at FE college, prior to university (higher education) entrance at around age 18.

In primary schools, pupils mainly have one class teacher for most lessons; in secondary schools, they will have specialist subject teachers. A school will be serviced by support staff such as educational psychologists, and secondary schools will have teachers with assigned responsibilities for pastoral care. There is little in the way of specialised school counselling services, though many schools have staff members who will have completed some training in counselling.

Pupils spend curricular time in lessons of about 50 minutes, and have a mid-morning play break (and sometimes a mid-afternoon play break) of 15–20 minutes, and a longer lunch-time break of some 60–90 minutes, only part of which is taken up with lunch (often on a shift system). The break times are not supervised by teachers, but by lunchtime supervisors (usually local mothers) who receive little pay and usually even less training for the task.

Most schools are in urban areas, ranging in size from London (*c.* 8 million) through large provincial cities (*c.* 0.5 to 1 million) to towns of several tens of thousands of inhabitants. Some of course are rural, especially in the primary sector. Urban areas, especially in England, may contain a racial mixture, with sizeable minorities (occasionally majorities) of pupils from Afro-Caribbean or Indian subcontinental origins, and smaller minorities from the Arab countries, or Far Eastern countries.

The population is socioeconomically quite diverse, with considerable range of wealth and housing. The private schooling sector has expanded over the last decade to around 7 per cent, higher in London and the south-east.

Lifetime expectations are for only 50 per cent of marriages to survive. Some 20 per cent of pupils may be in separated, divorced or single-parent families at any time; there are marked regional and racial variations in this (Clarke, 1992).

Attitudes to child-rearing remain somewhat punitive. Physical chastisement of children by parents or by child-minders is allowed, and was sanctioned by the previous government (early 1997). However, it is forbidden to teachers in schools. More traditional attitudes to physical punishment may be greater in lower social class groups and some racial minorities. There is however widespread concern about physical and sexual abuse of children in the family; and about bullying in schools.

Studies of school bullying in England and Wales

School bullying remained a low-key issue in the whole of the UK well into the 1980s; only in the last ten years has bullying appeared firmly on the educational agenda. Public and media attention became particularly focused on the issue in 1989 to 1990. In 1989 three books on the topic appeared: D. Tattum and D. Lane (eds), *Bullying in schools*; E. Roland and E. Munthe (eds), *Bullying: An international perspective*; and V. Besag, *Bullies and victims in schools*.

The Elton Report (Department of Education and Science, 1989) on discipline in schools, while primarily on teacher–pupil relations and discipline, did mention problems of bullying in a few paragraphs. It stated (pp. 102–103) that 'recent studies of bullying in schools suggest that the problem is widespread and tends to be ignored by teachers. . . . Research suggests that bullying not only causes considerable suffering to individual pupils but also has a damaging effect on school atmosphere.' It recommended that schools should encourage pupils to tell staff of serious cases of bullying, deal firmly with bullying behaviour, and take action based on clear rules and backed by appropriate sanctions and systems to protect and support victims.

No direct action on bullying was taken by the then Department for Education (DFE) in London as an immediate result of the Elton Report. However, the Gulbenkian Foundation set up an advisory working group on 'Bullying in Schools' in 1989. This funded several initiatives. One was a 32-page booklet, *Bullying: A positive response*, by Tattum and Herbert (1990), available at a low cost. With the launch of this booklet it also supported a three-month extension of the ChildLine telephone service to a special bullying line which received some 40–200 calls a day; an analysis of these was later published (LaFontaine, 1991).

In 1991 two edited collections on bullying appeared, both looking at practical approaches to help teachers – *Practical approaches to bullying* by Smith and

Thompson (1991), and *Bullying: A practical guide to coping for schools* by Elliott (1991). The Gulbenkian Foundation also funded the preparation of an annotated bibliography and resource guide on anti-bullying materials and strategies (Skinner, 1992; a second edition was published in 1996). Subsequently, it supported the preparation of *We don't have bullies here!*, a package of materials for schools by Besag (1992); *Cycle of violence*, video materials by Tattum, Tattum and Herbert (1993); and *Countering bullying*, a compilation of case studies by Tattum and Herbert (1993). The national charity Kidscape, with a long interest in child protection, has also produced materials and campaigned on the issue of school bullying. In the south-west of England, Maines and Robinson (1992) advocated a 'no blame' approach to tackling bullying. These varied support activities have contributed to not only keeping bullying on the agenda, but to providing sources of practical help for schools and teachers.

During this period the Gulbenkian Foundation also supported survey work at Sheffield University, which I directed. In this, we piloted ways of using anonymous questionnaires to gather information on the nature and extent of school bullying, basing our work on the questionnaire used by Olweus (1993) in Norway. This and other survey results, reported between 1989 and 1991, revealed the widespread nature of school bullying. There were even newspaper headlines asking whether Britain was the 'Bullying capital of Europe'. (The bullying statistics for Britain do appear to be higher than those in Norway, but no higher than in many other European countries, or Japan, as subsequent research has shown.) The survey findings and publicity led to the DFE funding the Sheffield Anti-Bullying Project, an intervention project inspired by that in Norway, and designed to evaluate just how useful particular interventions were. Funding for this commenced in April 1991 and continued until August 1993. This project will be described later.

In 1992, the BBC *That's Life* programme pursued the topic vigorously following the suicide of an adolescent girl due in part to bullying at school. Questions were asked in Parliament about what action the government was taking on bullying. At this point, the Sheffield Project was half-way through; while stating that the report of this project was awaited, the DFE decided in the interim to circulate a 'Scottish pack' to all schools in England and Wales. This pack, *Action against bullying* (1991), by Johnstone, Munn and Edwards of the Scottish Council for Research in Education (SCRE), had been circulated to schools in Scotland some months previously. (In 1993, the SCRE team produced a second pack, *Supporting schools against bullying*, with particular advice for parents and non-teaching staff; Mellor, 1993; Munn, 1993.) Also in 1993, Tattum produced an edited collection, *Understanding and managing bullying*.

The nature of bullying in England and Wales

In one of the first systematic studies, Arora and Thompson (1987) used a 'Life in School' checklist to define the nature of bullying in a secondary school in the north of England. Actions most often perceived as bullying included hurting, demanding money, breaking belongings, hitting and kicking. The 'Life in School' checklist is described in more detail in Arora (1994b). It has a 40-item list of behaviours, such as 'told a lie about me' or 'smiled at me', which the pupils complete depending upon whether these happened to them during the week. The checklist circumvents issues of pupils' understanding of what the term bullying means; this is an important issue, as Smith and Levan (1995) found, in a study of 6 year olds, that many young children over-interpreted the term bullying to include nasty acts generally. Issues of definition and measurement are discussed further in Ahmad and Smith (1990) and Arora (1996).

An alternative to the 'Life in School' checklist is the Olweus anonymous self-report questionnaire, which incorporates a standard definition of bullying. This was modified for use in the UK (Ahmad and Smith, 1990). It was used in the first large-scale survey in Britain, by Whitney and Smith (1993), carried out in 24 schools in Sheffield at the end of 1990. Over 6700 pupils took part in the survey; 2600 from primary and 4100 from secondary schools.

The results confirmed that bullying was extensive. Twenty-seven per cent of primary school pupils reported being bullied 'sometimes' or more frequently, and this included 10 per cent bullied 'once a week' or more frequently. For secondary schools, these figures were 10 per cent and 4 per cent respectively. Analyses by year group confirmed that there was a fairly steady decrease in reports of being bullied from 8 through to 16 years.

So far as reporting taking part in bullying others was concerned, this was admitted by some 12 per cent of primary school pupils 'sometimes' or more frequently, including 4 per cent who bullied 'once a week' or more frequently. For secondary schools, these figures were 6 per cent and 1 per cent respectively. For those who were bullied, most of the bullying was reported to have been carried out by pupils in the same class as the victim in primary schools. In secondary schools, pupils were slightly more likely to be bullied by pupils from a different class (but in the same year) than by pupils in their own class or in higher years than themselves, probably because secondary schools have more classes in a year group. Few seemed to be bullied by pupils from years below them.

The majority of the bullying was reported to have occurred in the playground, particularly by primary pupils. For secondary pupils this percentage was only slightly higher than being bullied in the classroom or in the corridors. Reports of being bullied going to or from school were less than half the reported incidence of being bullied in school.

Most of the bullying took the form of general name-calling. Being physically hit and being threatened were the next most frequent forms of bullying in both primary and secondary schools. Boys were more likely to be physically hit and threatened than were girls. Girls were more likely to experience indirect forms of bullying such as having no one talk to them, or having rumours spread about them. These sex differences were found in both primary and secondary schools.

Pupils were asked if they had either told a teacher at school or anyone at home about being bullied. There were three clear trends in this data. First, both primary and secondary school pupils were significantly more likely to tell someone at home that they had been bullied than to tell their teacher. Second, primary school pupils were significantly more likely than secondary school pupils to tell either their teacher or anyone at home that they had been bullied. Third, the percentage of pupils who did tell their teacher or anyone at home that they had been bullied increased fairly consistently with frequency of being bullied, especially for the highest frequency of 'several times a week'; but even for these, only about half of secondary pupils had told anyone at home.

Similar findings to the above were reported by Boulton and Underwood (1992) in a study of about 300 8 to 12 year olds, also in the Sheffield area. Other surveys elsewhere in Britain suggest incidence figures and general findings in line with the Sheffield survey (e.g. Miller, 1995). However, a survey by Mellor (1990) in a cross-section of Scottish schools reported lower levels of bullying, more in line with the Norwegian levels. The reason for this difference is not clear.

Analysis of school variations in the Whitney and Smith (1993) study suggested that size of school was not a factor. There was a modest effect of socioeconomic deprivation, accounting for about 10 per cent of the variance (more bullying in schools in more deprived areas). However, it is likely that school ethos and anti-bullying policies explain a much larger source of variance.

Racist bullying has been a particularly worrying feature in some schools (Kelly and Cohn, 1988); in one well-known case racist bullying resulted in a child's death (Burnage Report, 1989). Children can experience racist teasing and name-calling (Mooney, Creeser and Blatchford, 1991), and those of non-white ethnic origin have been shown to experience more racist name-calling (though not necessarily other forms of bullying) than white children of the same age and gender (Moran, Smith, Thompson and Whitney, 1993; Boulton, 1995b).

In secondary schools, it appears that children of different sexual orientation (gay, lesbian) are also likely to be bullied. Rivers (1995, 1996) obtained questionnaires from 140 gay and lesbian young people; 80 per cent had experienced teasing about their sexual orientation, and over half had been physically assaulted or ridiculed by other pupils or teachers.

Bullying and children with special educational needs

Certain children in England and Wales are seen as having special educational needs, either because of some disability such as partial sight or blindness, hearing impairment or deafness, or a physical disability; or because of emotional and behavioural disturbance; or certain learning difficulties, such as dyslexia. A child can be 'statemented', a process involving an evaluation of the child's needs and abilities by an educational psychologist. A small proportion of children with severe disabilities are educated in special schools. Another small proportion of children with severe behavioural difficulties and disruptive behaviour, who may have been excluded from mainstream schools, are educated in small 'pupil referral units'. However, the majority of statemented children are 'mainstreamed'; that is to say, they are educated in the same schools as the majority of pupils. However, they may be taken out of ordinary classes at certain times for special tuition. The process of statementing allows schools to claim some extra resources for these pupils, and some schools have special resources ('integrated resources') for certain disabilities (e.g. partial sight, hearing).

Several studies have shown that children with special educational needs are substantially more at risk of being involved in bully/victim situations. Martlew and Hodson (1991) compared mainstream children (without special needs) with children with special needs in a school in Sheffield with integrated resources for children with mild learning difficulties. The children with special needs were found to be teased significantly more, and to have fewer friends. Mainstream children showed a preference for social interaction with other mainstream peers rather than children with special needs.

Nabuzoka and Smith (1993) examined social relationships in two schools with integrated resources in Sheffield. Of 179 children interviewed, 36 had been statemented as having special needs (moderate learning difficulties). Each child was asked to nominate individuals from their class who best fitted eight behavioural descriptions, including 'bully' and 'victim'. Children with moderate learning difficulties were significantly more likely to be selected as victims (33 per cent) than were those without moderate learning difficulties (8 per cent).

Nabuzoka and Smith also looked at the degree of association with other behavioural nominations such as children who were thought to be 'shy', 'seeking help', 'disruptive' and 'starting fights'. Bullies were seen as being disruptive and starting fights. Victims were seen as being shy and needing help. This was true for both the children with and without special needs. This implies that the same criteria of vulnerability (implied by shyness and needing help) tend to be used to victimise other children, whether or not they have special needs. On the other hand, these children with special needs were more likely to be selected as victims of bullying than non-statemented children.

An important factor in making statemented children more vulnerable may be lack of protective peer relationships, which are generally found to be less in children with special needs. Indeed, Nabuzoka and Smith found children with special needs to be less popular and more rejected than peers who had no special needs, a finding similar to Martlew and Hodson (1991).

Are problems of bullying recognised by teachers? Nabuzoka and Smith found that while there was a high correlation between being a victim and 'shy' as well as 'help-seeking' behaviour in the perceptions of the children's peers, no such relationship was found with teacher ratings. The teachers however, like peers, significantly rated children with special needs as more shy and seeking help than children who had no special needs. The lack of association between being a victim of bullying and these behavioural characteristics by teachers indicate that teachers may not be aware of some factors putting certain children at risk of victimisation.

A study by Whitney, Smith and Thompson (1994), linked to the Sheffield intervention project, carefully matched children with special needs to mainstream children of the same school year group, age, race and gender. The results confirmed that children with special needs were two to three times more at risk of being bullied; they were also more at risk of taking part in bullying others. Teachers were reasonably accurate in recognising that these children were likely to be bullied, but tended to underestimate the frequency of such bullying as compared to the pupil's own self-report.

These studies point to at least three factors which increase the risk of children with special needs being victimised. First, they may have particular characteristics related to their learning difficulties or have other disabilities which may make them an obvious target; second, children with special needs in integrated settings are less well integrated socially and lack the protection against bullying which friendship gives; and third, some children with behavioural problems may act out in an aggressive way and become 'provocative victims'.

The particular situation of dysfluent children (children with a stammer) was reported on by Mooney and Smith (1995), on the basis of retrospective reports by adults who were members of the Association for Stammerers (now called the British Stammering Association). Dysfluent children are very often bullied, as not only is the stammering an obvious target for teasing – by teachers as well as pupils, at times – but it is also very difficult for the dysfluent child to respond verbally in an assertive way. Many adults reported that their school experiences had affected them very severely.

Dawkins (1996) compared experiences of bullying between two groups of children attending hospital clinics: some (CDC) were attending a child development centre with conditions affecting their appearance and/or gait and therefore had a visible abnormality; the contrast group (OPD) were attending a general paediatric clinic with conditions not associated with visible abnormalities. The CDC children were significantly more likely to experience bullying; in part, this appeared to be because of the extra help they received in school, which may have stigmatised them. For both groups, being alone at playtime and having few friends at school were risk factors for being bullied.

Characteristics and consequences of bully/victim status

A number of studies have looked at characteristics of children who are bullies, or victims, and at the possible consequences of such status. Two pioneering studies by Lowenstein (1978a, b) relied partly on teacher nominations to identify bullying and bullied children. Bullying children were found to be more likely to have parents with marital difficulties, and an inconsistent approach to discipline, and to be rated by teachers as hyperactive and of low IQ or underachieving. Bullied children were seen as less physically attractive, less assertive and less well adjusted on a number of measures. Some of these outcomes may be 'haloed' by the effect of using teachers' ratings, and most subsequent studies have used self-report or peer nomination to ascertain bully/victim status.

As part of a large longitudinal study of London children, Farrington (1993) has reported links between generations, with fathers who were aggressive and bullying at school being more likely to have sons who were also bullying at school. Bowers, Smith and Binney (1992, 1994) used several different assessment procedures to obtain children's own perceptions of their families. They compared perceptions of bullies, victims, bully/victims and control children (as designated by peer nomination). Many bullies and bully/victims perceived their families as relatively lacking in affection and having poor monitoring procedures, confirming Lowenstein's findings. However, this work also showed the need to distinguish provocative victims or bully/victims from both bullies and ordinary victims. Children involved only in bullying perceived the family more in terms of power relationships with siblings and other family members, whereas the bully/victims perceived difficulties with parental behaviour such as punitiveness and lack of involvement, and seemed to be more concerned with their own position in the family, sometimes defensively. So far as bullied children were concerned, there was some evidence of over-protective parenting. Perhaps children in over-protected family environments do not develop the same skills of independence as their peers and are more vulnerable to exploitation by potential bullies.

Boulton and Smith (1994) and Boulton (1995a) also used peer nominations in a study of middle school children. Boulton and Smith found moderate stability of both bully and victim status from one year to the next. Both bullying and bullied children were less popular than non-involved children; bullying children were often 'controversial' (liked by some, disliked by others), whereas bullied children were often 'rejected'. On self-esteem measures, bullying children scored lower on behavioural items of the Harter scale (i.e. they accurately perceived their behaviour to be less well accepted) but were not low in other respects; bullied children did score lower on several dimensions of self-esteem. Boulton (1995a) assessed the playground behaviour of these children; bullying children tended to be in larger groups, whereas bullied children spent more time on their own and less time in rule games.

Sharp (1995, 1996; Sharp and Thompson, 1992) has studied correlates and consequences of bullying in a sample of 723 secondary school pupils aged 13 to 16 years. Forty-three per cent of those interviewed reported having been bullied during the previous year. She found that 20 per cent of these pupils said they would truant to avoid being bullied; 29 per cent found it difficult to concentrate on their school work; 22 per cent felt physically ill after being bullied, and 20 per cent had experienced sleeping difficulties as a result of the bullying. Some of these students reported finding the bullying extremely stressful, and although half reported using constructive coping strategies, not all could do so. Not all those bullied had low self-esteem, but those who did also reported more passive response styles to the bullying and, perhaps as a result, more extensive bullying and greater stress.

This work indicates that experiences of bullying can lead to physical complaints. This is also suggested by a survey in east London carried out by Williams, Chambers, Logan and Robinson (1996). Nearly 3000 children aged 7 to 10 years were interviewed; 22 per cent reported they had been bullied. Bullied children were significantly more likely to report not sleeping well, bed-wetting, feeling sad, and experiencing more than occasional headaches and stomach aches. School doctors and nurses may well be presented with symptoms due to bullying, and the implications of this for school health services are discussed by Dawkins (1995).

Two large-scale studies have been on students who report fear of being bullied at school (which may not necessarily mean actually being bullied, although one would expect substantial overlap). Francis and Jones (1994), in a study of 11,535 pupils from 68 schools throughout England and Wales aged 13 to 15 years, found that 25 per cent of respondents admitted to fear of being bullied; these pupils had higher neuroticism and lie scale scores, and lower psychoticism and extraversion scores on the Junior Eysenck Personality Questionnaire.

Balding, Regis, Wise, Bish and Muirden (1996) surveyed 11,613 pupils aged 11 to 16 years from 65 schools in England with the Health Related Behaviour Questionnaire, which has over 100 questions. Again, the target question was reported fear of going to school because of bullying (rather than actual bullying). Twenty-seven per cent of the sample reported some fear of bullying, with 5 per cent often fearing it. With such a large sample, many associations with other variables were significant: generally, pupils who feared bullying were less satisfied with life; had lower self-esteem; saw themselves as less fit and having less personal control over their health; were less satisfied with their weight; reported less enjoyment of physical activities; had a higher frequency of illness and disease, and more referrals to the doctor; reported more breathing problems and loss of sleep; had less confidence in the presence of the opposite sex; perceived less adult support; and were less able to share problems with parents.

Action taken against bullying in England and Wales

Some of this has been described earlier, including the production of two packs by the SCRE in Scotland (which are available in England and Wales), and the interim circulation of materials in England in 1992. These materials were designed for teachers (and in the case of the second Scottish pack, in part for parents). They were based on existing knowledge and ideas, but not on an evaluation of the effects and relative success of different interventions.

An early case study of an intervention in a secondary school was reported by Arora and colleagues (Arora, 1989; Foster, Arora and Thompson, 1990; Thompson and Arora, 1991; Arora, 1994a). This was a whole-school programme against bullying which included increased liaison with parents, increased supervision of breaks, review of the pastoral care curriculum to incorporate anti-bullying work, and development of a non-punitive sanctions policy. The 'Life in School' checklist was used to assess levels of bullying after one and two years; a reduction of around 20 per cent in levels of bullying was obtained.

The whole-school approach aims to bring about a school climate in which pupils can trust adults, specifically teachers, to respond promptly and fairly but firmly with cases of bullying. A somewhat different philosophy has been to try to empower pupils themselves to tackle bullying, building on the findings from general attitude surveys that some 80 per cent of pupils do not like bullying (Whitney and Smith, 1993). A distinctive but controversial approach to school bullying has tried to give more power to pupils via school tribunals or 'bully courts'; the idea is that pupils themselves will hold a court to hear evidence about cases of bullying, and administer appropriate sanctions. The idea was first described by Laslett (1980, 1982) in the context of a day school for maladjusted children aged 7 to 12 years. This court existed for ten years, and Laslett reported (but without systematic evidence) some positive outcomes including some reduction in bullying.

'Bully courts' were advocated by Kidscape in 1990 (though without acknowledging Laslett's work). This received considerable press publicity, and there were reports – which have not been substantiated – that at least 30 schools had introduced bully courts and had reduced bullying as a result. The history of this publicity, and the very few systematic evaluations carried out, are described in detail by Smith, Sharp and Cowie (1994). Essentially, bully courts remain unevaluated as a pure intervention; but many teachers have severe misgivings about this procedure, as they feel the power of pupil courts could be misused and that it is an abdication of teachers' responsibilities.

By 1990 a number of ideas were being advocated for tackling bullying in England and Wales. These included the whole-school policy approach, bully courts and the Pikas Method of Shared Concern (Orton, 1982; Pikas, 1989), as well as assertiveness training, use of drama, and *The Heartstone Odyssey* (a story sequence including episodes of racist bullying; Kumar, 1985). Shortly thereafter, Maines and Robinson (1992; Robinson and Maines, 1997) advocated a 'no blame' approach to bullying, similar in its non-punitive, non-direct approach to the Pikas method; they report that this has been well received by teachers. There was also concern about bullying in playgrounds

(Mooney, Creeser and Blatchford, 1991). However, apart from Arora's one case study in progress, there had been little systematic evaluation of the claims made for these various methods.

The DFE Anti-Bullying project

During 1991 to 1993 the DFE funded an Anti-Bullying Project at Sheffield University, which was designed to carry out such an evaluation. It was also intended to develop suitable material for intervention packages capable of application in a wider context. The project worked with 23 schools (sixteen primary, seven secondary) which had received a survey portfolio on bullying, to support them in developing interventions against bullying, monitor their work, and evaluate their effectiveness with the help of a second survey carried out two years later.

The main or core intervention was developing a whole-school policy on bullying; a written document laying down clearly what is meant by bullying, what steps will be taken if it occurs, who will be informed and what records will be kept; and how the effectiveness of the policy will be monitored. Key principles for whole-school policy development were that the policy should:

1. Follow from a raising of awareness of the issue of bullying in the school.
2. Be developed through an extensive and thorough process of consultation which involved staff (including non-teaching staff), parents, governors and pupils.
3. Be accessible in content and include a clear definition of what bullying is, as well as precise guidelines for staff, pupils and parents detailing what they should do to prevent bullying and how they should respond if they become aware of bullying taking place. It should help create a climate where children can talk about their feelings and feel able to tell someone if they are being bullied or are aware of someone else being bullied.
4. Be well communicated throughout the school community to ensure mutual expectations and consistency in practice.
5. Be implemented effectively, and be seen to be implemented.
6. Be monitored and reviewed to ensure continued effectiveness over time.

In addition, schools were supported in a choice of optional interventions, covering:

- curriculum work – using video, drama and literature in the classroom to raise awareness and discuss bullying issues, and using quality circles for problem-solving bullying issues;
- playground interventions – training lunch-time supervisors in recognising bullying and dealing with it effectively, and improving the playground environment.

- working with individuals and small groups – the Pikas method of shared concern for working with bullies (Pikas, 1989), assertiveness training for victims and peer counselling (Cowie and Sharp, 1996).

Each school received some basic materials on school bullying, and if the school had chosen to implement an additional intervention, a copy of relevant material was provided; for example, a school which had chosen to use video work to explore bullying through the curriculum would receive a copy of the video *Sticks and stones* by Central Television (1990). Representatives from the schools were invited to attend a series of training sessions relating to each intervention.

Throughout an eighteen-month period from June/July 1991 to November/December 1992, schools were encouraged to establish their anti-bullying policy and implement additional interventions. Monitoring of the interventions and their effects took place over the four terms starting in September 1991. Selected groups of pupils and individual staff who had experienced particular interventions were interviewed or completed questionnaires to ascertain how they experienced the intervention, and whether they thought it had had any effect in reducing bullying, either immediately or in the longer term.

Interim playtime monitoring was carried out on certain year groups which would be present in the schools for the duration of the project. For five consecutive days at each half-term, these pupils completed a short questionnaire after lunch, which asked 'Have these things happened to you today?' These included: racist name-calling; name-calling for another reason; direct physical bullying; damage to possessions; threat or extortion; social exclusion; rumour-spreading; and 'being bullied in another way'. These monitoring data allowed us to compare rates of bullying in the same children over time.

The main analysis of the success of the interventions was based on the second whole-school survey. At the end of 1992 the large questionnaire survey was repeated, exactly two years after the first survey, in all 23 project schools. This survey was identical with the first, except that two extra questions asked pupils how much they thought the school had done about bullying, and whether bullying had generally got better or worse over the last year or so.

The results for each school were compared to identify any changes in levels of bullying. Obviously, as the second survey came two years after the first survey, the school composition had changed. Only about 50 per cent of the original pupils were still in the school, and they were in different classes or year groups. These results were therefore compared on a school basis; the outcomes are for the school as a whole.

Results of the DFE project

In general, the full process of consultation, development and implementation of a policy took more time than anticipated – about a year. All schools made progress on this, but some project schools did not get as far as implementation. About eight of the primary schools and four of the secondary schools could be said to have made good progress through all the stages of whole-school policy development by the time of the second survey.

In addition, all project schools tried out one or more of the optional interventions. The most popular was training of lunch-time supervisors (sixteen schools), followed by drama work (eleven), assertiveness training (seven), playground environment (six), video work (five), Pikas approach (five), quality circles (four), literature (four), and peer counselling (two). Schools varied considerably in how much effort they put into these interventions.

Interviews with pupils and teachers suggested that curriculum work – video, drama, literature – could be used successfully for awareness raising, but that the specific effects were quite short term. The best use for curriculum work seems to be as part of the introductory phase of developing a whole-school policy, and of maintaining it; and for renewing it especially for new pupils at the beginning of each school year. Quality circles were enjoyed by pupils and did often come up with useful suggestions.

Playground work was seen as important. Lunch-time supervisors reported that training was helpful, but to be most effective this should be integrated with whole-school policy development so that action by lunch-time supervisors was part of a larger, known framework. Improving the playground environment could be a promising longer term course of action, and involving the pupils as much as possible in planning changes and maintaining them appeared to produce the best effects.

Work with individuals and groups was also found to be useful. The Pikas method of shared concern was often effective in the short term and was a useful approach for dealing with a gang of bullies immediately, but may lose its effectiveness if repeated, unless part of a larger school policy. Assertiveness training was found to be helpful in empowering many children who may be bullied and is thus a useful extra approach, but was unlikely in itself to have effects on other children or on school climate.

The results from interim playtime monitoring were accumulated to give scores over each of the four terms. There were large reductions in all types of experienced bullying reported by pupils. These were statistically significant for direct physical violence, threats or extortion, being teased repeatedly, and spreading nasty rumours. An average reduction in total bullying behaviour of 46 per cent occurred between the first monitoring period in November 1991 and the final period in November 1992 (see Figure 5.1). From general survey findings, it is likely that about 15 per cent of the overall reduction shown here will be due to the pupils being a year older; it is likely that the remaining reduction of around 30 per cent could be ascribed to intervention work.

These data allow some inference as to when the most change occurred. For all forms of bullying, the largest reductions were between the latter part of the spring term and the first half of the summer term, often the time when schools active in the project were finalising policy development.

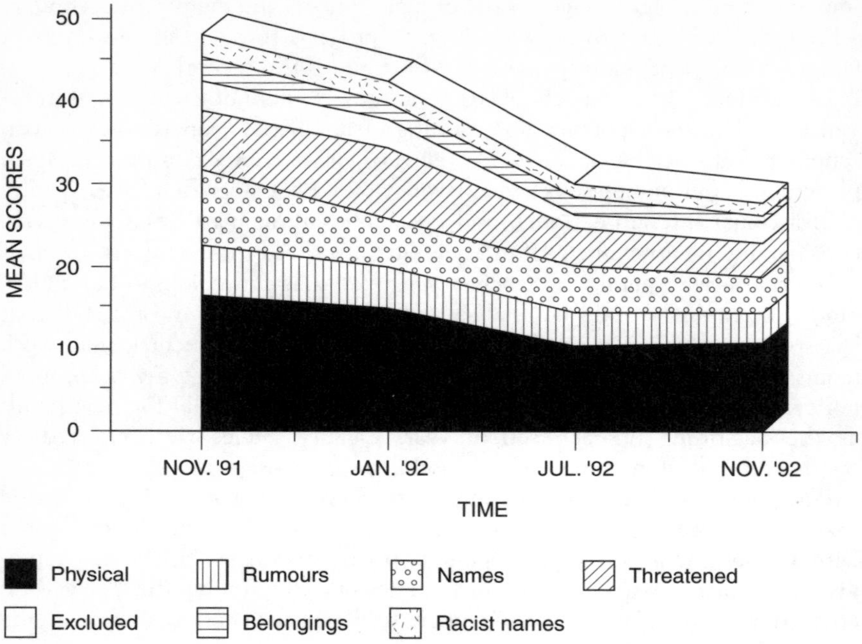

Figure 5.1 Changes in seven types of bullying behaviour, over four terms, from playground monitoring.

Source: Smith and Sharp, 1994

The comparison of first and second survey results confirmed that most schools had made progress in dealing with bullying. First, pupils generally reported (in their questionnaire responses) that their school had taken some action on bullying, and the extent of pupil ratings agreed well with ratings from the project team on this. The majority of pupils also felt that bullying in the school had generally declined.

The questionnaires also provided reports on whether individual pupils had experienced bullying that term. Twelve of the sixteen primary schools and five of the seven secondary schools showed clear improvements here. In general, the pattern of improvement in the primary schools was a reduction in the number of pupils reporting being bullied (mean 17 per cent; maximum 81 per cent) and a reduction in the frequency of bullying (mean 14 per cent; maximum 54 per cent). There was also a reduction in the number of pupils who reported bullying others (mean 7 per cent; maximum 51 per cent) and a reduction in the frequency of bullying others (mean 12 per cent; maximum 64 per cent). Some results were modest, others were quite substantial.

In the secondary schools the reduction in reports of being bullied and of bullying others was often small by the time of the second survey, typically being around 5 per cent. The major changes in secondary schools were in other indicators. There were usually very substantial increases in the proportion of bullied pupils who told a teacher about it (mean 32 per cent; maximum 79 per cent) and in the proportion of bullying pupils who said someone had talked to them about it (mean 38 per cent; maximum 99 per cent).

There were wide variations among schools in how quickly and thoroughly they implemented whole-school policies and how much effort they put into the other interventions. Generally, schools which put more time and effort into anti-bullying measures, and which consulted widely in whole-school policy development, had the best outcomes in reducing bullying. Success in taking action required the commitment of at least one member of staff as coordinator of interventions against bullying, and the clear support of senior management for that person.

The findings of the project are reported in Smith and Sharp (1994), with practical measures detailed in Sharp and Smith (1994); more details of whole-school policy work are given in Thompson and Sharp (1994).

A package *Don't suffer in silence* (Department for Education, 1994) was produced, drawing on the experience of the project schools and giving guidance to schools and teachers on the development of policies and use of other interventions. It includes details of carrying out a survey, case studies of project schools and lists of resources. There is also a video accompanying the text. The pack is free to schools requesting it, and so far about 19,000 schools out of 26,000 circulated have requested it.

An evaluation of responses of schools to the pack has been made by Smith and Madsen (1997); generally, it was found to be useful in developing school policies and anti-bullying strategies. From a sample of 155 schools replying, 29 per cent had a separate whole-school bullying policy, 58 per cent had a section on bullying as part of a wider behaviour or discipline policy, 10 per cent were in the process of developing a policy, while only 3 per cent did not have a policy (though this may be a biased estimate of the situation nationwide, as the school response rate was only 35 per cent). Schools also reported on the success of the different methods they had used. Most approaches were seen positively, with the exception of school tribunals or bully courts (which only six schools had attempted). Most schools felt that bullying had decreased since they had received the pack, basing this on observations and reports of incidents.

Research linked to the DFE project

Two other research projects were linked to the DFE-funded project. Many schools, especially primary schools, have somewhat bleak, uninteresting and unvaried outdoor play areas. Since so much bullying occurs in the playground, improving the playground environment might be a useful positive intervention. Work of this kind was supported by a grant from the Gulbenkian Foundation (1991–1992), with intensive work with four primary schools on the design of the playground environment, using plans developed by each school in collaboration with members of the Department of Landscape, Sheffield University. Outcomes showed that determined effort and high pupil involvement could bring considerable benefits (Higgins, 1994).

For schools catering for special needs children (either special schools or integrated schools which have special provisions for such children), the survey questionnaires were not so suitable. Nevertheless, bully/victim problems are likely to be just as prevalent in these schools, if not more so. Interviews with the children seemed to be the most appropriate method. This work was supported by a grant from the Economic and Social Research Council (1991–1992). Eight schools within the main DFE project had integrated resources for statemented children, and took part. Results showed that children with special needs were at much greater risk of being bullied than those without special needs. However, school policy development, as well as interventions such as assertiveness training, did bring about considerable reductions in this bullying (Whitney, Smith and Thompson, 1994).

A follow-up of some of the Sheffield project primary schools by Eslea and Smith (1998) points out the difficulties as well as opportunities facing schools in anti-bullying work. Of four schools followed up in detail beyond the second survey, two had reduced bullying further, in one there was little change, and in one it had become worse again. A relevant factor appeared to be how recent policy development was, and the extent to which the policy was 'kept alive' once initial project involvement had finished. Another conclusion was that girls' bullying, while less frequent than boys', may be more difficult to tackle; boys' bullying had continued to fall in all four schools, but girls' bullying only in one.

Other intervention studies

Two other studies have reported on evaluation of anti-bullying interventions since the Sheffield study.

One of these was funded by the Safer Schools – Safer Cities programme, and carried out in Wolverhampton. A three-year project with interventions (including a whole-school policy) in fifteen schools started in 1991. An adaptation of the 'Life in School' checklist was used for evaluation. This was an ambitious project carried out on a small funding base, with an interim report (G. Smith, 1991) and a report in a book chapter (G. Smith, 1997). It seems that reductions in bullying were rather small: of the order of 1 per cent to 4 per cent in the five secondary schools (summarised in Arora, 1994b). This project provided the video for use with the DFE pack *Don't suffer in silence* (1994).

Another study was funded by the Police Research Group of the Home Office from 1991–93, and is reported by Pitts and Smith (1995). The project was carried out in two deprived inner city areas, one in London and one in Liverpool. In each area, one primary school and one secondary school took part. There were high levels of violence and antisocial behaviour, both in the schools and the surrounding communities.

The researchers set up a staff–student anti-bullying working party in each school to bring about, implement and monitor a policy and strategies to facilitate communication and prevent bullying. In the primary schools a video was used and a peer support programme introduced. In the secondary schools there was more emphasis on assertiveness training and conflict mediation skills. A self-report questionnaire was used to assess levels of bullying.

There were reductions in bullying in both primary schools, modest at one year (around 10 per cent) but substantial by two years (around 40 per cent); attitudes had improved, and teachers and lunch-time supervisors were perceived as doing more about bullying. Bullying also decreased in the Liverpool secondary school by about 20 per cent. However, in the London secondary school, bullying actually increased by around 7 per cent over the two years; it seems that this school may have been affected by an increase in racial tension in the neighbourhood during this period, together with a group of ex-students hanging around the school gates and perimeter and undermining efforts of staff and students to increase safety at this school.

It is clear that the surrounding community may be an important factor in school bullying. In Hull, Randall (1996, 1997) has discussed work in communities to prevent bullying. Beyond school bullying, there has been recent interest in bullying in prisons (including young offenders' institutions) (Beck, 1994; Ireland and Archer, 1996; Tattum, 1997), and the links to school bullying (Devlin, 1995). Bullying in the workplace has also become a significant topic (Adams, 1992; Field, 1996; see P.K. Smith (1997) for a discussion of this in relation to school bullying).

Current perspectives

The DFE pack has provided advice to schools on a national basis. Regular inspections of schools are made by the Office for Standards in Education (OFSTED) about every four years, and the issue of whether bullying is a problem in a school, and whether the school has taken measures to combat it, including having a policy, is now on the agenda for these inspections. Many other materials are also now available to schools in the UK.

Telephone helplines continue to be one source of support, and the ChildLine bullying line received further funding for seven months in 1994 as part of a BBC Social Action project. It received a total of 58,530 calls; the majority of callers were within the age range 11 to 14 years, predominantly girls. A detailed analysis of the calls, and of an associated survey on bullying, is given in a report by McLeod and Morris (1996).

There is currently considerable interest in peer support and mediation as an approach to bullying. A television film was made of a London secondary school where these approaches were used (*Bullying*: Windfall Films, Hopeline Videos, PO Box 515, London SW15 6LO). These approaches still await proper evaluation (Cowie and Sharp, 1996). A survey of peer support schemes in nine schools by Cowie (1998) found that there were benefits to the peer helpers in terms of confidence and responsibility, and to the school atmosphere generally; but there were also problems due to some degree of hostility to peer helpers from other pupils, and to issues of power sharing with staff, and ensuring sufficient time and resources for proper implementation. These findings have been confirmed in a larger survey of 60 schools in which peer support schemes had been in place for at least one year (Naylor and Cowie, 1998). A newsletter, *Peer Support Networker*, is produced at the Roehampton Institute London (School of Psychology and Counselling, RIL, West Hill, London SW15 3SN).

In the last year or so, successful legal actions (as well as some unsuccessful ones) have been taken by pupils or their parents against schools in which they were persistently bullied. In November 1996, a London school was sued by a 20-year-old former pupil who had suffered four years of victimisation there; there was an out-of-court settlement of £30,000 (*Guardian*, 1996). In November 1997, an 18-year-old schoolgirl lost an appeal against a three-month jail sentence; she had led a gang attack on a pupil who had later committed suicide (*Guardian*, 1997). In February 1998, two 15-year-old boys received nine- and twelve-month detention orders for bullying, including demanding money with menaces (*Guardian*, 1998).

More knowledge and resources are available to schools and teachers in the UK, and progress has been made to reduce bullying following procedures which have been evaluated. Bullying, which had been almost a taboo topic for decades, is now much more openly discussed. Schools are more willing to admit it can be a problem, and are more willing to tackle it with the resources now available and with the incentive of OFSTED inspections and possible legal actions. The continuing difficulties facing schools as they tackle this issue should not be underestimated. Nevertheless, persistent and concerted action on their part can diminish the problem of school bullying, and thereby enhance the rights, happiness and welfare of pupils in the foreseeable future.

References

Adams, A. (1992) *Bullying at work*. London: Virago Press.

Ahmad, Y. and Smith, P.K. (1990) Behavioural measures: Bullying in schools. *Newsletter of Association for Child Psychology and Psychiatry*, 12, 26–27.

Arora, C.M.J. (1989) Bullying – action and intervention. *Pastoral Care in Education*, 7, 44–47.

Arora, C.M.J. (1994a) Is there any point in trying to reduce bullying in secondary schools? *Educational Psychology in Practice*, 10, 155–162.

Arora, C.M.J. (1994b) Measuring bullying with the 'Life in School' checklist. *Pastoral Care in Education*, 12, 11–15.

Arora, C.M.J. (1996) Defining bullying: Towards a greater understanding and more effective intervention strategies. *School Psychology International*, 17, 317–329.

Arora, C.M.J. and Thompson, D.A. (1987) Defining bullying for a secondary school. *Education and Child Psychology*, 14, 110–120.

Balding, J., Regis, D., Wise, A., Bish, D. and Muirden, J. (1996) *Bully off: Young people that fear going to school*. University of Exeter: Schools Health Education Unit.

Beck, G. (1994) Self reported bullying among imprisoned young offenders. *Inside Psychology*, 2, 16–21.

Besag, V. (1989) *Bullies and victims in schools*. Milton Keynes: Open University Press.

Besag, V. (1992) *'We don't have bullies here!'* 57 Manor House Road, Jesmond, Newcastle upon Tyne NE2 2LY.

Boulton, M.J. (1995a) Playground behaviour and peer interaction patterns of primary school boys classified as bullies, victims and not involved. *British Journal of Educational Psychology*, 65, 165–177.

Boulton, M.J. (1995b) Patterns of bully/victim problems in mixed race groups of children. *Social Development*, 4, 277–293.

Boulton, M.J. and Smith, P.K. (1994) Bully/victim problems among middle school children: Stability, self-perceived competence, and peer acceptance. *British Journal of Developmental Psychology*, 12, 315–329.

Boulton, M.J. and Underwood, K. (1992) Bully/victim problems among middle school children. *British Journal of Educational Psychology*, 62, 73–87.

Bowers, L., Smith, P.K. and Binney, V. (1992) Cohesion and power in the families of children involved in bully/victim problems at school. *Journal of Family Therapy*, 14, 371–387.

Bowers, L., Smith, P.K. and Binney, V. (1994) Perceived family relationships of bullies, victims and bully/victims in middle childhood. *Journal of Personal and Social Relationships*, 11, 215–232.

Burnage Report (1989) *Murder in the playground*. London: Longsight Press.

Central Television (1990) *Sticks and stones*. Community Unit, Central Television, Broad Street, Birmingham B1 2JP.

Clarke, L. (1992) Children's family circumstances: Recent trends in Great Britain. *European Journal of Population*, 8, 309–340.

Cowie, H. (1998) Perspectives of teachers and pupils on the experience of peer support against bullying. *Educational Research and Evaluation*, 4, 108–125.

Cowie, H. and Sharp, S. (1996) *Peer counselling: A time to listen*. London: David Fulton.

Dawkins, J.L. (1995) Bullying in school: Doctors' responsibilities. *British Medical Journal*, 310, 274–275.

Dawkins, J.L. (1996) Bullying, physical disability and the paediatric patient. *Developmental Medicine and Child Neurology*, 38, 603–612.

Department for Education (1994) *Bullying: Don't suffer in silence. An anti-bullying pack for schools*. London: HMSO.

Department of Education and Science (1989) *Discipline in schools: Report of the committee chaired by Lord Elton*. London: HMSO.

Devlin, A. (1995) *Criminal classes*. Waterside Press, Domum Road, Winchester SO23 9NN.

Elliott, M. (ed.) (1991) *Bullying: A practical guide to coping for schools*. Harlow: Longman.

Eslea, M. and Smith, P.K. (1998) The long-term effectiveness of anti-bullying work in primary schools. *Educational Research*, 40, 203–218.

Farrington, D. (1993) Understanding and preventing bullying. In M. Tonry (ed.), *Crime and justice: A review of research*, vol. 17 (pp. 381–458). Chicago, Ill.: University of Chicago Press.

Field, T. (1996) *Bully in sight: How to predict, resist, challenge and combat workplace bullying*. Wantage: Success Unlimited.

Foster, P., Arora, C.M.J. and Thompson, D.A. (1990) A whole school approach to bullying. *Pastoral Care in Education*, 8, 13–17.

Francis, L.J. and Jones, S.H. (1994) The relationship between Eysenck's personality factors and fear of bullying among 13–15 year olds in England and Wales. *Evaluation and Research in Education*, 8, 111–118.

Guardian (1996) School pays £30,000 to victim of bullying. 16 November.

Guardian (1997) School bully loses appeal. 14 November.

Guardian (1998) Judge orders detention for school bullies. 24 February.

Higgins, C. (1994) Improving the school ground environment as an anti-bullying intervention. In P.K. Smith and S. Sharp (eds), *School bullying: Insights and perspectives* (pp. 160–192). London: Routledge.

Ireland, J. and Archer, J. (1996) Descriptive analysis of bullying in male and female adult prisoners. *Journal of Community and Applied Social Psychology*, 6, 35–47.

Johnstone, M., Munn, P. and Edwards, L. (1991) *Action against bullying: A support pack for schools*. Edinburgh: SCRE.

Kelly, E. and Cohn, T. (1988) *Racism in schools: New research evidence* Stoke-on-Trent: Trentham Books.

Kumar, A. (1985) *The Heartstone Odyssey*. Allied Mouse Ltd, Longden Court, Spring Gardens, Buxton SK17 6BZ.

LaFontaine, J. (1991) *Bullying: The child's view*. London: Calouste Gulbenkian Foundation.

Laslett, R. (1980) Bullies: A children's court in a day school for maladjusted children. *Journal of Special Education*, 4, 391–397.

Laslett, R. (1982) A children's court for bullies. *Special Education*, 9, 9–11.

Lowenstein, L.F. (1978a) Who is the bully? *Bulletin of the British Psychological Society*, 31, 147–149.

Lowenstein, L.F. (1978b) The bullied and non-bullied child. *Bulletin of the British Psychological Society*, 31, 316–318.

McLeod, M. and Morris, S. (1996) *Why me? Children talking to ChildLine about bullying*. ChildLine, Royal Mail Building, Studd Street, London N1 0QW.

Maines, B. and Robinson, G. (1992) *Michael's story: The 'no blame' approach*. Lame Duck Publishing, 10 South Terrace, Redlands, Bristol B56 6GT.

Martlew, M. and Hodson, J. (1991) Children with mild learning difficulties in an integrated and in a special school: Comparisons of behaviour, teasing and teachers' attitudes. *British Journal of Educational Psychology*, 61, 355–372.

Mellor, A. (1990) Bullying in Scottish secondary schools. *Spotlight 23*. Edinburgh: SCRE.

Mellor, A. (1993) *Bullying and how to fight it: A guide for families*. Edinburgh: SCRE.

Miller, A. (1995) *Young people and bullying*. Liverpool: John Moores University Consumer Research.

Mooney, A., Creeser, R. and Blatchford, P. (1991) Children's views on teasing and fighting in junior schools. *Educational Research*, 33, 103–112.

Mooney, S. and Smith, P.K. (1995) Bullying and the child who stammers. *British Journal of Special Education*, 22, 24–27.

Moran, S., Smith, P.K., Thompson, D. and Whitney, I. (1993) Ethnic differences in experiences of bullying: Asian and white children. *British Journal of Educational Psychology*, 63, 431–440.

Munn, P. (1993) *School action against bullying: Involving parents and non-teaching staff.* Edinburgh: SCRE.

Nabuzoka, D. and Smith, P.K. (1993) Sociometric status and social behaviour of children with and without learning difficulties. *Journal of Child Psychology and Psychiatry*, 34, 1435–1448.

Naylor, P. and Cowie, H. (1998) *The effectiveness of peer support systems in challenging bullying in schools: A preliminary account of findings from a UK survey*. Report to the Prince's Trust, Roehampton Institute London.

Olweus, D. (1993) *Bullying at school: What we know and what we can do*. Oxford: Blackwell.

Orton, W.T. (1982) 'Mobbing'. *Public Health, London*, 95, 172–174.

Pikas, A. (1989) A pure concept of mobbing gives the best results for treatment. *School Psychology International*, 10, 95–104.

Pitts, J. and Smith, P. (1995) *Preventing school bullying*. Home Office Police Research Group, 50 Queen Anne's Gate, London SW1H 9AT.

Randall, P.E. (1996) *A community approach to bullying*. Stoke-on-Trent: Trentham Books.

Randall, P.E. (1997) *Adult bullying*. London: Routledge.

Rivers, I. (1995) Mental health issues among young lesbians and gay men bullied in school. *Health and Social Care in the Community*, 3, 380–383.

Rivers, I. (1996) Young, gay and bullied. *Young People Now*, 81, 18–19.

Robinson, B. and Maines, G. (1997) *Crying for help: The No Blame approach to bullying.* Lucky Duck Publishing, 34 Wellington Park, Clifton, Bristol BS8 2UW.

Roland, E. and Munthe, E. (1989) *Bullying: An international perspective*. London: David Fulton.

Sharp, S. (1995) How much does bullying hurt? The effects of bullying on the personal well-being and educational progress of secondary aged students. *Educational and Child Psychology*, 12, 81–88.

Sharp, S. (1996) Self esteem, response style and victimisation: Possible ways of preventing victimisation through parenting and school based training programmes. *School Psychology International*, 17, 347–357.

Sharp, S. and Smith, P.K. (eds) (1994) *Tackling bullying in your school: A practical handbook for teachers*. London: Routledge.

Sharp, S. and Thompson, D. (1992) Sources of stress: A contrast between pupil perspectives and pastoral teachers' perspectives. *School Psychology International*, 13, 229–242.

Skinner, A. (1992, 2nd edn 1996) *Bullying: An annotated bibliography of literature and resources*. Youth Work Press, 17–23 Albion Street, Leicester LE1 6GD.

Smith, G. (1991) *Safer schools – safer cities*. Unpublished report, Wolverhampton Education Department.

Smith, G. (1997) The 'Safer Schools – Safer Cities' bullying project. In D. Tattum and G. Herbert (eds), *Bullying: Home, school and community* (pp. 99–113). London: David Fulton.

Smith, P.K. (1997) Bullying in life-span perspective: What can studies of school bullying and workplace bullying learn from each other? *Journal of Community and Applied Social Psychology*, 7, 249–255.

Smith, P.K. and Levan, S. (1995) Perceptions and experiences of bullying in younger pupils. *British Journal of Educational Psychology*, 65, 489–500.

Smith, P.K. and Madsen, M. (1997) *A follow-up survey of the DFE Anti-Bullying Pack for Schools: Its use, and the development of anti-bullying work in schools*. London: DfEE.

Smith, P.K. and Sharp, S. (eds) (1994) *School bullying: Insights and perspectives*. London: Routledge.

Smith, P.K., Sharp, S. and Cowie, H. (1994) Working directly with pupils involved in bullying situations. In P.K. Smith and S. Sharp (eds), *School bullying: Insights and perspectives* (pp. 193–212). London: Routledge.

Smith, P.K. and Thompson, D.A. (eds) (1991) *Practical approaches to bullying*. London: David Fulton.

Tattum, D. (ed.) (1993) *Understanding and managing bullying*. Oxford: Heinemann Educational.

Tattum, D. (1997) Developing a programme to reduce bullying in young offenders institutions. In D. Tattum and G. Herbert (eds), *Bullying: Home, school and community* (pp. 159–172). London: David Fulton.

Tattum, D.P. and Herbert, G. (1990) *Bullying – a positive response*. Faculty of Education, South Glamorgan Institute of Higher Education, Cyncoed Road, Cardiff CF2 6XD.

Tattum, D.P. and Herbert, G. (1993) *Countering bullying*. Stoke-on-Trent: Trentham Books.

Tattum, D.P. and Lane, D.A. (1989) *Bullying in schools*. Stoke-on-Trent: Trentham Books.

Tattum, D.P., Tattum, E. and Herbert, G. (1993) *Cycle of violence*. Cardiff: Drake Educational Associates.

Thompson, D. and Arora, T. (1991) Why do childen bully? An evaluation of the long-term effectiveness of a whole-school policy to minimise bullying. *Pastoral Care in Education*, 9, 8–12.

Thompson, D. and Sharp, S. (with Rose, D. and Ellis, M.) (1994) *Improving schools: Establishing and integrating whole school behaviour policies*. London: David Fulton.

Whitney, I. and Smith, P.K. (1993) A survey of the nature and extent of bully/victim problems in junior/middle and secondary schools. *Educational Research*, 35, 3–25.

Whitney, I., Smith, P.K. and Thompson, D. (1994) Bullying and children with special educational needs. In P.K. Smith and S. Sharp (eds), *School bullying: Insights and perspectives* (pp. 213–240). London: Routledge.

Williams, K., Chambers, M., Logan, S. and Robinson, D. (1996) Association of common health symptoms with bullying in primary school children. *British Medical Journal*, 313, 17–19.

6 Scotland

Andrew Mellor

Overview

Scotland is a small northern European country, which is part of the United Kingdom but retains a separate education system. Research suggests that the incidence of bullying in Scottish schools is on a par with that in Scandinavia but slightly lower than in other parts of the British Isles. Action against bullying in Scottish schools was inspired by the Scandinavian example, and supported and encouraged by central and local government. This process has had five components:

- the creation of policy
- research
- the production and distribution of materials and resources
- the provision of training and support
- the embedding of anti-bullying into the fabric of the education system.

Schools across the country have been encouraged to develop anti-bullying policies which are suited to their own circumstances and needs, thereby driving forward a developmental process which has touched many aspects of school life including ethos, discipline, personal safety, parental partnerships, etc. The introduction of anti-bullying policies has been described as a benevolent Trojan horse which allowed new ideas about personal and social education to be smuggled into those schools which were resistant to a more direct approach.

Future developments may involve a more holistic approach which requires schools to make an examination of all existing policies and to bring together their common features in a statement about the relationships and rights of all members of a school community – children and adults.

Scotland – a country within a country

Scotland was an independent country until 1707 when it became part of the United Kingdom. It still retains a separate and distinctive education system, which is controlled from Edinburgh by a government department called the Scottish Office. (After 1999 control of the education system will be passed to the new Scottish parliament which is being established in Edinburgh.) Scotland also has its own legal system. The total population of the country in 1991 (according to the official census) was just under five million of whom 1.01 million were under 16 years of age. Since the previous census in 1981 numbers have fallen slightly and, although this is partly due to a falling birth rate, it may also be a continuation of the phenomenon of net outward migration which has seen millions of people leave the country since the middle of the nineteenth century (including Thomas Blake Glover, who left his Aberdeen home to become one of the founding fathers of modern Japanese industry).

In terms of ethnicity, the great majority of the population in 1991 was described as white. Only 6353 people were described as black or Afro-Caribbean and 47,411 people belonged to groups which originated in Asia, mostly in the Indian subcontinent. Eleven per cent of residents in 1991 were born outside Scotland, of which the greatest number were born in England (354,000), followed by Ireland (49,184).

Scottish people are very proud of their national identity and, although most speak and write in English, a related language called Scots is still sometimes used in conversation, and in poetry and literature. A completely different language, Gaelic, is spoken by about 65,000 people in the north-west of the country. Most people live in, or near, one of the four main cities – Aberdeen, Dundee, Edinburgh (the capital) and Glasgow (the largest, with a population of over one million). Less than 3 per cent of the workforce is engaged in the rural industries of agriculture, forestry and fishing.

The Scottish educational system

The Scottish people nurture a belief in the superiority of their own educational system which is not entirely without a historical basis. In the year 1600 there were eight universities in Britain, of which two were in England and six in Scotland. It is also true that the establishment of a country-wide system of elementary schools in Scotland happened 200 years before it occurred in England. However, a present-day visitor to the United Kingdom would probably observe more similarities between schools in Scotland, England, Wales and Northern Ireland than differences. Throughout the UK, education is compulsory for all children between the ages of 5 and 16. Most children are educated in state primary and secondary schools and can either leave school at 16 or stay on until 18 to study for university or college entrance qualifications.

However, Scottish education does have distinguishing features. Children transfer from primary to secondary school a year later than in England, at the age of 12. There are thus seven stages in primary school from Primary 1 to Primary 7. In the first two years of secondary school (S1 and S2) all pupils study a common course which is based on government guidelines. There is no national curriculum, as in England and Wales, so schools can, in theory, teach whatever they consider to be appropriate. In fact, because they are subject to inspection by Her Majesty's Inspectors of Schools, most tend to follow Scottish Office guidelines fairly closely. In S3 and S4, pupils study between seven and eight subjects for Standard Grade examinations which they sit when they are 16. Those who choose to stay at school study for Higher Grade examinations in up to five subjects in S5. If successful they can then enter university at age 17, but many now choose to stay on at school for a sixth year (S6).

A minority of children are educated in private schools, but most attend state schools which are run by 32 local education authorities under the overall direction of the Scottish Office Education and Industry Department (SOEID, previously SOED). Before a reorganisation in 1996 there were only twelve education authorities. In 1989 school boards were introduced. They have some similarities to boards of governors in England and Wales, but with fewer responsibilities. A system of promoted posts in guidance was introduced into secondary schools in 1974. This means that all secondary schools have a number of teachers responsible for the pastoral care of pupils and who are experienced in interviewing and counselling.

It is possible to overstate the differences between the Scottish educational system and that in the rest of the UK. But the distinctiveness of Scottish schools, and the small size of the country, has helped to facilitate the development of an approach towards bullying which is cohesive, widely supported and which is suited to the traditions and structures of our educational system.

Bullying – definitions and words

Most of the language used to describe bullying behaviour in playgrounds and classrooms in Scotland is similar to that used in the rest of the English-speaking world. A government sponsored anti-bullying package (Johnstone *et al.*, 1992) stated that bullying was 'the wilful, conscious desire to hurt or threaten or frighten someone else'. The authors advised that each school should encourage discussion among staff and parents about its own definition. This discussion 'itself is a valuable part of action against bullying'. Partly as a result of this *laissez-faire* attitude towards definitions, the word *bullying* is now used in Scotland to embrace many different types of behaviour and is increasingly used to describe abuse and harassment in the adult world. In the last few years well-publicised cases of alleged bullying have been reported in the armed forces, the fire service, the police and even in the offices of a local authority.

The only government sponsored quantitative research carried out in Scotland (Mellor, 1990) adopted a Scandinavian definition: 'bullying is long-standing violence, mental or physical, conducted by an individual or a group against an individual who is not able to defend himself or herself in that actual situation'.

Although the Scots do not seem to have developed a distinctive language of bullying, we do have an elaborate oral tradition which discourages victims from telling. The intensity of the scorn which the words carry may defy translation into Japanese – or even English:

> Tell-tale tit, your mammy cannae knit.
> Your daddy cannae go to bed without a dummy-tit.
> (Traditional children's rhyme)

The words that are used in Scotland to describe someone who tells convey strong disapproval. Scottish children run the risk of having the sharp monosyllabic label of 'clype' attached to them. One wonders if any other language but Scots has such a concise and cruel term for what should be a widely encouraged action.

> We are not encouraging clyping but the kids are told that they can come and see a guidance teacher at any time. . . . They usually manage to find you.
>
> (Secondary teacher)

Thankfully, the attitude of teachers is changing. Children are now much less likely to be rebuffed with a self-righteous phrase like 'I don't listen to tell-tales, John.' But this went on for so long that it is deeply embedded in the childhood code.

The history of interest in bullying

Before 1987 the only official advice available to Scottish teachers who were concerned about bullying was contained in the report of the Pack Committee (1977), which had been appointed by the Secretary of State for Scotland in 1974 to enquire into truancy and indiscipline in Scottish schools: 'When detected, bullying and extortion should be dealt with firmly and quickly.'

These few words constituted the sum of the advice available to teachers in 1987. There were no Scottish publications and no research into this topic. However, there was a widespread public concern in the mid-1980s about the physical and sexual abuse of children by adults. It could be argued that the resulting campaign against child abuse helped to sensitise public opinion to the plight of child victims in general, and legitimised the issue of bullying in schools as a topic that was both newsworthy and deserving of serious research and thoughtful intervention. Another factor was that some members of the Scottish educational establishment saw the development of anti-bullying policies as a benevolent Trojan horse which allowed new ideas about personal and social education to be smuggled into those schools which were resistant to a more direct approach.

Legal actions and press reports

In some countries campaigns against bullying have been triggered by press reports of particular incidents, but this has not been the case in Scotland. That is not to say that individual incidents have not attracted publicity, but rather that most such stories have emerged since the start of the government sponsored research and intervention programme.

Although a number of victims have threatened to take legal action against schools for failing to protect them against bullying, only one case has made any progress, albeit very slowly, through the legal system. This concerns events in 1989 when a 15-year-old girl is alleged to have been partially stripped of her clothing in an Edinburgh playground by a group of boys and girls. Photographs were then said to have been taken and passed around the school. The girl was reported to be so distressed by her experience that she took an overdose of tablets, from which she recovered, but she subsequently stopped attending school altogether. Nearly ten years on, lawyers for the girl are still arguing with lawyers representing the school.

Inspiration from Scandinavia

If anything can be identified as the main trigger for action against bullying in Scottish schools, it is the inspiration provided by the Scandinavian countries. In 1987 I was one of two Scottish teachers who attended the European teachers' seminar on bullying in schools in Stavanger, Norway. This was indeed a seminal event. It highlighted the anti-bullying work which had been carried out in Norway and Sweden since 1969. It also provided research evidence to show that it was possible to reduce the level of bullying in school. This challenged a fairly widespread assumption (in Scotland and elsewhere) that bullying was an inevitable part of growing up. The Scandinavians have provided a model which has enabled the process of developing strategies and resources to be telescoped into a comparatively short period in Scotland. At the same time Scottish educators have benefited from work carried out in other parts of the British Isles. Much of this was also inspired or informed by the Scandinavian example.

Scottish research

The first attempt to quantify the problem in Scotland was through a pilot project carried out among 12- to 16-year-olds in three secondary schools (Mellor, 1988). Six per cent of girls and 11 per cent of boys said that they had recently been bullied 'sometimes or more often'. Another finding from this small survey was that 40 per cent of the sample said that they would do nothing to help if they saw someone being bullied.

The 1989 study

The Scottish Office was sufficiently interested in these results to sponsor, in 1988, a study which attracted much media attention when its report was published (Mellor, 1990). This was the first government sponsored research into bullying in the United Kingdom. The project was carried out in ten secondary schools in 1989 with a sample of 942 12- to 16-year-olds. In order to allow comparisons, a Norwegian methodology and definition was adopted. We expected to find a higher level of bullying than had been discovered by Dan Olweus in his 1983 survey of Norwegian schools. In fact the pattern and incidence of bullying revealed was similar to that in Olweus' very much wider survey (1991). For example, 6 per cent of Scottish pupils said that they had been bullied recently 'sometimes or more often', the same figure as for the 12 to 16 age group in Norway. The number of children who said that they had bullied others was slightly lower in Scotland: 4 per cent as opposed to 7 per cent.

Comparisons were also made with an early study in Sheffield, England by Colin Yates and Peter Smith (1989). Although most subsequent English studies have produced lower figures they tend to be consistently higher than in this Scottish study (see Figure 6.1).

During their school career as a whole, boys and girls were equally likely to be the victims of bullying. But when pupils were asked how often they had been bullied recently there was seen to be an increasing gap between the number of boy and girl victims in the older age groups, as well as an

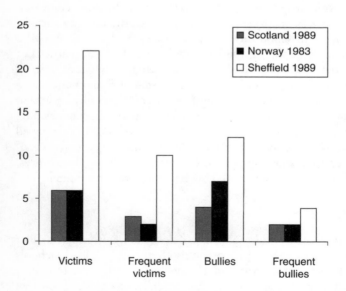

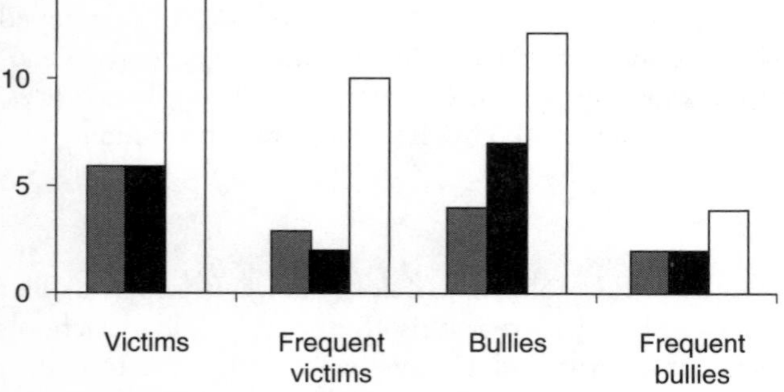

Figure 6.1 Pupils who said they had been bullied or bullied others recently.
Sources: Mellor, 1990; Roland and Munthe, 1989; Yates and Smith, 1989

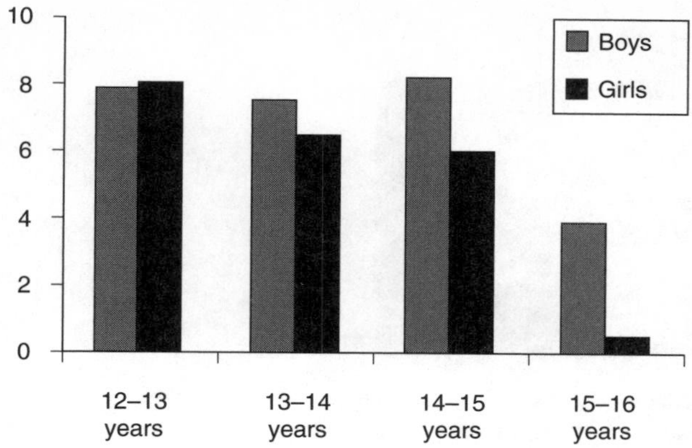

Figure 6.2 Recent victims, 'Sometimes or more often'.
Source: Mellor, 1990

overall decrease in the number of older victims (see Figure 6.2). In an attempt to determine the characteristics of victims and bullies, social and family information was collected. Although the children involved came from all backgrounds, there were some variations. The following statements must be regarded as tentative because of the relatively small sample.

Two groups of children were more likely to be victims of all the types of bullying that were measured: those living with their father only, and those living with someone other than their parents. Only children were slightly less likely, and children with two siblings least likely, to be victims. Children from larger families were more likely to feel rejected by others. Social class did not seem to be an important factor, although children of parents with professional and managerial jobs were less likely to be bullied, while those whose parents had skilled manual jobs were more likely to be victims.

Children from ethnic minorities said that racism was a major cause of bullying. There were also suggestions that children who usually successfully avoided bullies could become victims at certain times; for example, when changing schools or during a marriage breakup.

Half the boys and just over one-third of the girls admitted having bullied others at some time. The difference between the sexes was most marked among 15-year-olds. An alarming 12 per cent of 15- to 16-year-old boys said that they had recently bullied others and 5 per cent said that they had bullied someone every day (see Figure 6.3). How much this was due to an element of bravado is not clear.

Bullies came from virtually all social classes and family backgrounds but children who had three or more siblings, or who lived with someone other than their parents, were slightly more likely to bully others. Children whose

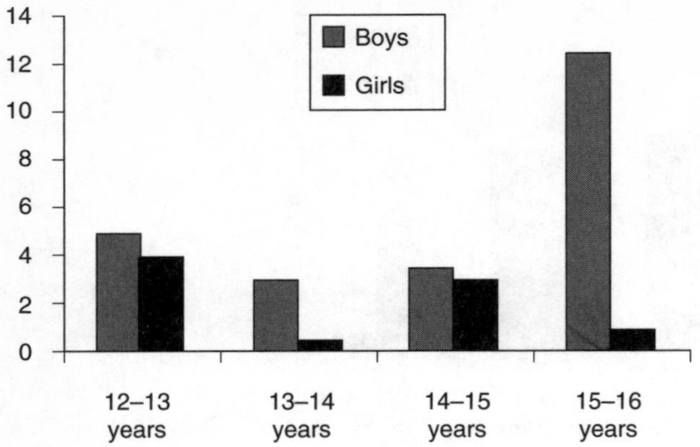

Figure 6.3 Recent bullies, 'Sometimes or more often'.
Source: Mellor, 1990

parents had professional and managerial jobs were less likely to be bullies, while those whose parents had skilled manual jobs were more likely to be bullies.

Children were asked, 'Where does bullying usually take place?' The most common location for bullying reported by the sample as a whole was the playground (48 per cent). However, since half of these pupils have never been bullied, the views of recent victims were examined. Forty-four per cent said that bullying usually takes place in the playground, while 28 per cent cited the classroom.

Perhaps the most important finding of this survey was that there were significant variations in the reported incidence of bullying between the ten schools. For example, the number of children who said that they had been bullied recently 'sometimes or more often' ranged from 2.4 per cent to 15.4 per cent. These differences could not be explained by the size of the schools, their academic achievements, their geographical locations or by the social class of the parents of their pupils. However, even though none of the schools had at that time developed a specific anti-bullying policy it seemed that some were succeeding in containing the level of bullying. After examining what these schools were doing and looking at the research which had been carried out in other countries, it was suggested in the report that there were three prerequisites for a successful anti-bullying policy:

- *Recognition*: schools must be honest about admitting that bullying exists
- *Openness*: opportunities must be provided for people to talk about bullying without fear of rebuff or retribution

- *Ownership*: if parents, teachers and pupils are involved in formulating an anti-bullying policy they will have a vested interest in making sure that it succeeds.

Other quantitative research

There have been few studies into the incidence of bullying in Scottish schools. Two possible reasons for this are firstly, because it was felt that this would have produced results similar to those found in Scandinavia and elsewhere. Secondly, having established with the 1989 study that the problem was serious enough to warrant attention, most efforts were aimed at developing intervention and reduction strategies. Many Scottish schools have implemented their own questionnaire surveys, with the aims of identifying problems and issues, and of informing the school's response. There have also been some surveys carried out as part of undergraduate and postgraduate studies. One of these (Leslie, 1993) examined pupil attitudes in seven Scottish primary schools. Seventeen per cent of these younger children reported that they had been recently bullied 'sometimes or more often' and that 'being called names' was the most common type of bullying (see Figure 6.4).

Another, larger survey has been carried out by the author of a package of development materials issued to schools in Strathclyde (Strathclyde Regional Council, 1994) but the report on this has not yet been published. However, some findings were revealed to the press in 1996. Eleven per cent of the pupils questioned said that they were put off school by bullying, 4 per cent reported being bullied every day and 6 per cent said that they had suffered for years.

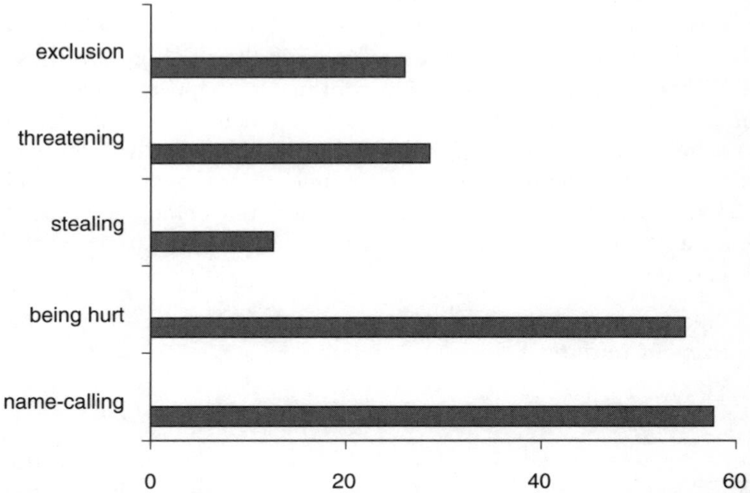

Figure 6.4 Types of bullying reported by primary schoolchildren.
Source: Leslie, 1993

Initiatives and interventions

This section and the next are based on a report produced by the national development officer (Mellor, 1995) using information collected during his secondment, and information from a questionnaire survey of local authorities and teacher education institutions. The full report is available from SCRE, 15 St John Street, Edinburgh EH8 8JR, Scotland (www.scre.ac.uk).

Scotland, being a small nation with limited resources, has developed action against bullying in a particularly cost-effective way. A small input of resources from central and local government has had a significant effect on the way schools respond to the problem. This has been achieved through a process which has had five interdependent components:

1 The creation of *policy* which is dependent upon, and which also helps to foster, a climate of concern.
2 *Research*, which has helped to establish the nature and scale of the problem and to point to possible solutions.
3 The production of *materials and resources* which can be used in schools to aid the process of developing strategies against bullying.
4 The provision of *training and support* to teachers and other professionals.
5 The *embedding* of anti-bullying strategies into the fabric of the Scottish educational system.

These five component parts exist and should continue to exist simultaneously, but it is the final one which presents the greatest challenge. Even the most successful Scandinavian programmes against bullying only claim to have reduced its incidence by 50 per cent. This sets a target for Scottish schools. They must introduce preventive measures designed to make bullying less likely, while at the same time continuing to improve their response to those episodes of bullying which will inevitably continue to happen. Given our present state of knowledge, bullying in school can neither be completely prevented nor reliably cured, but we know it can be significantly reduced.

This section will examine how central government, local government and the independent sector have aimed to fulfil the first four components listed above. Evidence of the fifth component – embedding – is discussed at the end of the section.

Central government initiatives

Policy

Speaking at a press conference in 1994 Lord James Douglas-Hamilton, the Minister for Education at the Scottish Office, said that schools should take a positive approach to this issue and that he wanted each school to have a clear policy to which staff, pupils and parents were committed.

Research

The Scottish Office Education Department has been concerned with all aspects of the process of the development of anti-bullying action, although its starting point was not the creation of policy but the commissioning, in 1988, of quantitative research (see Mellor, 1990).

Materials and resources

The first SCRE anti-bullying pack. In response to the findings of this research the SOED commissioned the Scottish Council for Research in Education to develop a pack which could be used by schools in the development of anti-bullying policies (Johnstone, 1992). It was distributed to all Scottish schools and subsequently to schools in England, Wales and Northern Ireland. In addition, large numbers have been sold elsewhere in countries such as New Zealand, Australia and Canada. To date, well in excess of 40,000 copies have been distributed.

The second SCRE anti-bullying pack. The success of the first pack produced a financial windfall which was used to finance the production of a second pack (SCRE, 1993a and b). This focuses on ways to involve families and non-teaching staff and it contains a number of support materials and two booklets. The first, written by Pamela Munn, is directed at headteachers. The second (Mellor, 1993) contains advice for families and is also available separately. Both the SOED and the Northern Ireland Education Department have bought copies of the pack for all their schools.

Other SOED publications. In August 1994 SOED issued multiple copies of a leaflet entitled *Let's stop bullying* to all schools, with extra supplies being available on request. The leaflet was aimed directly at pupils and accompanied a public information film, also aimed at young people, which the department issued at the same time to the television companies in Scotland. A leaflet with the same title was distributed to parents in 1995. As part of a series of Focus training papers for school boards, SOED also commissioned the production of *Focus on bullying* and issued it to all schools two months later. The Focus paper advised boards as to what they could do to support the development of school policy. It asked school boards to remember that 'acknowledging that bullying exists does not reflect badly on your school – it is a necessary and positive first step'.

Training and support

The Scottish Schools Anti-Bullying Initiative. After considering the responses to the publication of the SCRE pack, and the requests it had generated, the

SOED decided that there was a need for a back-up to the materials which had been distributed to schools. Late in 1992 a decision was taken to set up the Scottish Schools Anti-Bullying Initiative (SSABI) with myself as the UK's first Anti-Bullying Development Officer. My full-time secondment to SCRE began in April 1993 and finished in December 1995. The SSABI aimed to:

- provide advice, information and training to schools and teachers
- work with education authorities which are developing their own initiatives
- carry out school-based studies with the aim of producing support materials.

Local authority action

Until recently, state schools in Scotland were run by twelve local authorities of which the largest, Strathclyde, represented nearly half the population of the country. But in 1996 local government was reorganised into 32, mostly smaller, authorities. The analysis in this section refers to the pre-1996 authorities.

Policy

Given that effective action against bullying depends upon individual schools developing their own policies, with the involvement of the whole school community and tailored to suit local traditions and conditions, it is possible to categorise the various ways in which education authorities sought to encourage this:

- By distributing packs or materials produced centrally (notably the two SCRE packs) and endorsing the advice contained within them. All twelve authorities did this.
- By developing a discrete authority policy on bullying which advises or instructs schools to develop their own policies. Four of Scotland's twelve education authorities had policy statements or position papers on bullying which were approved by elected members of their councils. Being the largest authorities, they were, between them, responsible for the bulk of the country's schools.
- By explicitly incorporating a statement on bullying into a wider authority policy paper.

Only one authority – Fife – has thus far adopted a policy which ostensibly places bullying within a wider framework. In fact Fife's policy paper, *Making our schools safer*, is in all its essentials similar to those adopted by the authorities above. The philosophy which underpins all of these papers, including Fife's, is the promotion of positive relationships and the protection of young people from aggression by their peers. All stress the links that exist with other policies and issues. Opinions vary about precisely which issues anti-bullying should be linked with, or subsumed within, but the following were suggested: attendance; behaviour control and support; child protection; children's rights; discipline; equal opportunities; ethos; guidance; harassment; health education; multicultural and anti-racism education; personal and social education; partnership with parents; promoting positive relationships; pupil welfare; safer schools; values education; youth strategy.

Monitoring and evaluation

The sponsoring and conduct of educational research is not a prime function of local authorities. However, they do have a duty to ensure the quality of educational provision, and it is with this in mind that a number of them conducted investigatory exercises into anti-bullying strategies which helped to inform their own response and the response that they wished their schools to make. Activities which could be described as monitoring and evaluation included:

- Mapping exercises, aimed at tracing the development of policy in schools and assessing their training needs – Highland, Tayside, Grampian.
- Evaluation exercises designed to measure the success of initiatives and packages; for example, Fife's evaluation of its MOSS training course; Strathclyde's extensive survey of pupils carried out during the piloting of its *Promoting positive relationships* package; Tayside's (draft) reports on its bullying helplines and the 'Shared Concern' pilot project.

Materials and resources

A variety of Scottish Office anti-bullying materials have been distributed by local authorities to schools throughout Scotland. These include:

- 1990 *Spotlight 23 – bullying in Scottish secondary schools* (SCRE)
- 1992 *Action against bullying*, the first SCRE anti-bullying pack
- 1993 *Supporting schools against bullying*, the second SCRE anti-bullying pack
- 1994 *Let's stop bullying – advice for young people*
- 1994 *Focus on bullying* – A fact sheet for school boards
- 1995 *Let's stop bullying – advice for parents and families*

One authority, Strathclyde, built its response to this issue on a training package produced within the region – *Promoting positive relationships (bully-proofing our school)* (1994).

A wide variety of other documents, packs and audio-visual resources were cited by the authorities as having been found to be useful in the training of teaching and non-teaching staff. It should be noted that the great majority of these materials do not deal solely, or even mainly, with bullying. For example, *Turn your school round* (Mosley, 1993) describes the circle time technique, which was developed from the idea of quality circles as used in industry. The package makes very little mention of bullying, but the skills and values it promotes – self-esteem, positive behaviour, respect for others' feelings, assertiveness, working in groups – are central to all anti-bullying strategies.

Drama productions have been used as an awareness-raising exercise in a number of areas, and as such constitute a valuable resource. They have provided a catalyst for further discussion and action. However, where they have not been properly followed up by teachers their effect has not lasted. Examples of touring productions include:

- The Lothian Education Department Theatre in Education team toured schools in Lothian in 1993 with a programme entitled *Bully for you* for P7 and S1 pupils. Only those schools which had already started to develop anti-bullying strategies were included in the itinerary. A teaching pack was produced which contained follow-up ideas and material collected from a variety of sources.
- FAB in the Arts (FAB stands for Fight Against Bullying). This theatre group toured primary schools in Strathclyde in 1993 giving music, movement and drama workshops to upper primary pupils. There were a series of follow-up worksheets prepared for pupils.
- Borderline Theatre, Ayr: *Boxing clever*, a play using masks, toured 30 primary schools in Ayr Division of Strathclyde in March 1993. A large information pack including the script and ideas for classwork was produced.

Support and training

The main types of training which have been provided by schools and local authorities are:

- awareness-raising sessions which allow people to explore their own attitudes and experiences and which encourage the development of a climate of concern about bullying (whole school)
- detailed training in anti-bullying strategies (targeted)
- information-giving sessions which allow staff, pupils or parents the opportunity to learn about a school's anti-bullying policy and to comment on it (whole school).

SUPPORT FOR PUPILS AND PARENTS

The need to provide support for individual pupils is widely acknowledged and many of the strategies being tried out are designed to do exactly that.

Most of them operate within individual schools (for example, a 'buddy' system at Merksworth High School) but one authority, Tayside, provided, in partnership with ChildLine (a charitable organisation), a telephone helpline for children involved in bullying. Pupils in other parts of Scotland do, of course, have access to the normal ChildLine services but these are greatly oversubscribed and many callers cannot get through to a counsellor. The large number of calls received on both the Tayside number and the general ChildLine number from children who are being bullied in Scottish schools would seem to indicate that these lines provide a service which the callers consider their schools are not yet providing. Ultimately, the aim must be to make such lines redundant by ensuring that children who are being bullied find the support they need within their own schools.

Parents have been involved in action against bullying in a number of ways. A few, mostly school board and parents' association members, have helped to initiate the development of policy. Meetings and workshops for parents have used many of the materials and involved many of the trainers who have been working with school staff. Support for such activities has been fairly well provided and continues to be developed. For example, the Strathclyde pack contains workshop material especially designed for parents. However, the number and nature of the telephone calls from concerned parents to the National Development Officer would seem to indicate that it is not always easy to find the right person to contact about a child who is being bullied.

The independent sector

There is no evidence to suggest that the minority of Scottish children who attend independent schools are any more or less likely to be involved in bullying than those who attend state schools. What evidence there is suggests that the experience of pupils and the challenges facing schools which are developing anti-bullying policies are remarkably similar in both sectors. The differences which do exist are more related to organisational and institutional factors than to any fundamental differences in behaviour or relationships in the sectors. Particular challenges for independent schools include:

- the lack of access to a support network similar to that available to local authority schools
- the competitive nature of the market in which independent schools operate means that headteachers are sometimes reluctant to tackle this issue openly – happily there is increasing evidence that schools are now seeing the development of anti-bullying policies as an aid rather than a hindrance to the marketing of places
- the special difficulties faced by those independent schools which cater for pupils with social, emotional and behavioural problems

- the presence of large numbers of boarding pupils in some schools; boarders do not have easy access to parental support and cannot hide from any bullies
- the existence of single-sex schools and schools where one sex, usually girls, is in a very small minority
- the lack of a formal guidance system or a programme of personal and social education in some schools.

The Scottish Council for Independent Schools (SCIS) represents 95 per cent of the independent sector in Scotland. It coordinates educational and other developments, advises its member schools and organises in-service training for teachers. SCIS has helped to distribute the SOED and SCRE anti-bullying materials to schools and has been very supportive of the advice contained in them. It has organised two anti-bullying training days, in March and September 1994, which were led by the National Development Officer and which were attended by representatives from 41 of the 63 SCIS schools. Some schools sent as many as five delegates.

Some schools have organised in-house training, either using their own staff, the National Development Officer or consultants. Some have carried out questionnaire surveys, developed curricular material for pupils or held meetings for parents. Others have organised training for staff or have formed planning committees. It could be argued that this is all part of a re-examination of values, and represents an attempt to update the ethos of independent schools by challenging some of the attitudes of both pupils and teachers. One teacher in an independent school wrote: 'The school thrives on competition – one against the other. Perhaps this tends to almost encourage bullying.' Another said that 'power games are part of life' but added that bullying should 'not be tolerated'. Clearly there is a need and a desire to develop an ethos in which competition and caring are not incompatible, but this statement could equally be applied to schools in the state sector. All children deserve to be protected from bullying and other kinds of abuse, whatever type of school they attend.

Embedding – the evidence

The evidence to show the extent to which a concern about bullying and strategies for reducing it has become embedded in the fabric of the Scottish educational system is incomplete and subjective. There are a number of reasons for this, including:

- The difficulty of choosing a valid methodology to measure embedding. Counting the number of schools which have a written policy in place can give some indication of the extent to which the problem is being tackled. But it must be remembered that the existence of a written policy is no guarantee that a school is necessarily practising anything more than tokenism.

- The sheer size of Scotland, and the large number of schools it contains, makes it impossible for a survey of this type to be comprehensive.
- Even where authorities have systematically collected and provided evidence about the development of policy and the provision of INSET in individual schools it is very difficult for them to gauge the extent to which schools have taken action to implement policy.

For these reasons it is possible here only to make a few observations and to report on examples of local initiatives which are considered to be noteworthy. First the observations:

- Five out of twelve local authorities, which between them are responsible for providing education to 84 per cent of the population, have been sufficiently concerned about bullying for their Education Committees to spend time discussing policy papers and providing instructions or advice to schools. Strathclyde Education Committee chose to watch the seventeen-minute video which accompanies their new pack.
- Some authorities have spent considerable sums on anti-bullying materials and personnel. Strathclyde spent £35,000 on publishing and introducing their training pack. Tayside has spent a six-figure sum on its initiative, while the purchase by Shetland of 2500 copies of the SCRE families booklet represents a proportionately large outlay for this very small authority.
- Five authorities have produced or sponsored training materials and eight have organised training programmes.
- All those authorities which made an estimate of the proportion of schools that have developed anti-bullying policies reported that the process is more advanced in the secondary than the primary sector.
- Lothian cited the inclusion of anti-bullying policies in development plans and school handbooks, the demand for in-service training and the number of individual queries and telephone calls as evidence that a concern about bullying is becoming embedded in the system. Orkney describes a similar increase in interest following a visit by the National Development Officer.
- Against the previous observation must be set the fact that two of the smaller authorities, Western Isles and Dumfries and Galloway, said that there is no evidence that a concern about bullying is becoming embedded in the system.

Examples of current practice

Examples of significant local developments can be found all over the country. Many schools have tried to involve as many people as possible – pupils and parents as well as staff – in the development of policy. Some schools have undertaken questionnaire surveys in order to inform and inspire their own response to this issue. Others have carried out literature reviews as part of a process of deciding the most appropriate resources to purchase. A few have pioneered the introduction of new strategies in what could be described as action research. In the majority of cases the findings of such studies have not been disseminated beyond the school community where they have taken place which, given the newness of this issue, is a pity.

There is firm evidence that a degree of concern about bullying does now exist in local authorities and schools, but it is possible that this concern is fragile and insubstantial. If so, it might be blown away by a blast of hot air created by another issue which may even now be brewing up somewhere over the horizon. But given the foundations built by the people responsible for the initiatives in schools across the country, this seems unlikely to happen.

Future directions

What has been most effective?

As a starting point for the consideration of what future action needs to be taken, local authorities and teacher education institutions were asked which influences they considered to have been most effective in promoting the creation of a climate of concern and the development of strategies relating to bullying. Respondents were asked to indicate whether various influences, i.e. research, the SOED, local authorities , the media, charities or others, had played an effective role. This was a highly subjective poll of opinion, but it is possible to make the following observations about the returns:

- Both local authorities and teacher education institutions indicated that the publication of research reports, the work of the SOED and SCRE, and media reports had been most effective in helping to create a climate of concern.
- They agreed that the SOED, SCRE and education authorities could share the credit for what success there has been in the development of effective strategies.
- Schools themselves have played an important role in both processes, but particularly in the development of strategies.

Towards a more holistic approach

It would make life easier if there were a simple solution to bullying: a strategy that could be adopted every time it happened which ensured that it stopped. Such a strategy does not exist and never will, because bullying itself is not a simple phenomenon. Many different types of behaviour can be classed as bullying. Each may need a different response. Indeed, if we only think in terms of responding to bullying once it has happened, the size of the problem will never be diminished. Prevention is the only really effective cure. Having said that, some bullying will always take place however good pro-active strategies are, so there will always be a need for reactive strategies as well. Some such strategies may even act in a pro-active way if, for example, they encourage the development of a more open ethos in which the causes of bullying are discussed.

The lack of a universal remedy is one complication. Another is that effective anti-bullying action involves an examination of many themes and issues within a school – ethos, values, child protection, special needs, relationships, parental partnerships, guidance and so on. The linking of these themes makes bullying a powerful issue. The creation of an anti-bullying policy can drive forward a developmental process which affects many aspects of school life and it can help schools to measure the success of other policies by prompting questions such as:

- Do parents find it easy to contact the school if they are concerned about bullying? (Parental partnership)
- Can this really be described as a caring school if the concerns of the minority of children who are being bullied are not noticed? (Ethos)
- How do we deal with a child whose bullying behaviour is just one manifestation of a whole raft of problems? (Special needs)
- Do the victims of bullying find it easy to talk to a teacher? (Guidance)
- Does this school prevent bullying and provide a safe learning environment? (Child protection/personal safety)

However, the very fact that bullying interfaces with so many other issues can create problems. How can a parent tell the difference between a school which genuinely believes that bullying should be tackled within the context of, say, discipline and is doing so effectively, and another which says the same but which is using this as an excuse for doing nothing?

In addition, what do we say to a school which wants to tackle bullying, but which also wants to do something about child protection, racism, equal opportunities, etc.? Where is the time to come from? Developing an anti-bullying policy in a way which involves the whole school community takes a long time. To be effective this process must have a place in the school's development plan and it must include provision for evaluation and modification. This will take years rather than months.

Perhaps the answer lies in developing a more holistic approach to protecting children from bullying and abuse of all kinds. This would be an approach which examines all existing policies and brings together their common features in a statement about the relationships and rights of everyone in a school community – child and adult. This may also involve a re-examination of values and discipline, and a recognition that this process is central and not peripheral to the education of individuals and the success of our schools.

This holistic or unifying policy is not intended to be an easy way out. As with any policy, the final document is merely a certificate of completion. If the process which should lead up to the award of the certificate has not happened, then it is a worthless scrap of paper. It is necessary to go through the pain of looking at sensitive issues like discipline, child protection and bullying one by one if we are to see whether or not the rhetoric of the policy matches the reality which exists in a school. But we must also recognise that schools which have devoted large amounts of time and effort to the development of their anti-bullying policies will not be able to continue this indefinitely. The mechanism of the two- or three-year cycle of development which now operates in most Scottish schools will encourage them to move on to other things.

There is a real danger therefore that the concern about bullying which has welled up over the last six years will not be maintained. One senior education official said he thought that bullying was 'just flavour of the month'; the implication being that if he ignored the problem it would return to the shadows where it had always lurked, ignored and unseen until the late 1980s. Our task is to ensure that he is proved wrong.

References and Scottish materials

Brown, K. (August 1994) *Bully No More*. Glasgow: St Andrew's College.

Brown, K. (November 1994) *Bully No More – The Pupil Pack*. Glasgow: St Andrew's College.

Fife Regional Council (1994) *A Which Guide to Dealing with Bullying*. Glenrothes: FRC.

Grampian Regional Council (1994a) *Anti-Bullying Information Pack*. Aberdeen: GRC.

Grampian Regional Council (1994b) *Surveying Pupil Attitudes Towards Bullying*. Aberdeen: GRC.

Ironside, V. (1994) *The Huge Bag of Worries*. Edinburgh: The Royal Scottish Society for the Prevention of Cruelty to Children.

Johnstone, M., Munn, P. and Edwards, L. (1992) *Action Against Bullying*. Edinburgh: Scottish Council Research in Education.

Keighren, K. and Houston, A. (1994) *Tayside Region Bullying Helplines – The First Five Months*. Dundee: TRC. In draft form – not yet published.

Leslie, B. (1993) *A Survey of Bullying in Seven Scottish Primary Schools* (M.Sc. dissertation). Glasgow: University of Strathclyde.

Lothian Regional Council (1993) *Lothian Children's Family Charter*. Edinburgh: LRC.

Mellor, A. (1988) *Bullying* (unpublished dissertation). Glasgow: St Andrew's College.

Mellor, A. (1990) Spotlight 23 *Bullying in Scottish Secondary Schools*. Edinburgh: SCRE.

Mellor, A. (1993) *Bullying and How to Fight It*. Edinburgh: SCRE.

Mellor, A. (1994a) Spotlight 43 *Finding out about Bullying*. Edinburgh: SCRE.

Mellor, A. (1994b) Accentuate the positive – Scottish action against bullying. In *Children's Peer Relations – Conference Proceedings*. Adelaide: University of South Australia.

Mellor, A. (1995) *Which Way Now? – A Progress Report on Action Against Bullying in Scottish Schools*. Edinburgh: SCRE.

Mosley, J. (1993) *Turn Your School Round*. Wisbech: Learning Development Aids.

Olweus, D. (1991). *Bullying: What We Know and What We Can Do*. Oxford: Blackwell.

Pack Report (1977) *Truancy and Indiscipline in Schools in Scotland*. Scottish Education Department/HMSO.
Roland, E. and Munthe, E. (eds) (1989) *Bullying – An International Perspective*. London: David Fulton.
Scottish Consultative Council on the Curriculum (1992) *Speak Up – An Anti-Bullying Resource Pack*. Dundee: SCCC.
Scottish Council for Research in Education (1993) *Supporting Schools Against Bullying*. Edinburgh: SCRE.
Scottish Office Education Department/SCRE (1993a) *Action on Discipline in the Primary School*. HMSO.
Scottish Office Education Department/SCRE (1993b) *Action on Discipline in the Secondary School*. HMSO.
Scottish Office Education Department (1994a) Focus No. 4 *Focus on Bullying*. HMSO.
Scottish Office Education Department (1994b) *Let's Stop Bullying – Advice for Young People*. HMSO.
Strathclyde Regional Council (1994) *Promoting Positive Relationships (Bullyproofing Our School)*. Glasgow: SRC.
Tattum, D.P. and Lane, D.A. (eds) (1989) *Bullying in School*. Stoke-on-Trent: Trentham Books.
Tayside Regional Council (1992a) *Action Against Bullying in Tayside Schools – Support Material for School Based In-service*. Dundee: TRC.
Tayside Regional Council (1992b) *Action Against Bullying: Drawing from Experience*. Dundee: TRC.
Tayside Regional Council (1994) *Resolving Group Bullying in Schools – Anatol Pikas Shared Concern Method – Tayside's Experience 1993–94*. In draft form – not yet published.
Yates, C. and Smith, P.K. (1989) Bullying in two English comprehensive schools. In E. Roland and E. Munthe (eds), *Bullying – An International Perspective*. London: David Fulton.

7 Ireland

Brendan Byrne

Overview

Attendance in full-time education is compulsory for all pupils between 6 and 15 years of age. The state provides for free education up to the age of 18 years in most second level schools. In September 1993, the Department of Education published guidelines for countering bullying behaviour in primary and post-primary schools. These were distributed to all schools in the state. In those guidelines bullying is defined as 'repeated aggression, verbal, psychological or physical, conducted by an individual or group against others'. Since 1993 there has been intense media interest in bullying. Two major conferences on bullying have been held in Ireland, one national and one international. Very few court cases in relation to bullying have taken place in Ireland. The teachers' unions have also taken a keen interest in the subject. Initiatives to deal with and prevent bullying behaviour have been very varied. Schools have drawn up policies on bullying. The Garda (police) have a schools programme for primary schools, part of which deals with the issue. Theatre groups have also raised awareness. There is a recognition that bullying is not exclusive to schools and various youth organisations have drawn up measures to counter bullying.

Country summary

Ireland has a population of 3,621,035; 58 per cent live in urban areas, 42 per cent in rural areas. The main urban centres are Dublin (the capital), Cork, Limerick, Galway and Waterford.

Ireland has a small number of immigrant pupils and their wide residential scatter poses problems for the teaching of their mother tongue in schools in Ireland. Despite this, considerable provision is being made for such pupils. Most immigrant pupils acquire a knowledge of English through participation in classes at school and general community life. Most of these pupils also attend Irish-language classes in their schools. In 1994 there was a total of 1812 children of non-English-speaking immigrants from European Union countries at school in Ireland. The largest number (543) was German.

Immigrants from 84 non-EU countries accounted for a total of 2311 pupils in primary and secondary level; the largest group was Chinese (427).

The economy of Ireland has been traditionally agricultural: almost 81 per cent of the total land area is devoted to pasture and cropland. Since the mid-1950s, however, the country's industrial base has expanded, and now mining, manufacturing, construction and public utilities account for approximately 37 per cent of the GDP and agriculture for only 12 per cent. Private enterprise operates in most sectors of the economy. In the last ten years there has been a large increase in the tertiary (service) sector. Approximately one-third of the population lives within a 30-mile radius of Dublin. The greatest concentration of resources is in the east of the country. The western seaboard is the least economically developed area.

School summary

In accordance with the School Attendance Act, 1926, attendance in full-time education is compulsory for all pupils between 6 and 15 years of age.

First level

In Ireland the primary education sector comprises national primary schools, special schools and non-aided private primary schools. Although compulsory education does not start until age 6, some 54 per cent of Irish children aged 4 years and 99 per cent aged 5 attend primary school at pre-primary level. Education at primary level comprises standards 1 to 6 of national school as well as enrolment of 7- to 12-year-olds in special schools.

As far as possible primary schools have single-grade classes. However, in smaller schools it may be necessary to combine class levels with one teacher. Generally speaking, pupils progress to the next grade at the end of the school year, although exceptions do arise. There is no formal end-of-year examination. The average class size in primary schools (1994/1995) was 27.5. The number of national school pupils in ordinary classes classified by pupil size of school is shown in Table 7.1. The average primary school day lasts 5.5 hours, with a starting time between 9.00 a.m. and 9.30 a.m. There is a short break during the morning (usually fifteen minutes) with a lunch break of 30 minutes.

Second level

Education at the second level, first cycle (lower secondary) comprises the Junior Certificate Programme. Education at the second level (upper secondary) comprises all senior cycle courses including the Leaving Certificate Programme as well as all post-leaving certificate courses in second-level schools. The second-level education sector in Ireland comprises secondary, vocational, community and comprehensive schools.

Table 7.1 Number of first-level schools, and pupils, by pupil size of school

Pupil size:	*Below 50*	*50–59*	*100–199*	*200–299*	*300–499*	*500 +*	*Total*
Schools	695	887	860	352	285	124	3203
Pupils	23,230	65,271	120,292	86,678	108,072	75,583	479,126

Source: Department of Education, 1994/1995

Education is free of charge in all schools that are financially maintained by the state (vocational schools/community colleges, comprehensive and community schools) and also in the majority of (independent) secondary schools provided by the voluntary sector which participate in the scheme of free education established in 1967. Approximately 7 per cent of second-level schools charge fees. Second-level schools classified by enrolment size are shown in Table 7.2.

Third level

At this level the first stage can be either of a type that leads to an award not equivalent to a first university degree (e.g. a National Council for Educational Awards National Certificate or National Diploma course) or one which leads to a university degree or equivalent (including postgraduate diploma studies). The second stage of education at the third level leads to a postgraduate university degree or equivalent (Masters and Doctorate programmes).

Definition of bullying

The most commonly used definition of bullying, in Ireland, is that found in the guidelines on countering bullying behaviour in primary and post-primary

Table 7.2 Number of second-level schools of different type, by enrolment size

Enrolment size	*Secondary*	*Vocational*	*Community*	*Comprehensive*	*Total*
Under 100	9	21	—	—	30
100–150	7	20	—	—	27
150–200	18	22	—	—	40
200–250	23	26	2	—	51
250–300	33	14	—	—	47
300–500	141	81	13	6	241
500–800	185	46	28	8	267
800 and over	36	17	17	2	72
Total	452	247	60	16	775

Source: Department of Education, 1994/1995

schools published by the Department of Education in September 1993: 'Bullying is repeated aggression, verbal, psychological or physical, conducted by an individual or group against others.' The guidelines go on to speak about types of bullying, referring to physical aggression, damage to property, extortion, intimidation, abusive telephone calls, isolation, name-calling and 'slagging'. In an Irish context, 'slagging' usually refers to the good-natured banter which goes on as part of the normal social interchange between people. However, when this slagging extends to very personal remarks aimed again and again at one individual about appearance, clothing, personal hygiene or involves references of an uncomplimentary nature to members of one's family, particularly if couched in sexual innuendo, then it assumes the form of bullying. It may also take the form of suggestive remarks about a pupil's sexual orientation. The guidelines also refer to the fact that school personnel may be bullied by means of physical assault, damage to property, verbal abuse and threats to families. It is also pointed out that a teacher may unwittingly or otherwise engage in or reinforce bullying behaviour in a number of ways (Department of Education, 1993, p. 4).

History of interest in the topic

Until February 1993, there was sporadic interest in the topic of bullying, with occasional newspaper articles in response to bullying incidents. Between 1985 and 1992, I carried out research at primary and post-primary schools to confirm my suspicion that bullying is a problem in schools (Byrne, 1987, 1992). My research was influenced greatly by the work of Olweus in his 1978 book, *Aggression in the schools: Bullies and whipping boys*. Some of my work was a replication of Olweus' research, as well as original material (especially interviews with students and teachers on the topic of bullying behaviour). In addition, O'Moore and Hillery (1989) published results of research on bullying in some Dublin primary schools.

In February 1993 my book *Coping with bullying in schools* was published, and it generated considerable media and public interest. In March, the Minister for Education, Niamh Bhreathnach, announced the formation of a working group to draw up guidelines for countering bullying behaviour in primary and post-primary schools. The group consisted of a chairperson (Department of Education, Principal Officer), two school inspectors (one primary and one post-primary), a psychologist from the Department of Education, a parent representative, Mona O'Moore from Trinity College and myself. The guidelines were published in September 1993 and distributed to all schools.

In March 1993, the first National Conference on Bullying in Ireland was held. It was organised by Vivette O'Donnell and received considerable media attention. At the conference, the Sticks and Stones Theatre Company's schools programme was launched. In 1983, O'Donnell had founded the Campaign against Bullying (CAB), which set out to provide information and advice with the aim of reducing the incidence of bullying. Other support groups were also set up, including the National Association for Victims of Bullying and the Waterford Bullying Awareness Group. In addition, the National Parents' Council (primary and post-primary tiers) produced advice for parents, as did the National Association of Parents.

Since February 1993, there has been intense media interest in bullying, with stories about bullying on school buses and attacks on students on the way home from school. From time to time, newspaper stories have tried to make a link between bullying and suicide. However, it is virtually impossible to definitively link bullying and suicide. The case of 14-year-old Robert Brummer will illustrate the point. On 9 October 1996, Robert went to his bedroom with the family's .22 rifle and shot himself dead. Robert had attended school in the village of Killorglin, County Kerry. In a note which he left for his family, Robert wrote about the angst that most 14-year-olds go through. He mentioned the pressure of exams and the slagging he got about his height. He was apparently small for his age. There was also a reference to Kurt Cobain, the Nirvana lead singer who shot himself in 1994. There was speculation that Robert may have committed suicide because of bullying. He may have been the butt of jokes about his German father. His father is a German businessman working in the area and his mother is Irish. They have lived in the state for a number of years and Robert had been bullied in the school. Michael Kelleher, head of the National Suicide Research Foundation, says that it is almost impossible to identify a single cause for suicide and advised parents always to listen to their children, even when it sounds like a moody teenage melodrama. The Foundation researched 100 suicides in Cork. In those suicides under the age of 25, only one in five had received treatment.

In October 1994, the parents of a boy who suffered alleged bullying while attending an infant class agreed to a settlement offer of £1200 from the school to cover their medical and legal expenses. The case was heard in the Circuit Civil Court in Dublin. The judge was told the child's parents had to pay £700 in medical fees and finance their child's education at a private school. The parents decided not to go ahead with an action against the school for alleged negligence, as they believed that digging up the past would only harm their son. In addition, the boy's counsel pointed out that they did not have witnesses to the alleged bullying. It is important to note that the parents accepted the settlement offer without prejudice.

Initial interest in bullying in Ireland focused on schools. It was considered that bullying was exclusive to schools. It is now generally accepted that bullying needs to be placed in a wider community context. In October 1994 I published a book entitled *Bullying: A community approach*. It considers the role which parents, schools, young people, youth and sports clubs, employers and the police can play in tackling the problem. In August 1995, I presented a paper entitled 'Bullying: A community approach' at the World Federation for Mental Health, World Congress, held in Dublin.

In October 1996 an International Conference on Bullying was held in Trinity College. Mona O'Moore, who organised the conference, presented the results of the nationwide survey of bullying in Irish schools. Some 400 people attended the conference and included school principals, teachers and educationalists. The proceedings of this conference have been published in a special edition of the *Irish Journal of Psychology* (O'Moore, 1997).

Research on the nature and types of school bullying

O'Moore and Hillery (1989) and Byrne (1987), using similar definitions of bullying to Olweus, found figures of about 5 per cent of pupils involved as bullies and a similar number as victims. O'Moore and Hillery (1989) found that 16 per cent of children in primary remedial groups bully others, compared with 6 per cent in non-remedial groups. Byrne (1987) found 9 per cent in remedial classes compared with 5 per cent in ordinary classes.

Byrne (1992) discovered an overall incidence of 10.4 per cent of children involved in bullying behaviour, with 5.3 per cent as bullies and 5.1 per cent as victims. He also found that boys were more likely to be involved as bullies than girls (only 25.7 per cent of the bullies were girls). The victims were less forthcoming, more withdrawn and distressed than the bullies. Bullies tended to be more uncontrolled than the victims. They followed their own urges and were careless of social rules. The victims were significantly more neurotic than the bullies and often worried, unhappy and fearful of new situations. Byrne (1992) gives a detailed account of his findings on the characteristics of bullies and victims. The study showed that bullies have the highest rate of early school completion (36.6 per cent compared to 13.8 per cent for victims). It emerged that 26.8 per cent of the victims, 32.8 per cent of the bullies and 8 per cent of the control pupils were receiving remedial education of one form or another.

While the majority of teachers (80.5 per cent) considered bullying to be a significant problem in schools in general, only 39 per cent perceived it to be a significant problem in their own schools. The percentage was higher among secondary than among primary teachers (55 per cent compared to 26 per cent). The majority of teachers (66 per cent) believed that the incidence of bullying behaviour had remained about the same over the previous five years. However, 29 per cent believed that it had increased. Eighty-three per cent of teachers thought that the level of awareness of bullying as a problem in schools had increased over the same period.

Only 5 per cent of teachers felt that their teacher training had adequately prepared them to deal with the problem of bullying behaviour. In addition, being aware that a lot of the bullying takes place outside the classroom, many of them were unclear about the extent of their responsibility in dealing with the problem. Finally, all the principals referred to the lack of support services which they could call upon in cases of serious bullying (e.g. psychological services).

In November 1993, the Irish National Teachers Organisation (INTO) published a report of a nationwide survey on the question of discipline in schools conducted in May 1993. Chapter 5 refers to bullying and comments on the incidence of bullying in primary schools, analyses some of the causes for it, and examines some of the courses of action which are being used at present to combat it. The survey analyses the results for 452 schools, including various types of school (large, medium and small; boys, girls and mixed schools) in urban, suburban, rural and inner city areas, and in the various standards in primary schools. Fifty-seven per cent of schools had a policy on dealing with bullying but 77 per cent felt that bullying is becoming a more acute problem. The highest increase in the incidence of bullying appeared to be in the third and fourth classes. Name-calling was found to be the most common form of bullying. Ninety-nine per cent of teachers were of the opinion that bullying occurred in the playground. In order to improve the situation, the report raises the possibility of parents assisting with yard supervision but draws attention to the legal minefield with regard to responsibility. Increasing supervision by teachers would cause a deterioration in teachers' conditions of service and would therefore be impractical. Seventy-eight per cent of teachers felt that children had to contend with bullying on the way to and from school.

The INTO survey gives valuable information about bullying in schools from the teacher's perspective. It illustrates clearly that it is incorrect to look only for a school-based solution. The survey contends that bullying is caused by a combination of psychological and domestic factors. The school has a role to play as part of a broad-based approach supported by society in general.

In October 1996, the results of a nationwide survey, funded by the Gulbenkian Foundation and the Department of Education, and completed by O'Moore, Kirkham and Smith of the Anti-Bullying Research and Resource Centre at Trinity College Dublin were released. The study was carried out during the 1993/1994 school year with young people from 8 years of age in primary schools up to the sixth year in second-level schools completing questionnaires (using the Olweus Bully/Victim Questionnaire, 1989). Some 530 schools were involved – 320 primary and 210 secondary. This represented 10 per cent of all primary schools and 27 per cent of all post-primary. The study found that one in twenty primary school children is victimised once a week. The figure is one in 50 at post-primary level. Fifty-one per cent of pupils recounted that they would join in bullying a pupil whom they did not like. The number of pupils being bullied who would not tell anyone in school increases with age, from 54 per cent of third class pupils to 74 per cent of sixth class pupils. In second-level schools the level of non-reporting is as high as 92 per cent. The figures for telling someone at home show that in post-primary schools in the sixth year, 80 per cent of pupils said they had not done so. At primary level in sixth class the number is 54 per cent. The survey also indicated that bullying peaks in the second year of post-primary schools.

Initiatives

The Department of Education 'Guidelines for countering bullying behaviour in primary and post-primary school'

At the end of March 1993 the Education Minister announced the setting up of an expert working group to draw up guidelines for countering bullying behaviour in schools. The draft guidelines were completed by early July and teachers' unions, parents, and school management groups were consulted and their recommendations included in the final guidelines which were released in September 1993. The introduction emphasised 'that the issue of bullying behaviour be placed in general community context to ensure the cooperation of all local agencies in dealing appropriately with it'. It points out that 'Bullying behaviour affects everyone in the classroom, in the school community and, ultimately, in the wider community'. In an attempt to prevent bullying, the guidelines recommended 'a school policy which includes specific measures to deal with bullying behaviour within the framework of an overall school code of behaviour and discipline'. Cooperation and consultation are emphasised.

> The managerial authority of each school in developing its policy to counter bullying behaviour must formulate the policy in co-operation with the school staff, both teaching and non-teaching, under the leadership of the Principal, and in consultation with parents and pupils. In this way, the exercise of agreeing what is meant by bullying and the resultant development of school-based strategies for dealing with it are shared by all concerned.

In raising the awareness of bullying in its school community so that they are more alert to its harmful effects, schools could choose to have a staff day on the subject of bullying, complemented by an awareness day for pupils and parents/guardians. Within the school there should be definite procedures for dealing with incidents of bullying behaviour. Parents/guardians must also be informed of the appropriate person to whom they can make enquiries regarding incidents of bullying behaviour which they might suspect or that have come to their attention through their children or other parents/guardians. The non-teaching staff should be encouraged to report any incidents of bullying behaviour to the appropriate member of staff. Serious complaints should be reported to the principal or vice-principal who could impose the appropriate disciplinary sanctions and make contact with the parents if necessary.

The guidelines say that pupils involved in bullying behaviour need assistance on an ongoing basis. In conclusion, the guidelines refer to the desirability of the inclusion of a module on bullying behaviour in the pre-service training of teachers, which would be a positive step in alerting potential teachers to problems caused by such behaviour in schools. In addition, it considered that the expansion of in-service courses to teachers on aspects of bullying behaviour would be of considerable benefit to the teaching profession in the process of raising awareness and developing techniques to deal with such behaviour.

A case study of a community college

One community college adopted the following approach:

- A one-day seminar was organised. The following groups from the school community were represented: parents; board of management; teaching staff; non-teaching staff; students; youth workers from the local area; the Juvenile Liaison Garda; representatives of the bus company serving the school; local shopkeepers; local doctors.
- The first part of the day consisted of a general talk on bullying – types, causes, cases, ways of coping – followed by a question and answer session.
- In the afternoon, participants were divided into groups and asked to consider instances of bullying from their own experience and to answer a number of questions in relation to those instances.
- The day concluded with feedback from workshops.
- Based on this the school drew up an explicit policy for countering bullying.
- The most common forms of bullying were name-calling, slagging and jeering.

A statement was issued to all students and parents at the beginning of the following school year (see Table 7.3).

Anti-bullying project in a Dublin secondary school

This project, devised by a teacher, Justin Morahan, started in 1993 and is ongoing. Once a week, each student in the school is expected, on a day appointed by the form teacher, to write an answer to three questions on bullying. This note must be written at home whether or not the student has any information to offer on the subject of bullying. Each student places his or her letter in an envelope, which is then sealed. The student's name is written on the outside of the envelope. This envelope, containing the letter, is brought to school on the following day. The questions to be answered in this note are as follows:

1 Have you been bullied or hurt within the last week?
2 Do you know of anyone in your class who is being bullied or hurt?
3 Do you know of anyone in the school who is being bullied or hurt?

Table 7.3 Statement issued by community college

To each student:
Our first school rule says:
'Treat all staff and fellow-students with respect.'
Bullying breaks this rule, because if you hurt, threaten or frighten someone you are not treating them with respect.
Bullying is not acceptable and will not be tolerated.
You must not:

- hit, kick or push other students
- jeer at them or their families
- steal or damage their property
- threaten them in any way.

This applies in class, on corridors, in the playground and on the way to and from school.
A record will be kept of all bullying incidents.

1 If you are involved you will be warned to stop.
2 If you do not stop, your parents will be informed.
3 If the incident is particularly serious, you may be suspended or expelled.

If you are being bullied, or if you know of someone else who is being bullied, you must tell someone, a teacher or your parents, and you will be helped.

(signed) Principal . . . . Vice-Principal . . . . . .

On the day after the letters are written, each student places his or her letter in a locked, wooden letter-box presented to him or her by the class teacher. The class or form teacher ensures that the name on the outside of each envelope corresponds to the person putting it in.

The Anti-Bullying Co-ordinator (ABC) later opens and reads the notes as they are received. When they contain information about cases of bullying, the ABC interviews the alleged victim and the alleged bully or bullies and contacts parents if the bullying continues. The procedure here is that parents are contacted by telephone and invited to an interview. Victims of bullying receive ongoing support and counselling. The bully also receives help in an attempt to bring about a change in behaviour.

The Stay Safe Programme

The Stay Safe Programme (Lawlor and MacIntyre, 1991) is a teaching package designed for primary schools. It aims to prevent child abuse by equipping parents and teachers with the knowledge and skills necessary to protect children in their care. Children are then taught safety skills in the normal classroom context and these skills are reinforced through discussion with their parents. This approach increases community awareness and makes children less vulnerable to abuse of all kinds. The programme was developed and researched by the Child Abuse Prevention Programme and is the result of a two-year pilot study. The programme was designed on the basis of consultation with a teacher assigned to the project by the INTO, and ongoing discussions with the Departments of Health and Education. It consists of a video for children, two separate curricula for junior and senior cycles, a training course for teachers and an educational component for parents. The programme, which is now being made available to schools nationwide, contains a chapter on bullying and a lesson component for work with the pupils. During the piloting of the Stay Safe Programme, it became clear that bullying was an issue of major concern to teachers and parents, and that there was a need to tackle the problem in a structured way.

The section on bullying points out that 'children who are victims of bullying often feel shame, guilt or a sense of failure because they cannot cope with the bully. It is important that parents don't pass on a sense of disappointment in the child's inability to cope. They should acknowledge bullying as a problem that everybody comes across at some stage (and place the guilt firmly with the bully).' The rules of the Stay Safe Programme seem particularly appropriate when dealing with bullying: 'Say "No", get away, tell and keep telling.'

Meitheal

A youth programme called Meitheal has been developed in the diocese of Kildare and Leighlin. In the Irish language, the word 'Meitheal' refers to the old rural practice of groups of farmers coming together as a community to work on an individual farm at harvest time. In schools, Meitheal is about gathering a group of senior students who will work to create a more caring environment in the school. Meitheal works on the basic idea that everyone is special and unique. Over the years, the most successful and appreciated action of the Meitheal group has been in helping first years and trying to counteract bullying in the school. This concept of peer support has now been adopted by a number of schools in Ireland.

Home/School/Community Liaison Scheme

Since 1990, there has been a Home/School/Community Liaison Scheme in operation in selected schools. It now serves 384 schools in both primary and post-primary schools, each school having a home/school coordinator. One of the main aims of the scheme is to maximise active participation of the children in the schools in the learning process, in particular those who might be at risk of failure. Initiatives are focused on parents and teachers, but will impinge directly over time on children's learning. The thrust of the scheme is preventive rather than curative. While bullying is only one of many issues which will concern coordinators, it is a good example of how parents and the school can work together. Coordinators are doing this increasingly by making available information sheets for parents on bullying in the parents' room or when they visit homes.

In-service

The Association of Secondary Teachers in Ireland, the union which represents the majority of second-level teachers in Ireland, has been running an in-service programme for the last two years on implementing school policy on discipline and bullying. The objective of the programme is to provide information, to develop teachers' knowledge base, to impart skills and disseminate good practice in schools. All teachers participating in the in-service programme receive certification.

Comenius Action In-service Teacher Training Programme

Improving the Learning Environment in Schools through Bullying and Discipline Strategies (ILES) is a training programme for post-primary teachers designed to improve the learning environment in school by improving teachers' skills for promoting good discipline and preventing bullying in schools. The objectives of ILES are:

1 to raise educational achievement levels by improving the quality of the learning environment in schools
2 to provide teachers with the skills to develop effective anti-bullying and discipline policies
3 to develop a manual for effective anti-bullying and discipline policies
4 to provide teachers with information on how schools in other countries deal with discipline and bullying
5 to promote the European dimension in education by enabling the transfer of expertise and knowledge among teachers from EU member states.

The project is part of the Comenius Action In-service Teacher Training Programme sponsored by the European Union, and involves Ireland, Scotland and France.

The in-service training project is based on the 'training the trainers' model. The course will be designed by two teachers each from three countries, who will prepare a manual and a training programme during the first year of the project. In the second and third years of the project, these six teachers will then train a total of 120 teachers. The latter teachers will be subsequently available as a group of experts in their own countries to train other teachers under programmes initiated by the project partners using the manual already developed by the training programme. The Association of Secondary Teachers Ireland (ASTI) will act as overall coordinator of the project.

The role of the Garda (police) in countering bullying

In dealing with bullying behaviour, the emphasis of the Garda Siochana is on a preventive approach. Over 600 Gardai have received special training and are involved in a programme for primary schools. Junior liaison officers are being trained to deal with the problem in post-primary schools. As well as bullying, the schools' programme deals with vandalism, road safety and the investigation of crime. The involvement of the Gardai is very much in line with the recommendation of the Department of Education guidelines that the problem of bullying behaviour is best tackled using a whole-community approach involving parents, teachers, non-teaching staff, social and community workers and the Gardai where appropriate.

There is no offence listed as bullying and the Gardai have no direct legal powers in dealing with it. However, if there is an assault, formal action can then be taken. In certain situations a breach of the peace could be interpreted as an offence. In the case of a person demanding money this could be a form of larceny. It is the intention of the Gardai to deal with juvenile offences outside the court system if possible. In instances of bullying, the Gardai carry out their investigations in a very discreet manner, with the emphasis on trying to get the bully to change behaviour sooner rather than later. The role of the Gardai is to support the school policy on bullying.

Childline

Childline is a service provided by the Irish Society for the Prevention of Cruelty to Children (ISPCC). It is intended for any child in trouble or danger. By dialling 1–800–666–666 any child anywhere in the country can talk to a voluntary counsellor about anything they wish. The service is non-directional and non-judgemental and children can remain anonymous. Childline takes no action unless a child empowers it to do so. When a child asks for help, whatever the problem, the option of going to a trusted adult within his or her own community or being referred to an appropriate agency is discussed. Since the service was launched in 1988, it has received more than 277,000 calls. In 1992 there were 551 counselled calls in bullying. In 1993 this had risen to 1080, a 96 per cent increase. The chief executive of the ISPCC has stressed the need to get away from the adult attitude that it was 'part of growing up – it did us no harm'. The ISPCC also worked with Kidscape (UK), the Department of Education and the National Parents Council (Post-primary) in the production of *Stop bullying*, a set of guidelines for use by parents and teachers in an effort to prevent, identify and respond to the problem of bullying.

Sticks and Stones Theatre Company

The Sticks and Stones Theatre Company was established to heighten awareness of bullying and to help schools to cope more effectively with the problem. The programme for primary schools was launched in October 1994. The project was funded initially by the Gulbenkian Foundation and the Department of Education. A programme was devised to depict typical forms of bullying whether in the schoolroom, playground, *en route* to or from school, or outside school time. The presentation consists of scenes of movement, mime, music and dance; this is followed by discussion sessions involving participation by the children. Prior to the presentation, a facilitator talks to teachers and explains the use of the handbook (1994) which is an integral part of the programme. In September 1996 the company launched a programme for second-level schools.

Initiatives in a youth setting

Major advances have taken place in dealing with bullying behaviour outside the school setting. In April 1994, the National Youth Federation held a two-day seminar for youth leaders from all over the country. As a result of seminars and workshops the organisation developed a code of good practice for dealing with bullying behaviour, which was written up as *Dealing with bullying: Guidelines for youth workers* (1995).

In March 1995, the Order of Malta held a National Seminar for its members (cadets). Young people from all over Ireland attended and the Order of Malta bullying charter was drawn up as a result of the workshops. The great value of their charter is that it represents the feelings of the young people themselves; it was not imposed by adults. Such a charter can be used periodically to promote discussion and raise awareness of the unacceptability of bullying behaviour. The charter produced by the cadets is shown in Table 7.4.

Anti-Bullying Unit, Trinity College, Dublin

There is an Anti-Bullying Centre, Resource and Research Unit in Trinity College, Dublin, with Mona O'Moore as co-ordinator. The centre aims to create a greater awareness and understanding of bullying behaviour and to provide advice, guidance and counselling and resource material for parents, schools and organisations seeking to counter bullying behaviour. It also aims

Table 7.4 Charter devised by Order of Malta

Bullying Charter

1. We want the Order of Malta to be free from bullying.
2. There should be no name-calling.
3. There should be no physical abuse.
4. There should be no ganging up on people.
5. There should be no slagging.
6. Everyone should feel respected.
7. When one of us does something wrong they should not be laughed at.
8. Problems should be shared.
9. We all share the responsibility to ensure that bullying is not tolerated.

to conduct research into bullying behaviour. The centre provides in-service and staff development days for schools and organisations and day conferences and workshops for pupils, parents, teachers and adults in the workplace. There is also a reference library.

Future directions

Many schools in Ireland have either drawn up a school policy on bullying or are in the process of doing so. There is a growing emphasis on in-service training on bullying for school staff. School chaplains and guidance counsellors have been involved in training seminars to better equip themselves to deal with the problem. In recent years education departments in the universities and teacher training colleges have included modules on countering bullying behaviour in schools. In 1998, in response to a report on discipline in schools (Martin, 1997) commissioned by the Department of Education, the Minister announced a review of the 1993 guidelines on bullying. The report stated that bullying was evident and required redress.

References

Byrne, B. (1987) A study of the nature and incidence of bullies and whipping boys (victims) in a Dublin City post-primary school for boys. Unpublished M.Ed. thesis, Trinity College, Dublin.

Byrne, B. (1992) Bullies and victims in a school setting with reference to some Dublin schools. Unpublished Ph.D. thesis, University College, Dublin.

Byrne, B. (1993) *Coping with bullying in schools*. Dublin: The Columba Press.

Byrne, B. (1994) *Bullying: A community approach*. Dublin: The Columba Press.

Department of Education (An Roinn Oideachais) (1993) *Guidelines on countering bullying behaviour in schools*. Dublin: Stationery Office.

Department of Education (An Roinn Oideachais) (1994/1995) *Statistical Report*. Dublin: Stationery Office.

Irish National Teachers' Organisation (INTO) (1993) *Discipline in the primary school*. Dublin: INTO.

ISPCC/National Parents Council Post-Primary (1994) *Kidscape – stop bullying*. Dublin: ISPCC.

Lawlor, M. and MacIntyre, D. (1991) *Stay Safe programme, child abuse prevention programme*. Dublin: Department of Health/Eastern Health Board.

Martin, M. (1997). *Discipline in schools*. Dublin: Stationery Office.

National Youth Federation (1995) *Dealing with bullying: Guidelines for youth workers*. Dublin: Irish Youth Work Press.

Olweus, D. (1978) *Aggression in the schools: Bullies and whipping boys*. Washington, DC: Hemisphere.

Olweus, D. (1989) The Olweus Bully/Victim Questionnaire. Mimeo. Bergen, Norway.

O'Moore, A.M. and Hillery, B. (1989) Bullying in Dublin schools. *Irish Journal of Psychology*, 10, 426–441.

O'Moore, A.M., Kirkham, C. and Smith, M. (1997) Bullying behaviour in Irish schools: A nation-wide study. *Irish Journal of Psychology* 18, 141–69. (This special edition on the topic of bullying in schools also contains keynote papers given by contributors at the Bullying in Schools Conference held in Trinity College, Dublin, in October 1996.)

Sticks and Stones Theatre Company (1994, 1996) *Handbook*. Dublin.

Further reading

Byrne, B. (1994) Coping with bullying in schools in an Irish context. In *Conference proceedings, children's peer relations: Cooperation and conflict*. January. Institute of Social Research, University of South Australia, Adelaide, Australia.

Byrne, B. (1994) Bullies and victims in a school setting with reference to some Dublin schools. *Irish Journal of Psychology*, 15, 574–586.

Byrne, B. (1994) *Young people and bullying*. Dublin: Irish Youth Work Press.

Byrne, B. (1997) Bullying: A community approach. *Irish Journal of Psychology*, 18, 258–266.

O'Donnell, V. (1995) *Bullying: A resource guide for parents and teachers*. Dublin: Attic Press.

O'Moore, A.M. (1988) *Bullying in schools*. Council of Europe Report, DECS-Egt (88) S-E. Strasbourg: Council for Cultural Co-operation.

O'Moore, A.M. (1989) Bullying in Britain and Ireland: An overview. In E. Roland and E. Munthe (eds) *Bullying: An international perspective*. London: David Fulton.

O'Moore, A.M. (1995) Bullying behaviour in children and adolescents in Ireland. *Children and Society*, 9, 54–72.

O'Moore, A.M. (1997) *What do teachers need to know?* London: Pitman

O'Moore, A.M. and Hillery, B. (1991) What do teachers need to know? In M. Elliott (ed.) *Bullying: A practical guide to coping for schools*. London: Longman.

8 France

Dominique Fabre-Cornali,
Jean-Claude Emin and Jacques Pain

Overview

The wide scope of the concept of school bullying

In France the main approach to this phenomenon is often restricted to a legal one (through the definitions given to physical violence or offences by the Penal Code). However, there seems to be a continuum from the pupils' utter lack of concern towards what they are taught, the hard-living 'incivilities' (abuse, hustles and so on) towards the personnel, the feeling of injustice and arbitrariness mentioned by the pupils and finally the violence defined by the Penal Code. Hence a feeling of insecurity is often felt by both the pupils and the school staff.

The new situation of school bullying

Today, in an increasing number of schools (especially in lower secondary schools), offences have increased and are often committed by increasingly younger children. Stress and strain have also increased. At the same time the management of school bullying is now perhaps harder because of the loss of consensus of the opinion on the role of school in the future.

Country summary

France has a population (in 1996) of 58,300,000 inhabitants; 20,500,000 of these live in 29 large urban centres of over 200,000 inhabitants (this being about half the total urban population). The immigrant population (1990) was 3,597,000; immigrants constitute 6.8 per cent of the 0–19-year-olds, 6.9 per cent of the 20–64-year-olds and 3.4 per cent of the over 65s; in 1995, Portuguese were the most numerous of these (24 per cent), followed by Algerians (16 per cent), Moroccans (13 per cent) and people from black Africa (7 per cent).

So far as employment is concerned, 68 per cent of wage-earning employees are in the tertiary sector; 20 per cent in industry; 7 per cent in building, civil engineering; and 5 per cent in agriculture. Immigrants form 6.2 per cent of the labour force, but are more affected by unemployment than French people.

School summary

The primary sector has five levels, from ages 6 to 10, though many children attend pre-primary. The secondary sector has four levels in lower secondary schools, and three levels in upper secondary schools (which are split into general, vocational and other types).

In the primary education sector there are 6,884,000 pupils in public schools (933,000 in private schools). This is made up of 2,635,000 in pre-primary schools (2–5 years old) and 4,183,000 in primary schools (6–10 years old) with 66,000 in adaptation/integration to school.

In the secondary education sector there are 4,655,000 pupils in public schools (1,167,000 in private schools). This is made up of 3,430,000 in lower secondary schools (+11–15 years old); and in upper secondary schools (+16–18 years old) there are 1,537,000 pupils in general schools, 729,000 pupils in vocational schools and 126,000 pupils in other types of schools.

In the public schools (écoles publiques) the average size of lower secondary schools is 535 pupils, and of upper secondary schools, 1029 pupils. In the private schools (écoles privées) the average size of lower secondary schools is 361 pupils and of upper secondary schools, 354 pupils. In the vocational schools (lycées professionnels) the average size of public schools is 443 pupils, and of private schools, 185 pupils.

Regarding class sizes, in lower secondary schools this is 24.5 in public schools and 24.7 in private schools; in upper secondary schools it is 29.5 pupils in public schools and 25.5 in private schools.

Bullying in schools

The main data on school bullying given in this chapter are drawn from a joint research project launched by the Ministry of Education (Direction de l'Evaluation et de la Prospective) and the Home Office (Institut des Hautes Etudes de la Sécurité Intérieure) in 1994. The research selection committee was supervised by Bernard Charlot (Paris VIII Saint-Denis University); nine research teams were selected and ten others joined the committee. A summary of all these surveys was published in 1997 (Charlot and Emin, 1997).

How the term is defined

First, in France the meaning of school bullying is different from that in the Anglo-Saxon world. On the whole, the French term 'violence' has a much wider scope than the British term 'aggression'. In France school bullying primarily refers to 'faits de violence' and under this definition violence is what is defined as such by the French Penal Code.

School bullying in France includes all the different forms of misuse of power (crime and offences against people, or against personal or school property), all the forms of violence of the school itself, as an institution, and also all minor but frequent manifestations of 'incivilities' (incivilités) which disturb school life (such as impoliteness, noise, disorder, etc.). A translation of 'bullying' as 'malmenances' has been suggested.

A more 'phenomenological' definition of school bullying has also been developed by some sociologists: by this definition, violence is what is thought of or felt as violent by the victim. As for the perception of bullying it is relative, and differs from one person to another, from one area to another. Pupils do not share with the staff the same viewpoint on bullying. On the one hand, schoolchildren are very sensitive to unfairness or lack of respect towards them; on the other hand, teachers feel very badly about insolent remarks and abuse coming from their pupils.

Beyond all these definitions it has to be kept in mind that, as Jacques Pain and the CIEP teams have shown in a comparative study (Pain *et al.*, 1997), the pattern of education in France today is different from that in Great Britain or Germany. A French school is a place where pupils have to be taught; in Great Britain or Germany, pupils have to be brought up. In France, the school also aims at the integration of children from immigrant families.

The history of interest in the topic

Before the mass media began to focus their interest on school bullying in the 1980s, official reports first started to tackle the problem. Eric Debarbieux (1996) in his survey *Violence en milieu scolaire* showed that all those reports share a qualitative approach. One of the first reports was by Selosse (1971; see also Selosse, 1997), for the European Council. School bullying was not yet mentioned as such. The report tried to show the link between juvenile delinquency and academic difficulties at school.

At the same time (around 1975), the theme of insecurity was becoming central to the politicians' concern (cf. Peyrefitte's report in 1977).

The reports of the General School Inspection

Those reports coordinated by G. Tallon were issued in 1979; the figures given in these reports (school bullying in upper secondary schools and in vocational schools) are the same as those of Marc Rancurel's report in 1992. That shows the lack of reliable statistics on school bullying. The General School Inspection on school life thinks that violence in school really began in 1975, but one of the limitations of these surveys is that they only take into account schools with social and bullying problems. Moreover, the existence of school bullying does not give any information about its frequency.

Marc Rancurel, who has been overseeing the problem for ten years, has often emphasised the difficulty of quantifying school bullying (for example, for a long period heads of schools have felt it shameful to mention it). Nowadays, he asserts, 'School bullying may occur more often, but its very nature has changed deeply.' This assumption has to be confirmed, but nevertheless for about the last four years the Ministry of Education has admitted that school bullying is a real problem which needs to be solved. Here are two examples:

- The instruction 'Lang – Quilès – Glavany' (Ministries of Education and Home Office), issued in 1992, speaks of the conditions of security in schools.
- A map of schools with social and bullying problems was drawn up in 1992. Two new official reports have recently been partly published (cf. Philippe Barret's report in 1994, 'Aggressive behaviour in lower and upper secondary schools'). It emphasises the need for more severe penalties for violent behaviour, and a reinforcement of the proceedings of expulsion for bullies.

The last official report (Fotinos and Poupelin, 1995), *La violence à l'école – Etat de la situation en 1994*, also lacks a comprehensive view of the problem. On the whole, we must acknowledge that the figures issued by the Ministry of Education and the Home Office on school bullying are still partial. But new working habits have now started and joint projects begun between the Ministry of Education, the Home Office and the Ministry of Justice (for instance, the bids for the research on school bullying show a good example of this cross approach between the Ministry of Education and the Home Office).

School bullying: a social problem

School bullying is currently seen more and more as a social problem. Some factors can explain it:

- The progress of the economic and social crisis, with the increase in unemployment (especially among young people).
- The focus of the mass media (television, radio and newspapers) on tragic news items such as murder cases, rapes or assault and battery inside or outside school.

As Robert Ballion (1996) points out, between 1985 and 1990 school itself changed entirely: for instance, the increase in numbers at school was more than 30 per cent for this period. Nowadays, upper secondary school has turned into a mass education structure. At the age of 17, the rate of school attendance is 92.5 per cent, and at 18 it is still 85.5 per cent. In 1985, young people with 'baccalauréat' amounted to 30 per cent of their age class; in 1994 they amounted to 60 per cent. Hence many schools (and especially upper secondary schools) experience greater and greater difficulties because of the combination of three different elements: the academic heterogeneity of their pupils, their lack of motivation, and in particular their 'mal être'.

Suicides

There are no official statistics of suicides due to school bullying known as such. But we may have a glimpse of the stress experienced by teachers bullied at school through a recent survey by Dr Horenstein, a psychiatrist working at the 'Mutual Insurance Company of the Personnel of National Education' (see Charlot and Emin, 1997). This study showed that there was an over-representation of male teachers (between 50 and 60 years old), and of schools in an urban and underprivileged environment. The victims mainly suffered from deep psychological trauma (25 per cent of physical aggression came from the schoolchildren's family and 43 per cent from the schoolchildren themselves). The 15 per cent of teachers who did not lodge a complaint against those who bullied them (70 per cent of them do) were the most affected by the stress.

Research on the nature and types of school bullying

Data on types and frequencies of bullying

As we have already noted, figures on school bullying are often incomplete. Since 1993 the Home Office has issued statistics on the phenomenon. A new statistics index, which has largely developed over the last few years, has been created to take into account this long existing phenomenon. Assault and battery undergone by pupils, or damage and theft against the school or its personnel, have been counted. The unexpected result of this new rubric is a low rate of delinquency at school. Schools on the whole look rather protected from crime and offences according to the definition of the Penal Code.

In 1995 the figures on school bullying were as follows: 982 assault and battery on pupils; 176 on teachers.

It should be kept in mind that the general rate of crime and offences in the French population is 6.5 per cent. School, it has to be emphasised, is less open to penalised delinquency than French society on the whole, even if we take into account an important 'black hole' of unknown delinquent acts.

More precisely, those figures issued by the Home Office show:

- *An increase in 'racketeering'* (the most well-known indicator of school bullying; racketeering, or taxing, refers to intimidation in order to get money, clothes or food, or to get someone to do tasks for you such as carrying your satchel or doing homework). There was an increase from 1988 to 1992 (with a slight decrease in 1993). This increase may partly be explained by better management of the problem. More generally, there is a close connection between school bullying and the development of juvenile delinquency.

- *The different types of school bullying and their frequency* (1995 figures). Against pupils: Murder: two. Assault and battery: 982 (53 per cent inside the school; 40 per cent in the surroundings of the school; 7 per cent on the way to school: 59 per cent of these acts were committed without using weapons). School racketeering: 1223 (40 per cent inside school; 52 per cent in the surroundings of the school; 8 per cent on the way to school). Indecent assaults: 363 (including 26 rapes). In 1995, 1909 acts of violence against pupils were committed. Against personnel working in schools: Assault and battery: 176 (79 per cent in the school: 7.3 per cent of these acts were committed without using weapons). Damage against school buildings and equipment: 3441 (273 through fire; 3168 by other forms such as graffiti, disruption, etc.). Theft and robbery: 6661. However, one should add that all these figures do not include the very 'minor' delinquent acts – such as stealing educational stationery.

The sex of the bullies and of the bullied schoolchildren are important data. Girls are generally less often found among the bullies and victims of bullying. School bullying – at least according to the Penal Code definition – is more of a male 'business'. School bullies usually attend at the school at which the bullying occurs; they do not come primarily from outside the school.

A view of the problem of school bullying from the point of view of bullied pupils themselves is given by C. Carra and F. Sicot (1996), two young research workers who have conducted a study on children bullied at school selected from a representative sample of lower secondary schools in the French department (district) of Doubs. Eight categories of school bullying were studied: all these categories were defined as such by the victims themselves. These are: lack of respect; damage to personal property; theft; blackmail; blows; negative racial attitudes; racketeering; and sexual harassment.

Two questionnaires were filled in by children bullied at school. Some of the conclusions from this study are:

- There is no one single form of school bullying, but several.
- Pupils generally mention acts or facts which are often ignored when one speaks of school bullying. Lack of respect towards them, damage to their property or theft are felt more acutely and are more often mentioned by children bullied at school than are sexual harassment, aggression or racketeering (for instance, lack of respect towards them is mentioned by nearly 50 per cent of the bullied children, but only 5 per cent of them mention the racketeering).

- The importance of the feeling of being bullied. In this survey, 69 per cent of the pupils said that they had been bullied at least once.
- The over-representation of boys attending the final grade of the lower secondary school (between 12 and 13 years old).
- Children coming from large families (over four children), whose parents are divorced or unemployed, or whose mother is an immigrant, are more vulnerable than others. On the whole, the study shows that some children run a higher risk of being bullied than others.

Differences due to social class and ethnic group

Jean-Paul Payet (1996), an ethno-methodologist who has studied school bullying in some lower secondary schools, has also shown that – in opposition to what the mass media often say – school bullying does not come only from outside the school. He questions a number of assertions claimed by the mass media, for instance, that school bullies come from the suburbs and from immigrants' families. Another assertion questioned by Payet is that these immigrants' families abdicate their responsibilities in the academic field. Payet shows that bullying is inherent in the school system and emphasises two phenomena he observed: the increasing social and racial segregation and the 'social distance' between teachers and schoolchildren from the working classes. For Payet, academic segregation originates in urban segregation. In underprivileged areas the school's population is actually more homogeneous socially and ethnically than is the population living locally. There is also internal segregation due to the way classes are set up. For instance, in the first grade classes of lower secondary school with good academic standards, he noticed that girls are often more numerous than boys, and native French children more numerous than those from immigrant families.

Initiatives and interventions

Initiatives taken to tackle bullying

In 1996, the Secretary of State for Education adopted measures to prevent school bullying. Three main objectives have been set:

1 *The improvement and reinforcement of the pupils' supervision*
In schools with social and bullying problems, social workers, nurses, supervisors (150 for both boarding- and day-schools) and 2200 young volunteer conscripts (plus 2500 already appointed in some schools) were appointed at the beginning of the 1996 school term. Pupils with difficulties in academic fields will be supported. New structures will be tested in order to provide education for schoolchildren with academic difficulties and to help them to find an academic or vocational answer to their problems.

Each 'académie' (region) will be equipped with an audit and support unit for schools with bullying problems. An agreement between the state and some insurance companies has been signed to enable bullied staff to get quick and complete compensation. The teachers on training courses will be trained for teaching conditions in underprivileged areas; and young teachers will be supported.

2 *The help and support of pupils and of their parents*
The fight against pupils' absenteeism will take priority. At the beginning of the first term, the school's regulations will be read and studied by all classes in the school in order to foster a sense of civic responsibility among schoolchildren.

Before the beginning of the term, a meeting with the parents of the pupils going into the first year will be held in every lower secondary school. Recourse to mediators and interpreters will be automatic in order to develop a closer dialogue between teachers and immigrant families. The timetable may be modified in schools with social and bullying problems to enable children to do more sports, or fulfil some other achievements (artistic, musical, dramatic and so on).

3 *The preservation of the schools and the improvement of their environment*

- All the schools in ZEPs ('zones d'éducation prioritaire') will be evaluated.
- The map of all these ZEP schools could be modified.
- Measures to limit schools' size could be adopted in underprivileged areas.
- Intruders coming from outside the school might be prosecuted.
- Boarding schools will be built and tested in ten areas.
- Ultimately judges, police, and personnel from education should work together more frequently.

An example of a constructive answer to the problem of school bullying: 'intervention research' (la recherche-action)

For the last fifteen years, fieldwork on school bullying has been carried out in some lower secondary schools (mainly in ZEPs) and in the suburbs of big cities. Three examples of this fieldwork are given here. They all refer to what is called 'intervention research', and have in common three main characteristics:

- They aim to change working habits and practices of the school staff
- The school staff has gradually learned to work together on joint projects with other partners (police, town services and so on)
- The projects have been followed through for four or five years by some researchers (with a training in educational sciences).

For example:

ZEP Les Mureaux

Heads of vocational and lower secondary schools, city officials, policemen working in the area and members of associations have set up a group which has met regularly for five years (and jointly decided upon different types of action: seminars, offers of mediation, training courses on school bullying, etc.).

ZEP Trappes

In a lower secondary school, the headteacher and his staff have started different actions, such as the setting up of new school regulations and charter, specific training of the staff, and a pedagogy adjusted to the academic difficulties of the schoolchildren. Six years on, one may say that this school has turned into quite a standard one.

ZEP Mantes

In another lower secondary school, the headteacher has planned together with young voluntary teachers a new project for the school in order to prevent school bullying. These two last examples, and others, have shown the important role played by the head of the school in the prevention and management of school bullying.

Conclusion: an increasing need for intervention

France has for long favoured a legal approach to dealing with bullying in school, as compared with many European countries which manage their conflicts inside the schools. Nowadays the importance of a preventive management of school bullying is taken into consideration (cf. the measures taken by the Ministry of Education in 1996). For the future, emphasis should be put on the training of school personnel (to solve conflicts, negotiate, etc.), the reinforcement of the cohesion of the staff around the headteacher (who plays a leading part in building up a good 'climate' in the school) and the necessity of obvious reference points and regulations inside the school.

References

Ballion, R. (1996) Les difficultés des Lycées à travers les transgressions. Revue. *Migrants et formations*, 104, March.

Barret, P. (1994) *Les conduites agressives dans les lycées et les collèges*. Unpublished report of the Inspection Generale.

Carra, C. and Sicot, F. (1996) Pour un diagnostic local de la violence à l'école. Enquête de victimation dans les collèges du département du Doubs. Laboratoire de sociologie et d'anthropologie, Université de Franche-Comté.

Charlot, B. and Emin, J.-C. (eds) (1997) *La violence a l'école: état des savoirs*. Paris: A. Colin.

Debarbieux, E. (1996) *La violence en milieu scolaire, l'état des lieux*. Paris: ESF.

Fotinos, G. and Poupelin, M. (1995) *La violence à l'école, état de la situation en 1994, analyse et recommandations*. Paris: Ministère de l'Education Nationale/Inspection Générale de l'Education Nationale.

Pain, J., Barrier, E. and Robin, D. (1997) *Violences à l'école. Une étude comparative européene a partir de douze établissements du second degré en Allemagne, Angleterre et France*. Vigneux: Matrice.

Payet, J.-P. (1996) L'école et la violence – à propos de quelques tabous. Conférence, Université d'été, 'Violences à l'école'.

Peyrefitte, A. (ed.) (1977) *Réponse à la violence*. Paris: Documentation française/Presses Pocket.

Rancurel, M. (1992) *La violence à l'école: constats, réflexions, propositions*. Recueil de notes de l'Inspection générale de l'Education nationale, exemplaire dactylographié.

Selosse, J. (1971). *Le rôle de l'école dans le prévention de la délinquance juvenile*. Rapport au Conseil du L'Europe.

Selosse, J. (1997) sous le direction de Pain, J. and Villerbu, L. *Adolescence, violences et deviances*. Vigneux: Matrice.

Tallon, G. (1979) *La violence dans les collèges*. Ministère de l'Education Nationale et de la Culture.

Statistics

L'état de l'Ecole, n°6, Direction de l'Evaluation et de la Prospective, November 1996.

Repères et références statistiques sur les enseignements et la formation, 1996.

Tableaux de l'économie française, INSEE, 1996.

Further reading

Arendt, H. (1972) *Du mensonge à la violence*. Paris: Calmann-Lévy.

Bachmann, C. and Leguennec, N. (1996) *Violences urbaines. Ascension et chute des classes moyennes à travers cinquante ans de politique de la ville*. Paris: Albin Michel.

Ballion, R. (1991) *La bonne école, évaluation et choix du collège et du lycée*. Paris: Hatier.

Ballion, R. (1993) *Le lycée, une cité à reconstruire*. Paris: Hachette.

Bazin, H. (1995) *Le mouvement Hip-Hop*. Paris: Desclée de Brouwwer.

Bouamana, S. (1993) *De la galère à la citoyenneté. Les jeunes, la cité, la citoyenneté*. Paris: EPI / Desclée de Brouwer.

Cahiers de la Sécurité Intérieure (LES) (1994) Numéro spécial. *La violence à l'école*. IHESI / La Documentation française, 15.

Chamboderon, J.C. (1971) La délinquance juvénile, essai de construction de l'objet. *Revue française de sociologie*, 12.

Charlot, B. (1987) *L'école en mutation: crise de l'école et mutation sociale*. Paris.

Chesnais, J.C. (1981) *Histoire de la violence*. Paris: Hachette.

Choquet, M. and Ledoux, S. (1994) *Adolescents*. Paris: INSERM.

Cousin, O. (1994) *L'effet-établissement, étude comparative de douze collèges*. Thèse de sociologie (dir F. Dubet), Bordeaux: exemplaire dactylographié.

Crubellier, M. (1979) *L'enfance et la jeunesse dans la société française, 1800–1950*. Paris: Armand Colin.

Debarbieux, E. (1989) La place du maître dans la classe: imaginaire, espace, violence. In *Actualité de la Pédagogie Freinet* (sous la direction de P. Clanché et J. Testanière). Bordeaux: PUB.

Debarbieux, E. (1990a) L'enfant, le cru, le philosophe, orthopédie et sauvagerie dans les dialogues platoniciens. In *Recherche sur la philosophie et le langage*. Université de Grenoble/Vrin, 10.

Debarbieux, E. (1990b) *La violence dans la classe*, Paris: ESF éditeur.

Debarbieux, E. (1992) De la violence à l'école. Prolégomènes pour une recherche et des pratiques. In *Actes, psychanalyse et société*, Bordeaux: Presses Universitaires.

Debarbieux, E. (1994a) Ecole du quartier ou école dans le quartier, violence et limites de l'école. In *Migrants-formation*. CNDP, 97.

Debarbieux, E. (1994b) *La Pédagogie Freinet: mises à jour et perspectives* (sous la direction de P. Clanche, E. Debarbieux, et J. Testanière). Bordeaux: Presses Universitaires.

Debarbieux, E. (1994c) *Vingt-cinq ans de sciences de l'éducation, Bordeaux, 1967–1992* (sous la direction d'A. Jeannel, P. Clanché et E. Debarbieux). Paris: AESCE/ INRP.

Debarbieux, E. (1994d) Violence, sens et formation des maîtres. In H. Hannoun et Hans A.-M. Drouin (eds) *Pour une philosophie de l'éducation*, Dijon: CNDP.

Debarbieux, E. (1995) Pratique de recherche sur la violence à l'école par la médiation sociologique. In *Skhôlé*, 3 (IUFM Aix-Marseille).

Defrance, B. (1988) *La violence à l'école*. Paris: Syros.

Demailly, G. (1991) *Le collège, crise, mythes et métiers*. Lille: PUL.

Derouet, J.L. (1988) Désaccords et arrangements dans les collèges (1981–1986). Eléments pour une sociologie des établissements scolaires. *Revue française de pédagogie*, 83.

Derouet, J.L. (1992) *Ecole et justice, de l'égalité des chances aux compromis locaux?* Paris: Métailié.

Dhoquois, R. (1996) Civilité et incivilités. *Les cahiers de la sécurité intérieure*, 23.

Dirn, L. (1990) *La société française en tendances*. Paris: PUF.

Douet, B. (1987) *Discipline et punitions à l'école*. Paris: PUF.

Dubet, F. (1991) *La galère, jeunes en survie*. Paris: Fayard, 1987.

Dubet, F. (1994) *Sociologie de l'expérience*. Paris: Le Seuil.

Dufour-Gompers, R. (1992) *Dictionnaire de la violence et du crime*. Toulouse: Erès.

Dulong, R. and Paperman, P. (1992) *La réputation des cités HLM, enquête sur le langage de l'insécurité*. Paris: L'Harmattan.

Dumay, J.-M. (1994) *L'école agressée*. Paris: Belfond.

Gremy, J.P. (1996) La délinquance permet-elle d'expliquer le sentiment d'insécurité?, *Les cahiers de la sécurité intérieure*, 23.

Grisay, A., (1993) Le fonctionnement des collèges et ses effets sur les élèves de sixième et de cinquième. *Educations et formations*, 32.

Grosperrin, B. (1984) *Les petites écoles sous l'ancien régime*. Bordeaux: Sud-Ouest Université.

Guillon, M. (1995) Immigration et centres urbains: le cas de Paris. In *Les quartiers de la ségrégation: tiers-monde ou quart-monde* (R. Galissot et B. Moulin, dir.). Paris: Karthala.

Henriot Van Zanten, A. (1985) L'école en milieu rural: réalité et représentations. *Revue française de pédagogie*, 73.

Henriot Van Zanten, A. (1991) La sociologie de l'éducation en milieu urbain: discours politique, pratiques de terrain et production scientifique, 1960–1990. *Revue française de pédagogie*, 95.

Lagrange, H. (1995) *La civilité à l'épreuve. Crime et sentiment d'insécurité*. Paris: PUF.

Leger, A. and Tripier, M. (1986) *Fuir ou construire l'école populaire*. Paris: Méridiens.

Leon, J.-M. (1983) *Violence et déviance chez les jeunes: problèmes de l'école, problèmes de la cité*. Paris Ministère de l'Education nationale, exemplaire dactylographié.

Marchand, P. (1991–1992) La violence dans les collèges au XVIIIe siècle. *Bulletin de la commission historique du département du Nord*, 46, 23–40.

Meuret, D. (1995) Distribution des facteurs d'efficacité des collèges. In (coll) *L'école efficace*. Paris: Armand Colin.

Michaud, Y. (1986) *La violence*. Paris: PUF.

Migrants-Formation (numéros spéciaux) (1994) *Violences, conflits et médiations*, 92, 1993; *L'école dans la ville: ouverture ou clôture*, 97.

Ministère de l'Education Nationale (1988) *Regards des jeunes sur le système éducatif*.

Moser, G. (1987) *L'agression*. Paris: PUF.

Muchembled, R. (1989) *La violence au village*. Bruxelles: Brepols.

Pain, J. (1992) *Ecole: violence ou pédagogie*. Vigneux: Matrice.

Pain, J., Degois, M.P. and LeGoff, C. (1998) *Banlieues: les dégis d'un collège sensible*. Paris: ESF.

Payet, J.P. (1992) Civilités et ethnicité dans les collèges de banlieue. Enjeux, résistances et dérives d'une action scolaire territorialisée. *Revue française de pédagogie*, 101.

Payet, J.P. (1993) Ce que disent les mauvais élèves. Civilités, incivilités dans les collèges de banlieue. *Migrants-Formation*, 82.

Payet, J.P. (1995) *Collèges de banlieue. Ethnographie d'un monde scolaire*. Paris: Méridiens.

Pourtois, J.P., Desmet, H. and Lahaye, W. (1992) La pratique interagie de la recherche et de l'action en sciences humaines. *Revue française de pédagogie*, 105.

Roché, S. (1993) *Le sentiment d'insécurité*. Paris: PUF.

Roché, S. (1994) *Insécurité et libertés*. Paris: Le Seuil.

Roché, S. (1996) *La société incivile. Qu'est-ce que l'insécurité?* Paris: Le Seuil.

Rondeau, M.-C. and Trancard, D. (1995) Les collèges sensibles, description, typologie. *Educations et formation*, 40.

Testaniere, J. (1967) Chahut traditionnel et chahut anomique dans l'enseignement du second degré. *Revue française de sociologie*, 8.

Tichit, L. (1995) *De la rage au défi. Nouvelles formes de socialités juvéniles à travers l'approche ethno-sociologique de groupes de jeunes de banlieues populaires* (mémoire de DEA). Bordeaux: exemplaire dactylographié.

Vallet, L.-A. and Caille, J.-P. (1994) La qualité de l'information sur la nationalité dans les statistiques scolaires. *Rapport au directeur de la DEP*.

Viguerie, J. de la (1979) *L'institution des enfants. L'éducation en France, XVIe–XVIIe siècles*. Paris: Calmann-Lévy.

Vulbeau, A. (1993) *Du gouvernement des enfants*. Paris: EPI.

Wacquant, L.J.D. (1992) Pour en finir avec le mythe des cités-ghettos. *Les cahiers de la recherche urbaine*, p. 54.

Wievorka, M. (1992) *La France raciste*. Paris: Le Seuil.

9 Italy

Ada Fonzi, Maria Luisa Genta, Ersilia Menesini, Dario Bacchini, Silvia Bonino and Angela Costabile

Overview

After a general overview of country features – population, school system and distribution of resources – this chapter gives a brief history of the studies on school bullying in Italy, from 1993 when the anonymous questionnaire by Olweus was translated, to the more recent directions of bullying research. The nature of bullying has been investigated in five different cities in Italy (two in the north, one in the centre and two in the south). The average results confirm that bullying in Italian schools is very serious. Being bullied sometimes or more frequently in the last term is reported by 41.6 per cent of pupils in primary and 26.4 per cent in middle schools. Bullying other children occurs with 28 per cent of pupils in primary and 10.8 per cent in middle schools. The authors' opinion is that, besides some methodological differences between the Italian report and that of other European countries, in our culture some types of bullying seem to be more tolerated than in other western cultures.

As regards attitudes, the majority of children are opposed to bullying and supportive of victims, although there are differences according to age, gender and bully/victim status. Most Italian interventions in schools have been carried out as a result of local requests from a single school or from educational departments of city administrations. The majority of them have been directed at class level by means of curricular interventions, and were implemented for a short period of three months. The results are encouraging, and we hope they may lay the groundwork for a wider initiative against bullying in schools.

Social and educational background

According to the last census, the Italian population totals 57,300,000 inhabitants. In the last decade there has been a substantial decrease in the birth rate and an increase in immigration from other countries, mainly of Slavonic, African and North African people. Urban areas range in size from large conurbations (3.5 million (Rome and Milan)), to provincial cities (*c*. 0.2 to 1 million), and to towns of several tens of thousands of inhabitants. The population is socially and economically diverse, with a considerable range of wealth and housing according to economic status and to degree of development in different areas of the country. In fact economic resources present a clear-cut differentiation in the different areas of the country (i.e. northern and central versus southern Italy). Fifty per cent of the industrial and financial activities are concentrated in the north; in the centre, economic activities are based mainly on small enterprises of production and services; and in the south, there are more economic problems and a higher rate of unemployment.

The school system

In Italy schooling is compulsory from 6 to 14 years. The first sector of our educational system is called primary elementary school and covers a period of five years from ages 6 to 11. The second sector, called secondary middle school, covers a period of three years, from ages 11 to 14. After compulsory education pupils will continue into secondary education, articulated in humanistic, scientific, technical and professional schools for five years, prior to university entrance at around age 19.

On average, primary schools have classes of eighteen pupils ranging from age 10 to 25, with one or two classes in each year group. Around 50 per cent of Italian primary schools may be considered small, since they have fewer than 100 students. The rest have more than 100 pupils. School hours in Italy are different from many other European countries. A large majority of primary schools (85 per cent) work for 27–30 hours a week, organised over six days from 8:30 a.m. to 12:30 p.m., with pupils usually going home for lunch and returning for one or two hours in the early afternoon. Fifteen per cent of schools, mainly in northern and central Italy, have a schedule of 36–40 hours a week, with a timetable from 8:30 a.m. to 4:30 p.m. for five days, and a lunch break taken at school. Most schools in southern Italy (70 per cent) have a morning schedule of 27 hours a week with no classes in the afternoon. Middle schools usually have a schedule of 30 hours a week, from 8:30 a.m. to 1:30 p.m., with no lunch break.

On average, middle schools have classes of pupils ranging in size from fifteen to 28, with several classes in each year group and an average school size of 500 students. Around 20 per cent of students have longer school hours, with two or three afternoon curricular times and a lunch break at school.

Unfortunately, we have a high percentage of pupils who repeat school years in middle schools between ages 11 and 14 (around 15 per cent), and around 40 per cent of students leave school after completing compulsory education. The results of the educational system in Italy are not very satisfactory and they have a clear-cut differentiation according to social and economic factors and to different geographical areas of the country (i.e. northern and central versus southern Italy). For instance, around 76 per cent of young people belonging to low income families do not achieve a high school diploma. In southern Italy around 14 per cent of young people aged 15–19 years old do not finish compulsory education. This rate of school evasion in southern Italy is four times higher than that in northern Italy (Censis, 1995).

In primary schools, pupils have three or four teachers, each teaching a group of homogeneous subjects (i.e. written language, literature, painting and media languages). In middle schools they will have specialised subject teachers. In Italy we do not have school support staff such as educational psychologists working directly in schools; for help with pupils difficult to treat, schools may ask for assistance from health services where psychologists operate. Primary and middle schools have specialised teachers to support children with disabilities, and other specialists teaching the Catholic religion.

The private school sector covers around 10 per cent of students in primary schools and 8.4 per cent in middle schools. Private schools follow the same rules and curricular programmes as public schools, although they usually offer longer school hours (40 hours a week or more) than public schools.

Pupils spend curricular time in lessons of approximately 60 minutes, and in most primary and middle schools, break time is a short period of between ten and fifteen minutes once or twice a day. For those schools with longer school hours pupils usually have a lunch-time break of 90 minutes. Break times in Italy are supervised directly by teachers.

Most schools are in urban or small town areas and some are in rural or small villages, especially in the primary sector. In the last few years the Italian population has been growing due to increasing immigration from other countries; however, the proportion of students from other cultural and ethnic minorities is still very low in comparison with many other European countries (around 0.7 per cent in primary school and 0.4 per cent in middle school), with a higher rate in northern Italy and a lower rate in the south and on the islands.

Studies of school bullying in Italy

School bullying in Italy is a matter of recent interest. Our knowledge about the problem is still in the initial stages. In May 1993 a group of researchers from Florence and Cosenza universities collected data in some schools in order to investigate the presence of bullying and some qualitative aspects of the phenomenon.

Anonymous questionnaires which closely followed the design of Olweus (1993) and of Whitney and Smith (1993) were given to 784 pupils aged 8 to 14 in five primary schools and four middle schools in Florence (central Italy), and to 595 pupils from four primary schools and four middle schools in Cosenza (southern Italy). The questionnaire contained 28 single or multiple choice questions, filled in by pupils in the class. A definition of bullying was provided to give pupils a clear understanding of what they were to respond to; this was the Italian translation of the English definition:

> We say a child or a young person is being bullied, or picked on when another child or a young person, or a group of children or young people, say nasty and unpleasant things to him or her. It is also bullying when a child, or a young person, is hit, kicked, threatened, locked inside a room, sent nasty notes, when no one ever talks to them and things like that. These things can happen frequently and it is difficult for the child or the young person being bullied to defend himself or herself. It is also bullying when a child or a young person is teased repeatedly in a nasty way. But it is not bullying when two children or young people of about the same strength have the odd fight or quarrel.

Administration procedures also followed those of the English survey (Whitney and Smith, 1993; Smith, Chapter 5, this volume), with the exception of the time of the year when the data were collected: May in Italy and December in England. This difference between the two country reports has been discussed and investigated in subsequent studies focused on methodological issues. Another problem we found related to the translation of the term 'bullying' in Italy. In fact we do not have a term that can directly translate the meaning of bullying. Our word 'bullo' (bully) has two different meanings: one is related to an unusual way of behaving in order to make others notice you, and another relates to being aggressive towards other people. Moreover, the term was not very familiar among children. During the phase of translation and adaptation of the questionnaire, we presented the definition of bullying to a small sample (n = 45) of primary school children; they were asked to name this type of behaviour. The Italian term generally used by children was 'prepotenze', followed by 'violenze', which implies a more severe and often a physical negative action against the partner. 'Fare prepotenze' and 'essere prepotenti' seemed similar to the meaning of verbal, physical and indirect peer abuse given to the term by other authors (Olweus, 1993; Smith, 1991), and we decided to use it for the Italian version of the questionnaire.

In a second sample of 144 middle school children the effect of the semantic value of the Italian translation for bullying has been tested, administering the same questionnaire with the term 'violenze' instead of 'prepotenze'. The data indicate that the use of the term 'violenze' does not change the rate of the phenomenon, giving similar results to that obtained with the 'prepotenze' version of the questionnaire. From this methodological study, we concluded that probably the definition given at the beginning of the questionnaire might have affected the results more than the single word used to name it.

A preliminary presentation of the Italian survey on bullying in schools was published in a popular psychological magazine in May 1995 by Ada Fonzi (*Psicologia Contemporanea*). Immediately there was a major response to these data in the newspapers and on television programmes. Some reporters spoke of 'shock data', others interviewed some teachers in order to confirm the findings in the Florence and Cosenza schools. At the beginning of 1996 the survey findings appeared in the *European Journal of Psychology of Education* (Genta, Menesini, Fonzi, Costabile and Smith, 1996) and in an Italian scientific journal (*Età Evolutiva*) by Genta, Menesini, Fonzi and Costabile (1996).

What was surprising for the researchers and for media attention was that bullying was reported in both Italian areas (Florence and Cosenza) at a more substantial level than had been found in other European and western countries. The total percentages in our country were about twice as high as in England and almost three times higher than those in Norway.

In order to have more reliable data on the phenomenon in Italy, data on the nature and extent of bullying were also collected in other areas of the country (Turin and Bologna in the north, Rome in the centre, Naples and Palermo in the south) by local researchers supervised by members of the Florence Department.

At the end of 1995, two books on interventions against bullying, published abroad, were translated into Italian (Olweus, 1993; Sharp and Smith, 1994). Since then information about bullying in schools has reached a larger number of teachers and educational psychologists, creating more sensitivity to the problem. In fact, our team of researchers and other university colleagues now working on the same problem in Italy are receiving more and more requests to survey the phenomenon in schools and to train teachers to tackle the problem.

Since 1996 some intervention studies have been performed, mainly supported by local government grants. Some of them are still in progress and a few are in print or already published (Menesini, Argentieri, Baroni, Lazzari and Spadoni, 1996). In addition, a volume on the nature and extent of the phenomenon in Italy reporting data from several geographical areas, led by Ada Fonzi, was published late in 1997 (*Il bullismo in Italia*).

Parallel to interventions, some studies have been performed in order to analyse factors related to the phenomenon. Attitudes to bullying have been studied by Menesini and others (Menesini, Eslea, Smith, Genta, Giannetti, Fonzi and Costabile, 1996). Family factors have been investigated by Genta and Berdondini, using the family system test (FAST); emotion recognition and other social competence skills of bullies and victims have been studied by Fonzi, Ciucci, Berti and Brighi (1996). In other studies in progress, the role of moral disengagement (Fonzi, Menesini), of other family system variables (Fonzi, Genta, Giannetti), of sociometric and friendship status (Fonzi, Tomada) as well as some other personality and cognitive variables (Ciucci, Smorti and Fonzi, 1997) have been studied in a large school sample in two urban areas in Tuscany.

The nature of bullying behaviour in Italy

The data we present in this chapter are an average value among those found in five different Italian sub-samples. We averaged the data collected in two cities of northern Italy (Turin and Bologna), one of central Italy (Florence)

Table 9.1 The total Italian sample

	Primary			*Middle*		
	Boys	*Girls*	*Total*	*Boys*	*Girls*	*Total*
Florence	126	120	246	299	239	538
Cosenza	160	138	298	146	151	297
Bologna	86	89	175	—	—	—
Turin	204	175	379	464	443	907
Naples	442	479	921	523	407	930

and two of southern Italy (Cosenza and Naples). In Table 9.1 we present the sub-sample sizes in the five cities. In Turin, data were collected by a team of researchers supervised by Silvia Bonino. Other members were S. Ciarano, D. De Prosperis, T. Begotti and I. Vierin; the sample consisted of 379 primary school children and 907 middle school children. In Bologna, the team was led by Maria Luisa Genta, with Lucia Berdondini and Antonella Brighi; the sample consisted of 175 primary school children from one school located in a high-risk city neighbourhood. Although the number of this sub-sample is low in comparison with other cities, we decided to include this group of children, since their responses were not significantly different from those of the other sub-samples. In Florence the team was led by Ada Fonzi, with Maria Luisa Genta, Ersilia Menesini, Andrea Smorti, Enrichetta Giannetti and Enrica Ciucci; the sample consisted of 246 primary school children and 538 middle school children. In Cosenza data were collected by a team of researchers supervised by Angela Costabile, with Annalisa Palermiti, Flaviana Tenuta and Crescibene Teresa; the sample consisted of 298 primary school children and 297 middle school children. In Naples a team of researchers was coordinated by Dario Bacchini, with Paolo Valerio, Mario Bolzan, Annalisa Amodeo, Annalisa Ciardi, Roberto Vitelli and Luca Occhinegro; the sample comprised 921 primary school children and 930 middle school children. Excepting the Bologna sample, sub-samples were balanced in relation to different town districts (central area and suburbs) and to social and economic background (high-income and low-income families).

The average results from these five cities, presented in Table 9.2, confirm that bullying in Italy is very extensive in schools. Some 41.6 per cent of primary school pupils reported being bullied 'sometimes or more frequently in the last two or three months' and this value includes 17.5 per cent who were bullied once a week or more frequently. For middle schools, these figures were still very high, with 26.4 per cent reporting being bullied 'sometimes or more' and 9.5 per cent reporting 'once a week or more frequently'. Analyses by school levels and by year group confirmed that there was a significant decrease in reports of being bullied between the two schools and generally from 8 to 14 years. When children were asked to estimate the numbers of pupils involved as victims, 61.3 per cent of primary school and

Table 9.2 Percentages of boys and girls who reported being bullied, and bullying others, in the last term in primary and middle schools: average values in the five Italian sub-samples

	Primary			*Middle*		
	boys	*girls*	*total*	*boys*	*girls*	*total*
Being bullied:						
• Sometimes or more	42.9	40.2	41.6	25	27.8	26.4
• Once a week or more	20.1	14.7	17.5	10.2	8.7	9.5
Bullying others:						
• Sometimes or more	32.8	22.8	28.0	23.4	16.4	20.0
• Once a week or more	14.8	6.4	10.8	10.6	5.3	8.1

53.5 per cent of middle school pupils indicated three or more children being bullied in their class, with 30 per cent reporting six or more students being bullied in their class.

In the Naples sample, where the number of bullies and victims was estimated by both pupils and class teachers, a high incidence of agreement was found between the two judges. In Italy, bullying behaviour appears to manifest at high and substantial levels, both for those who considered themselves as victims and for adults and children not directly involved in the problem.

So far as reports of taking part in bullying others was concerned (Table 9.2), this was admitted by 28 per cent of primary school children 'sometimes or more frequently in the last two or three months', including 10.8 per cent of those who bullied others 'once a week or more frequently'. For middle schools, these figures were 20 per cent and 8.1 per cent respectively. These data on the extent of bullying in Italy seem to be fairly consistent across the country, since the data collected in three different cities confirm the initial figures found in the Florence and Cosenza samples.

Cross-cultural comparisons

If we compare our data on the amount of bullying with that from England (mainly Sheffield; see Whitney and Smith, 1993), the total percentages in our sample are about twice as high. For example, being bullied 'once a week or more' is almost twice as high in Italian primary schools as compared to English ones (17.5 per cent vs. 10 per cent) and even more so in Italian middle schools if we compared the English ones (9.5 per cent vs. 4 per cent). Bullying others 'once a week or more' is more than twice as high in Italian primary schools as in English ones (10.8 per cent vs. 4 per cent) and far higher in Italian middle schools (8.1 per cent in Italy vs. 1 per cent in England).

The high incidence of bullying in Italy, as compared to other European countries, seems to be a hard fact, only partly explained by cultural differences between Italy and other western countries. Our opinion is that, besides some

Table 9.3 Percentages of types of bullying behaviour experienced in primary and middle schools: average values for the five Italian sub-samples

	Primary			*Middle*		
	boys	*girls*	*total*	*boys*	*girls*	*total*
Called nasty names about colour and race	8.0	5.4	6.9	3.4	3.3	3.4
Called nasty names in other ways	49.7	52.8	51.0	44.9	45.3	45.0
Physically hurt	52.2	30.8	42.0	27.7	13.4	20.7
Threatened	22.0	14.6	19.2	17.7	8.4	13.0
No one would talk to me	16.4	18.0	17.2	6.8	6.2	6.4
Rumours spread about me	24.3	31.4	27.8	23.3	26.3	24.6
Belongings taken away from me	25.0	23.7	24.4	11.5	7.3	9.3

methodological differences between our report and that of other European countries, in our culture, some types of bullying seem to be more tolerated than in other western cultures. The same conclusion was made by Schneider and Fonzi (1996), comparing conflict display among children who are reciprocal friends in Canada and in Italy. Moreover, some forms of humour are well accepted in our culture; in particular, laughing at someone else or making fun of others is a frequent way of behaving among peers both in young and older age groups.

Types of bullying

The above interpretation would lead to the hypothesis that the most frequent form of reported bullying should be verbal. As presented in Table 9.3, for those who were bullied at least 'some time in the last term', most of the bullying took the form of general name-calling (51 per cent for primary school children and 45 per cent for middle school pupils). Being physically hurt and the victim of rumours were the next most frequent forms of bullying in both primary and middle schools. In middle schools there was a change, since being physically hurt decreases significantly from primary to middle schools (from 42 per cent to 20.7 per cent) and being the victim of rumours remains fairly stable (from 27.8 per cent to 24.6 per cent). Other common forms of bullying experienced are 'being threatened', 'having belongings taken away from me' and 'no one would talk to me'. The last two showed a consistent decrease from primary to middle school. Only 'called me nasty names about colour and race' is consistently low in primary (6.9 per cent) and in middle schools (3.4 per cent), and this probably reflected the low proportion of children from different cultures or race in the Italian schools.

Boys were more likely to be physically hit than girls. Girls were more likely to have rumours spread about themselves in primary school but in middle schools this difference disappears. Besides these data on the frequency of bullying behaviour, another study investigated children's perception of the degree of seriousness of different patterns of bullying (Menesini and Fonzi, 1997). A sample of 115 middle school children aged 11 to 13 rated the seriousness of the eight types of bullying presented in the anonymous questionnaire along a scale from 1 (not important) to 5 (very serious). Peer nominations of bullies and victims in the class were also collected. Results indicated that the least serious type of bullying is 'being called nasty names for reasons different from race', whereas 'being hit' and 'being threatened' are the most serious. Differences according to gender and bully/victim status are also present. Although, in our country, the figures for bullying behaviour seem to be consistently high across ages and different parts of the country, more than 50 per cent of it takes the form of verbal bullying, evaluated, by children themselves, as the least severe type of peer harassment.

Where bullying occurs

Table 9.4 shows results of questions about where bullying, reported sometimes or more, took place. For both primary and middle school children, the most frequent place was the classroom (57.2 per cent and 51.9 per cent respectively). For primary school pupils a large proportion of bullying was also reported to have been carried out in the playground (41.3 per cent), but the possibility of being bullied in the playground decreased consistently in middle schools (12.3 per cent). Other relevant places were corridors (around 19 per cent in both school sectors), and the toilets were often mentioned in an open-ended question.

Whether pupils tell

Pupils were also asked if they had either told a teacher at school or anyone at home about being bullied (cf. Table 9.5). For both primary and middle school pupils, those being bullied at least 'sometimes in the last term' were significantly more likely to tell someone at home than to tell their teachers at school (65.4 per cent vs. 51 per cent in primary school and 50.9 per cent

Table 9.4 Percentages for where in school the pupils were bullied in primary and middle schools: average values for the five Italian sub-samples

	Primary			*Middle*		
	boys	*girls*	*total*	*boys*	*girls*	*total*
Corridors	21.2	18.6	19.9	23.5	16.5	19.6
Playground	44.1	38.5	41.3	13.5	11.2	12.3
Classroom	52.3	62.5	57.2	49.9	53.9	51.9
Other	26.6	20.4	23.7	24.6	15.7	20.2

Table 9.5 Percentages for telling teachers or anyone at home about having been bullied: average values for the five Italian sub-samples

	Primary			*Middle*		
	boys	*girls*	*total*	*boys*	*girls*	*total*
Teachers	53.0	48.8	51.0	37.8	33.9	35.5
Family	62.4	68.8	65.4	46.1	55.8	50.9

vs. 35.5 per cent in middle school). In addition, primary school children were more likely than middle school pupils to tell either their teachers or someone at home that they had been bullied. Middle school girls were more likely than boys to tell someone at home about being bullied. Generally, around half of the victims do not report their experiences to someone at school or at home and, with age, there is a decrease in confidence that adults will help to tackle the problem.

Regional variations

In all of the sub-samples significant variations among different schools were found, as well as a significant effect of social and economic deprivation (usually we found more bullying, especially reports of having bullied others, in more deprived areas), although it is not easy to disentangle the role of school ethos and anti-bullying policies from those of social and economic factors. One of the most relevant differences across the country was that the rate of bullying problems was the lowest in Turin (being bullied sometimes or more is 34.8 per cent in primary schools and 17.9 per cent in middle schools), whereas it is the highest in Naples (being bullied sometimes or more is 47.6 per cent in primary schools and 30.6 per cent in middle schools). This seems to be related to the different distribution of resources in our country, especially family life conditions and educational levels. Naples has a very high level of school evasion and of young persons' unemployment, as compared with other cities in northern Italy. In addition, criminal organisations are particular factors in many city neighbourhoods, supporting a culture of bullying and individualism.

Attitudes to bullying

As regards attitudes to bullying, children's perception of bullies, victims and bystanders has been investigated by members of the Florence and Cosenza departments, together with a cross-national comparison between Italy and England (Menesini, Eslea, Smith, Genta, Giannetti, Fonzi and Costabile, 1996). The reference sample here is only the two sub-samples from Florence (784 primary and middle school boys and girls) and Cosenza (595 primary and middle school boys and girls).

Attitudes to bullying were measured in two specific areas:

1 How are teachers, and other children, perceived as reacting to bullying episodes?
2 What are children's attitudes towards bullying in terms of feelings, and inclination to act themselves in various ways?

For this purpose five attitude items from the same anonymous questionnaire (see above) were analysed. Two questions on who tries to stop bullying were considered: (1, 2) 'How often do the teachers [other children] try to stop it when a child is bullied at school?' As regards thoughts, feelings and inclination to act, children were asked: (3) 'What do you think about children who bully others?'; (4) 'How do you feel when you see a child of your age being bullied at school?'; and (5) 'What do you do when you see a child of your age being bullied at school?'

In relation to teachers' and children's intervention against bullying, children showed more confidence that teachers, rather than other children, would try to stop it. Teachers were generally seen to intervene 'sometimes' and 'almost always', whereas other children were seen to intervene 'almost never' and 'sometimes'. Girls were more confident of teachers' help than boys. Bully-victims are less confident of peer help than non-involved children.

As regards the attitudinal findings towards the issue, the majority of children are opposed to bullying and supportive of victims, although there are differences according to age, gender and bully/victim status of children. Children's attitudes related to age appear complex. In terms of intervention against bullying there is a decrease of reported help from primary to middle school, and these data are in line with a trend towards diminishing pro-victim scores with age found by Rigby and Slee (1991). In terms of perception and feelings, however, middle school children are more opposed to bullies and feel more than primary school children that bullying is an unpleasant experience.

Gender appears an important variable which can mediate children's attitudes towards bullying. Girls are usually more sympathetic than boys towards victims, they are more opposed to bullies and feel that the experience of bullying is unpleasant; this is in line with previous studies reporting that girls usually have a more pro-social attitude than boys (Hoffman, 1977). Only in relation to children's intervention did girls display similar attitudes in comparison with boys, and they did not say they would intervene on behalf of the victims more often than boys. In sum, girls reported being more affected emotionally, and being more upset by bullying, but when it comes to intervening the sex difference disappears.

In relation to gender and age differences a discrepancy exists between perception of the problem and inclination to act in support of the victims. This may also have a practical implication, since the majority of children are opposed to bullying, but they find it difficult to intervene. A challenge may be to empower these pupils to intervene against bullying.

The differences between bullies and victims are consistent with previous findings. Bullies are less inclined to intervene when they witness a bullying episode; they can understand those who bully others, and do not feel sympathetic towards the victim's suffering. These results confirm other studies on school-aged children and adolescents which stress the importance of beliefs in sustaining and orienting children's social behaviour (Dodge and Frame, 1982; Perry, Perry and Rasmussen, 1986; Slaby and Guerra, 1988). Many bullies see nothing wrong in their bullying behaviour; while they show little awareness of the victims' feelings, they assert that the victims in one way or another often deserve being bullied (see also Smith, Bowers, Binney and Cowie, 1993).

Initiatives and interventions

In May 1995 a national conference was organised by the Inter-University Centre for the study of pro-social and antisocial behaviour development (Psychology Departments of Rome, Florence, Milan and Naples) and supported by the Ministry of Education and the Ministry for Social Affairs. The topic of the conference was 'Il disagio giovanile: programmi di ricerca e di intervento' (Psycho-social difficulties in adolescence: research and intervention projects). At this conference Dan Olweus from Bergen University (Norway) was invited to speak about the research on bullying in Norway; other Italian scholars took part, presenting data on the Italian situation. The papers from the conference were published in *Età Evolutiva* (Fonzi, 1996).

Although awareness of teachers and families about the issue has been growing in the last two or three years, we have not yet had any national initiatives to tackle bullying in schools such as those carried out in some other European countries. Most Italian interventions in schools have been carried out as a result of local requests from a single school or from educational departments of city administrations. The majority have been carried out in Tuscany, while in other areas of the country some intervention projects have been implemented more recently. Some interventions have been evaluated and published (Menesini, Argentieri, Baroni, Lazzari and Spadoni, 1996; Menesini and Smorti, 1997), while some other experiences are still in progress.

In other European countries, anti-bullying projects have been characterised by a systemic approach to tackling the problem at several levels: from the school as a system, through the class, up to individuals who might have been involved as a bully or a victim; but in Italy the majority of our interventions have been directed to the class by means of curricular interventions.

Curricular interventions to develop children's awareness about bullying

One of the first interventions carried out in Italy was conducted by Menesini, Argentieri, Baroni, Lazzari and Spadoni (1996) and by Berdondini. It involved four classes in a primary school near Florence and six classes, plus three classes as a control group, in another city in Tuscany (Lucca). The same intervention has been replicated in 1995–1996 in some schools in southern Italy (Cosenza). The results of this second study are presently under analysis.

As regards the intervention which took place in Tuscany, it was a short-term intervention, lasting three months, from February to May 1995. Before and after the intervention the rate of the phenomenon was assessed by the anonymous questionnaire (Olweus, 1993; Whitney and Smith, 1993; Genta, Menesini, Fonzi and Costabile, 1996) and a peer nomination questionnaire (Fonzi, Ciucci, Berti and Brighi, 1996).

The intervention consisted of three integrated activities:

1 A story 'The bully' from *The Daydreamer* by I. McEwan was presented as a literary stimulus and children were invited to discuss problems, behaviours and feelings generated by it.
2 Children were also invited to tell and write about their own experiences of the issue.
3 Children took part in a cycle of role-playing activities which closely followed those presented in Sharp and Smith (1994). Drama activities offered children the opportunity to assume different perspectives on the problems and to explore possible consequences for bullies and victims.

A brochure explaining the project was provided for the teachers, and those participating in the intervention attended two or three initial training meetings. During the implementation phase, teachers were supervised by one of the two researchers responsible for the project. The intervention took place for approximately one or two hours every week for three months. In the middle school sample, activities were conducted by the teachers of Italian.

The questionnaire results indicate children's growing awareness of what adults can do about bullying. Being bullied generally decreased, whereas bullying others showed a tendency to increase. From peer nominations we found a tendency for bullies to improve their own position in the class. The results appear complex, since the decrease in being bullied signals a decrease of bullying activities, although bullies and bystanders seem to be more aware of their behaviour and refer to it more frequently than before. Generally, such curricular and short-term interventions on bullying seem to be more effective in raising awareness about the problem and in changing children's and adults' attitudes, but less effective in changing individual patterns of behaviour.

In the same middle school where literature stimuli and role-playing activities were implemented, the intervention also took place the following year based on video and movie stimuli. A video was produced, presenting a collection of film extracts and several activities to elaborate the issue of bullying from multiple perspectives (Menesini and Smorti, 1997). The general aims of this intervention were:

- raising awareness about bullying behaviour and its possible consequences for children as well as for the school community;
- developing a rule system against bullying and in favour of a more democratic life in the school.

The video consisted of three parts: part one focused on admiring or opposing attitudes towards bullies; part two showed possible relations between play-fighting and real fighting; part three offered stimuli for discussing the role of adult or peer bystanders.

The intervention took place from February to May (three months) and was preceded and followed by a survey on the problem using the anonymous questionnaire and the peer nomination measure (Fonzi, Ciucci, Berti and Brighi, 1996; Genta, Menesini, Fonzi and Costabile, 1996).

The results were encouraging and showed that the video stimuli can be a very powerful means to tackle the problem with children, allowing them to discuss in depth motivations and possible consequences of bullying and to develop a class rule system against it. In terms of how the intervention affected children's behaviour, the rates of being bullied and bullying others generally decreased in the four experimental classes in comparison with the control group (two classes). The decrease was around 8 per cent for being bullied and 5 per cent for bullying others, and it was consistent across the two measures (anonymous self-report, and peer nominations).

Developing a positive school climate against bullying

In a middle school in a small town near Florence (Pontassieve), teachers and children have been working on bullying for three years. This project was supervised by Enrica Ciucci and Andrea Smorti (see Menesini and Smorti, 1997). During the first year, teachers were trained to deal with the problem of psycho-social risk factors in schools, and data were collected on bully/victim relationships by anonymous questionnaires (Olweus, 1993; Genta, Menesini, Fonzi and Costabile, 1996; Whitney and Smith, 1993). In the second year a counselling service for teachers was provided in order to tackle problems and difficult children in schools. Teachers' and parents' meetings on bullying among schoolchildren were also organised.

In the third year an intervention was implemented at two different levels. At the school level, teachers, children, parents and other school members worked on developing a school policy against bullying and aimed to build up a positive school climate; on the class level, a group of teachers were trained on two types of curricular interventions: role-playing activities to raise awareness of the issue, and quality circles for problem-solving bullying issues.

The results showed that a short-term intervention such as this can affect social relationships among children, as well as bullying behaviour. In comparison to the control group, there was a significant decrease in reported bullying in the experimental group (relative decrease = 5.6 per cent) and a relevant increase in pro-social behaviours, feelings of belonging and number of friends. In the general evaluation of the intervention, the researchers also point out some problems mainly related to attitudes towards bullies, who received more understanding and tolerance among peers, whereas among adults they received less attention and opportunity for communication. Teachers and parents seemed to be more inclined to deal with the problems of victimised children than with the problems of bullies.

Another intervention project has been carried out by Lucia Berdondini in a primary school near Florence. The aim of this study was to analyse the role of emotional communication in bully/victim problems before and after an intervention. In particular, differences between bullies, victims and controls in displaying verbal and non-verbal emotions were measured before and after a year of anti-bullying intervention. The study started in October 1995 and has a three-year longitudinal design. The sample is composed of nine elementary school classes, six of which are experimental and three represent the control group. In the experimental group anti-bullying activities have been implemented by teachers during curricular and playtime activities. Some class activities have been videotaped and participants were interviewed according to a procedure proposed by Kagan and Kagan (1991): the 'interpersonal process recall' (IPR). The interviews have been videotaped as well. During the intervention period the control classes have been working with the normal school routine. Before and after intervention a peer nomination questionnaire has been used. Data have been collected for two years and results are now under analysis.

Summary

In conclusion, the Italian state of knowledge on bullying and on the effects of possible interventions is still at an early stage in comparison with some other western countries, but a group of researchers is very concerned and committed about it. As other European interventions have shown (Olweus, 1993; Smith and Sharp, 1994), we are aware that curricular and class interventions may only have a short-term effect. To have long-term effects a policy against bullying should be active in the school. Therefore our next steps for the future are:

- moving towards a more systemic and global approach as regards interventions on the problem;
- trying to obtain national funds for anti-bullying research in order to investigate psychological and social correlates of the phenomenon and to evaluate possible effects of interventions.

References

Censis (1995) *Rapporto sulla popolazione italiana*. Milano: F. Angeli.

Ciucci, E., Smorti, A. and Fonzi, A. (1997) Il rapporto bullo-vittima in soggetti di scuola media: Differenze di contesti ecologici. *Ricerche di Psicologia*, 2, 33–51.

Dodge, K. A. and Frame, C. L. (1982) Social cognitive biases and deficits in aggressive boys. *Child Development*, 53, 629–635.

Fonzi, A. (1995) Persecutori e vittime fra i banchi di scuola. *Psicologia Contemporanea*, 129, 4–11.

Fonzi, A. (ed.) (1996) Il disagio giovanile. Programmi di ricerca e di intervento. *Età Evolutiva*, 53, 70–115.

Fonzi, A. (ed.) (1997) *Il bullismo in Italia*. Firenze: Giunti.

Fonzi, A., Ciucci, E., Berti, C. and Brighi, A. (1996) Riconoscimento delle emozioni, stili educativi familiari e posizioni nel gruppo in bambini che fanno e subiscono prepotenze a scuola. *Età Evolutiva*, 53, 81–89.

Genta, M. L., Menesini, E., Fonzi, A., Costabile, A. and Smith, P. K. (1996) Bullies and victims in schools in central and southern Italy. *European Journal of Psychology of Education*, 11, 97–110.

Genta, M. L., Menesini, E., Fonzi, A. and Costabile, A. (1996) Le prepotenze tra bambini a scuola. Risultati di una ricerca condotta in due città italiane. *Età Evolutiva*, 53, 73–80.

Hoffman, M. L. (1997) Sex differences in empathy and related behaviors. *Psychological Bulletin*, 84, 712–722.

Kagan, N. and Kagan, H. (1991) IPR – A research training model. In P.N. Dowrick *et al.* (eds) *Practical guide to using video in the behavioural sciences*. Toronto, Ont.: J. Wiley.

Menesini, E., Argentieri, M., Baroni, L., Lazzari, R. and Spadoni, E. (1996) Le prepotenze tra ragazzi a scuola. Un'esperienza di ricerca intervento condotta con alunni di scuola media. *Scuola e Didattica*, 4, 29–34.

Menesini, E., Eslea, M., Smith, P. K., Genta, M. L., Giannetti, E., Fonzi, A. and Costabile, A. (1996) A cross-national comparison of children's attitudes towards bully/victim problems in school. *Aggressive Behaviour*, 23, 245–257.

Menesini, E. and Fonzi, A. (1997) Valutazione della gravità delle prepotenze subite in un campione di ragazzi della scuola media. *Psicologia Clinica dello Sviluppo*, 1, 117–133.

Menesini, E. and Smorti A. (1997). Strategie di intervento scolastico contra il fenomeno delle prepotenze. In A. Fonzi (ed.) *Il bullismo in Italia* (pp. 183–208). Firenze: Giunti.

Olweus, D. (1993) *Bullying at school. What we know and what we can do*. Oxford: Blackwell. (Trans. *Il bullismo a scuola*. Firenze: Giunti, 1996.)

Perry, D. G., Perry, L. C. and Rasmussen, P. (1986) Cognitive social-learning mediators of aggression. *Child Development*, 57, 700–711.

Rigby, K. and Slee, P. T. (1991) Bullying among Australian school children: reported behavior and attitudes towards victims. *Journal of Social Psychology*, 131, 615–627.

Schneider, B. and Fonzi, A. (1996) La stabilità dell'amicizia: Uno studio crossculturale Italia–Canada. *Età Evolutiva*, 54, 73–79.

Sharp, S. and Smith, P. K. (eds) (1994) *Tackling bullying in your school: A practical handbook for teachers*. London: Routledge. (Trans. *Bulli e prepotenti in classe*. Trento: Centro Studi Erikson, 1995.)

Slaby, R.G. and Guerra, N. (1988) Cognitive mediators of aggression in adolescent offenders: Assessment. *Developmental Psychology*, 24, 580–588.

Smith, P. K. (1991) The silent nightmare: Bullying and victimisation in school peer groups. *The Psychologist*, 4, 243–248.

Smith, P. K., Bowers, L., Binney, V. and Cowie, H. (1993) Relationships of children involved in bully/victim problems at school. In S. Duck (ed.) *Understanding relationship processes, Vol. 2: Learning about relationships*. Newbury Park, CA: Sage, pp. 184–212.

Smith, P. K. and Sharp, S. (eds) (1994) *School bullying: Insights and perspectives*. London: Routledge.

Whitney, I. and Smith, P. K. (1993) A survey of the nature and the extent of bullying in junior/middle and secondary schools. *Educational Research*, 35, 3–25.

10 Spain

Rosario Ortega
and Joaquin A. Mora-Merchan

Overview

We report on the bullying problem in Spain, a southern European country which is currently changing its education system. A brief description of the country and its sociocultural indicators is followed by a presentation of the study we carried out in five secondary schools from the state system in Andalucia, the southernmost region of the country. Using an adapted version of the Olweus Questionnaire (1989), which we translated into Spanish, we studied 859 pupils between the ages of 11 and 16. The study focuses on some questions taken from the questionnaire, which we analysed in order to highlight the following aspects of the problem: the extent of bullying in schools and the differences in the incidents with respect to gender and age; the forms which the bullying takes and the areas of highest risk in the schools; identification of the bullies and their way of behaving; a profile of the schoolchildren who are involved in these situations of interpersonal bullying, and the pupils' behaviour and attitudes towards these problems.

The results show that approximately 18 per cent of schoolchildren are frequently involved in bullying problems; this is a somewhat higher level of incidence than that given in the Norwegian and English studies. In terms of gender, we found that boys were more frequently involved than girls, and also that girls used more indirect forms of bullying than boys. The problem substantially decreases with age, particularly after 15 years. Insults, rumours, stealing, threats, physical violence and social isolation are, in that order, the most frequent forms of bullying. The classroom itself, the playground, and to a lesser extent the corridors, are the places in which bullying mainly occurs. With respect to behaviour and attitudes towards the problem, the study reveals that the victims are the most anti-bullying and the least capable of bullying other pupils. The pure bullies consider this type of behaviour to be normal and see themselves as potential bullies. The bully/victims nevertheless reveal a somewhat two-sided moral attitude in view of their dual participation in the problem.

Following this study, the authors planned a more extensive research and intervention project, which is currently under way in 23 schools in Andalucia.

Spain, a Mediterranean country in southern Europe

Spain, alongside Portugal, occupies the Iberian Peninsula, situated in the far south of western Europe. There are 39 million people in Spain, occupying just over half a million square kilometres, which means that there is a low population density: 77 inhabitants per square kilometre. The distribution of population, economic activity and wealth is not homogeneous between the seventeen politically autonomous communities which constitute the state of Spain. The most densely populated communities are also those with the highest economic activity, situated in the north and east of the peninsula; the communities with the lowest population density, in the centre, the west and the south, are also the poorest, with the exception of Madrid, which, being the capital of Spain, has its own singular characteristics.

Although the Spanish, with their typical sense of humour, will say that 'the country is going very badly but people live very well here', this does not mean that the Spanish settle for little, but rather that life in Spain is getting better and better. One example of this is that life expectancy for the Spanish is one of the highest in the developed world: 77 years is the average, with a noticeable difference in women, for whom life expectancy is over 80 years of age. A substantial general decrease in the death rate, and especially in infant mortality which now stands at less than eight deaths per 1000 births, is a reflection of the improved health conditions in Spain; today, Spain is one of the few countries in the world in which everyone has the right to public health care, which is generally indicative of a high quality of life.

As well as being healthier, the country is becoming more liberal, tolerant and varied, both ideologically and culturally speaking. The number of children born to unmarried mothers has multiplied by five and at the same time, people, especially women, are marrying for the first time later, and similarly having their first child later.

The average number of children per woman has decreased dramatically and is now 1.3, possibly one of the lowest in the world. The growing deficit of young people is already apparent in the population pyramid, in which we can also see a substantial increase in the number of people over age 65, many of whom are Europeans who are taking advantage of the benefits of living in Spain – it is still a cheap place in which to live, with efficient services and good weather.

Women are still socially discriminated against in comparison to men, and this is forcing many of them to reject the family in order to develop personally, socially and professionally. Therefore, while Spain is actually ninth in the world according to UNO's (1995) Human Development Indicator, it is actually 26th in terms of women's participation in work, and in an even worse position, 34th, on the indicator which rates inequality between men and women. This trend is changing, however, as today middle-aged women have an average level of education and young female students are achieving better results at university than men.

Women's undeclared work is possibly one of the reasons why Spain occupies 29th place worldwide in relation to Gross National Product per person, while in relation to total Gross Domestic Product we are in eighth place. When the so-called hidden economy in which many women are involved, without contract and without social security, is incorporated into the real economy, these indicators will change. On the other hand, perhaps this hidden economy, along with an extensive system of social protection, is what actually enables our society, with its relatively low levels of economic activity, to support a high rate of unemployment without too much social conflict.

In summary, Spain is one of the first ten countries in the majority of economic and social development indicators; it is also eighth in the world Index of Industrial Production and the fifth importer, the tenth producer of toxic and dangerous wastes and the tenth producer of greenhouse effect gases, but also the ninth contributor to the United Nations, the ninth country of the OECD (Organization for Economic Cooperation and Development) according to number of researchers, and tenth in terms of technological export earnings.

The school education system in Spain

The school education system in Spain is currently undergoing a major change. In 1990 the Spanish Parliament passed the LOGSE, the Ley Organica General del Sistema Educativo (General Constitutional Law of the Education System), which changed the existing structure and organisation of schools. This new law followed a wide social discussion on the nature and objectives of education in general and of each educational stage in particular.

The following stages of education have been established as a result of this law: preschool education which is voluntary for 0- to 6-year-olds; primary education which is compulsory for all children between 6 and 12 years of age; compulsory secondary education for 12- to 16-year-olds; and post-compulsory secondary education, which is again voluntary for children over age 16. This new structure has been accompanied by changes in curricula, all of which imply a different educational philosophy from the one existing before.

However, we still cannot say that this reform is anything other than an ongoing project, as it has not been totally introduced at all levels. Furthermore, the process is being carried out in a slightly unusual way in view of the fact that the country is divided into different autonomies, all of which have different degrees of self-government with regard to education policy.

The schools in the Andalucian study

The information presented here was gathered in 1991 and 1992 from a study in five schools within the state system (which is the largest in Spain), in the province of Seville, Andalucia, where the new education system had still not been introduced. Two of the schools were EGB, Educación General Basica

(Basic General Education). This was the only compulsory stage under the previous education system and was aimed at 6- to 14-year-olds. Within EGB there were two clearly different phases: in the first, which grouped together the first five grades (6 to 11 years), the pupils had only one teacher, who taught them everything on the curriculum (apart from physical education and religion or ethics). In the second phase, the curriculum was taught by teachers who were specialised in the various subjects, although with the same preliminary university training as the teachers in the first stage of EGB.

The aims of EGB corresponded to two main criteria. Firstly, education for everyone in all possible subjects (similar to what would happen in a comprehensive school). Secondly, to provide pupils with the necessary qualifications to enable them to enter post-compulsory secondary education (which in the later stages is similar to grammar school). The education policy in EGB schools was flexible and took emotional and social aspects into consideration, but was not very demanding in terms of academic results.

The remaining three schools were secondary education, which under the old system was not compulsory. There are two different types of secondary school: Formación Profesional (Technical School) and Bachillerato (Baccalaureate).

The main aim of the technical schools (which were represented in our report by only one centre) was to immediately incorporate students into the professional world; these courses lasted for five years, the first two of which included general curriculum subjects, while the remaining years were more career orientated. Baccalaureate courses were purely academic and clearly designed for students who would go on to study at university.

In both types of school, the teachers had specialist university training in their particular subject; however, this paid little attention to psycho-educational issues. These characteristics meant that education policy was largely centred on conceptual matters.

Bullying in our schools

A Portuguese teacher (Vieira) and two Spanish secondary school teachers (Fernandez and Quevedo) were responsible for carrying out the first study on bullying in the Iberian Peninsula (Vieira, Fernandez and Quevedo, 1989). The authors designed a questionnaire, which they gave to 1200 EGB and secondary school pupils from ten state and private schools in Madrid.

The results which they obtained showed that approximately 17 per cent of schoolchildren admitted to often being a bully, while 14 per cent admitted to often being a victim of bullying. The most frequent forms of bullying were verbal followed by physical attacks, then stealing and damage to personal belongings. There was a clear difference between boys and girls, as much in the extent to which they were involved as in the forms which they used: more physical bullying by boys and more social isolation by girls. In this study we did not find any differences between state and private schools.

This study was followed by one carried out by Cerezo and Esteban (1992). The research technique used was nomination of the people involved. This methodology enabled them to define what they called bully/victim types and to characterise the personality of each of the individuals involved according to their sociometric status.

Subsequently, our team, now linked to the one led by Peter K. Smith in England, completed a project co-financed by the Ministry of Science and Education (Spain) and the British Council; this was to assess the extent of bullying in five schools in Seville, Andalucia using our own adapted version of the Olweus Questionnaire. Various works have been published on this project (Ortega, 1992, 1994, 1995; Fernandez and Ortega, 1995; Mora-Merchan and Ortega, 1995; Ortega and Mora-Merchan, 1995, 1996).

The social attention that the mass media have given to bullying during the last five years has undergone a change, from indifference to an increasingly noticeable presence through the most important national newspapers and television channels. The first news items we collected were almost all in reference to dramatic cases of bullying among peers abroad, especially in Great Britain and the USA.

Throughout the years, the news has begun to focus on events taking place in our country and specific terms have come into use, such as bully, victim, social climate, etc. The range of aspects dealt with by the news has become progressively wider, and articles written by important figures have started to appear; at the same time, we are beginning to come across cases of group anti-bullying campaigns, and items referring to care schemes for children who are abused by their colleagues.

The education authorities have clearly not paid enough attention to the problem. It is only recently that direct intervention schemes and support programmes have been planned for the teams of teachers who are setting up anti-bullying projects. This has not been the case in research and university circles in which symposia on the topic of care for abused children have been organised and included in conferences on children's rights. The National Research and Development Plan itself, the largest supporting body of state research, has financed a project for our group to carry out large-scale research on the problem of bullying in our schools.

The Seville study on bullying

When we made the decision to study bullying and victimisation among schoolchildren, subsequent to the work that Peter K. Smith was carrying out at that time in England, the first problem we encountered was that of defining bullying within our cultural environment, as the concept just did not exist within our schools. This semantic failing merely proved the lack of social understanding towards the problem that we were studying. The situation was further complicated by adults' ignorance of or indifference to the problem. This meant that we had to explain the meaning and consequences of this type of behaviour beyond what the Olweus Questionnaire had done when outlining its characteristics: the behaviour of those involved, attitudes, persistence of the problem, effects on both victims and bullies, the lack of punishment for bullying, etc.

We finally defined the term 'bullying' as continuous abusive behaviour, harassment, or maltreatment, either physical or psychological, carried out by one student/students against another/others. However, we wanted to differentiate between what we considered to be real bullying – which makes the victim feel totally defenceless when faced by his or her peers without any means of avoiding the highly disturbing encounters – and simple interplay, mainly verbal, which does not produce the same level of anxiety and helplessness in the pupils but can even be seen as mere games or jokes between school mates. The issue remains open with regard to the forms of interplay which are culturally acceptable, while research provides us with information to further our understanding and characterisation of the problem we are studying.

The following information is from research which we conducted in Seville and its province, with the aim of determining the extent of bullying behaviour, and its main characteristics, in five schools. We decided to use data supplied by the pupils themselves, from which we hoped to obtain important information on aspects related to bullying/victimisation experiences from the point of view of those directly involved – the schoolchildren. With this idea in mind, we chose to use the Olweus Questionnaire (1989), in view of its worldwide circulation, and we translated it into Spanish under the supervision of Olweus himself. After some initial, more descriptive analyses (Mora-Merchan and Ortega, 1995; Ortega, 1992, 1994, 1995; Ortega and Mora-Merchan, 1995), we present a more in-depth and discriminatory analysis.

The sample

The sample chosen for this analysis was taken from five state schools in Seville and its province: three secondary education and two basic general education schools (the latter, as previously mentioned, are currently undergoing changes with the introduction of the new education system). Two of the secondary schools were Baccalaureate while the third was a technical school.

The participating schools were chosen because of their interest in the problem and their own offer to take part in this research. The schools were situated in areas of different socioeconomic status, from socioculturally deprived to middle and upper class. This fact was taken into consideration when analysing the differences between the various pupils' bullying experiences.

There were 859 pupils in total; their age range corresponds to what would be, at that time, as in the majority of European countries, compulsory secondary education (age 12 to 16). The age distribution was: 11-year-olds –

92; 12-year-olds – 96; 13-year-olds – 96; 14-year-olds – 350, and 15- to 16-year-olds – 225.

Analysis of the results

A classification of types to describe bullying problems among peers

Using the pupils' own answers to the Olweus Questionnaire, we were able to determine the following types according to the extent to which they were involved in bullying/victimisation problems: victims, bullies, bully/victims, observers and inconsistent types.

In order to make this distinction, we analysed the answers given by the students to the questions which referred to the type with which they identified themselves, within the problem of group bullying and abuse among school peers. These questions were the following:

- How many times have you been picked on this term?
- How many times have you been bullied and/or victimised in the last five days (not including the weekend)?
- How many times have you picked on other pupils in your school this term?
- How many times have you taken part in bullying or victimisation towards other pupils in the last five days (not including the weekend)?

We cross-checked the information obtained from the four questions. We repeated the procedure three times in order to find the consistency of the pupils' experiences, firstly as victims (first two questions), and secondly as bullies (last two questions); thirdly, we cross-checked the information that the previous analyses had given us in order to establish a profile of the types which participate in problems of group bullying and abuse among schoolchildren. These analyses provide us, as Olweus indicates, with data revealing a high level of internal consistency.

We defined as victims (1.6 per cent) those who consistently state that they strongly see themselves as being the object of bullying by their school mates. The bullies (1.4 per cent) reflect the contrary; they are defined as those who see themselves, equally as strongly, as being the cause of abuse towards their colleagues. We further identify a third type which shares the characteristics of the first two. The bully/victims (15.3 per cent) are defined as bullies who nevertheless are marked by their own experiences as victims of similar acts to the ones they perform against other students. The fourth type of student is defined by the distance which they maintain from the problem. They are students who do not seem to be involved in bullying behaviour but who at the same time play the role of observer, and this lends them their own characteristics and behaviour (77.4 per cent). There is a final type of individual who, due to the inconsistency of their answers, is difficult to include in any of the aforementioned types (4.3 per cent). Nevertheless, although the information they provide does not enable us to classify them as one type or another, we do appreciate the fact that they are also on the scene of bullying and victimisation incidents (sometimes even taking part in them).

Gender and age differences

In the schools we analysed, 18.3 per cent of pupils directly participate in bullying and/or victimisation. Nevertheless, gender and age are two important factors to be taken into consideration within this statistic. In terms of gender, girls and boys behave differently (chi-squared $p < 0.0005$). There are two main differences: first, more girls are observers of bullying/victimisation than boys (82.7 per cent vs. 73 per cent); second, more boys are bully/victims than girls (20.3 per cent vs. 9 per cent). The different characteristics of girls and boys are shown in Figure 10.1.

The aforementioned distribution of types is also highly affected by age; as we can see in Figure 10.2, age is a variable which must be taken into consideration when discussing bullying/victimisation problems. The results show the variations in the distribution of types in terms of age; these variations may be summarised as follows:

- The number of bullies remains constant throughout the research period.
- The number of victims, however, clearly tends to disappear among older children, although the number is quite stable among the younger pupils.
- The number of observers increases steadily, reaching a peak of 91.1 per cent among 16-year-olds.
- The bully/victims decrease steadily throughout the age range, from 47.8 per cent to 4.4 per cent.

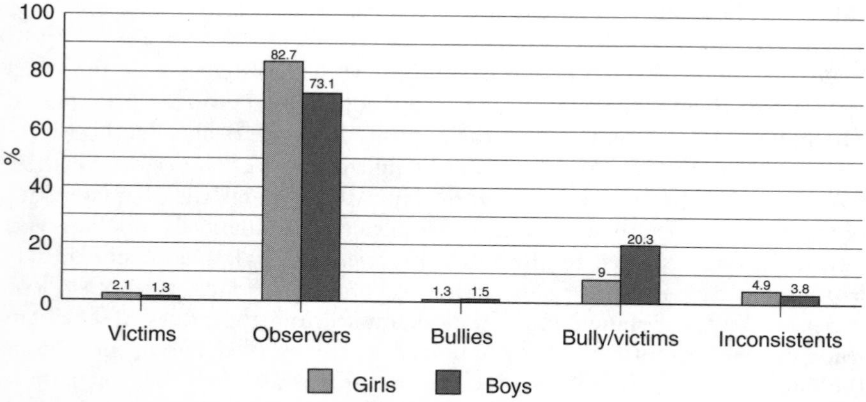

Figure 10.1 Classification of types by gender.

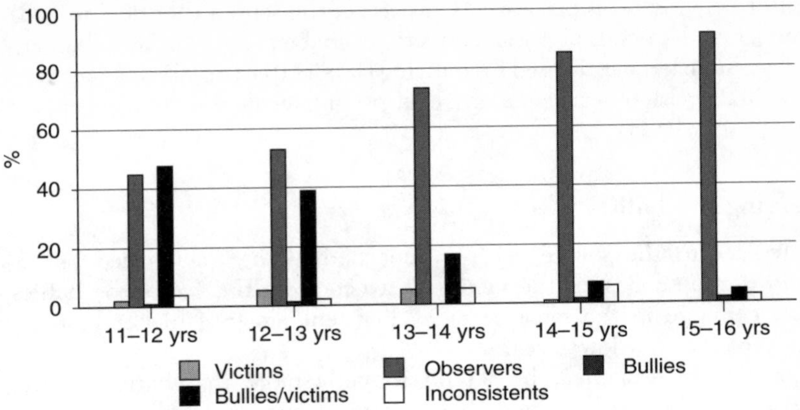

Figure 10.2 Classification of types by age.

- The number of individuals supplying inconsistent answers remains constant throughout the age range.

We also analysed the variations in types in relation to the pupils' socioeconomic status (according to the school they attended). However, the differences that we found were not attributable to the pupils' socioeconomic status but rather to their age.

We similarly analysed the degree of satisfaction the pupils showed with the time that they spent without a teacher (breaks, free time, changeover of classes, etc.). Every group showed a high level of satisfaction (between 80 to 90 per cent of the members of each type). Although the differences were not statistically significant, victims displayed the most dissatisfaction and the least satisfaction.

Forms of bullying and places of highest risk

Another interesting aspect is the forms of bullying used by the pupils. In our sample the most frequent forms were insults (31.1 per cent), rumours (12.2 per cent) and stealing (11.8 per cent), and the least frequent were threats (8.4 per cent), physical attacks (5.7 per cent) and isolation (5.5 per cent). However, and as we have previously found, gender is a determining factor when interpreting these results. Physical attacks and threats are much more usual forms of bullying in boys (chi-squared $p < 0.01$ and $p < 0.005$ respectively), while in girls the most frequent types of bullying are rumours (chi-squared $p < 0.05$) and isolation of the victim ($p < 0.02$) (see Table 10.1).

The Olweus Questionnaire also enabled us to obtain information on the locations where bullying usually takes place. These are in the following order:

the classroom, the playground and the corridors, although a considerable amount of bullying takes place in other parts of the school (not determined). The gender of the pupils also influences this variable. Corridors and the playground are more frequently used for bullying by boys than by girls (chi-squared, both $p < 0.05$); in other places there is no significant difference between genders (Table 10.2).

Identifying the bullies

With respect to the source, 41 per cent of bullying was carried out by pupils in the same class as the victim. If we consider the age of the bullies, 55.4 per cent are in the same year, 9.7 per cent are in a higher year and 5.6 per cent are in a lower year.

As previously explained, boys tend to bully more than girls – taking into consideration bullies and bully/victims – but the bullying is not always carried out by only one person. In fact only 54.1 per cent of bullying occurs in this form, while the rest of the time the bullies tend to act in groups (45.9 per cent).

One final factor that conditions and facilitates bullying and victimisation among peers is the amount of complaints the victims make regarding this behaviour. When we analysed this in those involved, we found that only 32.2 per cent of victims report the fact to their teachers, and 28.9 per cent to their families. This low percentage justifies to a certain extent the high

Table 10.1 Types of bullying reported: frequencies and gender differences

Forms of bullying	*Frequency (per cent)*	*Boys*	*Girls*
Insults	31.1	32.2	29.7
Rumours	12.2	10.2	14.7
Stealing	11.8	12.7	10.6
Threats	8.4	11.0	5.2
Physical attacks	5.7	7.6	3.4
Isolation	5.5	3.8	7.5

Table 10.2 Where bullying was reported to occur and gender differences

Place	*Frequency (per cent)*	*Boys*	*Girls*
Classroom	32.5	33.5	31.4
Playground	30.6	34.2	26.4
Corridors	17.5	20.3	14.0
Others	19.0	21.4	16.0

level of ignorance on the part of parents and teachers about these problems, and the surprise with which they greet the information when it is revealed. Without doubt, this lack of information on the part of parents and teachers makes it difficult to intervene in and break up the bullying/victimisation circles among peers.

Behaviour and attitudes towards the bullying problem

Another of the aspects that we analysed was the behaviour and attitudes that the pupils showed towards bullying/victimisation. We could best understand these attitudes and behaviour if we considered the pupils in terms of their respective types.

The first question we considered was how the pupils reacted, according to their respective type, when they witnessed a bullying problem. The results we discovered were highly significant (chi-squared $p < 0.0002$). As may be seen in Figure 10.3, the pupils who felt themselves to be victims are those who most often say that they would intervene in order to stop bullying and to help the other victim (between 51.9 and 57.1 per cent of victims). By contrast, very few bullies say they would try to do something to intervene (only 9 per cent) whereas many bullies say that bullying by other pupils is not their problem. It is also interesting to note what will without doubt be useful for future intervention in the problem; that is, the high number of pupils who do not directly take action against the problem but feel that they should (43.5 per cent).

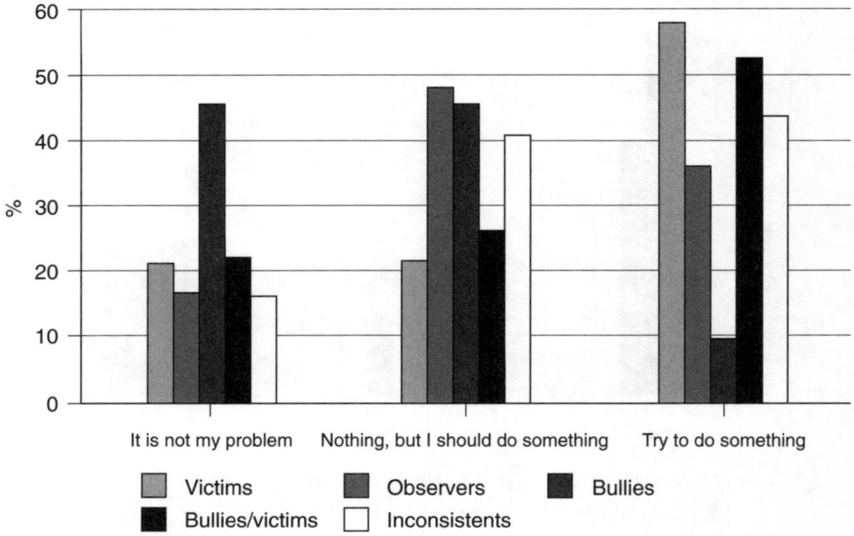

Figure 10.3 What do pupils say they do when they witness bullying?

The second question we analysed in relation to attitude was whether the pupils saw themselves as potential bullies should the occasion arise. Once again, considering the types that we have been using, we found some highly significant and interesting results (chi-squared $p < 0.00001$). This time, we found that the majority of victims rejected this possibility (64.3 per cent) and that only 7 per cent accepted that it would be possible. On the other hand, almost all the bullies (91.7 per cent) accepted the possibility of bullying should the occasion arise. The bully/victims provided a very interesting range of answers, considering their characterisation: 64.6 per cent acknowledged the possibility of becoming a bully should the occasion arise and only 15 per cent were certain that they would not (see Figure 10.4).

Finally, we have considered in our study the pupils' moral judgement towards bullies. We once again found significant differences ($p < 0.0002$) between the various types. The type of pupils who were most anti-bullying were the victims (71.4 per cent), while no bullies claimed they were radically opposed. If we look at the acceptance rate the figure is reversed: 25 per cent of bullies and no victims adopt an understanding position towards bullying behaviour. The bully/victim group provides the type of answer which is typical of their dual nature as bully and victim. On the one hand, they reflect the highest rate of understanding towards bullies (25.6 per cent), but at the same time there is a similar percentage of pupils within this group (24 per cent) who are totally anti-bullying (see Figure 10.5).

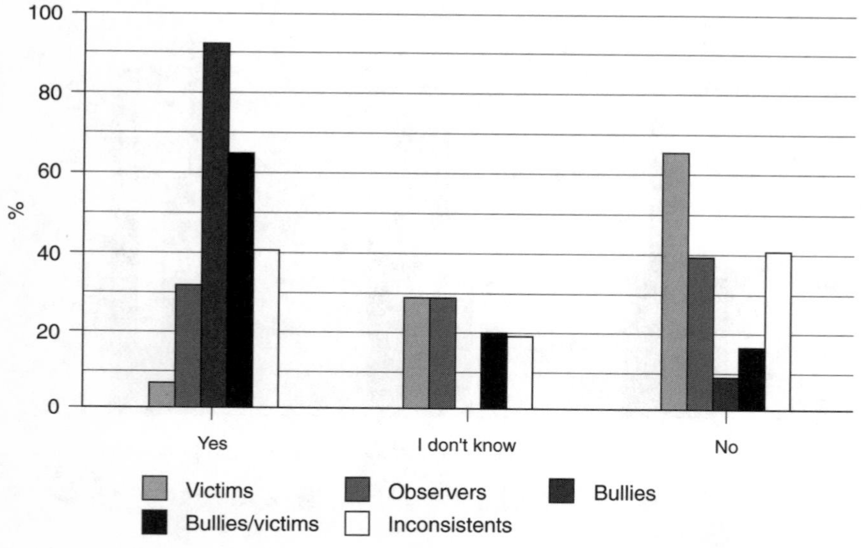

Figure 10.4 Would the pupil bully should the occasion arise?

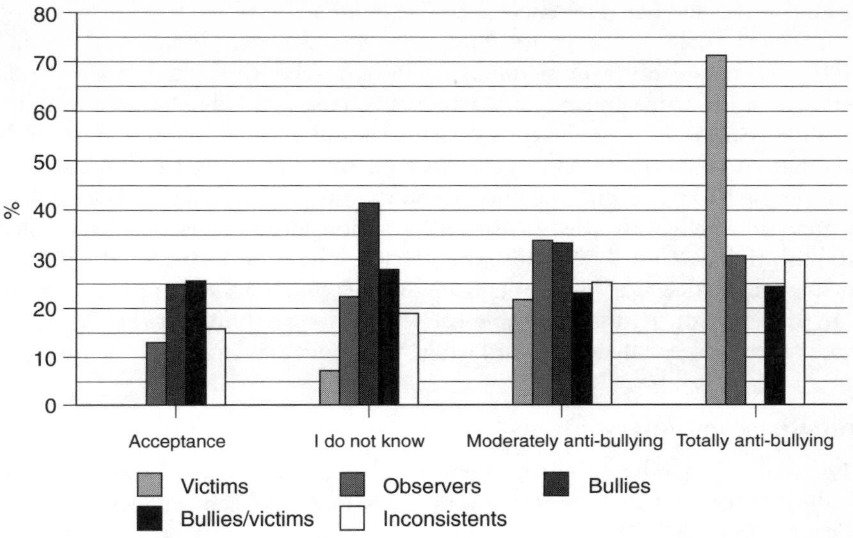

Figure 10.5 Moral judgement of bullying.

Comparison with other studies

The information we have obtained from this study is generally similar to that found elsewhere. In order to determine the main differences and similarities, we will compare our results with those of Olweus (1993) in Norway and Whitney and Smith (1993) and Smith and Sharp (1994) in England, in view of their international circulation.

The first similarity between the three studies may be found in the overall number of pupils involved. In each study the percentage of students is between

Table 10.3 Comparison of bully/victim problems in Spain with those reported from Norway and England

	Norwegian study (Olweus, 1993) (%)	*English study (Smith and Sharp, 1994) (%)*	*Seville study (%)*
Proportion of students involved	12.3	14	18.3
Victims	5.4	10	1.6
Bullies	6.9	4	1.4
Bullies/victims	1.6	Not stated	15.3
Age		Decreases with age	
Gender		More by boys than by girls	
Forms of bullying		Boys: more direct abuse	
		Girls: more indirect abuse	

14 and 18.3. However, when we analyse the number of victims and bullies we find some distinct differences (see Table 10.3).

Although there are no major differences between the Olweus and Smith studies, there are however significant differences between their studies and ours. There are three possible reasons for this. First is the differences in interpersonal relationships produced due to social and cultural reasons. A second explanation could stem from the different analyses performed on the answers; considering this possibility, we understand that we must examine the methods of analysis which were used on the information more precisely, in order to establish the most reliable means for possible comparisons. Thirdly, the differences could be due to a different concept of the types involved in the problem.

In the rest of the results (see Table 10.3) we find some similarities between the three reports, especially with regard to age and gender and forms of bullying.

Initiatives and interventions

The results, generally along the same lines as those of the Norwegian and English teams, and the scientific literature which has been produced on the subject during the last few years, indicated that it would be advisable to design a new large-scale research programme, which should include a wider survey in more schools. This new project has been financed by the National Research and Development Plan (SEC-95-0659) for the provinces of Seville and Madrid, and is currently under way.

For this new project we are using research methods designed by the team itself, in an attempt to determine the cultural characteristics of the school population, namely teachers and pupils (Ortega and Fernandez, 1993; Ortega, Mora-Merchan and Mora, 1996a, b, c). The latest questionnaire that we have designed in order to research the extent of the problem in our schools (Ortega, Mora-Merchan and Mora, 1996a, b), focusing on information given by the pupils themselves, includes the following areas: experiences as victim and/or bully; duration of the experiences; interpersonal relationships in the family circle; relationships between schoolchildren; and, with respect to the teaching team, the level of satisfaction with the different contexts of development, forms of bullying and the places in which it takes place; causes of bullying/victimisation; moral attitudes and behaviour; and proposals of solutions within the same school.

As well as researching the feelings, opinions, attitudes and behaviour of the schoolchildren in the project that we are currently carrying out in Madrid and Seville, we are researching the educational way of thinking, attitudes and behaviour and the teachers' own expectations of change in the schools in which they are working. Both lines of research are considered to be, in our study, an initial approach to the climate of coexistence in the schools with which we are working. These schools have been asked to develop an intervention plan against school bullying, following our proposals and along the general lines of the Sheffield Project (Smith and Sharp, 1994) but adapted to the characteristics of our environment.

To date, we have researched six schools in Madrid and 23 schools in Seville, which means that we have studied approximately 5000 schoolchildren between 10 and 16 years of age (the last year of primary education and the whole secondary education cycle). A preliminary analysis of these results is revealing – firstly, that bullying is a serious problem for coexistence at school, and for the correct social development of the children; secondly, that the methods of quantifying and analysing this subject should take into account the cultural characteristics connected to lifestyles and systems of coexistence in the family as well as at school. On the other hand, the preliminary results seem to confirm that we need to do more in-depth research into the interactive nature of the problem and into the complex psychological elements which are interrelated with bullying; similarly, we must ensure that all educational agents are involved in the intervention process, and that their actions are incorporated into the curriculum and into the whole range of school processes. The whole-school policy model which was applied in the Sheffield project in England (see Chapter 5, this volume) would be a very good alternative, provided that it is adapted to the specific processes of each school culture.

Our intervention proposal against bullying: the Seville anti-bullying model

Our proposal for educational intervention is characterised by the incorporation of all the educational agents: parents, teachers and pupils, in a model of curriculum development which acts along three different but at the same time connected lines:

- activity in the classroom, for which we have proposed work groups;
- control of coexistence in the classroom, and in the school, for which we have proposed classroom forums and periodic assemblies;
- transversality in the curriculum (this is a teaching technique whereby students are introduced to social/emotional themes through the normal curriculum subjects, not as subjects in themselves) for which we propose specific programmes of education in values.

The schools which we are studying receive intermittent attention from the research team by means of visits from the team itself; the first phase of the visits is to attempt to heighten awareness and understanding of the problem, this phase to include research by means of questionnaires to teachers and pupils. A second phase continues with meetings in which we provide a comprehensive explanation of the results of the research, and at the same time we propose the use, with our advice, of one specific intervention programme or the whole range.

When the teaching staff decides to take action in order to change the situation, we propose in our project that they develop different intervention programmes adapted to their particular sociocultural environment, with continual advice and support from our team. Whenever possible, we bring the school counsellor from the area to which the school belongs into the teachers' programmes, and he or she acts as adviser to the work group, and on many occasions takes on a specific programme of direct intervention with pupils who are actually implicated in serious problems of interpersonal bullying or those who are at risk. The research team advises the school counsellors by means of periodic training and tutoring seminars.

Fifteen schools are currently taking part in this process, with an average of fifteen teachers per school, and twelve school counsellors from the state education system. All the schools belong to areas of low or very low socio-cultural and economic level and are considered by the education authorities to be areas of preferential treatment. We will finalise the project once the intervention programmes have been under way for two years with a reappraisal of the bullying problem in the 23 schools, of which only fifteen are carrying out the intervention stage.

This new study has been a major challenge for the joint research team (Madrid and Seville) and is proving to be quite successful in terms of its implementation, but we will need to evaluate all aspects of the study to be able to report on its real effectiveness. In any case, we have no doubt that it means an increase in the level of social awareness of the bullying problem and in this sense is already proving to be positive.

Acknowledgements

We gratefully acknowledge the Inter-Ministerial Board of Science and Technology (SEC 950659) for financing the Seville School Anti-bullying Project. Similarly, we wish to thank Professor Ramón Fernandez of the University of Badajóz for his kind assistance with the sociological references related to the State of Spain.

References

Cerezo, F. and Esteban, M. (1992) La dinámica bully–victima entre escolares: Diversos enfoques metodológicos. *Revista de Psicología Universitas Tarraconensis*, 14, 131–145.

Fernandez, I. and Ortega, R. (1995) La escuela ante los problemas de maltrato entre companeros y violencia interpersonal: Un proyecto de intervención ligado a la reforma educativa en curso. Paper presented at the Fourth Congreso Estatal sobre Infancia Maltratada, Sevilla, pp. 284–289.

Mora-Merchan, J.A. and Ortega, R. (1995) Intimidadores y víctimas un problema de maltrato entre iguales. Paper presented at the Fourth Congreso Estatal sobre Infancia Maltratada, Sevilla, pp. 271–275.

Olweus, D. (1989) Prevalence and incidence in the study of antisocial behavior: Definition and measurements. In M. Klein (ed.) *Cross-national research in self-reported crime and delinquency*. Dordrecht, The Netherlands: Kluwer.

Olweus, D. (1993) *Bullying at school. What we know and what we can do.* Oxford: Blackwell.

Ortega, R. (1992) Violence in schools: Bully-victims' problems in Spain. Paper presented at the fifth European Conference on Developmental Psychology, Seville, September.

Ortega, R. (1994) Violencia interpersonal en los centros educativos de Educación Secundaria: Un estudio sobre maltrato e intimidación entre compañeros. *Revista de Educación*, 304, 253–280.

Ortega, R. (1995) Las malas relaciones interpersonales en la escuela: Estudio sobre la violencia y el maltrato entre compañeros de Segunda Etapa de EGB. *Infancia y Sociedad*, 27–28, 191–216.

Ortega, R. and Fernandez, I. (1993) *Cuestionario sobre actitudes intimidatorias y violencia personal.* Seville: Universidad de Sevilla.

Ortega, R. and Mora-Merchan, J.A. (1995) Bullying in Andalucian adolescents: A study about the influence of the passage from primary school to secondary school. Paper presented at the Seventh European Conference on Developmental Psychology (August), Krakow, Poland, p. 347 in book of abstracts.

Ortega, R. and Mora-Merchan, J.A. (1996a) El aula como escenario de la vida afectiva y moral. *Cultura y Educación*, 3, 5–18.

Ortega, R., Mora-Merchan, J.A. and Mora, J. (1996a) *Cuestionario sobre intimidación y maltrato entre iguales (Primaria)*. Seville: Universidad de Sevilla.

Ortega, R., Mora-Merchan, J.A. and Mora, J. (1996b) *Cuestionario sobre intimidación y maltrato entre iguales (Secundaria)*. Seville: Universidad de Sevilla.

Ortega, R., Mora-Merchan, J.A. and Mora, J. (1996c) *Cuestionario para Profesores.* Seville: Universidad de Sevilla.

Smith, P.K. and Sharp, S. (1994) *School bullying: Insights and perspectives*. London: Routlege.

Vieira, M., Fernandez, I. and Quevedo, G. (1989) Violence, bullying and counselling in the Iberian Peninsula. In E. Roland and E. Munthe (eds) *Bullying: An international perspective*. London: David Fulton.

Whitney, I. and Smith, P.K. (1993) A survey of the nature and extent of bullying in junior/middle and secondary schools. *Educational Research*, 35, 3–25.

11 Portugal

Ana Maria Tomás de Almeida

Overview

Basic education in Portugal is from 6 to 14 years: ages 6 to 9 in the first cycle or primary, ages 10 to 11 in the second cycle or preparatory, and ages 12 to 14 in the third cycle. A specific feature in Portugal is the grade retention scheme, whereby (at least until recently) many pupils are retained in a grade for one or more years if they underachieve in school.

Bullying and aggression have been of concern in Portugal mainly in recent years, and especially since 1994, when a campaign against violence involving children was supported by the wife of the then President, Mrs Mario Soares. The Prodignitate Foundation has supported work against such violence.

Initiation rituals in schools are a particular instance of violence and bullying behaviours. A survey of the extent of bullying, using a modified Olweus Questionnaire, was carried out in 1993 in Braga, in the north of the country. Eighteen schools and about 6200 pupils took part. Over 20 per cent of pupils reported being bullied, and over 15 per cent reported bullying others (more boys than girls). Typical sex differences were obtained. The playground was the most frequent location for bullying. An analysis of predictive factors showed that grade retention was a predictor of being involved in bullying. Similar findings have since been obtained from a survey in the Lisbon area. Some teacher training and intervention work is currently being carried out in some of the Braga schools.

Country description

Portugal is a Mediterranean country, a member of the European Union, geographically situated on the southwest European coast, covering an area of 91,985 km^2 and having a residential population of 9.8 million. Our town, Braga, is located in the northern province of Minho, a region characterised by a high population density, and also with the youngest population in the EU. Experiencing today a fast pace of industrialisation and a wealthier economic situation, Portugal has known rapid political, social and economic changes in the last two decades since the April revolution in 1974. An ageing population is not yet a serious problem in Portugal; according to the available national statistical reports of 1992, 37.6 per cent of the population are below 25 years of age, 49.3 per cent are between 25 and 64 years and 13.1 per cent are 65 years or older.

Employment has increased in recent years for both sexes, together with a rise in demand for qualifications. There has been a shift to the tertiary sector linked to a continuous rise in the more highly qualified levels of the employed population. The unemployment rate is 4.1 per cent with a relatively higher participation rate for men (55 per cent) than women (42 per cent) in the workforce.

Educational system

According to the latest statistical releases from the Education Ministry, in 1992 there were 9258 public schools for the first cycle and 964 for the second and third cycles of basic education and the secondary school sector. There were fourteen public universities and fourteen polytechnics. Since then the number of private universities and polytechnics has doubled.

The educational system comprises preschool, school and extra-curricular education. The actual structure of the school educational system derives from the Basic Law of the Educational System of 1986, which states that basic education is universal, compulsory, free of charge and lasts for nine years. Compulsory school education comprises three sequential cycles and covers children and adolescents between 6 and 15 years of age; that is, through the first (primary), second (preparatory) and third cycles of schooling.

Attendance at preschool is voluntary, from 3 to 6 years of age. In its formative aspect, it is meant to play a supplementary role to the family's educational role, with which close cooperation should be established. The preschool network is comprised of its own institutions, promoted by central, regional and local bodies, some private and some government subsidised.

School education integrates basic and secondary education as well as higher education. In the first cycle, lasting four years (6 to 9 years of age), teaching is all-encompassing, and the responsibility of a single teacher who may be assisted in specific areas, namely special educational needs. The second cycle, lasting two years (10 to 11 years of age), functions on a multiple teacher basis, with one teacher for each subject or group of subjects. The curricular plan is organised according to multidisciplinary areas, based on a standardised curriculum. The third cycle lasts three years (12 to 14 years of age). The curriculum comprises several subjects organised in disciplinary areas. In the ninth year it allows students some choice of optional subjects.

After compulsory education students may opt for secondary school courses included in the regular school system, or for vocational or artistic courses as an alternative. Along with courses mainly oriented to the continuation of studies, the system provides vocational and technological courses aimed at an earlier entry into an active working life. Both courses last three years, constituting a single cycle of studies from tenth to twelfth grade (15 to 17 years of age), and are divided into four areas: natural sciences, arts, socio-economic studies and humanities.

Higher education is made up of university and polytechnic attendance. University higher education is provided in universities and non-integrated university schools. Polytechnic education is taught in institutes of higher education specialising in the fields of technology, arts and education, among others.

Extra-curricular education is integrated into a framework of lifelong education and aims at complementing school training or to compensate for its lack. It may be an initiative of the state or of local authorities or a variety of associations: cultural, recreational, civic, parents, students and youth organisations.

A specific aspect of the Portuguese school educational system is the educational retention regulations which applied until 1992. These regulations allowed a school to retain a student in the same school grade until he or she met the requirements for the next grade. This retention system led to significant age differences in the same grade and to a significant number of over-age students in the class. The problem tends to get worse in higher grades as the number of students that fail in the current school grade accumulates. In 1990 to 1991, some 21 per cent of students were retained in the first cycle, 30 per cent in the second cycle, and some 56 per cent in the third cycle. Over the total school system, in the third cycle 26 per cent of students have been retained by one year, 17 per cent by two years, and 14 per cent by three years. From 1992 onwards, due to the implementation of the new guidelines that ruled out student school achievement as a basis for retention, retention has drastically dropped in the compulsory levels. However, some indicators from the school inspection department show that the tenth year of education is registering higher rates of retention.

School attendance rates vary from 30 per cent in preschool to 99 per cent in the first cycle, diminishing to 70 per cent in the second cycle, 55 per cent in the third cycle, 38 per cent in secondary, and 22 per cent in higher education. Compulsory schooling rate in the nine years is 44 per cent with an estimated school drop-out rate of 40 per cent after the sixth year of schooling. This unexpected drop-out rate probably reflects the recency of a nine-year system of compulsory education. Only the students that enrolled in the first grade after 1987 were compelled to register for nine years of education. Although the period of compulsory education is now extended to nine years, traditionally, and not so long ago, until 1987, compulsory education lasted only four years. With semi-rural families and regions where poverty is more dramatic, the school drop-out rate is more aggravated and related to high rates of child and young juvenile employment. Moreover, drop-out control policies are difficult to implement in overcrowded schools and are inefficient in most cases.

Social awakening to the problem of bullying

Bullying and peer aggression have become a recent topic of concern for Portuguese educators and researchers. The problem has begun to be analysed in studies of student disruptive behaviour causing disciplinary problems between teachers and pupils in the classroom, and also studies of vandalism against school buildings and equipment (Vieira da Fonseca, Garcia and Perez, 1989). This pattern of aggressive behaviour is still largely under-researched, and its magnitude as well as the personal and social effects of the problem are not yet fully understood. Nevertheless, in 1994, peer aggression gained public recognition because of the publicity given to cases of child and juvenile violence in Norway and in the UK, sometimes with mortal consequences for the young children involved.

Violence involving children and the ways children are affected by violence in society, in violent familial environments and through the media have become a major social issue. A national campaign to raise consciousness about the effects of television violence on children was launched by Mrs Soares and, the debate was broadcast on the radio, in the press and on television. Soon after, throughout the country, numerous teacher and parent associations, teacher corporative associations and more creditable science education institutions (e.g. the Institute for Innovative Education) held thematic seminars on violence in schools and related problems, mainly concerned with prevention. At the beginning of 1995, Mrs Soares commissioned the Prodignitate Foundation, the first national foundation which aimed at scanning and preventing political, social, familial and school violence. Awareness of the problem motivated politicians to create specialist committees to prepare well-documented recommendations to be disseminated among child and youth care services in health, education and social domains. For instance, an inter-ministerial commission joined nine entities, including the national council for education, representatives of psychology associations, the church, as well as law, education and mass media expertises. Accordingly, an amendment was published consisting of a major set of proposals and suggestions to regulate the dissemination of violence on television.

Throwing light on peer aggression and victimisation in schools

In parallel with these broadcasting and public debates, the discussion spread to the school arena where aggressive behaviour problems among children are a common occurrence. In general, teacher concerns arise from serious peer aggression that systematically affects the school routine causing disturbance in the classroom and the playground, in the corridors and at lunch-time. School perceptions are mainly centred on the behaviour problems and, in these circumstances, some pupils are seen as its primary agents and perpetuators. Teachers frequently state that one major difficulty is to handle the students' claims about bullies and to have effective and durable solutions at hand to keep the situation under control. Much less sensitivity and attention is felt towards the victims and their families. Typically, few specific measures are taken by schools in these situations apart from general warnings, suggesting avoidance of possible encounters, and/or appealing to patience, and tolerance of what is considered to be the nature of children in general.

For instance, in recent years there has been a rapid upsurge of initiation rituals in Portuguese schools. Particularly in new universities, younger students are holding reception meetings involving violent practices (so-called 'praxes académicas' from the Latin *praxis academia*) and a few serious incidents have caught the attention of the media (e.g. seriously injured people, a female rape and a male being blinded). In secondary and primary schools, these rituals are also known as 'praxes'; some of them seem to be more frequent at the beginning of the school year and take the form of a group expression of violence against a helpless student. One of the most 'popular' expressions of this type of group violence consists of 'going to the post', where a younger person is held by his mates with his legs open, and is pulled hard with his legs fork-like against a post. Although these practices are more common among boys, girls seem to know about them and may have observed them.

Considering examples such as this, bullying in schools is seen as part of the peer culture and something that is natural in children and young people but which they will leave behind as they grow older. Such phenomena are partly taken as a natural expression of aggressiveness, and this includes the majority of direct physically aggressive behaviours. Teachers often disregard types of aggressive behaviours that can cause severe consequences or which are even harmful crimes.

Perceptions and meanings of school bullying

Various studies in Europe, North America, Australia and Japan have indicated that bullying and aggression among schoolchildren is a widespread agonistic pattern of behaviour and its incidence is surprisingly high (e.g. Whitney and Smith, 1993). A clear definition of bullying is difficult and a direct translation from the Anglo-Saxon term 'bullying' is not found in the Portuguese lexicon. Nevertheless, related terms capture the meaning of the concept, and closely synonymous terms are peer abuse ('abusar dos colegas'), victimisation ('vitimar'), intimidation ('intimidar') and violence in schools ('violência na escola'). In the current state of the definition of the term, the Anglo-Saxon term 'bullying' is frequently referred to and its use is associated with physical or psychological violence persistently occurring against someone who is more fragile or vulnerable in power or strength. This type of aggressive behaviour is different from tough or rough playful behaviour, since there is a clear intention to harm or torment the other, and usually older, stronger or more powerful or numerous bullies pick younger, isolated and weaker victims.

Children's perceptions of bullying episodes appear in early childhood. Young children of around 5 and 6 years old report experiences of bullying and acknowledge that bullying is not playful behaviour (Smith and Levan, 1995). Children's definitions are quite extensive, including various forms of teasing and dominance, with an emphasis on fighting and aggressive episodes. However, they do not necessarily understand that bullying involves repeated or unprovoked actions against weaker persons (Madsen and Smith, 1993).

Extensive perception of bullying behaviour is not necessarily accompanied by efficient coping strategies and may even perpetuate inadequate ways of dealing with the problem. It is doubtful whether young children are being socialised not to bully others. Indeed, age trends show only a slight decrease in bullying others as children grow older. The decline is more steady for bullied children, dropping more drastically in secondary schools (i.e. adolescent years). Nevertheless, some severely bullied children continue to be victimised all through their school years (Olweus, 1993).

The Portuguese research project on bullying and peer aggression in schools

Taking into account the novelty of bullying issues in Portuguese schools, our first study on bullying aimed at raising awareness of the problem among the teacher community through information about its nature and extent, its causes and consequences, in order to give a better understanding about the phenomenon. This first research project was initiated at the Institute of Child Studies of Minho University in Braga, in collaboration with the Sheffield team in England and coordinated by Peter Smith, with funding from the Treaty of Windsor. Launched in a teacher training department, with a multidisciplinary staff, the Portuguese team integrated researchers from heterogeneous scientific backgrounds and a wide range of educational fields: Beatriz Pereira, from the physical educational section, Ana Almeida, from child psychology, and Lucília Valente, from expressive arts in education, who coordinated the project.

The project study began by addressing the issue in the first two cycles of compulsory education. Accordingly, we drew attention to bullying problems at younger ages and thus hoped to be able to characterise the phenomenon at the beginning of schooling and further elaborate on preventive strategies under the scope of personal and social curricula and teacher education courses.

This project began in the spring of 1993. It aimed at surveying the nature and magnitude of the problem in the first and second cycles. Later, at the beginning of the school year in September and through to the end of April, the project began a second phase aimed at involving teachers. A teacher training course was organised, fully licensed and approved by the National Council for Teacher Continuing Education and involving 36 teachers. The course was organised on a basis of weekly three-hour sessions, totalling 66 hours of training. The curriculum brought together recent theoretical issues on aggression and victimisation, information about the Norwegian and English intervention programmes, and details about intervention methodology. In addition, the training included practical and direct approaches on counselling, drama work, social skills training and cooperative team work, playtime organisation facilities, and some specific approaches to working with school bullies. Final assignments included the presentation of an anti-bullying intervention proposal designed to be compatible with the particular characteristics of the school.

Rather than just being sensitised to the problem, trained teachers took action in the following year. In a few schools bullying was chosen as the theme of the school educational project, which is similar to a whole-school policy. The school educational project is usually specified as a one-year project and its development is aimed at a wider involvement of the school staff, students, parents and local authorities. Other teachers carried out more focused interventions in the area of student counselling, and some ran drama activities with smaller groups of children. In addition, a monitored intervention has been done, under the supervision of Beatriz Pereira, in partial fulfilment of her Ph.D. project.

Nature and extension of bullying in Portuguese schools

The aims of the pupil survey were to give a more detailed account of the dimension of bully/victim behaviours in primary and preparatory schools; the differences in types of bullying and contexts of occurrence, and bully/victim patterns in relation to age, gender, area of school, underachievement and socioeconomic background.

A total of eighteen schools (about 6200 students, 2846 from primary and 3341 from preparatory schools) completed a modified version of the Olweus Questionnaire, taken from the English study of Smith and Sharp (1994). The age range was 6 to 15 years in the first cycle and 9 to 17 years in the second cycle. (The large age interval in each cycle is due to the educational retention regulations discussed earlier; underachievers can be held back for one to three years. Codifying this variable, we differentiated students as 0 for no retentions, 1 for one retention, 2 for two or more retentions.)

The sample was drawn from the school population of the Braga district, a high-density region in the northwest of Portugal. The schools were located in urban, industrialised and rural areas; their size varied considerably, from 150 pupils in some primary schools, to over 1000 students in four preparatory schools. All the schools were integrated in the public system of education but socioeconomic background varied. Urban primary schools had middle–high income families and suburban and rural schools had middle–low income families. In the urban and suburban preparatory schools the socioeconomic levels were more evenly distributed. Socioeconomic level was codified using a Portuguese classification scheme (level 1 high to level 4 low), taking account of the educational background of both parents, and occupation.

For younger children the Olweus Questionnaire was modified into a pictorial form and phrased in short and simple questions. Each item was read aloud and its completion was followed by adult supervision. The same version was used in the primary and preparatory schools; the questionnaires were filled in by students anonymously. A clear and simple definition of bullying was stated, stressing that bullying was not incidental playful behaviour, but rather nasty and harmful behaviour going on for some time and causing physical or emotional pain. Questions about being bullied and bullying others referred to the current school term.

The question on types of bullying was codified according to the following categories: *physical* (includes being physically hurt, assaulted or having belongings stolen); *direct verbal* (includes being called nasty names and threatened); *indirect* (includes being socially excluded, having rumours spread about oneself). The frequencies of being bullied and of bullying others during the school term are shown in Table 11.1. Response options were never, once or twice, three or four times, or five times or more. We only considered the last two response options of 'three or four' and 'five or more' as bullying.

Overall, no significant differences were found when comparing the extent of being bullied in primary and preparatory schools. However, a higher percentage of boys than girls reported being bullied. This difference between boys and girls is significant in both primary ($p < .001$) and preparatory schools ($p < .001$).

Reports of bullying others indicated a higher incidence in primary schools. Between primary and preparatory schools, boys showed a significant decrease in the percentage of bullying others ($p < .001$), whereas for girls this difference was nonsignificant. Unusually, compared to studies elsewhere, the percentage of boys who report bullying others in primary schools exceeded the percentage of boys who report being bullied. At least twice as many boys as girls admit to bullying others, significant in both primary ($p < .001$) and preparatory schools ($p < .001$).

Differences in the type of bullying behaviour experienced by boys and girls, separately for primary and preparatory pupils, are shown in Table 11.2. Direct physical aggression was the most frequent type of bullying experienced by

Table 11.1 Percentages of being bullied and bullying others: for boys and girls, in primary and preparatory schools

	Primary (years 1–4)			*Preparatory (years 5–6)*		
	Boys n = 1409	*Girls n = 1337*	*Overall n = 2746*	*Boys n = 1739*	*Girls n = 1531*	*Overall n = 3270*
Been bullied three or more times	25.7	18.0	21.9	24.2	18.7	21.6
Bullying others three or more times	27.2	11.7	19.6	20.5	9.6	15.4

Table 11.2 Percentages for types of bullying behaviour: by school and gender

	Primary schools (years 1–4)			*Preparatory schools (years 5–6)*		
	Boys n = *1044*	*Girls* n = *927*	*Overall* n = *1971*	*Boys* n = *1201*	*Girls* n = *1122*	*Overall* n = *2323*
Direct physical (hitting, punching, taking belongings)	76.5	67.6***	72.3	63.1	46.7***	55.2
Direct verbal (called nasty names, threatened)	67.0	60.5**	63.9	65.5	66.5 *ns*	66.0
Indirect (rumours, no one talked to me)	47.7	61.8***	54.3	29.8	54.5***	41.7

Notes: Figures are percentages of those children who were ever bullied. Total percentages exceed 100 since children could check more than one response.
** $p < 0.01$
*** $p < 0.001$

both boys and girls in primary schools. However, direct verbal aggression was the most common type of bullying reported for both sexes in preparatory schools. Girls tended to use more indirect forms earlier than did boys.

In general, all types of bullying declined with age, except for girls who reported verbal aggression. There were clear sex differences, with boys consistently experiencing more physical bullying, and girls more indirect bullying (all significant at $p < .001$ on chi-square), with little sex difference in verbal bullying (this is consistent with the English data of Rivers and Smith, 1994).

Data on who was reported to do the bullying are shown in Table 11.3. According to pupils' reports, bullying was perpetrated most often by 'one boy' or 'several boys', followed by 'both boys and girls'. Girls were signalled as bullies to a much lesser extent, although more frequently by other girls than by boys. Similar to Whitney and Smith (1993), about half of the bullying experienced seemed to result from a particular bully/victim relationship, and half from a group phenomenon (i.e. 'mobbing') .

An analysis of which class the bullying child was in, relative to the victim, is given in Table 11.4. This shows that most bullying was reported to have been carried out by other pupils in the victim's class, and by older pupils. Few pupils reported that they had been bullied by younger pupils. Boys more frequently admitted to having been bullied by older boys both in primary and preparatory schools. In contrast, girls seem to have been bullied by other pupils from their own class both in primary and preparatory schools.

An analysis of where bullying was reported to have taken place is given in Table 11.5. In both primary and preparatory schools, bullying took place mainly in the playgrounds. For pupils in primary schools, the classroom was

Table 11.3 Percentages of who does the bullying: by school and gender

	Primary (years 1–4)			*Preparatory (years 5–6)*		
	Boys n = 1015	*Girls n = 823*	*Overall n = 1838*	*Boys n = 1128*	*Girls n = 1053*	*Overall n = 2181*
Mainly one boy	48.1	44.2	46.4	57.8	39.3	48.9
Several boys	36.8	25.2	31.6	35.5	23.2	29.6
Mainly one girl	1.9	7.8	4.5	1.2	10.8	6.0
Several girls	2.9	4.1	3.4	1.0	9.8	5.2
Both boys and girls	10.3	18.7	14.1	4.5	16.9	10.5

Table 11.4 Percentages of when the bullying was carried out: by schools and gender

	Primary (years 1–4)			*Preparatory (years 5–6)*		
	Boys n = 1014	*Girls n = 849*	*Overall n = 1863*	*Boys n = 1031*	*Girls n = 1049*	*Overall n = 2180*
In the victim's own class	54.5	63.8	58.8	50.1	65.5	57.5
Different class but same year	39.5	34.0	37.0	35.9	33.7	34.9
In years above	67.5	50.9	59.9	73.5	49.8	62.1
In years below	14.4	19.3	16.6	5.5	7.8	6.6

Note: Figures are percentages of those children who were ever bullied. Total percentages exceed 100 since children could check more than one response.

the second place where bullying most frequently happened, but the results showed a shift from the classroom to the corridors in the preparatory schools. These trends were similar both for boys and girls.

In subsequent analyses, we examined how bully/victim incidence related not only to gender and age, but to school area, school year, 'underachievement' and social class. To do this, logit models were fitted to the proportion of children reporting as having been bullied or having bullied others, including the factors mentioned.

So far as the likelihood of *being bullied* was concerned, only two variables were significant; namely, gender ($p < .001$) and school area ($p < .02$). There was an increased risk of being bullied for boys attending school in a suburban area. After controlling for gender and school area variables, no significant variations were found across social class, school year and 'underachievement'.

Table 11.5 Percentages for where in school boys and girls were bullied in primary and preparatory schools

	Primary (years 1–4)			*Preparatory (years 5–6)*		
	Boys n = 1000	*Girls n = 802*	*Overall n = 1802*	*Boys n = 1120*	*Girls n = 1019*	*Overall n = 2139*
Corridors	24.9	21.8	23.5	28.0	35.2	31.5
Playground	79.6	75.9	78.0	80.7	75.4	78.2
Classroom	44.1	46.3	45.1	19.3	27.1	23.0
Other places	23.3	18.0	20.9	18.1	14.7	16.5

Note: Figures are percentages of those children who were ever bullied. Total percentages exceed 100 since children could check more than one response.

So far as the likelihood of *bullying others* was concerned, significant variables were gender ($p < .001$), school area ($p < .05$), school year ($p < .001$), 'under-achievement' ($p < .001$) and social class ($p < .001$). Additionally, a significant first-order interaction was found between gender and social class ($p < .05$). There was an increased risk of bullying others for boys attending school in a suburban primary school, which rises with increasing 'underachievement'. For boys only, this risk is higher in lower social class groups.

General discussion

This survey shows that bullying is a substantial problem in Portuguese schools, and that its magnitude is similar to other southern European countries, namely Italy (Genta, Menesini, Fonzi, Costabile and Smith, 1996) and Spain (Garcia and Perez, 1989) (although these two studies refer to relatively older samples from age 8 upwards).

So far as the incidence of bullying in primary schools is concerned, the results show that children report considerably high levels of bullying. From primary to preparatory school, the extent of being bullied remains relatively stable. In addition, a high percentage of boys and girls in primary schools admit to bullying others and a small decline by preparatory school is probably not enough to alleviate the problem. Among the factors that contribute to age changes are maturity, socialisation, being in a position to bully or to be bullied, social skills or lack of them, accrued sensitivity and undifferentiated representation of bullying (Smith and Levan, 1995). It is very possible that many pupil reports of bullying, contributing to the high figures of bullying in Table 11.1, correspond to a lot of fighting, pushing and hitting. Yet dominance relations in early childhood do involve this type of behaviour and the significance of these aggressive episodes in the peer group has to be recognised in the development of cognitive, social and emotional control skills.

Another finding of interest is the difference in types of bullying between boys and girls. Here the socialisation codes seem to give some credit to the old saying 'Boys are tough and girls are nice', at least in the sense that girls are using more hidden and socially conforming forms of bullying. Of particular interest in our sample is that underachievers retained for one year or more are more at risk of becoming bullies.

A first replication of the Braga survey, carried out in four preparatory schools in Lisbon (Pereira, Mendonça, Neto, Almeida, Valente and Smith, 1996), shows a consistency across preparatory schools in Braga and Lisbon (the mean age of this sample was 11.5 years). Particularly in the comparative study of Braga and Lisbon preparatory schools, we found significant differences in the incidence of bullying according to sex, school year, years of underachievement and social class. Bullies were significantly more likely to be boys (21 per cent) than girls (10 per cent); the problem was greater in the sixth grade than in the fifth grade; children who had school retentions were more likely to bully others, as were children from lower social class groups. None the less, no differences were found in relation to school area. In addition, in this replication study we found significant differences in the incidence of being bullied according to sex and social class. More victims were boys (24 per cent) than girls (18 per cent), and more victims were from lower socioeconomic backgrounds. There was no effect of school area, school year or retention.

Taking into account these findings, we tend towards the conclusion that peer aggression is most probably perpetuated by older pupils often stronger than their peers, and thus in an advantageous position to bully others with impunity. It is not certain whether their lack of school achievement also contributes to this risk. In any event, the finding suggests a negative aspect of grade retention; hopefully the implementation of recent regulations of academic achievement will bring about a drastic reduction in the percentage of pupils being retained in compulsory levels of education. Accordingly, we expect to find a significant decrease in bullying rates in the near future in Portuguese primary and preparatory schools.

Conclusion

Taken together, these research findings allow us to call attention to the magnitude of bullying in Portuguese schools. Optimistically, schools reforms, information about the effects of bullying in personal life trajectories and in the school ethos, and interventions aiming at preventing and reducing bullying will have positive results. Nevertheless, bullying is neither a new school problem nor is it even now much acknowledged by teachers. My personal perception after several discussions of this phenomenon with teachers is that much staff resistance to intervening in a more active way against peer aggression and victimisation is, in large part, associated with the coexistence of several separate spaces/contexts in the school. To mention a few more relevant ones: the academic context where teachers and students relate in a rather authoritarian way, and the extra-curricular activities where teachers and pupils interact in a more relaxed and authoritative form. Aside from these two adult–child contexts of interaction is the student's space, where children have to cope and learn how to handle both tolerance and toughness. In spite of the reality of growth, socialisation is a two-way process and separation and rigid frontiers in between these and other contexts in school can draw adults and younger pupils apart, with an increasing distance between adult and child contexts. Whether we can prevent bullying or not, educational contexts have to be strongly committed to improving ways of interacting, building trust and reciprocity among children.

References

Garcia, I. F. and Perez, G. Q. (1989) Violence, bullying and counseling in the Iberian Peninsula: Spain. In E. Roland and E. Munthe (eds) *Bullying: An international perspective*. London: David Fulton.

Genta, M. L., Menesini, E., Fonzi, A., Costabile, A. and Smith, P. K. (1996) Bullies and victims in schools in central and southern Italy. *International Journal of Educational Research*, 11, 97–110.

Madsen, K. and Smith, P. K. (1993) Age × gender differences in participants' perception of the concept of the term 'Bullying'. Paper presented at Sixth European Conference in Developmental Psychology, Bonn.

Olweus, D. (1993) Victimisation by peers: antecedents and long-term outcomes. In K. H. Rubin and J. B. Asendorf (eds) *Social withdrawal, inhibition, and shyness in childhood*. Hillsdale, NJ: Lawrence Erlbaum.

Pereira, B., Mendonça, D., Neto, C., Almeida, A., Valente, L. and Smith, P.K. (1996) Facts and figures of the first survey on bullying in Portuguese schools. Paper presented at European Conference on Educational Research, Seville.

Smith, P. K. and Levan, S. (1995) Perceptions and experiences of bullying in younger pupils. *British Journal of Educational Psychology*, 65, 489–500.

Smith, P. K. and Sharp, S. (eds) (1994) *School bullying: Insights and perspectives*. London: Routledge.

Whitney, I. and Smith, P. K. (1993) A survey of the nature and extent of bullying in junior/middle and secondary schools. *Educational Research*, 35, 3–25.

Vieira da Fonseca, M., Garcia, I. and Perez, G. (1989) Violence, bullying and counselling in the Iberian Peninsula. In E. Roland and E. Munthe (eds) *Bullying: An international perspective*. London: David Fulton.

12 Belgium

Nicole Vettenburg

Overview

This chapter describes the problem of bullying in Belgium, the existing studies, the initiatives taken and the materials developed.

Belgium is a small, densely populated and relatively prosperous European country. It has a federal structure consisting of three communities. The competence for education lies with the communities: each community has its own education system.

Research into the problem of bullying in schools in Belgium was not undertaken until recently, and only in Flanders has the problem been given any explicit attention. There is an unmistakable influence of Scandinavian and Dutch publications, media reports and articles in the professional press, studies and materials developed.

Public interest in the problem of bullying is regularly aroused by a publication on the problem, the conclusion of a concrete project or the occurrence of a serious event.

Four studies provide relevant information on the problem of bullying. Of particular interest is the study conducted by Stevens and Van Oost, a large-scale project focusing on the problem of bullying. The results of four studies can be summarised as follows: in elementary education, 16 per cent of children reported bullying other children; 23 per cent reported being a regular victim of bullying. A certain stability in time was found: this year's bullies and victims are likely to be next year's bullies and victims as well. Conversely, it was also found that both phenomena decrease with age: in secondary education, 12 per cent report bullying others regularly and 15 per cent report being bullied regularly. Contrary to what is often assumed, there are few or no differences between the distinct types of education, although more severe forms of bullying are reported to occur in vocational education. Furthermore, boys are reported to be more often involved in bullying than girls; indirect bullying, however, is more frequent among girls. Finally, it was found that bullying is a phenomenon involving several children, that it mainly takes place during playtime and among children of the same year group. Only a small majority of the victims is given help, mainly by friends and class mates.

In the past few years, a relatively extensive supply of materials has been developed to work on the problem of bullying at school level, class level and individual level, as well as together with the parents. Education policy in Belgium has opted – also for the future – for an overall approach to specific school problems. Measures are implemented to give schools sufficient room to take initiatives fitting in with their pedagogical project and aiming to prevent and/or tackle problems (including bullying, drug abuse, truancy, etc.).

Socioeconomic and sociodemographic information

Belgium is located at the heart of the European Union and is surrounded by densely populated regions and highly industrialised zones. This central location, and the fact that Brussels is also the capital of Europe, makes Belgium the crossroads of international contacts. With an area of 30,518 km^2 and over ten million inhabitants, Belgium is a small but densely populated country (332 inhabitants/km^2). The northern part, Flanders, is Dutch-speaking and has the largest number of inhabitants (5.9 million). The southern part, Wallonia, is French-speaking and has 3.3 million inhabitants. About 9 per cent of the total population is of foreign extraction, with concentrations greatly differing per region: 5 per cent in the Flemish region, 11 per cent in the Walloon region and 30 per cent in the Brussels capital region. Italians and Moroccans constitute the largest groups of foreigners.

Between 1970 and 1993, Belgium evolved from a unitary to a federal state structure. The federal structure comprises three policy levels: the federal state, the communities and the regions. There is no hierarchy between these levels: each level has its own competencies. There are three communities: the Flemish, the French and the German-speaking community. Communities are responsible for cultural and personal affairs within a linguistic area, including education, culture, audiovisual media and youth protection.

There are three regions: the Flemish, the Walloon and the Brussels capital region. The regions are based on economic areas and are responsible for economic affairs, agriculture, housing, water policy, transport, etc. The communities and regions have their own parliament and government. More than three-quarters of the Belgian population (77 per cent) live in communes belonging to urban units with an average population density of 499 inhabitants/km^2. About 40 per cent of them live in five major urban regions with more than 390,000 inhabitants; 17 per cent in twelve urban regions with at least 80,000 inhabitants, while 20 per cent live in commuter residential zones.

The working population represents about 50 per cent of the total population. As in other industrialised western countries, the tertiary sector has been constantly gaining in importance, to the detriment of the other sectors (in 1993, working population in the tertiary sector: 70.2 per cent, in the secondary sector: 27.3 per cent, and in the primary sector: 2.5 per cent). With a net national income of BEF 610,000 per capita, Belgium ranks among the more prosperous countries. However, unemployment has been a negative constant in the Belgian economy. In 1995, the number of unemployed accounted for about 14 per cent of the working population.

The education system

The recent institutional reforms transferred the responsibility for education to the communities (compulsory school attendance, the minimum requirements for delivering diplomas and teachers' pensions remain the responsibility of the federal government). Since 1989, each community has had its own education system. These systems cover 57.5 per cent (Dutch-speaking scheme), 42 per cent (French-speaking scheme) and 0.5 per cent (German-speaking scheme) of the total number of pupils (Ministry of the Flemish Community, 1996; Ministère de l'éducation, de la recherche et de la formation, 1996).

The 1983 Compulsory School Attendance Act obliges parents to send their children to school for twelve years, starting from September in the year of the child's sixth birthday until the end of June of the year in which they turn 18. Compulsory attendance is full time until the age of 15 if the pupil has completed primary education and the first two years of secondary education with full curriculum. If this is not the case, it is full time until the age of 16. From the age of 15/16, compulsory school attendance is part time. The pupil can partially attend classes and partially work. However, full-time education remains a possibility and is opted for by the large majority of pupils. Education is free during the period of compulsory school attendance.

Constitutional freedom allows the organisation of educational networks and umbrella organisations. Traditionally, three such networks are distinguished:

- Community education, organised by the communities; the Belgian constitution obliges this network to be neutral.
- Subsidised official education, organised by the provinces and the municipal authorities; schools in this network can be either denominational or non-denominational.
- Subsidised private education, based on private initiative; this includes denominational (mainly Catholic) education, non-denominational private education and pluralist private education. The private educational network accounts for the largest share of the pupil population.

The networks have far-reaching autonomy. They are free to choose their pedagogic methods, curricula and schedules. They have pedagogic counsellors who are in charge of the external guidance of schools and staff. In addition, the guidance centres (PMS) are network-related; they play a complementary role in counselling and in pupils' study and career guidance. The guidance centres work in teams consisting of psychologists, educationalists, social workers, physicians and paramedics.

Nursery education is provided for children aged 2.5 to 5. It is not compulsory and it is free. Nearly all children (90–95 per cent) attend nursery school. There are three years. The 3-, 4- and 5-year-olds are usually brought together in the first, second and third nursery classes respectively.

Primary education (6 to 12 years) consists of six consecutive years. The year-class system is used, each class having its own form teacher. The five-day school week consists of nine half school days (there are no classes on Wednesday afternoons); there are 28 periods of 50 minutes (four in the morning, two in the afternoon).

Secondary education (12 to 18 years) also consists of six consecutive years, divided into three grades of two years each. The first grade is largely common for all pupils. From the second grade (third year) onwards, four education types are distinguished: general secondary education, technical secondary education, artistic secondary education and vocational secondary education. In secondary education, 32 or 34 periods are organised.

Besides full-time secondary education, there is also part-time vocational secondary education. This is organised into two grades, at the level of the second and third grades of full-time vocational education respectively. Pupils taking part-time education are expected to work part time as well.

The size of classes greatly varies by level, education type, form and school. For instance, 1A classes in secondary education have on average twenty pupils (between twelve and 26); for 1B classes, the figure is 10.6 (between four and sixteen) and the sixth forms (all education types) have an average size of 14.3 (between nine and 25) (Verhoeven *et al.*, 1992).

In comparison with other countries, Belgium has a relatively high percentage of children in education: 61 per cent of youngsters aged 2 to 29, compared with 62 per cent for France, 58 per cent for the Netherlands, 57 per cent for Japan, 54 per cent for Germany and 50 per cent for Switzerland (De Groof and Van Haver, 1993). Possible explanations include: compulsory education until the age of 18, a more substantial participation in nursery education, and a relatively open access to higher education. The school population totals 2.2 million pupils/students: 19 per cent in nursery education, 33 per cent in primary education, 36 per cent in secondary education and 13 per cent in higher education. In secondary education (age 12 to 18), 43 per cent of the pupils take general education, 29 per cent technical education and 27 per cent vocational education from the second grade onwards.

The number of pupils of foreign nationality varies greatly between the Flemish (4.5 to 6 per cent) and the French community (about 18 per cent).

Research on bullying

In order to obtain a comprehensive view of the problem of 'bullying in school' (including existing studies, initiatives and materials in both parts of the country), the following research work was carried out: a systematic study of the last six years of the most relevant (educational) journals (about twenty);

study of the press articles of the past five years; telephone contacts with researchers involved in school problems; and contacts with the major organisations developing and disseminating material.

In the course of data collection, we found that more attention is being paid to the problem of bullying in Flanders than in Wallonia. The attention paid in Flanders is quite recent (first publication in 1989; a growing number of publications from 1993 onwards); and frequent use is made of research data and concrete material from Norway (e.g. Olweus, 1991) and The Netherlands. In Wallonia, we found no research and no material concerning the specific topic of bullying. In Wallonia as well as in Flanders, related or broader school themes received due attention in the press, in research and in material development; these themes include violence in school, drug abuse, drop-out, and development of relationships (see Vettenburg, 1994). This chapter is confined to literature and data specifically relating to the theme of 'bullying in school'; as a result, the following report is largely based on the Flemish situation.

Definition of bullying

In Flemish, there are several terms to denote what is called 'mobbning' or 'mobbing' in Scandinavian countries and 'bullying' in English. The most common term is 'pesten', although 'treiteren' and 'plagen' also do occur. 'Pesten' and 'treiteren' are generally used as synonyms, while the term 'plagen' (teasing) is usually given a slightly different content (De Meyer *et al.*, 1994; Van Mossevelde, 1996).

In Wallonia, the problem of bullying receives little attention; accordingly, there are few real designations for the phenomenon. In newspaper articles we came across 'brimades', 'rackets', 'chahuter (un professeur)', 'violence à l'école' and 'harceler'. Sometimes the English term 'bullying' is used as well. However, the problem of 'violence at school', which includes 'bullying', is given considerably more attention (e.g. Dekeyser, 1993).

The most frequently used definition of bullying is that used in the 'Klasgenoten Relatie Vragenlijst' (Classmates Relationship Questionnaire) developed by Olweus in 1991: 'A person is bullied or being picked on if he or she is repeatedly over time exposed to negative actions of one or more persons' (Stevens and Van Oost, 1994b). Van Mossevelde (1996) adds to this definition: 'who always gain(s) the upper hand'. This addition makes explicit the imbalance of power described by Olweus (1991).

Negative actions may be verbal (e.g. threatening, mocking, calling names, gossiping), physical (e.g. hitting, beating, kicking, scratching) or directed against the victim's possessions (e.g. taking away books, puncturing a bicycle tyre). Besides this direct form of bullying, an indirect form (namely social isolation or exclusion from the group) is mentioned as well. The term 'bullying' most often refers to bullying of pupils. In some cases, bullying of teachers by pupils was also examined, for instance, in the preliminary research by Stevens and Van Oost (1994a, b) and in a thesis by Tyriard (1995). Given the limited amount of information on this issue, we will only deal with the bullying of pupils.

Interest in the problem

There has been a surge of public interest in the problem of bullying in Belgium over the past few years. Newspapers and magazines regularly publish articles carrying titles referring directly to bullying. Some examples: 'Les brimades à l'école' (Bullying at school) (6/2/90), 'Pesten op school: 1 op 5 is slachtoffer' (Bullying at school: 1 out of 5 is victim) (15/11/93), 'Vooral het beroepsonderwijs telt pestkoppen en overdraagzamen' (Bullying mainly in vocational education) (25/8/93), 'Pesten gebeurt vaker dan je denkt' (Bullying: more frequent than you think) (26/10/94), 'Jongere pleegt zelfmoord na pesterijen op school' (Boy commits suicide after bullying in school) (28/2/96), 'Rosten, schele, bonestaak, blokbeest' (Red-head, squinter, beanpole, swot) (29/3/96). A television broadcast on bullying (1993) elicited much response. Following a serious case of extortion of a pupil by fellow-pupils, a question was raised in the Flemish Council concerning 'bullying in school – data and measures'. The academic world is also paying increasing attention to the phenomenon. Explicit questions on bullying were included in broader research enquiries (on school experiences, health behaviour), and a study into bullying is currently under way (see below).

There are several reasons for this public interest: the announcement of publications (e.g. Vandersmissen and Thys, August 1994; Van Oost and Stevens, October 1994; Deboutte, June 1995), the presentation of (prevention) material (Educative Project, September 1994), the initiation or conclusion of a project (project in school in Ghent, March 1994), specific events (suicide, February 1996; threatened suicide, March 1994). (Our limited analysis of newspaper articles has shown that the problems of suicide and bullying in Flanders were related to one another in two specific cases: March 1994 – a 14-year-old boy threatens to commit suicide after serious bullying at school; the parents report this to the police; February 1996 – a 13-year-old boy commits suicide (by hanging) in his parents' garden after persistently being bullied; a press release by the Public Prosecutor's Office reports that 'the repeated beatings and acts of bullying exasperated the boy' and were the probable cause of his suicide. In addition, Wallonia witnessed two cases of serious bullying resulting in the death of the victim.)

Research was initiated as a result of self-experienced problems (children and youngsters' helplines, guidance centres) or problems reported by the social and educational sectors to the scientific world. Education policy, both in Flanders and in Wallonia, is interested by the problem of bullying, but an overall approach has been opted for (e.g. as part of comprehensive care provision, pupil guidance, attainment targets, mediators, migrant policy, etc.). The general aim is to improve mutual relationships and the climate at school.

Such measures undoubtedly affect the problem of bullying within school. They also give the school the opportunity to develop concrete initiatives within its own pedagogical project to prevent and/or tackle the problem of bullying.

Research studies

Since 1989, four major studies have been undertaken that are of particular interest to the problem of bullying. Of these four studies, two explicitly concern the theme of bullying; the other two cover a wider field (pupils' well-being and health) but do include relevant questions on bullying. We will first give a brief description of these studies, followed by an integration of their major findings.

Children and youngsters' helplines (KJT)

In 1989, six children and youngsters' helplines conducted a study about victims of bullying. For this purpose, 113 calls were analysed. On the basis of this material, a brochure was published for parents and teachers (Lambrechts, 1989). It was the first, albeit limited, study into the problem of bullying, and it was given wide coverage in the press and in several professional journals. Since the sample used was very limited (in number and involving only children calling the children and youngsters' helplines), the results are not comparable with the questionnaire data from the other studies. However, the same trends can be discerned as those revealed by subsequent studies.

The World Health Organisation Study (WHO)

Flanders participated in an international investigation into the health and health behaviour of schoolchildren carried out under the auspices of the World Health Organisation. On two occasions (1990 and 1994), a large-scale school inquiry was organised which included some questions relating to bullying. The results obtained in 1994 were compared with those of 1990. In 1994, the emphasis was on school experiences. The questions concerned the relationship with class mates and teachers, fear of one or more pupils, and loneliness. These analyses were effected on a reduced sample (11- to 18-year-olds): they included 3716 pupils in 1990 and 9256 pupils in 1994 (Peeters *et al.*, 1995).

Central Board for Study and Career Guidance (CSBO)

During the school year 1991–1992, the Central Board for Study and Career Guidance (CSBO; it groups the guidance centres active in Catholic education) performed a study into the well-being of pupils in secondary education.

For this purpose, an inquiry was organised among 1054 sixth-form pupils in ordinary full-time secondary education. Part of this inquiry focused on contacts with fellow-pupils, with questions concerning the atmosphere in class and during school breaks, the bullying problem, and pupils' attitudes towards migrant youngsters. This part was reported by Vandersmissen and Thys (1993).

Behaviour and Health Research Group (RUG)

In early 1993, Ghent University (RUG) launched a project on bullying in school as part of its health promotion scheme. The aim was to develop an action programme on the basis of the key issues derived from the research. The investigation was conducted with 10,000 pupils between 10 and 16, drawn from 84 primary and secondary schools. It used the Classmates Relationship Questionnaire in the Dutch translation by Van Lieshout of the instrument developed by Olweus (1991), slightly adapted to the Flemish context. The research was carried out by Stevens and Van Oost of the Behaviour and Health Research Group at Ghent University. This research resulted in several publications and was given broad media coverage. In Belgium, it is the most extensive study to focus on the topic of bullying. At present (1996) the action programme has been finalised; its implementation and evaluation are under way. The report of the second part is scheduled for 1997.

Research findings

Since the RUG study provides the most comprehensive information, we have taken this study as the starting point for the report on research results. The RUG information will be complemented by data from the other three studies (referred to by the abbreviations indicated above).

Bullying and being bullied

Bullies

The studies by Stevens and Van Oost (1994a, b; 1995a, b) show that 15.9 per cent of pupils in primary education bully other pupils regularly or often; 5.6 per cent do so at least once a week. In secondary education, these figures are 12.3 and 3.9 per cent respectively.

Victims

Twenty-three per cent of pupils in elementary education report that they are victims of bullying regularly or often; with 9.1 per cent of them, this is at least once a week. In secondary education, the percentages are 15.2

per cent and 6.4 per cent respectively. The CSBO study shows that 18 per cent are being bullied to a lesser extent; 2.6 per cent of them report being bullied badly.

The phenomenon of bullying and being bullied also appears to be relatively stable in time. Pupils bullying others or being bullied themselves one year are more likely to continue the same bullying behaviour or to become victims again the following year (a correlation of 0.53 and 0.41 respectively). This appears to apply more to bullied boys than to bullied girls (CSBO).

Types of bullying

The CSBO study shows that the most frequent form of bullying is ridiculing (60 per cent). Name-calling (22.4 per cent) and exclusion (20.5) are quite frequent, followed by hitting and pushing around (11.7 per cent), threatening (9.8 per cent) and destruction of possessions (6.3 per cent). 'Verbal' types of bullying are clearly predominant. This also appears from the list of 'others', in which types of bullying such as giving nicknames, making humiliating remarks, mocking, etc. prevail. Feeling alone at school and in the playground is more frequent with pupils from elementary education than with those from secondary education (8.4 per cent and 4.8 per cent respectively) (RUG). This decrease with age is confirmed by the WHO study.

Age

Bullying and being bullied decrease with age. In the RUG study, the frequencies decrease significantly between ages 10 and 16. In the CSBO study, bullying among boys decreases by about 10 per cent per grade (32 per cent, 22 per cent and 11 per cent respectively); this trend is less pronounced among girls, since bullying is less frequent at a lower age (16 per cent, 10 per cent and 10 per cent respectively). The WHO study investigated the fear of one or more pupils. Among boys, the fear of class mates decreases from 18 per cent (11- to 12-year-olds) to 5 per cent (17- to 18-year-olds); among girls the percentages are 11 per cent and 4 per cent respectively.

Types of education

The findings of the RUG and the CSBO studies are not totally in agreement in this regard. The RUG study found no differences between general, technical and vocational education (second grade), either with regard to bullying or to (directly or indirectly) being bullied. In the first grade, bullying and being bullied seems to be slightly more frequent with pupils in the B classes than in the A classes. This is confirmed by the CSBO research for less serious bullying among boys, but not for more serious types. Of the pupils in vocational education, about 4.5 per cent describe themselves as being bullied badly, both in the second and the third grades. In general and technical education this percentage is 1 to 1.5 per cent.

Sex

Boys are found to be more often victimised and to bully others more frequently than girls. The situation is different, however, with regard to indirect bullying: more girls say that they have fewer friends in class and that they feel more alone at school.

The CSBO study found no difference between boys and girls within the group feeling badly bullied; less serious forms of bullying occur more frequently with boys than with girls (confirmation of the RUG study), but in vocational education, girls in the third grade are bullied more often than those in the other types of education, and this in the very age group in which milder bullying is usually least frequent.

Number of pupils involved

Bullying and being bullied is a phenomenon involving several pupils. In general, groups of pupils from the same class take part in bullying. About half of bullying behaviour occurs in the pupil's own year group, the other half in other year groups; see Table 12.1 for details.

Places where bullying occurs

Most bullying occurs in the playground (elementary education: 77 per cent; secondary education: 60 per cent). Bullying pupils also occurs in class (during lessons and breaks) and on the journey to and from school. Bullying in class occurs more frequently in secondary education than in elementary education (15 per cent and 4.6 per cent).

Bullying of migrant children

No study into this problem has been undertaken in Belgium to date. However, the CSBO study did contain the question 'Would you like migrant youngsters to take classes in your school?', which was put to youngsters in schools with and without migrant children. The answers indicate that intolerance towards migrant children is much higher among boys than among girls (20 per cent against 5 per cent), and that this percentage is twice as high in technical education compared with general education, and again twice as high in vocational education compared with technical education, irrespective of sex. The factor 'familiarity with migrant children' seems to be of lesser importance. These data suggest that bullying of migrant children is probably most frequent in vocational education.

Table 12.1 Pupils involved in bullying

	Elementary school (%)	*Secondary school (%)*
Whom were you bullied by?		
• several boys	36.9	39.5
• one boy	24.9	27.5
• several girls	13.5	16.5
• one girl	9.7	10.2
• boys and girls	14.9	6.3
How many pupils in your class are being bullied?		
• no one	8.8	14.2
• 1 pupil	10.9	17.4
• 2 or 3 pupils	30.8	39.4
• 4 or 5 pupils	26.7	18.4
• 6 or more pupils	22.7	10.5
In which class is/are the pupil(s) that you have been bullied by?		
• my own class	53.1	50.5
• a parallel class	11.0	14.3
• a higher class	11.4	18.7
• a lower class	6.6	1.7
• different classes	17.9	14.7

Source: Stevens and Van Oost, 1995b

Reactions to bullying

About two-thirds of boys and girls say they defend themselves against bullying. About 40 per cent of the victims receive no help at all; the others are helped mainly by friends and class mates and to a much lesser extent by teachers, the school board and parents (CSBO).

The questions on pupils' attitudes towards bullying revealed that a majority have a negative attitude. In elementary education, 62 per cent of the children say they attempt to intervene whenever they notice cases of bullying; in secondary education, this figure drops to 39 per cent. There is a clear correlation between the attitude towards bullying and (non-)intervention. Individual interviews also showed that pupils are more likely to intervene when friends are being bullied; that they do not know how to intervene; and that they are afraid of ending up alone against the bullies, and becoming victims themselves.

Pupils say that in general, teachers do not often intervene: only 37.6 per cent of the teachers in elementary education and a mere 16.2 per cent of teachers in secondary education intervene regularly.

Working on the problem of bullying

Flanders has a relatively large supply of materials designed to tackle the problem of bullying (BDJ-Jeugd and Vrede; Deboutte, 1995; Dekeyser, 1993;

De Meyer *et al.*, 1994; Project Group K.U. Leuven, 1996; Stevens and Van Oost, 1995a, b). In addition to material on bullying in education, there is much useful material on bullying in youth work (Project Group K.U. Leuven, 1996).

There is, however, a substantial difference in the extent to which these materials are disseminated. Some material is poorly publicised and disseminated (e.g. a set of working documents developed by a school and available on request); other material has been published and is widely known but is not disseminated because it is too expensive; finally, some material is widely known, relatively cheap and is hence well disseminated.

Furthermore, it should be noted that schools are calling increasingly often on the welfare sector to work preventively (e.g. improvement of the school climate) or curatively (e.g. referral to individual aid) on social and psychosocial problems (Vettenburg, 1991; Vettenburg and Biermans, 1995).

What is described below only applies to Flanders; in Wallonia, very little material was found. However, Ufapec (the Catholic parents' association of Wallonia) is translating and distributing the book *Pesten, gedaan ermee! Hoe omgaan met pesterijen? Tips voor ouders, leerkrachten en begeleiding* (Bullying, stop it! How to deal with bullying? Tips for parents, teachers and counsellors' (Deboutte, 1995) in French. Furthermore, the Université de Paix has developed material designed to deal with conflicts, cooperation and the stimulation of group awareness, communication, etc.

The project by Van Oost and Stevens aimed to develop the action programme 'bullying in school'. Here are some elements of particular interest:

- Action on bullying can be both *curative* and *preventive*. Curative action implies that strategies are developed to put an end to bullying. Conversely, preventive action aims at making the phenomenon of bullying debatable within the whole school before (serious) cases of bullying occur.
- A distinction is also made between working with *short-term objectives* and working with *long-term objectives*. Working with short-term objectives implies the search for a strategy that puts an immediate stop to bullying. Working with long-term objectives affects the background factors of both the bully and the victim, as well as the factors contributing to the integration of a strategy against bullying in a comprehensive school plan.
- When working on bullying in education, one should not only address the bully and the victim. It is of capital importance that the other pupils (the middle group), all the teachers, the rest of the school staff and the parents should also be involved in the actions undertaken (Stevens and Van Oost, 1995b).

We will first examine how concrete material can be used in school, and then how the role played by the parents is currently conceived.

Action in the school

In order to obtain results, it is important to operate at three different levels: the school level, the class level and the level of the individual pupils. Existing material and initiatives are discussed below depending on the level they are aimed at.

School level

Working on bullying at the school level aims to involve the whole school (that is, all the pupils and the whole school staff). It is mainly preventive and has a long-term effect. The objectives of action at the school level include informing and sensitising the whole school staff about bullying in school, and motivating them into making an active contribution towards reporting and intervening. Another objective is to work out a concrete school policy against bullying by implementing and supporting the necessary measures and structures at the school level (Stevens and Van Oost, 1995b).

In several publications, action at the school level is concretised in the establishment of a school plan. A school plan is a set of regulations relating to behaviour and contacts in school. The aim of such a plan is to improve the climate in the school and the class (De Meyer *et al.*, 1994) and to sensitise all sections of the school to the problem of bullying.

When drawing up a school plan, particular attention should be paid to an unambiguous definition of bullying; but it is equally important to determine the attitude of teachers, school board and pupils towards bullying, to draw up rules concerning bullying and violence at school and to formulate measures *vis-à-vis* offenders (De Meyer, Heurckmans and Vanbilloen, 1994). It is also suggested that it is essential to involve all sections of the school in the school plan and to discuss the plan with pupils and parents.

Finally, it is pointed out that several concrete measures may be taken at the school level to prevent bullying. Surveillance during breaks and playtimes may be tightened, for instance, the more so since it has been found that it is then that most bullying occurs.

Measures at the class level

Action at the class level can be both curative and preventive. Not only should the bullies and the victims be involved but the whole class, since it has been found that the middle group plays an important part in bullying. Indeed, the middle group often joins the bully, either directly or indirectly (the latter by remaining indifferent to bullying, or by not daring or being able to react).

The main aim of these measures is to make pupils understand the importance of their attitude towards bullying, and to make them realise that bullying cannot be tolerated. Action at the class level implies that pupils should be sensitised to the problem of bullying, should be convinced that bullying will not be tolerated in their school and should realise the importance of their own attitude towards bullying.

An additional aim is to encourage pupils to react against bullying and to report bullying behaviour. All this can be concretised in a code of behaviour which clearly states what is to be done in case of bullying.

Much material exists for action at the class level. Examples are informative series of lessons, role play, questionnaires to take stock of bullying in the class, texts and juvenile books on the theme of bullying, plays, videos and informative games.

Measures at the individual level

Action at the individual level is aimed mainly at developing interventions designed to react to actual cases of bullying; hence it is mainly curative. The measures proposed at the individual level are the incident interview, the recovery interview, the supportive interview and the guidance interview (Stevens and Van Oost, 1994b).

A key person in tackling the problem of bullying is the 'core teacher', i.e. the teacher responsible for monitoring bullying problems within the school. He or she should be permanently accessible for reporting cases of bullying.

A first measure is the *incident interview*. The aim of this interview is to put an immediate end to a concrete case of bullying. An incident interview may be conducted by any adult person working at the school.

A second measure is the *recovery interview*. During this interview, the core teacher and the victim talk through the incident. The main aim is to seek ways of repairing the damage sustained and to ensure that the rules laid down by the behaviour code are applied whenever infringements occur. The core teacher should also see to it that the measures taken in view of the pupil's recovery are implemented.

In addition, a *supportive interview* may be conducted between the core teacher and the victims. The incidents should be talked through with the victims so that they can express their feelings and find support; they should not have the feeling that they are alone with their problem. The core teacher and the pupil may also reflect on ways of improving the situation. The incident interview, the recovery interview as well as the supportive interview have short-term effects.

The *guidance interview*, conversely, aims at long-term effects. Both the victimised child and the bully can be counselled by, for instance, the core teacher or a member of a guidance centre (PMS) or the Centre for Mental Health Care (CGGZ), in order to tackle the victim's lack of social skills in his response to bullying on the one hand, and the bully's maladjusted social behaviour on the other.

The role to be played by the parents

The group of parents to be reached is a heterogeneous group: it includes the parents of victimised children, the parents of children bullying others, as well as the parents of children from the middle group.

Parents should first of all be sensitised to the problem of bullying. Their cooperation is important if a consensus is to be reached on communication and rules in both the school and the home environment. Besides, it is equally important that the school should encourage parents to report cases of bullying. Parents should be involved in the action programme at the school level, so that they can be informed, sensitised and motivated into making an active contribution towards reporting bullying behaviour.

Finally, a number of tips are given to the parents as regards intervening in bullying. There are tips for the parents of children from the middle group (e.g. discussing bullying, indicating that it is normal to react to bullying), for the parents of bullies (e.g. censuring bullying, keeping an eye on the situation if one knows one's child is a bully) as well as for the parents of bullied children (e.g. the recognition of signals, contacting the school) (Deboutte, 1995; Stevens and Van Oost, 1995b).

Conclusion

Concrete action in the field of bullying implies sensitisation, reporting and intervening. Sensitising boosts the involvement of pupils and adults, so that the problem of bullying is taken seriously and the school climate is positively affected. Encouraging reporting is equally important, since it makes the children realise that bullying is not tolerated; besides, it improves the communication on bullying in school and stimulates the victims of bullying to talk things over with their parents or teachers. Finally, it is important to intervene at all the distinct levels with a view to preventing and/or tackling the problem of bullying. The extent to which this method yields results is being investigated by Stevens and Van Oost; the results of this evaluation research are expected in late 1998.

Acknowledgements

Our special thanks to Barbara Walgrave and Anita Rimaux for their assistance in data collection for this chapter.

References

BDJ-Jeugd and Vrede, *Pesten – Educatieve set.* [This set consists of a series of lessons for teachers concerning bullying, the software package 'Pestkop' (Bully), the role play 'Lode and Louise'.] BDJ-Jeugd en Vrede, Van Elewijckstraat 35, 1050 Brussels.

Centrum voor Informatie en Documentatie (Departement Onderwijs) (1997) *Pesten op school: een bloemlezing, knipsels uit dag- en weekbladen, 1991–1996* (Bullying in school: a collection of cuttings from dailies and weeklies, 1991–1996). Brussels.

Deboutte, G. (1995) *Pesten, gedaan ermee! Hoe omgaan met pesterijen? Tips voor ouders, leerkrachten en begeleiding* (Bullying, stop it! How to deal with bullying? Tips for parents, teachers and counsellors). Brussels: BDJ-Jeugd en Vrede, Bakermat uitgevers.

De Groof, J. and Van Haver, T. (1993) *De school op rapport* (The school taken to task). Kapellen: Pelckmans.

Dekeyser, F. (1993). *Violence à l'école: Un point de vue enseignant* (Violence in school: A teacher's point of view). Brussels: Direction générale de l'enseignement secondaire.

De Meyer, A., Heurckmans, N. and Vanbilloen, E. (1994) *Pesten, een preventiepakket voor het onderwijs* (Bullying, a preventive set for schools). Leuven/Amersfoort: Acco.

Lambrechts, A. (1989) *Word je ook gepest? Een handleiding voor ouders en leerkrachten* (Are you also being bullied? A manual for parents and teachers). Brussels: Overleg Kinder- en Jongeren telefoons.

Ministère de l'éducation, de la recherche et de la formation (1996) *Le système éducatif en communauté française de Belgique* (The educational system in the French community of Belgium). Brussels: Secrétariat Général.

Ministerie van de Vlaamse Gemeenschap, Departement Onderwijs, Ministère de l'éducation, de la recherche et de la formation, Verwaltung der Deutschsprachigen Gemeinschaft, Abteilung Unterricht (1991) *Het educatief bestel in België. Van convergentie naar divergentie* (The educational system in Belgium. From convergence to divergence) (OESO: doorlichting van het educatief overheidsbeleid) (OECD: a study into educational government policy). Brussels/Eupen.

Ministerie van de Vlaamse Gemeenschap (1996) *Het onderwijs in Vlaanderen* (Education in Flanders). Brussels: Administratie Buitenlands beleid.

Nationaal Instituut voor de Statistiek (1996a) *Enquête naar de beroepsbevolking* (Enquiry into the working population). Brussels.

Nationaal Instituut voor de Statistiek (1996b) *Statistische Studiën* (Statistical studies). Brussels.

Olweus, D. (1991) *Treiteren op school* (Bullying in school). Amersfoort/Leuven: College Uitgevers/Acco (Dutch edn).

Peeters, R., Maes, L. and Van De Mieroop, E. (1995) *Jongeren en gezondheid in Vlaanderen* (Youngsters and health in Flanders). Ghent/Antwerp Universities.

Project Group K.U. Leuven (1996) *Pesten in jeugdwerk. Hoe omgaan met pesterijen? Tips voor jeugdwerkers* (Bullying in youth work. How to deal with bullying? Tips for youth workers). Brussels: BDJ-Jeugd en Vrede.

Stevens, V. and Van Oost, P. (1994a) Pesten op school: Een eerste deelonderzoek naar het optreden van pesten en gepest worden bij kinderen tussen 10 en 14 jaar (Bullying in school: A monograph on the incidence of bullying and being bullied among children aged 10 to 14). *Tijdschrift voor Klinische Psychologie*, 3, 239–259.

Stevens, V. and Van Oost, P. (1994b) *Pesten op school. Een actieprogramma* (Bullying at school. An action programme). Ghent University.

Stevens, V. and Van Oost, P. (1995a) Pesten op school: de rol van de PMS centra (Bullying in school: the role of the guidance centres). *Caleidoscoop*, 3, 34–37.

Stevens, V. and Van Oost, P. (1995b) Pesten op school: Een actieprogramma (Bullying in school: An action programme). *Handboek leerlingenbegeleiding. Probleemgedrag aanpakken* (Manual for pupil guidance. Tackling problem behaviour), Kluwer, 15, 93–100.

Tyriard, W. (1995) *Leerkrachten als slachtoffer van criminaliteit en afwijkend gedrag van leerlingen* (Teachers as victims of criminality and deviant behaviour). Eindverhandeling: Ghent University, School voor Criminologie.

Vandersmissen, V. and Thys, L. (1993) Onderzoek naar de schoolbeleving in Vlaanderen. Omgang met medeleerlingen (Study into school experiences in Flanders. Contacts with fellow-pupils). *Caleidoscoop*, 4, 4–9.

Van Mosseveld e, E. (1996) *De klas in de hand. Omgaan met en (bege)leiden van leerlingen* (Controlling the class. Dealing with, leading and guiding pupils). Leuven: Acco.

Van Oost, P. and Stevens, V. (1994–1995) Pesten op school: ontwikkelen en introduceren van een actieprogramma. Achtergronden, structurele voorwaarden, de rol van het beleid (Bullying in school: development and introduction of an action programme. Backgrounds, structural conditions, the role of policy). *Tijdschrift voor onderwijsrecht en -beleid*, 2, 100–108.

Verhoeven, J., Vandenberghe, R. and Van Damme, J. (1992) *Schoolmanagement en kwaliteitsverbetering van het onderwijs. Een empirisch onderzoek in secundaire scholen* (School management and quality improvement in education. An empirical study in secondary schools). Leuven: Departement Sociologie – Sociologisch Onderzoeksinstituut.

Vettenburg, N. (1991) *Welzijnswerk en onderwijs. Mogelijkheden en moeilijkheden in de samenwerking* (Welfare work and education. Possibilities and problems in cooperation). Leuven: Onderzoeksgroep Jeugdcriminologie.

Vettenburg, N. (1994) Geweld in de school (Violence in the school). *Pretekst*, 2, 20–22.

Vettenburg, N. and Biermans, N. (1995) *Samenwerking onderwijs en welzijnswerk* (The cooperation between education and welfare work). Leuven: Onderzoeksgroep Jeugdcriminologie.

Further reading

Comite Bijzondere Jeugdzorg (1995) Pesten (Bullying). In *Probleemgedrag op school. Een handleiding*. Brugge.

De Cock, J. (1994) *Pesten op school: preventieproject voor een pestvrije school* (Bullying in school: prevention project for a bullying-free school). Leuven: Licentiaatsverhandeling Criminologie, K.U. Leuven.

Eykerman, M. and Thijs, L. (1991) School: harde of zachte sector? Of: oorzaken en gevolgen van een 'ik-laat-me-niet-doen' stijl (School: the social sector? Or: causes and consequences of an 'I-will-not-be-bullied' style). *Welwijs*, 2, 17–19.

Feys, R. (1996) Pesten, agressie ... op school: plaag van de stoute leraars? (Bullying, aggression ... in school: plague of the naughty teachers?). *Onderwijskrant*, 92, 20–34.

Ganty, J. (1996) *La violence scolaire en Communauté française de Belgique* (Violence in school in the French community of Belgium). Academia Bruylant.

Nuytemans, A. (1993) Een verpest klasklimaat: over pestkoppen en de kop van jut in de klas (A ruined climate in the class: about bullies and victims). *Caleidoscoop*, 4, 10–15.

Vaillant, M. (1996) Violences et écoles (Violence and schools). *Journal du droit des jeunes*, 155, 205–210.

Vandenbroeck, M. (1992) Pesterijen op school. *Handboek voor leerlingenbegeleiding. Probleemgedrag aanpakken* (Bullying at school. Manual for pupil guidance. Tackling problem behaviour), 5, 1–17.

Van der Meer, B. (1994) Een vijfsporenaanpak van het pestprobleem op school (A five-track approach to the problem of bullying in school). *Caleidoscoop*, extra edn, 62–66.

Vanhaelemeesch, P. (1992) Pesten op school: een ware pest (Bullying in school: a real plague). *Pedagogische periodiek Christene School*, 6, 48–56.

Watson, A. (1992) 'De zondebok' op school ... Wat doe je eraan? ('The scapegoat' at school. What to do about it?). *Pedagogische periodiek Christene School*, 3, 16–20.

Wielemans, G. (1996) Pesten op school. Over zin en onzin van preventieprojecten (Bullying in school. On the (non)sense of preventive projects). *Welwijs*, 2, 38–41.

Wilkins, J. (1995) Pesten bij jongeren, V.C.O.V. biedt preventiepakket aan (Bullying among youngsters. V.C.O.V. offers preventive set). *Brug*, 3, 6–8.

Periodicals

(1991) De zondebok: schoolpesten (The scapegoat: bullying in school). *Klasse*, 19, 19.

(1993) Pesten op school. Aanpakken voor het te laat is (Bullying in school. Do something before it is too late). *Klasse*, 35, 4–5.

(1993) De pestkoppen krijgen vrij spel (Bullies at large). *Klasse*, 38, 12.

(1994) Leraars kunnen pestkoppen stoppen (Teachers can stop bullies). *Klasse*, 49, 24–25.

(1995) Slachtoffer: leraar (Victim: teacher). *Klasse*, 58, 28–29.

13 The Netherlands

Josine Junger-Tas

Introduction: social and cultural background of The Netherlands

Some demographic data

The Netherlands is a small country (34,000 km^2), but with fifteen million inhabitants it is – like Japan – densely populated. An important development is the so-called "greying" of the population. The proportion of persons of age 50 and over is increasing, while the juvenile population declines. The age group 12 to 17 was about 1,500,000 in 1980 and 1,100,000 in 1992, a decline of 27 percent. This demographic change has an impact on the number of juveniles who come into conflict with the law, although this impact should not be overstated.

Social, economic and cultural changes in western society in general and in The Netherlands in particular have produced important changes in the family structure and the family culture. Divorce rates have increased, one of the consequences of which is a growing number of single-parent households, generally headed by the mother. Moreover, young people wait longer before getting married as well as having children. Many of them live together without being married, and although most of them marry eventually when there is a child on the way, the number of couples living together outside wedlock has been increasing. Only 40 percent of the population were living as a family in 1994 and the prognosis is that this proportion will decrease to 35 percent in 2010. About 5 percent of all households are single-parent families, which is 12 percent of all families (SCP, 1994). A parallel phenomenon is the increase in small households in the large cities. Families with children are disappearing and are moving to the suburbs, while the cities are increasingly populated by single- and two-person households: in 1994 in Holland's large cities this proportion was 60 percent.

Another change in this respect is the declining birth rate: not only do women wait longer before having their first child, but families are considerably smaller than they were in the 1950s: 81 percent of all families have an average of one or two children.

One of the consequences of these widespread population changes is that modern western countries – and The Netherlands is no exception – grow increasingly dependent on immigrant populations for the maintenance of a balanced buildup of their population. In my country the immigrant population is essentially composed of people coming from Turkey, Morocco, Surinam and the Dutch Antilles, as well as a growing number of asylum seekers from Africa and Central Asia. These ethnic minority groups made up about 7.6 percent of the population in 1994, but as they have higher birth rates than the Dutch, the prognosis is that their share will be 13.5 percent of the total population by 2010. As ethnic minority groups are heavily concentrated in the large cities, it is expected that by 2010 immigrants will make up 15 percent of the adult city population and 45 percent of the population under age 20. This is considered to be a problematic development, as ethnic minorities are characterized by poverty, low educational attainment and a high level of unemployment.

The socioeconomic context

The average education level of the Dutch population has substantially increased since the Second World War. In 1960, 90 percent of the population had at most some extension of primary education; in 1975 this was still 75 percent, but in 1990 it was no more than 40 percent.

Until the 1990s low-skilled jobs were still available for those who could not meet the requirements of postmodern society, but unfortunately these jobs are disappearing at a fast rate. In most of the OECD countries employment increased in the 1960s, stabilized in the 1970s, declined in the 1980s, then recovered somewhat at the end of the 1980s, to fall again at the beginning of the 1990s. Unemployment rose from 0.7 percent of the labor force in 1960 to 6.5 percent in 1994. Unemployment has struck mainly industrial enterprises, construction companies and the transport sector and it is the low-skilled, low-paid, full-time jobs that have disappeared. About 35 percent to 39 percent of the total population is employed, which means that every worker must earn a living for 1.5 to two other persons. This has always been the case since the beginning of the twentieth century; what has changed, however, is the nature of the support: informal support by the family or the church has been replaced by formal social security benefits. According to data from our Central Bureau of Statistics, these benefits have increased from 1 percent in the 1930s to 28 percent in 1989. The share of the welfare system in Holland's net national income in the 1990s is about 31 percent. Its share in the administration's spending has been stable since the 1970s and amounts to about 43 percent. The system has led to some redistribution of income and to the flattening of the total income curve. However, in the last fifteen years the number of households living below the povery line has increased from 4 percent to 7 percent. These households are found essentially among single-parent families, low-skilled persons, the elderly, and ethnic minorities.

Actually, the government is reforming the welfare system by trying to increase employment possibilities, to reduce the recourse to state assistance in cases of long-term illness or invalidity, to shift a number of risks from a collective responsibility to private insurance, and to (slightly) lower the benefits.

Finally, we should mention the growing participation of mothers in the labor force. The participation rate of married women with children in The Netherlands increased by (depending on age) 10 percent to 15 percent during the last five years. For women under 30 with one child, participation has risen from 17 percent in 1980 to 53 percent in 1992. However, more than half of the women are working in predominantly low-paid, semi-skilled, part-time jobs, which allows them to combine family responsibilities with paid work. Indeed, most of the burden of household chores and the upbringing of children continues to be borne by women. Although the participation of fathers in their children's education is growing, progress in this respect is slow.

Some sociocultural variables

Dutch society is characterized by growing individualization and secularization. Individualization touches every sphere of life including the family: in 1965 only one person in six had no objection to paid labor for mothers with school-age children; in 1991 three-quarters of the Dutch population approved of working mothers. The family as a center of recreation and consumption has lost influence, while growing emphasis is placed on individual recreational activities and individual consumption patterns. It is clear that these changes make it considerably harder for parents to exercise control and supervise their children. Juveniles spend more time without any adult supervision than ever before. Parents often do not know their children's whereabouts nor who their companions are.

In a study on changing patterns of social control (Junger-Tas and Terlouw, 1991) it was found that since 1960 young people spend practically every weekend away from home: they go out at night more frequently than before, not with adults but with large groups of peers; they come home at ever later hours, their mobility has increased dramatically so they often go to bars or discos in neighboring cities, and their consumption of alcohol, soft drugs and different kinds of pills has increased. As a consequence of the combination of diminished adult control and increased use of alcohol and stimulant (soft) drugs, much delinquency is committed at night and on weekends, of which parents are not aware.

Secularization is expressed in a decline of religious beliefs, less frequent church-going and the demise of church life in general: it touches both the Protestant and the Roman Catholic church and above all young people. Many churches have been transformed into cultural centers, which shows the extent of the change in traditional religious and cultural values in The Netherlands.

The school system

The Dutch school system is not very different from other systems in Europe. Compulsory schooling stretches from age 5 through age 16; for children aged 4 to 6 there are nurseries. Primary school includes six school grades and thus covers roughly ages 6 through 12. Secondary education may include four, five, or six grades, depending on what follows in terms of education. Four years of secondary education will either consist of vocational training or lead to some more elaborate form of professional education, while five years of secondary schooling is a preparation for higher professional training in, for example, nursing, social work, or technical professions. Finally six years of education will almost always lead to further studies at university.

School violence in The Netherlands: nature of the problem

Violence in schools may take different forms: it may mean violence by teachers towards students, violence of students against teachers, school bullying of students directed at some other students, vandalism, and destruction of school property.

Violence against teachers

This problem has not been extensively studied, particularly in Europe. It has been studied in the United States (Kratcoski, 1985); a nationwide opinion poll by the National Institute of Education in 1978 found that more than 5 percent of teachers in average schools and 7.7 percent in large schools had been victims of violence in the twelve months before the survey. Since these proportions had been lower in the past it seems there is a rising trend in violence against teachers. In Europe there is some impressionistic evidence of this problem in France (Defrance, 1994), England (Newman, 1980), and The Netherlands (press reviews). A small Dutch survey among university freshmen revealed that 25 percent of them knew at least one teacher in their secondary school who had been the victim of threats, while 15 percent knew at least one teacher who had been a victim of physical assault (Zandbergen and Hauber, 1992). The students attributed the violence to the weak character of the teacher and the fact that he or she was unable to keep order in the classroom. Some students considered the violence as a consequence of the authoritarian attitude of the teacher. This type of school violence seems to be more frequent than would appear, but unfortunately we lack valid research in this field.

School bullying

According to Farrington (1993), bullying is "repeated oppression, psychological or physical, of a less powerful person by a more powerful one." Bullying includes physical, verbal, or psychological attack or intimidation that causes fear, distress, or harm to the victim and may include name-calling, pushing, shoving, hitting or kicking, mocking, rejecting or threatening one or more pupils.

One of the earliest European studies of bullying among boys aged 12 to 16 has been done in Sweden by Olweus (1978). Olweus based his information on peer nominations and teacher ratings. Olweus found that about 5 percent of the boys were pronounced bullies and 5.3 percent less pronounced ones, as well as 5.4 percent who were pronounced victims and 6.1 percent less pronounced ones. Later studies have been based on self-reports both of bullying and victimization. Such studies have been done in Ireland (O'Moore and Hillary, 1989), Scotland (Mellor, 1990), France (Choquet *et al.*, 1990), England (Smith, 1991; Smith and Levan, 1995), Germany (Bach *et al.*, 1984; Holtappels, 1985; Schwind *et al.*, 1995) and The Netherlands (Junger, 1990; Mooij, 1992, 1994).

At this point a word of caution seems necessary. Whether we talk about school violence or about school bullying, most of these behaviors are not isolated but are part of more generalized delinquent behavior. Many studies have demonstrated that juvenile delinquent behavior is not characterized by specialization; that is, one does not find juveniles who specialize either in property offenses or in violent offenses. Juvenile delinquency is versatile, which means that delinquent juveniles commit all types of offenses (Hindelang *et al.*, 1981; Junger-Tas *et al.*, 1983). This simply means that in most cases school bullying will be part of a broader pattern of antisocial and aggressive behavior and this fact has implications for the type of causal explanations one is looking for.

In The Netherlands two major studies have been conducted by Mooij, the first in primary schools and secondary schools (1992) and the second exclusively in schools for secondary education (1994). The first study examined 66 schools with 88 classrooms; 1065 pupils in primary school and 1055 in secondary schools participated in the survey. The study made use of the questionnaire developed by Olweus (1987), although some adaptations were made to the Dutch situation. Following suggestions by Olweus, six bullying scales were constructed:

- *Direct bullying:* being bullied for a long time, in school, in the playground and on the way to or from school in different ways, including verbal and physical bullying;
- *Indirect bullying:* involves social exclusion (having few friends, being shunned, feeling isolated);
- *Bullying other children:* bullies for a long time, frequently, and everywhere;
- *Rejecting bullying:* implies hating children who bully, and helping children who are bullied;
- *Bullying the teacher:* one or several children participate in annoying one of the teachers;

- *Stopping the process:* efforts by the teacher, by some of the children or by someone else (on the way to and from school) to stop bullying.

Mooij found that being a bully and being a victim were not related, which means that bullies are usually not victims of bullying by another pupil. However, where bullying becomes a collective group process the two phenomena are related.

Bullying appears to be related to age: the proportion of pupils claiming that they have not been bullied during the school year is 39 percent in primary schools, but 71 percent in secondary schools. Young children appear to bully more often and are also bullied more often than older children. However, within the classroom it is the relatively older boys (and not girls) who are the bullies. Being bullied appears to be related to having a somewhat isolated position in the group; that is, victims tend to be not accepted socially by the other children. On the other hand, victimization does not seem to be related to any deviation from the average intellectual level in the classroom; that is, victims were no more or less intelligent than class mates. Finally, on the basis of a continuum according to the frequency of being bullied, Mooij made some estimations as to the number of children in the education system who were bullied. These are shown in Table 13.1.

Mooij also looked at school factors that were related to bullying. He found that task differentiation, i.e. introducing a number of different learning tasks involving various small groups working on these tasks, was related to less frequent bullying. Although there was no relationship between the number of pupils in the classroom, it appeared that a teacher who carefully coaches social group processes can control bullying. Moreover, a high level of supervision in the school is related to less bullying and being bullied.

The second study (1994) was limited to secondary schools: 71 schools, 100 classrooms, 130 teachers and 1998 pupils aged 15 to 16 participated in this study. It looked at a broader topic than the first study and was extended to all "violence in schools." Mooij distinguished three kinds of perpetrators of school violence:

Table 13.1 Estimates of the number of children bullied in the Dutch education system by bullying frequency: school year 1990–1991

Bullying frequency	*Primary schools N = 1,442,902 (%)*	*Secondary schools N = 916,485 (%)*
From time to time	23	6
Once a week or more	8	2
Several times a week	4	2

Source: Mooij, 1992, p. 103

- verbal violence (name-calling, creating disorder, bullying);
- more serious behavior, including vandalism, theft, blackmail, extortion, or using a weapon;
- planned violence, which includes physical violence with weapons in or outside the school, and/or sexual harassment of girls.

I found this distinction rather confusing, because I do not think mixing violence against persons with vandalism and property offenses provides us with good measures of (school) violence. So with respect to our topic I will restrict myself to verbal and physical violence against pupils.

According to teachers' reports, over a period of six months 8 percent of the pupils were sometimes victims of bullying, 7 percent sometimes used verbal or physical violence against other pupils and 18 percent disrupted the lessons. According to the pupils, 15 percent of them had been victims of physical violence at some time. Victims were generally seen as less sympathetic, while bullies enjoyed some popularity. Contrary to his earlier study, Mooij now found a relationship between bullying and victimization. Many bullies were occasionally victims and vice versa.

In Junger's study (1990), which included 800 boys aged 12 to 18 from different ethnic groups, 20 percent of the boys interviewed were physically harassed from time to time and 6 percent quite often. The prevalence of verbal abuse was 26 percent from time to time and 7 percent very often. Her results do not differ greatly from what had been found by Mooij. An interesting finding was that there was no difference in victimizations by bullying between the various ethnic groups: Turkish, Moroccans, Surinamese and Dutch.

Bullies and victims: background factors

In order to get a clear picture of possible causes of bullying it seems useful to distinguish between three different types of causal factors: child factors, family factors and school factors. However, it should be clear that there is no one particular factor that could explain the problem of bullying. Different factors are operating in producing the outcomes and there is generally considerable interaction between them. But let us review the evidence shown in research.

Child factors

According to Olweus (1978), bullies are boys who have an aggressive personality. They are confident, strong, and have positive attitudes towards violence. They get considerable attention because of their violent behavior which gives them pleasure, and they recruit other boys to participate. They are not doing very well in school and they do not like the teachers. Bullies are rather popular among their co-students although in secondary schools popularity also seems to be related to school achievement. Mooij also found in secondary schools that bullies did not like school, were troublesome in class, often carried some sort of weapon – often a knife or a stick – and used soft drugs (Mooij, 1994).

Farrington (1993) warns us that bullying is not an isolated phenomenon, but is an expression of more general aggressive tendencies that show considerable stability over the years, and are part of a larger syndrome of antisocial behavior. Indeed, bullying tends to persist over time: Olweus (1978) found that nearly two-thirds of bullies at the time of the study were also bullies the following year. Others also showed that bullying does not stand on its own but is part of a more general aggressive behavior pattern. For example, in my country Verhulst and Althaus (1988) have collected information from 1412 parents of children aged between 4 and 14 in 1983, and then again two years later at age 6 to 16. A number of aggressive or aggressive related behaviors, such as starting fights, bullying, arguing, disobedience, impulsivity, stubbornness, screaming, demanding attention, showed significant stability. Reports from teachers on aggressive and externalizing behaviors were also quite stable over a period of four years (Verhulst and van der Ende, 1991). Fortunately, most children become less aggressive over the years although differences in aggressiveness between children remain.

Victims have low confidence and low status in the group: they are physically weak, fearful, unsure and nervous. They are often physically less attractive. They sometimes have a physical handicap, such as wearing glasses, small stature, hearing problems, or obesity (Farrington, 1993). They are often too intimidated to ask parents or teachers for help, fearing retaliation from their aggressors. Other Dutch research (Verhulst and Althaus, 1988) showed that victims tend to feel lonely, persecuted, anxious, and depressed. However, these feelings were less stable than aggressive behavior patterns. Over a period of two years these children tended to become less anxious, depressed, shy, or withdrawn.

Family factors

Bullies come from a troubled family situation and have parents who use erratic and harsh discipline methods. They are often rejected by their parents and disciplined by physical punishment. Moreover, violence (fighting, hitting and kicking) is often encouraged by parents (Bach, 1984; Holtappels, 1985). Bullying is related to a lack of affective relationship with parents. Farrington (1993) found in his own longitudinal research among 411 London boys aged 8 to 12 that the most important predictors of bullying were physical neglect by the age of 8, convicted parents by the age of 10, low school attainment at the age of 11 and low interest of the father in the boys' leisure activities at the age of 12. It is important to mention again that these factors also predict delinquency and violence in general and not only bullying. As for victims, parents are often not aware of what is happening at school, because their children do not tell them and their teachers rarely intervene.

Farrington and West showed considerable intergenerational continuity in bullying. For example, bullying at age 14, being unpopular at ages 12 to 14, having poor reading skills and gambling heavily at age 18 all predicted having a child who bullies at age 32 (Farrington and West, 1990). As for victimizations, Farrington and West also found that boys who were unpopular, who had few friends, who suffered poor child-rearing at age 8 to 10, who were nervous and regular smokers at age 14, tended to have victimized children at age 32.

School factors

According to Mooij's study children in primary school are often bullied on the way to and from school. Other studies found that most bullying takes place in the playground when supervision is minimal (Farrington, 1993). School size or the number of children in the classroom does not seem to make any difference with respect to the extent of bullying (Mooij, 1994; Olweus, 1978), although schools do differ in the amount of bullying that takes place. Important factors in this respect are the quality of the teaching and the intensity of supervision in the classroom and playground. An increase of school violence appeared to be related to teachers who are either too strict or unable to keep order in the classroom, and pupils who have a strong dislike of school. School violence shows a relationship to less attachment to the family as well as to the school, although negative school experiences seem to play a very important role.

With respect to secondary schools, Mooij created the following typology based on his data. It shows a scale ranging from schools with little violence to schools that have considerable violence problems (Mooij, 1994, p. 174):

- *Low level of school violence:* large, public grammar schools, which have contacts with social and psychological agencies in the community; schools where the pupils are not very interested in education, but which are considerably "pupil-oriented."
- *Medium level of school violence:* schools with a rather high degree of truancy, smoking, drinking and disturbances; "special" vocational education schools in large cities serving pupils with learning difficulties.
- *High level of school violence:* schools in the four largest Dutch cities with problems of school motivation and achievement, a high degree of delinquent behavior, including violence, soft drug use and the presence of weapons. Schools where teachers consider the pupils as violent; pupils are said to use hard drugs.

This typology seems to suggest that schools in socially disadvantaged and inner-city areas where unemployment, poverty, drugs and crime and family problems are rampant would present more problems of violence and bullying than schools in quiet middle-class areas. In fact this suggestion is confirmed by research in Canada (Ziegler and Rosenstein-Manner, 1991) and in England (Whitney and Smith, 1993).

Problems at home, such as divorce and unemployment, are related to problems in school, such as repeating classes and soft drug use. This may lead to contacts with other, possibly violent, soft drug users. In this respect it appears that a school climate of pupil-orientation and monitoring social processes in the classroom is very important in maintaining school attachment and a low level of violence. In particular, acceptance and respect for individual pupils and social support in the case of school problems are crucial. If these are absent, the pupil can only choose between two negative alternatives: either truant or drop-out of school, or participate in violent behavior in order to protect him- or herself.

An English study also showed considerable variation in bullying between schools (Stephenson and Smith, 1989); headteachers in low bullying schools tend to express clear views on bullying and attach importance to its control and prevention. The important question here is whether the influence of the school would be more strongly related to bullying than the characteristics of the children when they enter the school. For example, Farrington found that despite great variation among schools in rates of delinquency, the influence of schools on delinquency levels disappeared once pupil intake variables were taken into account (Farrington, 1972). However, Rutter *et al.* (1979) concluded that secondary schools did have an impact on delinquency rates independently of pupil intake with respect to social class and intelligence.

Considering the fact that in the life of young people situational variables and opportunity do play a considerable role in committing offenses and showing violence (Felson, 1994), it would seem that schools should be able to have a serious impact on bullying. However, teachers cannot intervene unless they have been told about bullying incidents. Different studies indicate that many children do not tell teachers what has happened (Mellor, 1990; O'Moore and Hillary, 1991; Ziegler and Rosenstein-Manner, 1991). In fact only up to half of the victims turn to teachers for help. This is a serious matter in view of the long-term effects that bullying and victimization may have on later life. If nothing is done, victims may find it difficult to concentrate on their school work and may be more and more afraid to go to school. Olweus found in his Norwegian study that even seven to ten years later, victims tended to have low self-esteem and feelings of depression. Moreover, bullies may be encouraged by the impunity of their aggressive behavior and develop a criminal career. Olweus also found that 60 percent of the bullies were convicted of a criminal offense up to age 24 and their re-conviction rate was four times higher than that of non-bullies (Olweus, 1991).

The prevention and control of bullying

One of the reasons that supports the idea that schools have an impact on the behavior of children is the fact that the school is so important in the life of the child. The school has the same meaning for children as a job has for their parents: they learn very quickly that school performance determines to a large extent their school status, they are rewarded for their achievements and punished for their failures, they learn what social hierarchy is like and know their own place in that hierarchy, they find friends or companions in misfortune, and finally they function in a social community that transmits important cultural values and behavioral norms (Junger-Tas, 1987).

In that respect a first question one might ask is what specific factors make a school effective in terms of teaching as well as of social environment. Some answers can be given on the basis of research (Edmonds, 1986; Mooij, 1992, 1994; Rutter *et al.*, 1986).

A first important element is the *quality of the principal* of the school. The principals of effective schools are instructional as well as social leaders.

A second set of factors has to do with *school focus*; that is, the instructional emphasis and the social and moral mission of the school. The school focus should be known and supported by all staff. The emphasis on academic performance should involve setting clear standards, imposing and controlling homework and soliciting pupil initiative and responsibility. The school should set high standards both in school achievement and in social behavior.

A third set of factors relates to *school climate* or *school ethos*: effective schools are safer, cleaner, more orderly, and quieter than ineffective schools. Considerable attention is given to the environment in which the children work. Broken windows, burnt out light bulbs, and dirt in the corners are quickly dealt with and there is a comfortable and well-cared-for school environment. In effective schools teachers set high standards in personal relations by way of their own behavior. When the children trust their teachers they are willing to consult them about personal problems and accept their counseling.

A final dimension is *classroom observation and classroom management*. Teachers in ineffective schools vary considerably in the imposition of discipline, making it a function of pupil characteristics, such as sex, race, and social class. Some are more lenient, others are harsher according to pupil characteristics. Teachers in effective schools make it clear that they expect that *all* children are capable of reaching a certain level of academic achievement, social competence and classroom behavior. Disciplinary dealing with disruptions should be swift and efficient. Feedback should continuously be given as well as frequent and appropriate use of praise for good achievement and behavior. There are ample opportunities for children to take responsibilities and participate in the running of the school.

Summing up the main characteristics of the effective school with respect to bullying one may mention the following three elements: a school-wide set of standards or norms of school performance and behavior; an acceptance by the pupil body of these norms, and a positive teacher response to good pupil behavior and achievements (Rutter *et al.*, 1986).

Returning to the Dutch situation, Mooij's research on school violence and bullying has demonstrated that not all schools are effective, and that unfortunately school bullying is a problem in many schools. An additional question therefore is how to prevent and control bullying. A useful way of coping with the problem is to distinguish different degrees of intensity of prevention measures and addressing these to offenders, to victims and to the school situation in which bullying occurs (Mutsaers, 1995).

With respect to (potential) offenders, attention should be given to school attendance, learning problems, and discipline. Truancy control and the control of school rules are important, followed by remedial teaching or special programs for children with learning problems. The school should also have good relations and communication with social and psychological agencies in the community and with the (juvenile) police. Unfortunately, Dutch policy measures in this field have been introduced only recently and there are as yet not many effect evaluations that can tell us what programs are the most effective.

Such studies have been conducted in Britain (Rutter *et al.*, 1979, 1986; Smith and Sharp, 1994), in the United States (Hawkins *et al.*, 1991) and in Canada (Tremblay *et al.*, 1991). In the Hawkins study the experimental classes received special treatment at home and school, designed to improve their bonding both to their families and to school. The parents were trained to reinforce socially desirable behavior. The teachers were trained in adequate classroom management, such as to provide clear instructions and expectations to children, to reward positive behavior and to teach children pro-social ways of solving problems. Eighteen months later the boys in the experimental classes were significantly less aggressive than the boys in the control group (see Chapter 17).

Tremblay and his colleagues conducted a study on a group of disruptive boys aged 7 to 9. Bullies as well as victims received social skills training and were then followed for a number of years. Social skills training for bullies included themes such as "what to do when I am angry." Victims were taught "how to react to teasing." Parent training included monitoring the child's behavior and giving positive reinforcements for pro-social behavior and negative reinforcements for negative behavior. Outcome data indicated that the experimental group scored considerably lower on bullying than the control group (see Chapter 18).

Social skills training can be very helpful for victims, as the study by Tremblay demonstrates. It might also help to have special "confidential persons" within the school to whom children can turn when they have problems. These problems may be anything, ranging from troubles at home, such as divorce or physical and sexual abuse, to school problems, such as (sexual) harassment or being bullied by other pupils. Social skills training might make children more assertive and capable in handling aggression, while a neutral confidant gives them the opportunity to make complaints under the guarantee of anonymity.

A third and final aspect is the *school context*. We have already mentioned the importance of surveillance, classroom management, discipline, the control of school values and norms, and the involvement of pupils in the organization and running of the school. A "whole-school approach" has been tested by Olweus in Norway, combining general information on bullying to parents and pupils, a video about bullying, a self-report questionnaire and teacher training (Olweus, 1991). The effects of the program were evaluated in 42 Bergen schools. Both the prevalence of victimizations and of bullying had substantially decreased (see Chapter 1).

A similar study has been reported by Smith and Sharp (1994) on 23 schools in Sheffield, England. All the schools introduced a whole-school policy. In addition, each school chose from a menu of other interventions, primarily classroom based (e.g. drama or video work), playground based, or focused on individuals in need (e.g. assertiveness training, Pikas method). Most schools registered decreases in victimization, and an increased willingness of pupils to seek help. Generally, pupil involvement seemed important, plus a high level of activity and involvement by staff (see Chapter 5).

General prevention and intervention in Dutch schools

An important policy plan from the Dutch Ministry of Education stresses the following:

> It should be realized that lack of safety in schools cannot be viewed in isolation from the social environment of the school: the families in which the children are growing up, the neighborhood or area in which they live, the friends with whom they spend their leisure hours and the violence television introduces into their homes. The violence that manifests itself in schools has its origins mainly outside them. It reflects a general problem for which society as a whole is responsible.
>
> (Ministry of Education, 1996)

However, the Ministry adds, schools have a responsibility of their own and should not tolerate unsafe conditions. Of course schools do not operate in a vacuum. Table 13.2 shows how schools are situated within the general social structure.

It is clear that schools must play an active role in creating "safe schools." Different actions may be taken depending on the nature of the problem. When members of staff or pupils are subjected to physical threats or violence, the school should take immediate *ad hoc* measures to make sure that safety and order are restored. Action has to be taken by the school principal, teachers and support staff. However, in serious situations (for instance, in some of our inner-city schools), the school should seek assistance from the police and (if necessary) from judicial authorities. In cases of endemic pupil

Table 13.2 Structural embedding of schools in The Netherlands

Support structures	*Schools*	*Policies*
Police and judicial authorities	School board	Organization of school boards
National educational advisory centers/ Counseling services	Teacher–parent participation council	Ministry/Inspectorate
Local sociocultural work, sports and recreational organizations	School principal	Local authorities
Youth social work agencies	Teachers and educational support staff	Teaching unions
School medical service	Pupils	National pupils' action committee
Parent counseling services	Parents	National parents' association

violence school principals, teachers and support staff should attend special social skills training in order to improve effective intervention and to prevent escalation. Where schools as well as pupils suffer from vandalism and destruction, situational preventive measures related to the building, the premises around and access to the building should be taken.

With respect to bullying in schools the following measures should be considered in particular:

- the creation of a code of conduct, which should be supported and enforced by all participants in the school;
- social skills training for pupils (to some extent integrated in normal lessons); research has shown that good results may be achieved by these programs (Tremblay and Craig, 1995);
- the creation of "confidential mediators" to whom pupils, parents and teachers may turn with complaints of intimidation or violence;
- one or more staff members who liaise with social support structures outside the school;
- one or more staff members who liaise with parents who do not speak Dutch, and whose role it is to inform them, to explain to them the Dutch school system and to assist them when they want to speak with teachers or staff;
- the creation of telephone helplines to which pupils, parents and school staff may turn and ask for advice.

Some specific projects

Mental Health Agency project

The first program discussed here has been addressed to elementary schools only. A specialized folder with a set of educative activities was developed by the Mental Health Agency in one of the big cities for children aged between 10 and 12 years.

The elements in the folder include: a code of conduct for teachers and students; standard norms for surveillance in school and playground; a student mentor system whereby older students take care of younger ones; teacher staff meetings with feedback on problem solving; social skills training; classroom discussions about bullying; integration of anti-bullying teaching material and special projects about bullying; meetings and discussions with parents; individual counseling with offenders and victims, eventually followed by a referral to social work or mental health agencies. Evaluation research in eleven experimental primary schools and eleven control schools, four to nine months after a pre-test, showed that schools made their own selection of the program elements included in the folder and did not apply all of them. However, most schools adopted teacher meetings, classroom discussions and individual counseling with both bullies and victims. All other elements were rarely applied.

With respect to victimization, the situation in the experimental schools had clearly improved: according to pupils there were 13 percent less victims of bullying, while according to teachers this was 17 percent. In particular, destruction of the victim's property, verbal and physical violence and psychological pestering (ridiculing, social exclusion) had decreased. Reactions to bullying did not change much except for the fact that victims in the experimental schools more often turned to their peers for support and found themselves less often in an isolated position. Other school measures showed improvements in general pupil relationships and less social vulnerability of victims.

Considering the bullies, the research noted an increase in bullying in the control schools and a decrease in the experimental schools. According to the bullies' self-reports there was a decrease of 11.5 percent; according to the teachers this was even 27 percent (but the teachers' answers may be biased by a tendency to positive self-presentation). However, when asked about specific types of bullying, the bullies mentioned a decrease of similar types of bullying to those mentioned by the victims.

The researchers concluded that there was not one measure responsible for the positive change. It seems the fact that so much attention was given to the topic was in itself sufficient to produce change. In addition, individual counseling with bullies and victims in particular appeared to reduce verbal and physical violence, while surveillance reduced destruction of victims' property.

Ministry of Justice projects

A different approach has been taken by the Ministry of Justice and the (four) largest cities in The Netherlands. The Ministry of Justice has made contracts with the city boards, funding broad prevention programs addressed to children and young people. The programs include a number of projects in primary schools and secondary schools, the objectives of which are generally wider than just the prevention of bullying. Although one of the aims is to prevent or eliminate bullying, other objectives include the prevention of delinquent behavior, such as petty theft and aggressive acts.

One example of such an agreement is a contract made between the Minister of Justice, the chief prosecutor of the court district and the Mayor of The Hague, including such programs as the intensification of a project diverting young petty offenders from the Juvenile Justice system, assistance to victims and prevention activities in schools. The latter project is organized by the Hague Advisory Educational Center (HAEC), which has also been associated with the introduction of the "bullying folder." The HAEC has developed a number of successful methodologies in the field of prevention, such as: to reduce prejudice and discrimination in schools; to channel aggression through sports and discussions; to teach students to deal creatively with school frustrations; to reduce anonymity and to increase social control; and to make students more responsible, enabling them to participate in establishing school rules.

With respect to the prevention of delinquent and bullying behavior the HAEC has developed a special curriculum for teachers, containing essentially the following features:

- an analysis of the school: what happens in that particular school in terms of different kinds of problems; what are the school's strong and weak points;
- how can the school contribute to the development of (desired) norms and values;
- what is the pedagogical climate, and what are the school characteristics;
- what should be the role of the school in case of truancy, school dropout and bullying;
- the training of teacher skills to improve classroom climate;
- special forms of pupil guidance to improve pupils' self-image, to value their own background, to make positive choices and to use behavior alternatives;
- integration of the program with that of other youth agencies in the community;
- to make a plan of action and to evaluate the results.

The program, which will be run over three years, aims at long-term changes in pupil behavior as well as in teacher skills with respect to preventive school policies and improved school climate. The HAEC wants to achieve this by requiring compulsory attendance of two program participants per school in the city of The Hague. These participants will have to make a school analysis and a plan of action. Moreover, they will have to put the plan into operation, evaluate it and modify and improve it. In addition, participants are expected to instruct their colleagues so that they will also take part in the program.

Conclusion

We may conclude that as far as The Netherlands is concerned, the problem of school bullying has been the object of research, and its seriousness has been recognized. However, in most of the research bullying is considered as part of a more general pattern of deviant or delinquent behavior. Preventive measures have been taken or are in preparation. In a common effort both national authorities – the Ministry of Education, the Ministry of Welfare and Health and the Ministry of Justice – and municipal authorities are designing programs, some of which have been already evaluated. Considering the broad range of troublesome and antisocial behavior shown by bullies, many of the programs that have been designed have wider aims than merely the reduction of bullying. These programs strive to influence the schools' moral climate, to improve their teaching environment, to further the social behavior of bullies and victims, and to create safer and happier schools where children can perform well and can develop their cognitive and social potential, so as to become capable and responsible adults.

References

Bach, H. and Knöbel, R. (1984) *Verhaltensauffälligkeiten in der Schule*. Mainz.

Choquet, M., Menke, H. and Manfredi, R. (1990) Les conduites violentes et la consommation de drogues licites et illicites parmi les 13–16 ans. *Journal d'Alcoologie*, 2.

Defrance, B. (1994) La violence à l'école. *Revue de la Gendarmerie Nationale*, 173.

Edmonds, R. (1986) Characteristics of effective schools. In U. Neisser (ed.) *The school achievement of minority children*. Hillsdale, NJ: Erlbaum.

Farrington, D.P. (1972) Delinquency begins at home. *New Society*, 21, 495–497.

Farrington, D.P. (1993) Understanding and preventing bullying. In M. Tonry (ed.) *Crime and justice: A review of research*, vol. 17, 381–459. Chicago, Ill.: University of Chicago Press, pp. 381–458.

Farrington, D.P. and West, D. (1990) The Cambridge Study in delinquent development: A long-term follow-up of 411 London males. In H-J. Kerner and G. Kaiser (eds) *Criminality: Personality, behavior and life history*. Berlin: Springer Verlag, pp. 115–138.

Felson, M. (1994) *Crime and everyday life – insights and implications for society*. Thousand Oaks, CA: Pine Forge Press.

Hawkins, J.D., Von Cleve, E. and Catalano, R.F. (1991) Reducing early childhood aggression: Results of a primary prevention program. *Journal of the American Academy of Child and Adolescent Psychiatry*, 30, 208–217.

Hindelang, M., Hirschi, Tr. and Weis, J. (1981) *Measuring delinquency*. Beverly Hills, CA: Sage Publications.

Holtappels, H.G. (1985) Schülerprobleme und abweichendes Schülerverhalten aus der Schülerperspektive. *Zeitschrift für Sozialitionsforschung und Erziehungssociologie*, 5.

Junger, M. (1990) Intergroup bullying and racial harassment in The Netherlands. *Sociology and Social Research*, 74, 65–72.

Junger-Tas, J. (1987) School en criminaliteit. *Justitële Verkenningen*, 4, 7–34.

Junger-Tas, J., Junger, M. and Barendse-Hoornweg, E. (1983) *Jeugddelinquentie: Achtergronden en Justitiële reactie*. Den Haag: WODC/Ministerie van Justitie.

Junger-Tas, J. and Terlouw, G.J. (1991) Het Nederlandse publiek en het criminaliteitsprobleem. *Delikt en Delinkwent*, March/April.

Kratcoski, P.C. (1985) School disruption and violence against teachers. *Corrective Social Psychiatry*, 3.

Mellor, A. (1990) *Bullying in Scottish secondary schools*. Edinburgh: Scottish Council for Research in Education.

Ministry of Education (1996) Safe Schools (Report to Parliament). Zoetermeer: Ministry of OCW.

Mooij, T. (1992) *Pesten in het Onderwijs*. Nijmegen: Instituut voor Toegepaste Sociale Wetenschappen.

Mooij, T (1994) *Leerlinggeweld in het Voortgezet Onderwijs*. Nijmegen: Instituut voor Toegepaste Sociale Wetenschappen.

Mutsaers, M. (1995) Preventie van leerlinggeweld. *Tijdschrift voor Leerlingbegeleiding*, 18, 2.

Newman, J. (1980) From past to future: School violence in a broad view. *Contemporary Education*, 52.

Olweus, D. (1978) *Aggression in the Schools*. Washington, DC: Hemisphere.

Olweus, D. (1991) Bully/victim problems among schoolchildren: Basic facts, and effects of a school-based intervention program. In D.J. Pepler and K.H. Rubin (eds) *The development and treatment of childhood aggression* (pp. 411–448). Hillsdale, NJ: Erlbaum.

O'Moore, A.M. and Hillary, B. (1989) Bullying in Dublin schools. *Irish Journal of Psychology*, 10, 426–441.

Rutter, M., Maugham, B., Mortimore, P. and Ousten, J. (1979) *Fifteen thousand hours*. London: Open Books.

Rutter, M., Maugham, B., Mortimore, P. and Ousten, J. (1986) The study of school effectiveness. In J.C. van der Wolf and J.J.Hox (eds) *Kwaliteit van het Onderwijs in het geding*. Lisse: Swets and Zeitlinger.

Schwind, H-W. *et al.* (1995) Aggression at German schools – the example of Bochum. *EuroCriminology*, 8–9, 163–180.

Smith, P.K. (1991) The silent nightmare: Bullying and victimization in school peer groups. *The Psychologist*, 4, 243–248.

Smith, P.K. and Levan, S. (1995) Perceptions and experiences of bullying in younger pupils. *British Journal of Educational Psychology*, 65, 485–500.

Smith, P.K. and Sharp, S. (1994) *School bullying: Insights and perspectives*. London: Routledge.

Sociaal Cultureel Planbureau (SCP) (1994) *Sociaal en Cultureel rapport – 1994*. Rijswijk: SCP.

Stephenson, P. and Smith, D. (1989) Bullying in the junior school. In D. Tattum and D. Lane (eds) *Bullying in schools* (pp. 45–57). Stoke-on-Trent: Trentham Books.

Tremblay, R.E., McCord, J., Boileau, H., Charlebois, P., Gagnon, C., Leblanc, M. and Larivée, S. (1991) Can disruptive boys be helped to become competent? *Psychiatry*, 54, 148–161.

Tremblay, R.E. and Craig, W. (1995) Developmental crime prevention. In M. Tonry and D.P. Farrington (eds) *Building a safer society – strategic approaches to crime prevention. Crime and Justice*, vol. 19, 151–237. Chicago, Ill.: University of Chicago Press.

Verhulst, F.C. and Althaus, M. (1988) Persistence and change in behavioral/emotional problems reported by parents from children aged 4–14: An epidemiological study. *Acta Psychiatrica Scandinavica*, 77, suppl. no. 339.

Verhulst, F.C. and van der Ende, J. (1991) Four year follow-up of teacher reported problem behaviors. *Psychological Medicine*, 21, 965–977.

Whitney, I. and Smith, P.K. (1993). A survey of the nature and extent of bullying in junior/middle and secondary schools. *Educational Research*, 35, 3–25.

Zandbergen, J.G.A. and Hauber, A.R. (1992) Geweld in pedagogische relaties. *Justitële Verkenningen*, 1, 86–89.

Ziegler, S. and Rosenstein-Manner, M. (1991) *Bullying in school.* Toronto: Board of Education.

14 Germany

Friedrich Lösel and Thomas Bliesener

Overview

Although an Independent Governmental Commission on the Prevention and Control of Violence was already addressing the problem of school bullying at the end of the 1980s, the topic only began to gain broad public attention in the 1990s. This was partly due to spectacular acts of violence as well as problems with xenophobia and the unification of the two Germanies. As a result, numerous empirical studies and preventive measures have been initiated in recent times.

Results of empirical research are largely in line with international findings (Besag, 1989; Olweus, 1991, 1993; Smith, 1991); there is a predominance of verbal aggression and mild physical assaults that often possess a playful character. However, the prevalence rates for frequent and persistent bullying are considerable. Depending on age, area, and definition, they vary between 4 percent and 12 percent. Similar rates of school students are victims of frequent bullying. Boys are much more widely involved both as bullies and as victims. Bullying seems to peak from the eighth to tenth grades (approximate ages 14 to 17 years). Grammar schools show lower bullying/victim prevalence than secondary general schools. The size of schools and classes is not related or only weakly related to bullying. The same holds for non-German nationality. Frequent bullies tend to be somewhat older than their victims. In comparison with other students, their families of origin hardly differ in socioeconomic status, but they show more deficits in emotional relations and education. The bullies' academic achievement is below average, and their attitudes toward schools and teachers tend to be negative. In their social behavior, they are relatively dominant, impulsive, and unafraid, but well integrated into peer groups with whom they share a hedonistic, sensation-seeking, and delinquent life-style. Typical victims tend to be outsiders, relatively fearful, shy, and depressive. They exhibit little self-confidence and suffer more frequently from psychosomatic complaints. The group of combined offenders/victims (provocative victims) is smaller than the other two groups. They are highly aggressive, but less dominant and not as socially accepted as bullies.

Measures of prevention and intervention in Germany often do not just address bullying, but are directed more generally toward youth violence as well as hostility toward foreigners. A variety of programs and activities has been initiated on federal, state, and local levels. These include information and further training courses for teachers; tackling aggression and conflicts in class; improving school life and encouraging commitment against violence; informing and increasing the sensitivity of students and their parents; counseling by school psychologists; and extra-curricular social work. There are also approaches that address several levels simultaneously. However, most measures have not been evaluated systematically. There are only a few small-scale evaluations of specific programs; a large-scale study on Olweus' program is currently in progress.

The following proposals are made for future research and practice: (1) to specify and differentiate the phenomenon of violence in schools more clearly; (2) to carry out longitudinal studies on prevalence and individual development of bullies and victims; (3) to use a broader variety of research methods; (4) to relate research more strongly to integrative bio-psycho-social theories of antisocial behavior; (5) to improve and differentiate the theoretical and empirical foundations of concepts of prevention and intervention; and (6) to expand controlled process and outcome evaluation.

The country and its school system

The Federal Republic of Germany (FRG) is a federation of sixteen individual states. In 1995, it had a population of 81.8 million with an area of 366,974 km^2. The two German states were united in 1990. The unification of the former German Democratic Republic (GDR; 16.1 million residents) with the FRG led to massive social and economic changes due to the transformation of the political system in the so-called new German states.

In unified Germany, 8.7 percent of the residents are not German nationals. Turkish nationals represent the largest group of employed foreigners at 28.5 percent, followed by Italians (9.4 percent) and Greeks (5.6 percent). In 1995, the FRG had a gross domestic product of DM 3,459,000 million (IW, 1996), 89.1 percent of which was produced in the so-called old states (the original FRG). The average unemployment rate across the year was 10.4 percent, although it was much higher at 14.9 percent in the new federal states. The estimated education budget for 1995 was DM 171,000 million, corresponding to DM 2090 per resident. Approximately half of this budget (DM 85,000 million) or 2.5 percent of the gross domestic product was spent on schools.

The structure of the school system and the administration of schools is the responsibility of each federal state. As a result, school systems show some differences from state to state. The basic structure of the education system is that primary school covers four years (ages 6 to 10), followed by secondary education stage I (five or six years, starting with two years in orientation stage, ages 10 to 12, followed by three years in secondary general schools, and four years in intermediate and grammar schools). Most pupils with handicaps or learning disabilities attend special schools. The secondary education stage II is quite diversified, ranging from vocational schools for less academic pupils (with in-company training and part-time vocational schooling) to extended intermediate schools, specialized, and general grammar schools (ages 15 or 16 to 18 or 19). Some comprehensive schools combine secondary stages I and II. In all German states, full-time school attendance is compulsory up to the age of 16. The number of students attending general schools was 9.8 million in 1995 (BMBF, 1996a). Their distribution across the different types of school is reported in Table 14.1.

In 1995, there were 9245 vocational schools, of which 1422 were privately run. In all, approximately 2.4 million students were attending some kind of vocational school, 27.5 percent of them full-time students.

Teaching hours at German schools are not standardized. Lesson plans are worked out individually for each class. In general, students attend school in the mornings; afternoon lessons commence only in secondary schools. School meals are generally not provided. All-day schools are rare and more frequent in the private sector.

School bullying as a public concern

In Germany, the discussion on school bullying is generally embedded within the broader framework of violence among the young. This topic had already received some public attention during the 1970s and 1980s, triggered by

Table 14.1 Number of general education schools, proportion of private schools, number of students, proportion of foreigners, and student–teacher ratios in various types of school

Type of school	*Number of schools*	*Proportion of private schools (%)*	*Number of students (thousands)*	*Proportion of foreign students (%)*	*Number of students per teacher*
Elementary	17,910	1.5	3,634.3	9.2	20.9
Orientation stage	2,358	2.2	374.7	7.7	16.4
Secondary general	6,132	2.9	1,123.5	18.8	14.8
Intermediate	3,504	7.3	1,175.2	6.6	17.7
Integrated secondary general and intermediate	1,280	0.4	368.2	0.8	15.0
Comprehensive	978	18.8	571.6	10.7	13.5
Grammar	3,168	11.2	2,164.6	3.9	14.8
Evening school/college	291	32.6	31.2	14.5	9.1
Special education	3,397	15.7	391.1	14.3	7.0

reports in the mass media on individual spectacular acts of violence by youths. Teachers also believe that school students have become more aggressive (e.g. Franz and Schlesiger, 1974), although systematic teacher surveys in the early 1980s indicated a prevalence of only approximately 2 percent of aggressive students (Bach *et al.*, 1984). The main topics in the public discussion on violence at schools were aggression between students and vandalism. Violence toward teachers or exercised by teachers, in contrast, remained marginal topics. German teachers are not allowed to use physical punishment to discipline students. Although the suggestion arose in the public discussion that violence had increased in schools, little empirical research was available during the 1970s and 1980s. A few studies addressed the problem within the broader framework of deviant behavior (Brusten and Hurrelmann, 1973; Fend and Schneider, 1984; Holtappels, 1985; Lösel, 1975). Others referred to specific phenomena such as vandalism (e.g. Klockhaus and Habermann-Morbey, 1986) or aggression in class (Tennstädt *et al.*, 1984).

At the end of the 1980s, an Independent Governmental Commission on the Prevention and Control of Violence (Commission on Violence) was established (Schwind *et al.*, 1990). It addressed the following areas: violence in the family, violence in schools, violence in the stadium, violence in the streets and public places, and politically motivated violence. Regarding violence in schools, the Commission concluded that the severity of the problem had not yet attained the levels indicated by, for example, reports from the USA. However, a large deficit in research was ascertained in this field. The Commission assumed a multifactorial approach to explain violence, in which familial, school, peer group, mass media, and personality factors interact (Lösel *et al.*, 1990). One particularly important cause within school was considered to be educational climate. Proposals for prevention and intervention were based on the principles that the school must remember its educational mission, the responsibility of teachers and students for their school must be reinforced, and the frustrations of school failure must be reduced through the provision of adequate support (Schwind *et al.*, 1990).

The 1990s have seen a major increase in mass media reports on violence in schools. Brutal fights, extortion, threats, and carrying weapons dominate these reports. Vandalism is receiving less attention than before. There is also increasing emphasis on the fears of victims. In individual cases, youth suicides are linked to their victimization (e.g. "Driven to suicide: Youth gang subjects Hamburg schoolboy to extortion and threats." *Süddeutsche Zeitung*, 8–9 February 1997). School bullying is increasingly being viewed as a social problem in Germany. A relevant factor here is also that young persons are those who are caught most frequently committing crimes, and it is particularly this group that is showing a further rise in crime rates in the 1990s according to police statistics (Pfeiffer *et al.*, 1996). Another aspect is that, since unification, the crime rates in the formerly communist part of Germany have risen, and this negative aspect of free societies is accompanied by pronounced fears of crime (Bilsky *et al.*, 1993; Kury, 1993). A third factor is that young persons have repeatedly been involved in serious acts of violence toward foreigners in the 1990s (Willems *et al.*, 1993). As a result, the specific phenomenon of school bullying is part of a general impression of increasing antisocial behavior among the young (Lösel, 1995a).

The 1990s have seen a strong increase not only in public attention to violence in schools, but also in research and efforts at intervention. In the last five years, far more empirical studies have been carried out on the topic than in the previous twenty years. Because schools in Germany are the responsibility of individual states and not the national government, these studies have focused on single federal states, districts, or cities. There is no representative survey for the whole of Germany. The studies tackle not only the prevalence of aggressive behavior in schools but also its correlates and causes such as type of school, size of school or classes, educational climate, teacher attitudes, students' age, family characteristics, peer group relations, personality variables, attitudes toward violence, leisure-time behavior, use of mass media, and so forth. Most studies contain surveys of students; however, several of them also examined teachers, school principals, parents, or school janitors (e.g. Ferstl *et al.*, 1993; Schwind *et al.*, 1995). Observations of behavior in natural settings or controlled interaction analyses are rare (Krappmann and Oswald, 1995). The majority of studies deal generally with violence in schools, and also include vandalism or aggression toward teachers.

The increase in empirical research has resulted in a more differentiated professional discussion. Some of the issues addressed are: (1) Has there really been an objective increase in violence in schools, or is it simply that people have become more sensitive in their perceptions and evaluations of violence? (2) Is the concept of violence applied too broadly so that it includes problems that have more to do with disciplinary difficulties and a decrease in politeness? (3) Are forms of play fighting that are normal and functional in developmental terms being dramatized inappropriately? Although there are indicators that violence in schools has somewhat increased in quantitative or qualitative terms (e.g. Dann, 1997; Freitag and Hurrelmann, 1993; Lösel *et al.*, 1996; Tillmann, 1997), it is hard to obtain unequivocal answers to such questions. One reason for this is the lack of empirically sound longitudinal studies using non-reactive methods. Another reason is that studies vary greatly in terms of their underlying concepts, theories, violent phenomena assessed, research instruments, and samples. Only a few studies refer specifically to the concept of bullying as defined by Olweus (1993, 1994): aggressive behavior or intentional injury of other students that is exercised repeatedly and over a longer period of time within relationships characterized by an imbalance of power. An exact translation of the term into German is not possible. Questionnaires use terms such as "Schikanieren" (harassment; Schäfer, 1996), "Quälen" (tormenting; Lösel *et al.*, 1995), or the non-German word "mobbing" (Hanewinkel and Knaack, 1997a).

Research on the nature and type of school bullying

Frequency and types of bullying

Most estimations on the prevalence of interpersonal violence among students are based on self-reports. These are taken from surveys of samples of school students that differ in terms of geography and urban density, types of school, and age. Furthermore, some studies assess bullying with global behavior categories, whereas others use concrete actions. There are also differences in the contexts and time intervals surveyed. Despite this heterogeneity, the findings on prevalence are relatively consistent. Studies show that a majority of students report at least one or two acts of bullying in the typical reference periods of six months or one year (e.g. Funk, 1995; Hanewinkel and Knaack, 1997a; Lösel *et al.*, 1997b; Melzer and Rostampour, 1996; Schäfer, 1996; Schwind *et al.*, 1995). However, frequent bullying is much more unusual. Using a criterion like "at least once a week", studies vary between *c.* 4 percent and 12 percent prevalence. For example, Hanewinkel and Knaack (1997a) found 9.7 percent of frequent bullying in a sample of 14,788 students from all grades in Schleswig-Holstein. Schwind *et al.* (1995) reported approximately 10 percent of frequent and intensive aggressive behavior for a sample of 934 students from all grades in the city of Bochum. In a sample of 1163 students from the seventh and eighth grades in the cities of Erlangen and Nuremberg, Lösel *et al.* (1997a) found a prevalence rate of 6.5 percent for frequent physical bullying and 11 percent for frequent verbal bullying. From a short-term longitudinal study of 1567 fifth to ninth grade students in North Hesse, Todt and Busch (1996) reported 8 percent of frequent verbal aggression and approximately 4 percent of frequent physical aggression. Tillmann *et al.* (1996) investigated 3540 students from secondary schools in Hesse. In single items they found that approximately 5 percent had several fights per week and 12 to 13 percent had teased or called others names with the same frequency. Aggregating physical and verbal forms, Freitag and Hurrelmann (1993) observed about 6 percent of frequent aggressors in a sample of 973 students from secondary schools in the cities of Essen and Osnabruck. Schäfer (1996) found about 7 percent of frequent bullying in a combined sample of 392 sixth and eighth graders from Munich; however, as in other studies, there were clear differences between the two age groups (3 percent vs. 11 percent). In a sample of more than 4000 students in the sixth and ninth grades of schools in the new federal state of Saxony (Melzer and Rostampour, 1996), the prevalence rate of unspecified "frequent" bullying was 4.1 percent.

This range of frequent bullying agrees broadly with reports by teachers on the number of students in whom they see intensive aggressive symptoms (Dann *et al.*, 1994; Schwind *et al.*, 1995). When surveys ask more specifically about various forms of aggression, milder forms such as teasing, harassment, insults, pulling faces, and spreading lies about others are practiced most frequently (Ferstl *et al.*, 1993; Funk, 1995; Lamnek, 1995; Lösel *et al.*, 1997a; Schwind *et al.*, 1995; Todt and Busch, 1996). Physical aggression takes second place, and these occurrences often have a more playful character. Thus far, most German studies have come to the conclusion that forms and degrees of violence should be differentiated thoroughly.

Prevalence rates for students who are repeatedly and massively subjected to violence are similar to the data on active bullying. Hanewinkel and Knaack (1997a) found 9.2 percent and Schäfer (1996) reported 5.3 percent who became victims at least once a week. Using the same time category, Lösel *et al.* (1997a) reported frequent victimization rates of 11.7 percent for verbal bullying and 5.7 percent for physical bullying. The analysis of single items from Tillmann *et al.* (1996) showed that approximately 2 percent were beaten and 6 percent teased or insulted several times a week. In Melzer and Rostampour (1996), 5.7 percent were frequently victimized; and in Freitag and Hurrelmann (1993), this rose to 16 percent. The latter study, however, used a broader definition ("more or less frequently"). If various forms of violent experience are differentiated, there is a similar rank order as in offender data. The focus of passive victimization lies in verbal provocation, attacks, and threats, whereas physical assaults or threats with weapons tend to be experienced more rarely (Funk, 1995; Lösel *et al.*, 1997a; Schwind *et al.*, 1995). This is in line with the data obtained from general questions on the occurrence of violence in schools. Here, first place is taken by disruptions of teaching/lack of discipline, rude insults, and nonverbal provocation. Massive aggression such as extortion, violent conflicts between groups of students, and the carrying of guns are, in contrast, found at the bottom of the list (Schwind *et al.*, 1995).

The prevalence data for students who are not only repeatedly aggressive to others but also report that they are themselves persistent victims of violence is relatively heterogeneous. Melzer and Rostampour (1996) found a rate of 54 percent of offenders who had also been victims of aggression. In another study by Diehl and Sudek (1995), 60 percent of students who threatened others reported that they were threatened themselves. A similar relation of 50 percent has been reported by Dettenborn and Lautsch (1993) among the victims who were also offenders. In contrast, when comparable criteria are used in defining victim and offender, and a massive repeated experience of violence is applied as the criterion in each case, prevalences are lower. For example, Melzer and Rostampour (1996) found only 5 percent among their victims who also reported that they were frequent offenders. In Lösel *et al.* (1997a), there was a rate of 2.1 percent of the total sample for students who were frequently aggressive and simultaneously victimized. These results indicate that the group of bully/victims or pro-active victims (Olweus, 1994) is smaller than the other two groups.

A few student surveys have also provided information on the growth of violence among school students. For example, Mansel and Hurrelman (1998) have found a general increase in frequency when comparing surveys carried out in Westphalia in 1988 and 1996. Tillmann (1997) has compared a sample from the state of Hesse in 1995 with older data collected in Bielefeld. This study also revealed an increase in physical aggression, and this was particularly marked among students attending secondary general schools. Lösel *et al.* (1998) have presented a cohort study of identical school classes: data collected at two inner-city secondary general schools with high frequencies of violence in 1973 showed that in 1995 18 percent more male students reported that they had caused physical injury.

Sexual harassment

The available studies indicate that physical assaults on sexual self-determination tend to be observed rather infrequently. Verbal sexual harassment, in contrast, was observed frequently by 43 percent of the students surveyed (Schwind *et al.*, 1995). None the less, 6.6 percent of the male students reported that they had frequently grabbed at a girl's breasts or between her legs (Tillmann *et al.*, 1996). When evaluating these prevalence data, it none the less has to be considered that a survey carried out in Berlin (Unabhängige Kommission, 1995) revealed that 57.2 percent of male and female students who reported sexual harassment said that they had experienced this outside the school.

Bully–victim relationship

Bullies frequently appear in a group (Böttger, 1996), but these are rarely organized youth gangs (Mölleken and Steinke-Schmickler, 1995). However, the views of students, teachers, and parents differ here: whereas teachers more frequently view the origins of youth violence in individual students and less frequently in groups, students and parents believe that violence tends to derive from youths in groups (Böttger, 1996). In a survey of victims among students in the city of Cologne (Diehl and Sudek, 1995), only one-third reported that they had been victims of group violence. The majority of offenders in this study were peers or older students. This finding is also replicated in other studies (e.g. Lösel *et al.*, 1997b).

Sex differences

The most clearly confirmed finding in research on bullying is a stronger prevalence among boys (e.g. Freie und Hansestadt Hamburg, 1993; Fuchs *et al.*, 1996; Funk, 1995; Lamnek, 1995; Lösel *et al.*, 1997b; Melzer and Rostampour, 1996; Schwind *et al.*, 1995; Todt and Busch, 1996). Boys exhibit markedly higher rates both as offenders and victims. However, differences between the sexes become less clear in verbal aggression and particularly in so-called relational violence (exclusion from groups of friends, defamation, spreading lies; Lösel *et al.*, 1997a; Schwind *et al.*, 1995).

There are also differences in the victim–offender constellation. Boys are usually teased by one or more boys; very rarely, in contrast, by one or more girls. Girls, on the other hand, are usually teased by one or more boys, by one or more girls in about one-third of cases, and more frequently by mixed groups (Diehl and Sudek, 1996; Schäfer, 1996).

Age differences

The prevalence of bullying does not remain constant across various school age groups. Regarding the active use of violence, many studies have noted an increase in around the eighth to tenth grades (Fuchs *et al.*, 1996; Hanewinkel and Knaack, 1997a; Lamnek, 1995). However, the forms of bullying seem to change as well: whereas physical confrontation is predominant among younger students, verbal or psychological aggression becomes more prominent among older ones (Lamnek, 1995; Melzer and Rostampour, 1996). A similar age trend may be seen in vandalism (Funk, 1995). The low exposure to violence reported in the highest grades studied (eleventh to thirteenth) has to be evaluated against the background that such students are a positive selection. They are all attending grammar school and taking university entrance examinations. Bullying is also generally not so high in the lower grades of these schools. For students in other types of school, who are generally involved in the dual vocational training system (part-time vocational school), data from accident statistics indicate particularly severe confrontations (Bayerische Staatsregierung, 1994).

Where and when it occurs

According to a study carried out in Saxony-Anhalt (Kultusministerium des Landes Sachsen-Anhalt, 1994), teachers report that most violence among students occurs in the playground (60.1 percent), followed by the journey to and from school (17.3 percent), school corridors (10.4 percent), and classrooms (9.2 percent). In a study by Ferstl *et al.* (1993), teachers reported the following rank order: (1) playground; (2) corridors; (3) classrooms; (4) journey to and from school; (5) washrooms and toilets. In most surveys covering the perspective of students, the playground also took first place (Diehl and Sudek, 1995; Ferstl *et al.*, 1993; Mölleken and Steinke-Schmickler, 1995; Schwind *et al.*, 1995). Compared with teachers, students see a further focus of violence in the classrooms (Schäfer, 1996). Students also view the journey to and from school as being comparatively problematic. Although the prevalence of violence on the journey to and from school is lower than in the playground (Lösel *et al.*, 1997b), it is where approximately one-third of students feel unsafe (Mölleken and Steinke-Schmickler, 1995; Schwind *et al.*, 1995). The journey home seems to be more of a problem than the journey to school (Diehl and Sudek, 1995; Ferstl *et al.*, 1993). As far as times are concerned, the experience of violence is concentrated above all in the breaks, the time after the end of school and before school begins, and during periods between lessons. Approximately one in eight students reported that they experienced the majority of violence during class hours (Ferstl *et al.*, 1993).

Who is told

Up to now, only a few studies in Germany have examined who is informed about the students' experience of violence. According to a study by Dettenborn (1993), 74 percent thought it was meaningful to talk to parents about it. The willingness to do this among victims was slightly lower (69 percent) whereas among offenders it drops to 58 percent. There is a clear dependence on the type of school: willingness to talk to parents is highest among students attending grammar school and lowest among students attending secondary general school. Reasons for not talking to parents were (in rank order) that they would not understand the problem, they would not know what to do, and helplessness. The survey revealed that 82 percent confirmed that they would talk to a teacher about their violence problems. The main reason for not talking here was a lack of trust in the relationship. According to Wustmans and Becker (1996), the willingness to inform a teacher or person in charge declines with increasing age. In addition, those students who perceive themselves as being less competent in dealing with conflict seem to talk to teachers (Wustmans and Becker, 1996).

Attitudes toward bullying

The majority of students unequivocally reject acts of aggression (Funk, 1995; Tillmann *et al.*, 1996; Todt and Busch, 1996). None the less, there are differences between the sexes. In line with sex roles, boys are more in favor of using violence to assert their own goals (Funk, 1995). They also exhibit a greater willingness to join in bullying (57.4 percent vs. 28.7 percent) or a higher level of understanding for fellow students who pester others (27.0 percent vs. 8.1 percent; Schäfer, 1996). In the group of those who are frequent bullies, a positive attitude toward aggression prevails (Schwind *et al.*, 1995; Todt and Busch, 1996). They see aggression as a more or less indispensable instrument for attaining their goals.

According to the differences in attitudes, both sexes also differ in their fear of violence in schools. Although girls are less frequently victimized than boys, they are more afraid of being bullied (Bliesener, 1997). This is in accordance with results on sex differences in fear of crime (Bilsky *et al.*, 1993; Kury, 1993), and may be due to more pronounced feelings of vulnerability.

Characteristics of bullies, victims, and bully/victims

Only a few studies in Germany have worked out detailed characteristics of the person and of the social environment of bullies and their victims. These findings reveal that bullies tend to be slightly older than their victims (Bliesener, 1997; Melzer and Rostampour, 1996). In comparison to their non-bullying school mates, they more often come from disadvantaged milieus with cumulative risk factors such as divorce, alcohol abuse, unemployment, or parental conflict (Lösel *et al.*, 1997b). Offenders exhibit more dissatisfaction with school, see less sense in learning, and are frequently bad students (Melzer and Rostampour, 1996). They have a negative image of teachers and perceive the social climate in their class and school as less satisfactory (Averbeck *et al.*, 1996; Todt and Busch, 1996). Their relationships to their parents as well as their family climate are also described as more negative (Lösel *et al.*, 1996; Melzer and Rostampour, 1996). Bullies tend to be socially dominant, impulsive, and inattentive (Lösel *et al.*, 1997b). They are less anxious – even when engaged in risky activities (Todt and Busch, 1996) – and in no way socially isolated (Krappmann and Oswald, 1995; Lösel *et al.*, 1997a). Their social information-processing mechanisms in conflict situations are more egocentric and impulsive and less de-escalating than in other students (Bliesener, 1997). Bullies tend to have a hedonistic value orientation (Kuhnke, 1995). They are frequently committed to cliques and get into conflicts with other groups. In their leisure time, they look for more strongly stimulating and "action-filled" situations such as discotheques and amusement arcades (Kuhnke, 1995; Lösel *et al.*, 1996). They also view more violence or horror movies than other students (Funk, 1995; Lösel *et al.*, 1996) and are more aggressive and delinquent outside the school (Lösel *et al.*, 1997b).

Victims of bullies are frequently isolated and unpopular in their classes (Lösel *et al.*, 1997b; Melzer and Rostampour, 1996). They describe themselves as being more withdrawn, anxious, depressive, lacking self-confidence, and suffering more psychosomatic complaints than their class mates (Lösel *et al.*, 1997b). They come from similar family milieus as bullies and also tend to have poor relations with their parents, who, in contrast to the situation of bullies, are more interested in their school achievement (Melzer and Rostampour, 1996). Their perception of family climate suggests that they do not come from a favorable and overprotective milieu (Lösel *et al.*, 1996). Victims' school grades are below average just like those of offenders. Melzer and Rostampour (1996) found a somewhat higher level of achievement among their victim group compared to bullies; however, in Lösel *et al.* (1997a), both groups were similarly below average. Contrary to a widespread stereotype, victims are not "swots" who are stigmatized by other students because they are jealous of their academic achievements. However, they tend to be worse at sports than bullies (Lösel *et al.*, 1997b).

Bully/victims or provocative victims have not been studied much in Germany up to the present. According to our own analyses, these students form the group with the most and the greatest range of behavioral and emotional problems (Lösel *et al.*, 1997b). Regarding their general aggressiveness outside the school context, they do not differ from bullies. They also have similar aggression-facilitating cognitions in conflict situations (Bliesener,

1997). However, they tend to be less dominant and socially accepted, but more depressed, anxious, and inattentive. Compared with young persons who are not conspicuously aggressive, they have more emotional problems and difficulties with self-esteem (Lösel *et al.*, 1997b). Taking these characteristics into account, they seem to walk into their aggressive conflicts through their own undercontrol and initial provocations (see Besag, 1989).

Sociodemographic and ethnic differences

Some studies have examined the relationship between bullying among students and socioeconomic status (Funk, 1995; Holtappels, 1985; Hurrelmann and Pollmer, 1994; Niebel *et al.*, 1993). These revealed no or only weak relations between student violence and SES or family income. Although these variables are partially confounded, emotional and educational characteristics of the family seem to be more conducive to bullying than material ones.

Various studies also showed no significant differences in prevalence between foreign and German youth in bullying or the experience of violence at schools (Ferstl *et al.*, 1993; Fuchs *et al.*, 1996; Funk, 1995; Lösel *et al.*, 1997a; Niebel *et al.*, 1993). These results are in contrast to police statistics reporting a higher rate of delinquency among foreign adolescents (Pfeiffer *et al.*, 1996). German students only have a somewhat higher rate of victimization (Lösel *et al.*, 1997a). It may be that a stronger involvement in peer groups among foreign youth protects them from victimization. On the other hand, in secondary general schools, non-German students are not small minorities but form a large part of the classes. Most foreign students have grown up in Germany and speak fluent German. Those who are ethnically most different and have language difficulties (mainly asylum seekers and refugees) are educated in special classes.

Objective school characteristics

At comparable ages, bullying is most frequent in secondary general schools or special schools and least frequent in grammar schools (Fuchs *et al.*, 1996; Funk, 1995; Schwind *et al.*, 1995). Intermediate schools lie in between. This relationship is partially confounded with differences in intelligence, SES, and other sociodemographic variables. Violence is also relatively frequent in comprehensive and vocational schools and less frequent in elementary schools (Schwind *et al.*, 1995). Ecological school characteristics have hardly ever been studied. They seem to correlate with vandalism (Klockhaus and Habermann-Morbey, 1996) but not with bullying (Niebel *et al.*, 1993).

Subjective patterns of explanation

The patterns used to explain the causes of violence among students differ according to the perspective of the group surveyed. The teachers' perspective emphasizes representations of violence in the mass media and conditions in the parental home. In contrast, school conditions or a lack of leisure-time facilities and future perspectives are less important to them (Fuchs *et al.*, 1996; Schwind *et al.*, 1995). Teachers in the new federal states, however, consider changes in their society to be the main cause for an increase in violence (Kultusministerium des Landes Sachsen-Anhalt, 1994).

The parents' perspective is different. They consider inadequate teacher training as a main reason for violence at schools. Causes under their personal control (such as child-rearing practices, television watching, etc.) were viewed as secondary (Schwind *et al.*, 1995).

Surveys of students reveal a stronger emphasis on situational and interactional factors. These include boasting, jealousy, and working off frustrations. Problems, conflicts, or violence in the family are only moderately important from their perspective. Students also consider that the consumption of violence in the mass media has only a minor impact (Diehl and Sudek, 1995; Mölleken and Steinke-Schmickler, 1995; Schwind *et al.*, 1995; Unabhängige Kommission, 1995).

Similarly, different attribution patterns can be seen among other relevant groups. Respondents from public youth service institutions particularly mentioned experience of violence and exclusion in the family and in public domains (Freie und Hansestadt Hamburg, 1993). In our own study of approximately 500 teachers and school principals, child psychiatrists and clinical psychologists, judges and public prosecutors, and forensic psychologists we found five subjective explanatory factors (Lösel and Hylla, 1996): (1) cold and depriving society; (2) educational and family deficits; (3) personality problems; (4) drugs and domestic violence; and (5) violence in the mass media. Teachers and school principals particularly emphasized the role of educational and family deficits as well as violence in the mass media. In contrast, child psychiatrists and clinical psychologists placed relatively more emphasis on personality problems and – like law professions – on drugs and domestic violence.

These studies suggest that causal attributions reflect everyday experiences and role socializations. On the other hand, responsibility for violence tends to be attributed more to others. Although such tendencies are rather common, they are dysfunctional for intervention, because they lead to inconsistent reactions and do not encourage people to modify their own behavior. It is therefore necessary to make different subjective theories transparent and coordinate them with each other (see Averbeck and Lösel, 1994; Lösel and Bliesener, 1989).

Prevention and intervention

As outlined above, the Commission on Violence has already made recommendations for prevention and intervention in schools (Schwind *et al.*, 1990). Increased public interest in the topic has since led to a variety of programs.

However, many measures have not focused specifically on school bullying, but on the broader topic of violence among young persons. Due to several serious acts of violence toward foreigners and Germany's Nazi history, particular attention has been given to this field.

Because not only schools but also the police and the justice system are regulated on a state level, numerous different regional programs have been initiated. The Federal Government has also launched some national programs. It has published information about violence among young persons (e.g. Der Bundesminister des Innern, 1993; Mischkowitz, 1994), commissioned empirical surveys (e.g. Willems *et al.*, 1993), implemented further training courses for teachers, and also commissioned brochures for students. For example, the campaign *Fairständnis* (an artificial word combining the concept of fairness with understanding and empathy) published youth magazines on the prevention of violence ("Enough: Say no to violence"). These magazines discuss aggression and prejudice and demonstrate nonviolent behavior options in conflict situations, and are accompanied by teaching aids, methodological suggestions, and handbooks for teachers (e.g. Arbeitsgemeinschaft Jugend and Bildung e.V., 1996a, b). When working on the topic of violence at school, case reports are used to discuss typical aggression toward fellow students, the problems of outsiders, and how conflicts escalate. Students should look for potential solutions together during class. While doing this, they work out and practice basic rules for social behavior. However, the program is not mandatory and has not yet been subjected to a systematic evaluation.

Another measure initiated by the Federal Government was an action program against aggression and violence (*Aktionsprogramm gegen Aggression und Gewalt*, AgAG; see Informationsdienst AgAG, 1996) which was funded with 90 million German Marks from 1992 to 1996. The AgAG program particularly targeted young persons endorsing violence, violent young persons, and young persons at risk in the new German states. A major link was also violence toward foreigners. The program was not school based but focused on social work and the youth services. It was also used to expand and consolidate the introduction of federal youth services and social work structures in the new German states. Approximately 140 projects were set up to prevent and reduce violence in 30 selected regions. Between 6500 and 8000 children and adolescents participated in them. An integrative approach was applied that included measures such as contact-seeking street work, individual counseling, clique and group work, adventure and vacation programs, youth club and leisure-time provisions, sports facilities, mass media projects, and social training courses. These were accompanied by further training for personnel as well as research and publications on social work with violent youth (see Reitmajer, 1996). After the end of the AgAG program, nearly all projects were taken over by state and district authorities. As persistent school bullies are frequently also aggressive and delinquent in other contexts (Lösel *et al.*, 1997b; Olweus, 1994), the AgAG program could have an impact on violence between students. However, it has not been evaluated systematically.

The various activities in individual states can only be outlined here. The Bavarian State Government, for example, set up an inter-ministerial work group on youth and violence (Bayerische Staatsregierung, 1994). Like the Federal Government's Commission on Violence, this group proposed numerous measures for prevention and intervention. These addressed not only schools but also the family and residential care, day-care centers, youth services and social work, the protection of minors in the mass media, or the police and the justice system. The following goals were formulated for schools: (1) placing more attention on the child-rearing tasks of schools, emphasizing value orientations and social learning; (2) communicating a feeling of belonging, experience of community, and responsibility within the life space of the school; (3) promoting individual competencies and interests through more differentiation in schools; (4) enabling peaceful coexistence in ethnic, national, and cultural multiplicity; (5) providing special interventions for disadvantaged young persons and those with behavioral difficulties; (6) supporting and motivating school principals and teaching staff; and (7) promoting cooperation between schools, parents, and extra-curricular organizations.

The goals should be met through school-based measures that were, in part, already being practiced and, in part, still needed to be initiated. These included:

- Increased attention to ethical issues in the school curriculum; more cooperative forms of teaching such as project lessons; consistent interventions when rules are violated; prohibition of bringing dangerous objects into the school.
- Designing the school to be a life space through joint ventures; encouraging students to take responsibility for each other; making school buildings aesthetically more attractive.
- Further development of the differentiated school system and academic career counseling; measures to promote students with learning difficulties.
- Experimental trials on the integration of foreign students in regular classes; intercultural education in class and school life; strengthening political education.
- Further promotion of the school as a child-rearing aid; mobile special education teachers; intensification of school counseling; cooperation with other social services.
- In-service further training for teachers to improve their competence in dealing with violence; more consideration of the child-rearing tasks in teacher assessments; fixed teaching hours to care for students in social risk situations.
- Cooperation between school and parents, youth services, the police, the justice system, and further potential partners.

Some pilot tests were financed, for example, a school trial on further in-service training for teachers, a project on education in the use of the media at secondary general schools, a project to expand all-day care; an experiment with violence-related theater productions for students; multilingual brochures for non-German parents; and so forth. Controls over their implementation and systematic evaluations of the measures do not exist.

Similar initiatives to those in Bavaria can also be found in the other federal states (see, for example, Freie und Hansestadt Hamburg, 1993; Kultusministerium des Landes Sachsen-Anhalt, 1994; Niedersächsisches Kultusministerium, 1992; Senatsverwaltung für Schule, Berufsbildung und Sport Berlin, 1992). As the above examples show, very complex bundles of measures are suggested or being implemented. However, they also contain specific school-based concepts that are oriented toward similar key principles to those emphasized by Olweus (1991): (1) creation of a school environment characterized by warmth, positive interest, and involvement from adults; (2) firm limits to unacceptable behavior; (3) in cases of violations of limits and rules, consistent application of non-hostile, non-physical sanctions; (4) a certain degree of monitoring and surveillance of the students' activities in and out of school; and (5) adults acting as authorities at least in some respects. To disseminate such principles, a German version of Olweus' book (1995) has been distributed to schools in Berlin and Schleswig-Holstein. Further training courses for teachers have been held in most federal states. A number of schools have organized open education days in which the school principals, teachers, parents, and (sometimes) students work on the problem of violence at their school. External experts have been invited to contribute research findings on bullying. Our experience has been that such sessions are well received, and they stimulate internal prevention measures at schools. However, it has to be noted that schools that are open to such activities are not necessarily those in which violence is particularly marked.

Parts of the information material and actions are none the less too unspecific and insufficiently oriented toward the empirical findings on bullying. For example, it is sometimes claimed that physical features of schools, low self-esteem, achievement pressure, or a lack of freedom are important causes of bullying. Various intervention concepts are restricted to general information and do not focus sufficiently on aggressive activities at a specific school. Others prefer only non-directive measures. It can also be seen that the type of measures proposed and the ways in which they are discussed among teachers, parents, and others are related to sociopolitical attitudes. As mentioned above, problems can be anticipated arising from inconsistency in the implementation of measures and in organizational development.

A common feature of recent prevention concepts is that programs should not be too narrow but should address school life in general (Dann, 1997; Hensel, 1993; Lösel *et al.*, 1990; Schwind *et al.*, 1995; Todt and Busch,

1996). Specific measures against bullying can be implemented on different levels and be integrated into a broader concept of positive school life. Such specific programs on the prevention of violence had already been developed in the 1980s. In contrast to the more complex approaches, at least some systematic evaluations are available. One example is a social learning program for the prevention of juvenile delinquency and aggression from Lerchenmüller (1986, 1987). It is designed to improve the social competence and non-aggressive conflict solving of students through role play, teamwork, and so forth. A control group study was able to confirm short-term effects on social attitudes and behaviors (Lerchenmüller, 1986). However, these did not prove to be stable in a follow-up study. The author attributed this to deficits in modifying teacher behavior. Another example is the training program with aggressive children introduced by Petermann and Petermann (1990). It is based on behavioral programs like that of Patterson *et al.* (1992). A series of positive single case evaluations is available (see Petermann and Bochmann, 1993). However, this program is primarily designed for work in child guidance centers and is not so suitable for school classes. A third example is the teacher training scheme introduced by Tennstädt *et al.* (1984). This is designed to improve the teacher's educational problem-solving competencies through information, practice, and joint supervision. By modifying the teacher's communication and reinforcement behavior, the aim is to reduce aggression and disturbances in classes and schools. A comparative evaluation study has shown, among others, effects on the subjective aggression theories of teachers, their action competencies in test situations, their perception of aggression, as well as their experiences of school and classroom climate (Tennstädt and Dann, 1987). However, controlled studies of the impact on aggressive bullying behavior are not available. Some findings, such as a lower norm transparency from the student perspective, suggest that the program effects cannot be directly transferred to this problem.

A more recent and multi-level program was investigated by Todt and Busch (1996) in three schools at North Hesse. The program is based on systematic surveys on violence in the respective schools. It addressed empirically found risk factors for bullying as well as protective factors against it. The intervention measures included clear rules against bullying, further in-service training of teachers, discussions with parents, students' engagement in a bicycle workshop, concentration and relaxation exercises, open education school days, and a model of offender–victim mediation. A particularly interesting feature of this program was that it differentiated between subtypes of bullies and suggested specific measures for the various groups. Annual survey data showed a moderate decline in verbal and physical aggression from 1993 to 1995. Unfortunately, the design included no comparison group.

Despite such positive examples, there is a lack of controlled large-scale evaluations of complex programs for the prevention of school bullying in Germany. The most important exception is the recent program on "Mobbing:

Prevention of violence in schools in Schleswig-Holstein" (Die Ministerin für Frauen, Bildung, Weiterbildung und Sport des Landes Schleswig-Holstein, 1994). This consists of a state-wide implementation and controlled evaluation of Olweus' program (1994). The program has been running since 1994, following an empirical survey on violence at schools in Schleswig-Holstein (Ferstl *et al.*, 1993). As in the original, the program is based on principles of social learning theory and is applied on three levels (see Olweus, 1990). Schleswig-Holstein is concentrating on the following elements:

1 *School level:* Better supervision of recess; more attractive school playgrounds; contact telephone; teacher training groups for developing school climate; cooperation between parents and teachers; parent working groups.
2 *Class level:* Clear class rules against bullying; clarification, praise, and sanctions; regular class meetings; behavior-oriented treatment of the topic in class; cooperation between parents and teachers.
3 *Individual level:* Serious talks with bullies and their victims; serious talks with the parents of the children involved; discussion groups with parents of bullies and their victims; change of class or school (if necessary).

Following the introduction of the program, the 47 participating schools were surveyed with a German adaptation of the Bully/Victim Questionnaire (Olweus, 1989). Participants were 14,788 male and female students from all types of school (Hanewinkel and Knaack, 1997b). After completing the initial survey, an open education day was held at all schools. The purpose was to discuss the results of the survey, to promote awareness of the problem and the motivation to get involved, and to prepare consequences. Alongside the school principals and teachers, external experts such as school psychologists were also present. The open education day was followed by a school conference at which each school worked out its own prevention and intervention program. The program was then put into force with the support of external experts. There were also working meetings for the schools in the project as well as an in-service further training for teachers. After approximately one year, a second assessment was carried out with the Bully/Victim Questionnaire in 37 schools (n = 10,610). According to preliminary evaluation data, the program has led to a reduction in the prevalence of victimization in its less frequent forms and in the lower grades. However, there has also been a small increase in the prevalence of being bullied in grades 11 and 12. Organizational problems in the implementation may have contributed to this negative effect, because teaching in these grades is based on a course system and not on fixed classes. As with the treatment of antisocial behavior in other contexts, considerable attention must be paid to consistency in implementation and organizational development in order to ensure sufficient integrity in treatment implementation (see Lösel, 1996).

Perspectives

Although public awareness of school bullying in Germany has increased during the 1990s and there has also been an expansion of research, a series of problems still has to be tackled in the future. These include:

1 *Defining the phenomena more precisely.* Most research in Germany is oriented more generally toward the concept of violence in schools. This lumps together widely differing phenomena ranging from disciplinary difficulties across vandalism up to serious injuries to other students. Although there are clear correlations between these behaviors, different concepts may well be indicated as far as causes and adequate interventions are concerned. Regarding aggression between students, on the one hand, more attention should be paid to the concept of bullying defined as relatively frequent and long-lasting aggressiveness within relationships characterized by an imbalance of power. On the other hand, forms of play fighting or rough-and-tumble play should be differentiated more clearly and not be dramatized unnecessarily.

2 *Longitudinal research.* Some of these controversies arise from the lack of long-term follow-up studies on prevalence. Just as there are regular surveys on juvenile delinquency (Elliott *et al.*, 1989) or crime victimization (van Dijk *et al.*, 1990), repeated, representative cohort studies are needed on school bullying in Germany. This would permit a better estimation of prevalence trends. When possible, different informants and data sources should also be included (see below). However, more longitudinal research is needed not only on prevalence rates, but also on the individual development of school bullies and victims. Hardly any information on this is available in Germany. Such research would clarify how bullying problems are embedded within long-term and more general forms of antisocial behavior (Olweus, 1994).

3 *Broader variety of research methods.* Bullying research in Germany still concentrates mainly on student and teacher reports (see Krumm, 1997). A general problem in developmental psychopathology is that there are, at times, only moderate correlations between different data sources (Achenbach *et al.*, 1987; Bliesener and Lösel, 1993). In bullying research as well, this means that more studies with multi-setting–multi-informant approaches are desirable. For example, peer reports, direct behavior observations, as well as laboratory experiments, role plays, and non-reactive data should also be included.

4 *Relation to general research on antisocial behavior.* In terms of empirical studies and in theoretical explanations, bullying research is restricted to schools. Although school factors are certainly important for maintenance and prevention of the problems, numerous studies have shown that bullies also exhibit persistent antisocial behavior outside of schools (Farrington and West, 1993; Lösel *et al.*, 1997b; Olweus, 1993). The theoretical

approaches in German research pay little attention to this. Descriptive research or structural and demographic explanatory variables prevail. Efforts should be made to integrate more general explanations of anti-social behavior, for example, on information-processing mechanisms (Crick and Dodge, 1994; Huesmann, 1994) or bio-social interactions (Moffitt, 1993; Raine *et al.*, 1997). Taking into account various contexts of aggressiveness and integrative bio-psycho-social explanations will lead to more well-founded approaches in diagnosis and intervention as well.

5 *Prevention and intervention.* Concepts on prevention and intervention are still sometimes too non-specific and not always oriented toward the current state of empirical research on causes of bullying. As in the treatment and prevention of crime and delinquency, there is a risk that, despite the best of intentions, programs may not only be ineffective, but even counterproductive (Lösel, 1995b; McCord, 1978). It is also becoming clear that measures should not be applied in too much isolation, but on multiple levels (e.g. school, class, individual, parental). In this context, one should include preventive programs that already address antisocial behavior at preschool age (Tremblay and Craig, 1995; Yoshikawa, 1994).

6 *Program evaluation.* Compared with the numerous proposals for intervention, there is a distinct lack of controlled evaluations. Generally only qualitative studies accompanied the programs. Valid quasi-experimental or randomized evaluations are rare and restricted to individual teacher or student training. Without doubt, controlled evaluations are hard to implement with more complex programs. However, a problem in Germany is that no fixed percentage of program funding is specified for sound evaluation. Research on programs tackling school bullying should also not just be restricted to outcome evaluation. The numerous problems in implementation, monitoring, and organizational development that may impact on program integrity indicate a need to strengthen process evaluation as well (Hollin, 1995; Lösel, 1996).

Although such improvements in research and practice in the field of school bullying are not only a question of funding, the question of cost cannot be ignored. However, this is probably an investment that will not only reduce the current suffering of victims and help make schools more human, but may also reduce future costs for bullies in the criminal justice system.

Acknowledgments

Preparation of this chapter was supported by a grant from the German Federal Criminal Police Office (Bundeskriminalamt). We also wish to thank Jonathan Harrow for his help in translation.

References

Achenbach, T.M., McConaughy, S.H. and Howell, C.T. (1987) Child/adolescent behavioral and emotional problems: Implications of cross-informant correlations for situational specificity. *Psychological Bulletin*, 101, 213–232.

Arbeitsgemeinschaft Jugend and Bildung e.V. (1996a) *Basta – Nein zur Gewalt.* Wiesbaden: Universum Verlagsanstalt.

Arbeitsgemeinschaft Jugend and Bildung e.V. (1996b) *Pädagogische Handreichung 96/97. Methodische Vorschläge und Begleitmaterial.* Wiesbaden: Arbeitsgemeinschaft Jugend and Bildung e.V.

Averbeck, M., Bliesener, T. and Lösel, F. (1996) Gewalt in der Schule: Zusammenhänge von Schulklima und Schulleistungen mit unterschiedlichen Typen der Konfliktlösung. In E. Witruk and G. Friedrich (eds) *Pädagogische Psychologie im Streit um ein neues Selbstverständnis* (pp. 584–591). Landau: Verlag Empirische Pädagogik.

Averbeck, M. and Lösel, F. (1994) Subjektive Theorien über Jugendkriminalität. Eine Interview-Studie im Justizsystem. In M. Steller, K.P. Dahle and M. Basque (eds) *Straftäterbehandlung. Argumente für eine Revitalisierung in Forschung und Praxis* (vol. 2, pp. 213–226). Pfaffenweiler: Centaurus.

Bach, H., Knöbel, R., Arenz-Morch, A. and Rosner, A. (1984) *Verhaltensauffälligkeiten in der Schule.* Mainz: Hase and Koehler.

Bayerische Staatsregierung (1994) *Jugend und Gewalt. Kinder und Jugendliche als Opfer und Täter – Situation, Ursachen, Maßnahmen.* München: Bayerische Staatsregierung.

Besag, V. (1989) *Bullies and victims in school.* Milton Keynes: Open University Press.

Bilsky, W., Pfeiffer, C. and Wetzels, P. (1993) Feelings of personal safety, fear of crime and violence and the experience of victimization among elderly people: Research instrument and survey design. In W. Bilsky, C. Pfeiffer and P. Wetzels (eds) *Fear of crime and criminal victimization* (pp. 245–267). Stuttgart: Enke.

Bliesener, T. (1997) Konflikte und Aggressionen zwischen Jugendlichen: Zusammenhänge mit situationsbezogenen Informationsverarbeitungen und Reaktionsmustern. In Bundeskriminalamt (ed.) *Informationen aus der kriminalistisch-kriminologischen Forschung Forum 1996* (pp. 97–125). Bundeskriminalamt: Wiesbaden.

Bliesener, T. and Lösel, F. (1993) Verhaltensbeobachtung psychischer Auffälligkeiten in der Schule: Eine Studie zur Adaption und Validierung der Direct Observation Form der Child Behavior Checklist. *Diagnostica*, 39, 138–150.

Böttger, A. (1996) *Schule, Gewalt und Gesellschaft. Kritische Anmerkungen zu einer kontroversen Diskussion und Ergebnisse empirischer Forschung.* Hannover: Kriminologisches Forschungsinstitut Niedersachsen.

Brusten, M. and Hurrelmann, K. (1973) *Abweichendes Verhalten in der Schule.* München: Juventa.

Bundesministerium für Bildung, Wissenschaft, Forschung und Technologie (BMBF) (1996a) *Grund und Strukturdaten 1996/97.* Bonn: BMBF.

Bundesministerium für Bildung, Wissenschaft, Forschung und Technologie (BMBF) (1996b) *Zahlenbarometer 1996/97.* Bonn: BMBF.

Crick, N.R. and Dodge, K.A. (1994) A review and reformulation of social information processing mechanisms in children's social adjustment. *Psychological Bulletin*, 115, 74–101.

Dann, H.D. (1997) Aggressionsprävention im sozialen Kontext der Schulen. In H.G. Holtappels, W. Heitmeyer, W. Melzer and K.J. Tillmann (eds) *Schulische Gewaltforschung: Stand und Perspektiven* (pp. 351–366). Weinheim: Juventa.

Dann, H.-D., Heubeck, E. and Strak, R. (1994) Aggression und Störungen im Unterricht. *Unterrichten/Erziehen*, 1, 53–57.

Der Bundesminister des Innern (1993) *Texte zur inneren Sicherheit. Extremismus und Gewalt*. Bonn: Der Bundesminister des Innern.

Dettenborn, H. (1993) Gewalt aus der Sicht der Schüler. Ergebnisse einer Untersuchung in Berlin. *Pädagogik*, 3, 31–33.

Dettenborn, H. and Lautsch, E. (1993) Aggression in der Schule aus der Schülerperspektive. *Zeitschrift für Pädagogik*, 39, 745–774.

Diehl, F. and Sudek, R. (1995) Gewalt unter Schülern. Eine Fallstudie an einem Gymnasium. In R. Harnischmacher (ed.) *Gewalt an Schulen. Theorie und Praxis des Gewaltphänomens* (pp. 85–181). Rostock: Hanseatischer Fachverlag für Wirtschaft.

Dijk, J.J.M. van, Mayhew, P. and Killias, M. (1990) *Experiences of crime across the world. Key findings from the 1989 international crime survey*. Deventer: Kluwer.

Elliott, D.S., Huizinga, D. and Menard, S. (1989) *Multiple problem youth*. New York: Plenum.

Farrington, D.P. and West, D.J. (1993) Criminal, penal and life histories of chronic offenders: Risk and protective factors and early identification. *Criminal Behaviour and Mental Health*, 3, 492–523.

Fend, H. and Schneider, G. (1984) Schwierige Schüler – schwierige Klassen. Abweichendes Verhalten. Sucht- und Delinquenzbelastung im Kontext der Schule. *Zeitschrift für Sozialisationsforschung und Erziehungssoziologie*, 4, 123–142.

Ferstl, R., Niebel, G. and Hanewinkel, R. (1993) *Gutachterliche Stellungnahme zur Verbreitung von Gewalt und Aggression an Schulen in Schleswig-Holstein*. Kiel: Die Ministerin für Bildung, Wissenschaft, Kultur und Sport des Landes Schleswig-Holstein.

Franz, M. and Schlesiger, H. (1974) *Probleme der Arbeit in der Hauptschule. Eine Querschnittuntersuchung in den Schulen des Schulaufsichtsbezirks 21, Altona/Elbgemeinden*. Hamburg: Behörde für Schule, Jugend und Berufsbildung.

Freie und Hansestadt Hamburg. Behörde für Schule, Jugend und Berufsbildung (1993) *Gewalt von Kindern und Jugendlichen in Hamburg*. Hamburg: Freie und Hansestadt Hamburg.

Freitag, M. and Hurrelmann, K. (1993) Gewalt an Schulen: In erster Linie ein Jungen-Phänomen. *Neue Deutsche Schule*, 8, 24–25.

Fuchs, M., Lamnek, S. and Luedtke, J. (1996) *Schule und Gewalt. Realität und Wahrnehmung eines sozialen Problems*. Opladen: Leske & Buderich.

Funk, W. (1995) *Nürnberger Schüler-Studie*. Regensburg: Roderer.

Hanewinkel, R. and Knaack, R. (1997a) Mobbing: Eine Fragebogenstudie zum Ausmaß von Aggression und Gewalt an Schulen. *Empirische Pädagogik*, 11, 403–422.

Hanewinkel, R. and Knaack, R. (1997b) Prävention von Aggression und Gewalt an Schulen. Ergebnisse einer Interventionsstudie. In H.G. Holtappels, W. Heitmeyer, W. Melzer and K.J. Tillman (eds) *Schulische Gewaltforschung. Stand und Perspektiven* (pp. 299–313). Weinheim: Juventa.

Hensel, R. (1993) Auf dem Weg zu weniger Gewalt – auch durch das Leben in der Schule. In M. Spreiter (ed.), *Waffenstillstand im Klassenzimmer. Vorschläge, Hilfestellungen, Prävention*. Weinheim: Beltz.

Hollin, C.R. (1995) The meanings and implications of "programme integrity." In J. McGuire (ed.) *What works: Reducing reoffending* (pp. 195–208). Chichester: Wiley.

Holtappels, H.G. (1985) Schülerprobleme und abweichendes Schülerverhalten aus der Schülerperspektive. *Zeitschrift für Sozialisationsforschung und Erziehungssoziologie*, 5, 291–323.

Huesmann, L.R. (ed.) (1994) *Aggressive behavior: Current perspectives*. New York: Plenum.

Hurrelmann, K. and Pollmer, K. (1994) Gewalttätige Verhaltensweisen von Jugendlichen in Sachsen – ein speziell ostdeutsches Problem. *Kind, Jugend, Gesellschaft*, 1, 3–11.

Informationsdienst AgAG (1996) *Projekte im Aktionsprogramm gegen Aggression und Gewalt*. Berlin: Informations-, Fortbildungs- und Forschungsdienst Jugendgewaltprävention.

Institut der Deutschen Wirtschaft Köln (IW) (1996) *Zahlen zur wirtschaftlichen Entwicklung der Bundesrepublik Deutschland*. Köln: Deutscher Instituts-Verlag.

Klockhaus, R. and Habermann-Morbey, B. (1986) *Psychologie und Schulvandalismus*. Göttingen: Hogrefe.

Krappmann, L. and Oswald, H. (1995) *Alltag der Schulkinder. Beobachtungen und Analysen von Interaktionen und Sozialbeziehungen*. Weinheim: Juventa.

Krumm, V. (1997) Methodische Ansätze und Methodendefizite in der schulischen Gewaltforschung. In H.G. Holtappels, W. Heitmeyer, W. Melzer and K.J. Tillmann (eds) *Schulische Gewaltforschung. Stand und Perspektiven* (pp. 63–79). Weinheim: Juventa.

Kuhnke, R. (1995) Gewalttätige Jugendliche. Ergebnisse einer Längsschnittstudie bei Jugendlichen im Raum Leipzig. In S. Lamnek (ed.) *Jugend und Gewalt. Devianz und Kriminalität in Ost und West* (pp. 155–170). Opladen: Leske & Budrich.

Kultusministerium des Landes Sachsen-Anhalt (1994) *Konflikte – Aggressionen – Gewalt. Prävention und konstruktiver Umgang*. Magdeburg: Kultusministerium des Landes Sachsen-Anhalt.

Kury, H. (1993) Crime in East and West Germany – results of the first intra-German victims' study. In W. Bilsky, C. Pfeiffer and P. Wetzels (eds) *Fear of crime and criminal victimization* (pp. 213–230). Stuttgart: Enke.

Lamnek, S. (1995) Gewalt in Massenmedien und Gewalt von Schülern. In S. Lamnek (ed.) *Jugend und Gewalt. Devianz und Kriminalität in Ost und West* (pp. 225–256). Opladen: Leske & Budrich.

Lerchenmüller, H. (1986) *Evaluation eines sozialen Lernprogramms in der Schule mit delinquenzpräventiver Zielsetzung*. Köln: Heymanns.

Lerchenmüller, H. (1987) *Soziales Lernen in der Schule: Zur Prävention sozial-auffälligen Verhaltens. Ein Unterrichtsprogramm für die Sekundarstufe I*. Bochum: Brockmeyer.

Lösel, F. (1975) *Handlungskontrolle und Jugenddelinquenz*. Stuttgart: Enke.

Lösel, F. (1994) Deviancy, crime and disorder among young people. *Criminal Behaviour and Mental Health*, 4, 1–11.

Lösel, F. (1995a) Entwicklung und Ursachen der Gewalt in unserer Gesellschaft. *Gruppendynamik*, 26, 5–22.

Lösel, F. (1995b) The efficacy of correctional treatment. In J. McGuire (ed.) *What works: Reducing reoffending* (pp. 79–111). Chichester: Wiley.

Lösel, F. (1996) Working with young offenders: The impact of meta-analyses. In C.R. Hollin and K. Howells (eds) *Clinical approaches to working with young offenders* (pp. 57–78). Chichester: Wiley.

Lösel, F. and Bliesener, T. (1989) Psychology in prison: Role assessment and testing of an organizational model. In H. Wegener, F. Lösel and J. Haisch (eds) *Criminal behavior and the justice system* (pp. 419–439). New York: Springer-Verlag.

Lösel, F. and Hylla, R. (1996) The impact of professional roles on subjective explanations of juvenile crime and violence. Paper presented at the Sixth European Conference on Psychology and Law, Siena, August.

Lösel, F., Averbeck, M. and Bliesener, T. (1997a) Gewalt zwischen Schülern der Sekundarstufe: Eine Untersuchung zur Prävalenz und Beziehung zu allgemeiner Aggressivität und Delinquenz. *Zeitschrift für Empirische Pädagogik*, 11, 327–349.

Lösel, F. Bliesener, T. and Averbeck, M. (1995) *Gewalttätiges und gewaltfreies Konfliktlösungsverhalten in der frühen Jugend: Eine Bedingungs- und Prozeßanalyse. 1. Zwischenbericht.* Erlangen-Nürnberg: Institut für Psychologie und Sozialwissenschaftliches Forschungszentrum der Universität Erlangen-Nürnberg.

Lösel, F., Bliesener, T. and Averbeck, M. (1996) *Gewalttätiges und gewaltfreies Konfliktlösungsverhalten in der frühen Jugend: Eine Bedingungs- und Prozeßanalyse. 3. Zwischenbericht.* Erlangen-Nürnberg: Institut für Psychologie und Sozialwissenschaftliches Forschungszentrum der Universität Erlangen-Nürnberg.

Lösel, F., Bliesener, T. and Averbeck, M. (1997b) Gewalt an Schulen: Erlebens-und Verhaltensprobleme von Tätern und Opfern. In H.G. Holtappels, W. Heitmeyer, W. Melzer and K.J. Tillmann (eds) *Schulische Gewaltforschung. Stand und Perspektiven* (pp. 137–153). Weinheim: Juventa.

Lösel, F., Bliesener, T. and Averbeck, M. (1998, in press) Hat die Delinquenz von Schülern zugenommen? Ein Vergleich im Dunkelfeld nach 22 Jahren. In M. Schäfer and D. Frey (eds) *Aggression und Gewalt unter Kindern und Jugendlichen? Von Medien suggeriertes Problem oder empirisch belegtes Faktum?* Göttingen: Hogrefe.

Lösel, F., Selg, H., Schneider, U. and Müller-Luckmann, E. (1990) Ursachen, Prävention und Kontrolle von Gewalt aus psychologischer Sicht. Gutachten der Unterkommission I. In H.-D. Schwind *et al.* (eds) *Ursachen, Prävention und Kontrolle von Gewalt, Bd. 2, Erstgutachten der Unterkommissionen* (pp. 1–156). Berlin: Duncker & Humblot.

McCord, J. (1978) A thirty-year follow-up of treatment effects. *American Psychologist*, 33, 284–289.

Mansel, J. and Hurrelmann, K. (1998) Aggression und delinquentes Verhalten Jugendlicher im Zeitvergleich. *Kölner Zeitschrift für Soziologie und Sozialpsychologie*, 50, 78–109.

Melzer, W. and Rostampour, P. (1996) Schulische Gewaltformen und Täter-Opfer-Problematik. In W. Schubarth, F.-U. Kolbe and H. Willems (eds) *Gewalt an Schulen* (pp. 121–148). Opladen: Leske & Budrich.

Ministerin für Frauen, Bildung, Weiterbildung und Sport des Landes Schleswig-Holstein (1994) *Mobbing: Gewaltprävention in Schulen in Schleswig-Holstein.* Kiel: Die Ministerin für Frauen, Bildung, Weiterbildung und Sport.

Mischkowitz, R. (1994) *Fremdenfeindliche Gewalt und Skinheads. Eine Literaturanalyse und Bestandsaufnahme polizeilicher Maßnahmen, Bd. 30.* Wiesbaden: Bundeskriminalamt.

Moffitt, T.E. (1993) Adolescence-limited and life-course-persistent antisocial behavior: A developmental taxonomy. *Psychological Review*, 100, 674–701.

Mölleken, R. and Steinke-Schmickler, C. (1995) Gewalt an Kölner Schulen. Ergebnisse einer Umfrage. In R. Harnischmacher (ed.) *Gewalt an Schulen. Theorie und Praxis des Gewaltphänomens* (pp. 41–84). Rostock: Hanseatischer Fachverlag für Wirtschaft.

Niebel, G., Hanewinkel, R. and Ferstl, R. (1993) Gewalt und Aggression in Schleswig-Holsteinischen Schulen. *Zeitschrift für Pädagogik*, 39, 775–798.

Niedersächsisches Kultusministerium (1992) *Frieden schaffen in den Klassen. Mit Alpträumen in die Schule oder Alp-Traum-Schule?* Hannover: Niedersächsisches Kultusministerium.

Olweus, D. (1989) *The Olweus Bully/Victim Questionnaire*. Bergen: mimeograph.

Olweus, D. (1990) Bullying among school children. In K. Hurrelmann and F. Lösel (eds) *Health hazards in adolescence* (pp. 259–297). Berlin: de Gruyter.

Olweus, D. (1991) Bully/victim problems among school children: Basic facts and effects of a school based intervention program. In D.J. Pepler and K.H. Rubin (eds) *The development and treatment of childhood aggression* (pp. 411–448). Hillsdale, NJ: Lawrence Erlbaum.

Olweus, D. (1993) *Bullying at school*. Oxford: Blackwell.

Olweus, D. (1994) Bullying at school: Long-term outcomes for victims and an effective school-based intervention program. In L.R. Huesmann (ed.) *Aggressive behavior: Current perspectives* (pp. 97–130). New York: Plenum Press.

Olweus, D. (1995) *Gewalt in der Schule*. Bern: Huber.

Patterson, G.R., Reid, J.B. and Dishion, T.J. (1992) *Antisocial boys*. Eugene, OR: Castalia.

Petermann, F. and Bochmann, F. (1993) Metaanalyse von Kinderverhaltenstrainings: Eine erste Bilanz. *Zeitschrift für Klinische Psychologie*, 22, 137–152.

Petermann, F. and Petermann, U. (1990) *Training mit aggressiven Kindern*, 4th edn. München: Psychologie Verlags Union.

Pfeiffer, C., Brettfeld, K., Delzer, I. and Link, G. (1996) Steigt die Jugendkriminalität? In C. Pfeiffer and H. Barth (eds) *Forschungsthema "Kriminalität." Interdisziplinäre Beiträge zur kriminologischen Forschung* (vol. 5, pp. 19–53). Baden-Baden: Nomos.

Raine, A., Farrington, D.P., Brennan, P. and Mednick, S.A. (1997) *Biosocial bases of violence*. New York: Plenum.

Reitmajer, V. (1996) *Pädagogischer Leitfaden zum Abbau ausgrenzender und abwertender (verbaler) Praxen bei Jugendlichen im Kontext von rechtsextremistischer Orientierung, Ausländer- und Minderheitenfeindlichkeit*. Thalhofen: Bauer-Verlag.

Schäfer, M. (1996) Aggression unter Schülern. Eine Bestandsaufnahme über das Schikanieren in der Schule am Beispiel der 6. und 8. Klassenstufe. *Report Psychologie*, 21, 700–711.

Schwind, H.D., Baumann, J., Lösel, F., Remschmidt, H., Eckert, R., Kerner, H.J., Stümper, A., Wassermann, R., Otto, H., Rudolf, W., Berckhauer, F., Kube, E., Steinhilper, M. and Steffen, W. (eds) (1990) *Ursachen, Prävention und Kontrolle von Gewalt. Analysen und Vorschläge der Unabhängigen Regierungskommission zur Verhinderung und Bekämpfung von Gewalt (Gewaltkommission)*. Berlin: Duncker & Humblot.

Schwind, H.D., Roitsch, K., Ahlborn, W. and Gielen, B. (1995) *Gewalt in der Schule. Am Beispiel Bochum. Mainzer Schriften zur Situation von Kriminalitätsopfern* (vol. 10). Mainz: Weißer Ring.

Senatsverwaltung für Schule, Berufsbildung und Sport Berlin (1992) *Gruppengewalt und Schule*. Berlin: Senatsverwaltung für Schule, Berufsbildung und Sport.

Smith, P.K. (1991) The silent nightmare: Bullying and victimisation in school peer groups. *The Psychologist*, 4, 243–248.

Tennstädt, K.C. and Dann, H.D. (1987) *Das Konstanzer Trainingsmodell (KTM), Bd. 3: Evaluation des Trainingserfolgs im empirischen Vergleich*. Bern: Huber.

Tennstädt, K.C., Krause, F., Humpert, W. and Dann, H.D. (1984) *Das Konstanzer Trainingsmodell (KTM). Neue Wege im Schulalltag: Ein Selbsthilfeprogramm für zeitgemäßes Unterrichten und Erziehen, Bd. 1: Trainingshandbuch*. Bern: Huber.

Tillmann, K.J. (1997) Gewalt an Schulen: Öffentliche Diskussion und erziehungswissenschaftliche Forschung. In H.G. Holtappels, W. Heitmeyer, W. Melzer and K.J. Tillmann (eds) *Schulische Gewaltforschung. Stand und Perspektiven* (pp.11–25). Weinheim: Juventa.

Tillmann, K.J., Holtappels, H.G., Meier, U. and Popp, U. (1996) *Erste Forschungsergebnisse einer Repräsentativerhebung im Land Hessen über Gewalt an Schulen*. Universität Bielefeld: Sonderforschungsbereich 227.

Todt, E. and Busch, L. (1996) *Wissenschaftliche Begleitung des Modellversuchs "Schule ohne Gewalt" im Lahn-Dill-Kreis. Bericht über drei Untersuchungen an Schülern und Schülerinnen der Jahrgangsstufe 5 bis 9*. Gießen: Fachbereich Psychologie der Justus-Liebig-Universität Gießen.

Tremblay, R.E. and Craig, W. (1995) Developmental crime prevention. In M. Tonry and D.P. Farrington (eds) *Building a safer society: Strategic approaches to crime prevention* (pp. 151–236). Chicago: University Press.

Unabhängige Kommission zur Verhinderung und Bekämpfung von Gewalt in Berlin (1995) *Endbericht der Unabhängigen Kommission zur Verhinderung und Bekämpfung von Gewalt in Berlin*. Berlin: Arno Spitz.

Willems, H., Eckert, R., Würtz, S. and Steinmetz, L. (1993) *Fremdenfeindliche Gewalt: Einstellungen, Täter, Konflikteskalationen*. Opladen: Leske & Budrich.

Wustmans, A. and Becker, P. (1996) *Strategien von Schülerinnen und Schülern zum Umgang mit Gewalt in der Schule*. Beitrag zum 40. Kongreß der Deutschen Gesellschaft für Psychologie in München, September.

Yoshikawa, H. (1994) Prevention as cumulative protection: Effects of early family support and education on chronic delinquency and its risks. *Psychological Bulletin*, 115, 28–54.

15 Switzerland

Françoise D. Alsaker
and Andreas Brunner

Summary

The reputation of Switzerland, at least in Europe, is that it is expensive, perfectly organised, clean and very beautiful. Violence does not belong to Switzerland's reputation. In this chapter, we show that violence, in terms of victimisation, belongs to the daily life of schoolchildren in Switzerland as well as in other countries. In fact, even if there is no agreed upon word for bullying or victimisation, the media have often reported on 'violence at school' during the last five years or so. Fairly often the type of violence described fits well with the concept of bully/victim problems in schools. The first author uses the term 'plagen' in her contacts with schoolchildren, teachers and parents. It is a common word in most Swiss dialects and corresponds roughly to 'pester' in English. The term 'mobbing' is generally used for harassment in the workplace.

We first give some information on Switzerland as a country and on the educational system, which is rather complex. Second, we report on an informal survey conducted among the directorates of education in each canton as well as centres for school psychology and adolescent psychology. Finally, we report some results from a study conducted in 1994 among adolescents in Switzerland and, in fact, also in Norway. Presenting the first results from this project, we will focus mainly on the Swiss data and use the Norwegian data only in some comparisons. First, we present the percentages of girls and boys reporting being bullied or bullying others. Second, we present data on where bullying occurs. Finally, we address the issue of differences in occurrence of bully/victim problems among different school types in Switzerland.

General information on the country and its population

Switzerland, which lies in southern central Europe between Germany, Austria, Liechtenstein, Italy and France, has an area of about 41,000 km^2. The Alps cover approximately 60 per cent of the total area. The country consists of 26 cantons of varying size and population. Bern is the capital; Zürich, Basel,

Geneva and Lausanne are the other large cities. The Swiss Confederation is organised as a federal and democratic republic. The federal constitution of 1874, which is presently being totally revised, explicitly grants the federal government only the rights conferred by the cantons. The cantons, with their own governments and constitutions, have the benefit of extensive sovereignty, of which they make good use, as we will see when it comes to the educational system.

A distinctive feature of Switzerland is its four official languages: German, French, Italian and Rhaeto-Romanic. About 64 per cent of the population have German as their native language, about 19 per cent French, almost 8 per cent Italian and only 0.6 per cent Rhaeto-Romanic.

The population of Switzerland was 7,084,800 in 1996. About 20 per cent of the constant population of Switzerland are foreign nationalities. About a quarter of the foreign population is Italian, about 21 per cent come from ex-Yugoslavia and about 10 per cent from Portugal. Those seeking political asylum are not included in the figures of the constant population (75,200 at the end of 1995). About 46 per cent of the population are Roman Catholic and 40 per cent are Protestant.

The average national income per inhabitant is approximately 45,000 Swiss francs (1 CHF = 0.65 US$). In Switzerland, 56 per cent of the women and 79 per cent of the men over 15 years old are employed. In 1997 the level of unemployment was approximately 5 per cent, which is eight times higher than in 1990; this amounts to 185,000 registered unemployed persons, of whom about 40 per cent are women.

Education system

In Switzerland, the cantons are basically responsible for education. According to their various political, economic and cultural situations, each of the 26 cantons has developed its own education system. Thus, an overall view always means simplification (for details, see Bundesamt für Statistik, 1992). Mandatory school lasts for nine or ten years.

Classification/terminology

In order to give an overall view of the Swiss school system, the Swiss classification scheme used for the national school statistics is explained below. This scheme groups educational courses according to two main criteria: school level (standard: number of school years in the normal course) and programme (goal of the educational course).

Preschool

Preschool consists of institutions which, among other tasks, prepare the children for mandatory school. It is optional.

Primary school level

The primary school level covers the first years of mandatory school; it ends with the selection of pupils on the basis of educational achievement.

Secondary level I

Secondary level I covers the remaining school years after primary school to the end of mandatory school. According to the different achievement requirements for the pupils, three types are distinguished: schools with basic requirements, schools with broader requirements (the pupils have fulfilled specific criteria of selection) and schools without selection (schools which do not include different tracks).

Secondary level II

Secondary level II is the first phase after completing mandatory school education; it includes all vocational and general education courses. Adolescents attending secondary school level II have a choice between 'matura' schools (e.g. gymnasium), the prerequisite for attending a university, diploma middle schools, which prepare for specific vocational training, other general education schools, vocational schools for teaching, for vocational trainers and apprenticeships. Furthermore, the course for further vocational education is set very early in numerous cantons on a selective basis after the first four or six school years. A chosen course may only be modified at great expense; there is hardly any free interchange between the various types of school.

In 1989/1990, the average number of pupils per school class was 18.9 in primary school and 17.7 in secondary school.

Characteristics of the school system

Two points are characteristic of the Swiss education system: The first – as mentioned above – is federalism. This allows a great variety in the Swiss education scene. Within mandatory schools, for example, there are distinct differences: primary school can last four, five or six years, depending on the canton; secondary level I can include two, three or four types of school with varying requirements; the total amount of required school lessons during mandatory school can vary between 7200 and 9000 hours.

The second characteristic is linked to vocational education. It has a special status in the Swiss education system: about 70 per cent of the adolescents complete some kind of vocational education after mandatory school. Most of them serve an apprenticeship, which means receiving practical education in a company and theoretical education at vocational school. After their basic vocational education, about 80 per cent start working and one-fifth continue education at level III.

Bullying at school – survey among educational institutions

To get an idea of the present situation in Switzerland as to bullying statistics and intervention, we conducted an informal survey. In each canton, we wrote to the directorate of education as well as to centres for school psychology and adolescent psychology. Bullying was defined according to Olweus' (1993) general definition. That is, bullying was introduced as a specific form of violence among peers that presupposes that a student is 'exposed, repeatedly and over time, to negative actions on the part of one or more other students' (p. 9). The direct or indirect forms of bullying were made explicit and the following questions were asked:

- Is bullying at school considered to be a current problem in your institution/centre? If so, in what way?
- Are there any data on the frequency and forms of bullying at school in your canton?
- Are or were there any measures or programmes for prevention or intervention concerning (1) bullying, and (2) violence at school in your canton? Are such steps being planned?

In all, we approached 203 offices of which 60 responded: a response rate of almost 30 per cent. This included replies from 22 of the 26 cantons. Our main goal was to find out how much action was taken against bullying or 'violence at schools' in the different cantons. We assumed that institutions which had done something specific would be eager to show that they were active and would have answered our enquiry. Therefore we assume that the answers we have received include everything that exists on bully/victim problems in Switzerland. The main results of the survey are presented below descriptively.

Is bullying a current problem?

A clear majority of the sample considered 'bullying at school' as a current problem from both a quantitative and a qualitative perspective. Especially in larger cities and conurbations, the phenomenon is considered as becoming more widespread. In some cantons consisting mostly of rural areas a similar trend was observed, although usually only 'isolated cases' were reported. In other cantons, bullying was observed but was considered to be a constant phenomenon without being an acute problem. In a few cantons no bullying was registered. The reasons given for this were strong social control in rural areas and the direct settlement of such problems between teachers and parents without professional help.

Besides a larger number of registered cases, increasing brutality was also remarked on in several cantons. There was a large spectrum of forms and an increase in bullying in groups and outside cities was noted. The consulting centres reported sometimes being confronted with the problem in connection with other symptoms, such as sinking levels of achievement at school, skipping school, etc.

In sum, bully/victim problems in schools were generally perceived as existent, staying at least at a constant level, or often increasing.

Statistics

Although the phenomenon is obviously a current problem, hardly any data on bullying have been collected in Switzerland. According to information from the Federal Office of Statistics and from the Swiss Conference of the Cantonal Directorates of Education, there are no nationwide data. At the level of the cantons the situation is similar: seventeen of the 22 cantons which responded to the survey have no statistical data at all. Three cantons knew of certain enquiries, for example, by a school administration or by the police, but there are no complete and systematic data which are generally accessible.

The exception comprises two studies which do not specifically deal with bullying, but rather with violence at school in a general sense.

In the first study (Mülli, 1992), 631 high school pupils in three communities in eastern Switzerland were questioned about physical violence. It was observed that 12 to 15 per cent of the boys had been injured by weapons (knives) or by implements used in Asian martial arts. About 10 per cent of both genders also reported their genitals had been touched against their will by others who applied violence. In the canton of Waadt, Woringer (1994) studied violence in primary school; 86 children from four classes were questioned: 45.8 per cent of the children reported they were generally subjected to violence at school quite frequently or very frequently, 14.4 per cent were excluded from games, 19.3 per cent of the children never or very seldom had been victims, and a little more than half of the children had never committed violent acts against peers.

In several cantons, a large number of unregistered cases can be assumed. The problem of defining or precisely registering the phenomenon was given as a reason for the lack of statistics by a few cantons. Another problem is that the local school authorities have a large amount of autonomy, and schools and consulting centres work very independently. Centralised data collection is therefore always tied to a great amount of effort and is rather difficult. In addition, the relevant authorities are only just beginning to be interested in the phenomenon.

Prevention/intervention against bullying at school

In most cantons, 'bullying at school' is not treated as a separate topic for preventive measures, but is usually integrated into the programmes against violence at school in general. In a few cases, the phenomenon is discussed as a topic of its own in teachers' further education courses or at school meetings with parents. There are also a few schools which discuss the problem in more detail.

Concerning interventions, there is quite a different picture. There are specific actions in the sense of individual interventions. One single canton has specially trained professionals, and theoretical foundations and potential types of intervention are specifically documented.

Prevention/intervention against violence at school

For 'violence at school', which explicitly or implicitly includes bullying in many cantons, prevention programmes are more numerous and varied. Teams draw up expert reports, catalogues with lists of prevention and intervention strategies, handbooks and leaflets (e.g. Brechbühl, Brünggel, Iseli, Joray and Mathys, 1996). Projects such as touring exhibitions, special thematic weeks or school festivals are organised and there are further education courses for teachers and information meetings for parents. One canton reports having two specially trained psychologists in this field, another canton is planning a counselling centre for questions regarding violence and two other cantons successfully use mediators.

However, these numerous strategies are not always actually practised. A few cantons note with regret a lack of sensitivity among teachers or even their conscious or unconscious resistance to external professionals. Other cantons report simply having too few professionals for effective prevention.

As far as interventions are concerned, they are usually isolated. Only one canton has a specially trained team of professionals which functions as a 'task force' for crisis interventions (Guggenbühl, 1992). In another canton, a crisis intervention group which was recommended by professionals was considered unnecessary by the authorities.

Results from a recent survey among Swiss adolescents

In 1994 a survey on 'Everyday school life and stress in school pupils in Switzerland and Norway' was conducted. Among other things, the students were asked questions about victimisation. These are the first results from a larger Swiss sample explicitly addressing the question of victimisation. The results from the Norwegian students are included only in order to give some basis of comparison for the Swiss figures.

Participants and procedure

Data were collected on six adjacent age cohorts (in grades four through nine) in the German-speaking part of Switzerland (n = 1262), in the French-speaking part of Switzerland (n = 592) and in Norway (n = 1117). The two

Swiss samples are pooled together in the following analyses. All three samples were composed of approximately half girls and half boys. In both countries the samples were selected in urbanised communities of about the same size located near a larger city of about the same size (Berne in Switzerland and Bergen in Norway). Children in the Norwegian sample came from 62 classes. According to national regulations, only students could participate for whom explicit consent from the parents was obtained. Consent letters were received from 82 per cent of the parents in the originally drawn sample. The Swiss sample was drawn from 96 classes. Parents were informed about the study and had the opportunity to deny participation. This happened for fewer than 1 per cent of the students.

A questionnaire was administered to the students in their ordinary classrooms by two research assistants. Teachers were usually absent from the classroom. Anonymity was guaranteed.

Instrument

Six items were used to measure 'being bullied by others' and 'bullying others'. Three different forms of victimisation were assessed: physical, verbal and indirect victimisation (i.e. exclusion). The students answered each question separately, and a score was calculated for each of these three forms of victimisation. Given that there is no special word for 'bullying' in Switzerland (see above) and that we wanted the data from both countries to be as comparable as possible, we decided to use very similar formulations in both countries and we therefore did not use the specific Norwegian word for bullying (see Alsaker and Flammer (in press) for a discussion of the challenges of cross-national research). In order to make a comparison of our results to results using other instruments easier, the formulations used for being victimised (English translation on the basis of the Norwegian items) are given here:

- *Physical victimisation*: 'I have been pestered, hit, had my hair pulled, kicked, or attacked in a mean way at school or on the way to school.'
- *Verbal victimisation*: 'I have been made a fool of, teased in a mean way, or someone has said nasty things to me in school or on the way to school.'
- *Isolation*: 'Sometimes other pupils deliberately keep you out of things; they refuse to let you take part. Has this happened to you?'

The questions concerning bullying were formulated in a similar way. The answering categories to all six questions were: Such things have (1) never happened, (2) happened once or twice, (3) about once a week, (4) two or three times a week, and (5) even more often during the *past two months*. In the following analyses we consider only the percentages of students who were bullied or bullied others *at least once a week*. This cut-off point was chosen, first because we were interested in more tenacious bullying situations, and second, in order to compare our results with other published results using the same precise cut-off point.

Results

Frequencies of being bullied and bullying others

The percentages of Swiss girls and boys who reported that they had been bullied or had bullied peers at least once a week during the past two months are recorded and illustrated in Figure 15.1. As we can see, the percentages clearly differed between the three forms of bullying. In addition, girls reported significantly less often being verbally or physically bullied than boys ($\text{chi-square}_{verbal} = 7.38$, $p < 0.01$ and $\text{chi-square}_{physical} = 13.44$, $p > 0.001$; $df = 1$ in both cases). As expected they were also significantly less active than boys in bullying others verbally, physically, and also indirectly ($\text{chi-square}_{verbal} = 30$, $p < 0.00001$, $\text{chi-square}_{physical} = 20.76$, $p < 0.0001$ and $\text{chi-square}_{indirect} = 4.03$, $p < 0.05$; $df = 1$ in all analyses).

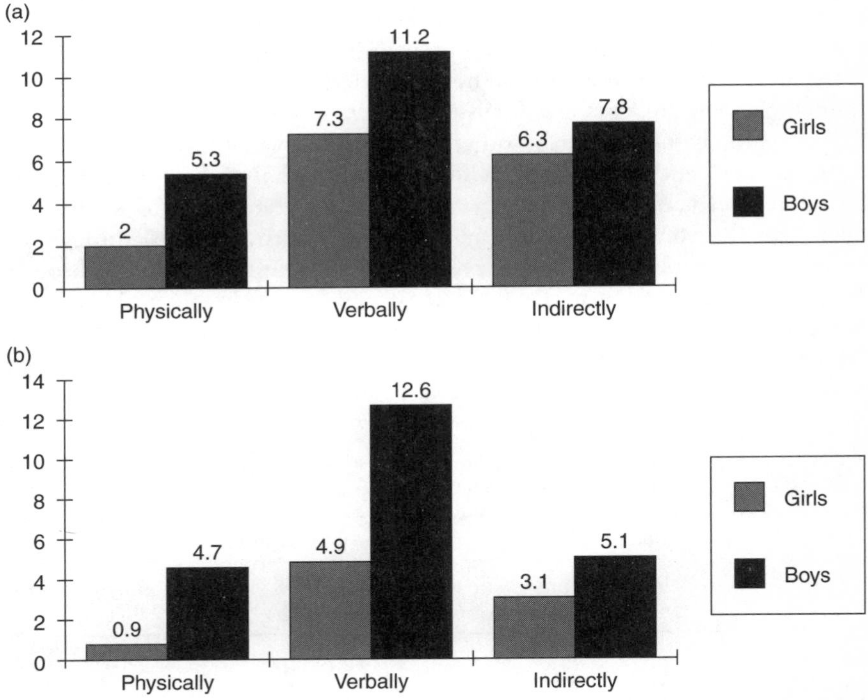

Figure 15.1 Percentages of Swiss girls and boys reporting (a) being bullied by peers and (b) bullying peers at least once a week.

The percentages reported in Figure 15.1 were similar to the percentages obtained from the Norwegian students. Table 15.1 contains the values for both countries. The data were compared using cross-tabulations separately for each gender. In ten out of the twelve comparisons, there were more Swiss students reporting victimisation than Norwegian students. However, there were only two significant results. Swiss girls reported being bullied indirectly more often than their Norwegian peers ($\text{chi-square}_{indirect} = 4.44$, $p < 0.05$; $df = 1$) and they also reported bullying others indirectly more often than the Norwegian girls ($\text{chi-square}_{indirect} = 7.96$, $p < 0.01$; $df = 1$). A compound score based on the three victimisation variables was computed. A student was categorised as being bullied or bullying others when she or he had reported experiencing (or doing) one of the three types of bullying at least once a week. The figures from the two countries were compared separately for each gender and pooled together. Swiss students consistently yielded somewhat higher percentages, but the differences were never significant.

In order to compare our results with other studies (see below), the data from the girls and the boys were pooled together and the average percentage of students bullied or bullying others at least once a week was calculated. The figures cannot be compared directly, since we have used separate questions for the three main forms of bullying, whereas most other studies report results based on one global question without mentioning any differentiation. Apart from the differences in girls as to indirect bullying (see above) the Swiss and Norwegian students did not differ significantly. Therefore, only the results for Swiss students are discussed here.

As regards being bullied by others, the pooled percentages were 3.7 per cent, 9.3 per cent and 7 per cent for physical, verbal and indirect victimisation respectively. Since the age range varies from study to study, the figures for the younger students (fourth through sixth grade, 10 through 13 years) and the older students (seventh through ninth grade, 13 through 16 years) are also given in Table 15.2.

Figures from Olweus' (e.g. 1991) study in Norway in 1983 were lower, with an average of 3 per cent of the students reporting being bullied at least once a week. It should be noted that the age range in his study was somewhat

Table 15.1 Percentages of Swiss and Norwegian students reporting being bullied or bullying others at least once a week, according to gender

	Bullied by peers				*Bullying their peers*			
	Girls CH[1]	*Girls N*[1]	*Boys CH*	*Boys N*	*Girls CH*	*Girls N*	*Boys CH*	*Boys N*
Physically	2	1.5	5.3	4.5	0.9	1.3	4.7	2.7
Verbally	7.3	5.1	11.2	11.3	4.9	4.2	12.6	9.7
Indirectly	6.3	3.6	7.8	6.6	3.1	0.8	5.1	3.3

Note: 1 CH = Switzerland, N = Norway

Table 15.2 Percentages of Swiss and Norwegian students reporting being bullied or bullying others at least once a week according to age

	Bullied by peers				*Bullying their peers*			
	Younger[2] *CH*[1]	*Younger* *N*[1]	*Older*[3] *CH*	*Older* *N*	*Younger* *CH*	*Younger* *N*	*Older* *CH*	*Older* *N*
Physically	5.8	3.5	2.3	2.4	3.7	2.2	2.3	1.8
Verbally	10.8	8.3	8.2	8.2	8.3	4.7	9.2	10
Indirectly	9.5	6.6	5.3	3.1	3.4	1.7	4.6	2.4

Notes: 1 CH = Switzerland, N = Norway
2 Younger = 4th through 6th grade, 10 through 13 years
3 Older = 7th through 9th grade, 13 through 16 years

wider than ours, and included second and third graders. O'Moore and Hillery (1989) reported 8 per cent Irish (Dublin) students (between 7 and 13 years of age) being bullied at least once a week. Whitney and Smith (1993) reported 9.8 per cent of the English children aged 7 through 11 years (junior and middle school) being bullied with the same frequency, whereas the percentage was 4.1 per cent in adolescents aged 11 through 16 years (secondary school). Perry, Williard and Perry (1990) reported 10 per cent of the American students being bullied (age 8 through 12).

In sum, our results fit fairly well with previous findings. Earlier figures (global measure) are in between the figures we report for physical (lowest percentages) and verbal victimisation (highest percentages). One might ask whether the format of our questionnaire can have heightened the figures concerning verbal and indirect bullying more than if we had used a global question. It could be argued that the students are pushed towards reporting less severe events, which would not have been mentioned as bullying if we had used the global method. On the other hand, earlier studies using a global question and a follow-up question on the type of victimisation have shown that students also report being bullied if it is 'only' verbally or through exclusion (indirectly); also, our use of the once a week cut-off point indicates the severity of the reported episodes. Being verbally attacked or excluded once a week is clearly considered to be a serious offence to one's integrity.

The figures for bullying others physically (2.8 per cent) and indirectly (4.1 per cent) also fit well with previous studies. The figures for verbal bullying (8.8 per cent) are higher than expected. This can be interpreted in a similar way to reports on being bullied. Again the results may indicate a clearly rougher climate among peers than what we know is adequate for a healthy social development.

The fact that Swiss girls reported significantly more indirect victimisation (exclusion) than their Norwegian peers, whereas all other differences are small and nonsignificant, is interesting. This may reflect a cultural difference in the way children and adolescents express aggression, since the Swiss girls also reported bullying in that way more than the Norwegian girls. It may also reflect a higher sensitivity for exclusion. In both cases it probably indicates a cultural difference in the importance of social integration.

Where does bullying occur?

The students had the opportunity to indicate several places where bullying occurred at school: on the way to and from school, in the playground (or at the entrance), in the classroom, in the corridors, and in the toilets. Considering only the answers from students who reported having been bullied at least sometimes during the last two months, percentages were calculated for where they indicated having been bullied. A corresponding analysis was conducted for bullying others. The figures are presented in Table 15.3.

As we can see, victims and bullies agree to a very high degree as to where bullying occurs. In Switzerland, on the way to and from school, playground and classrooms are nominated to a similar extent as locations for bullying to happen. Every one of these categories is mentioned by around one-third of the students. Corridors follow with approximately 20 per cent and toilets are negligible. The picture differs in Norway as regards the playground; most bullying seems to occur there, being mentioned by more than 55 per cent of the Norwegian students. This difference is interesting because it may point to a difference in the way breaks are organised, playgrounds are structured, or in the extent to which recess is supervised by adults. This is an issue to follow up.

School type and bullying. Does it make a difference?

We earlier summarised the selection system in schools. The students in the present study were at the primary level (fourth through sixth graders) and at the secondary level I (seventh through ninth graders). The types of schools included in the project can be divided into three categories: Primarschulen (schools with basic requirements), Sekundarschulen (schools with certain

Table 15.3 Percentages (multiple responses) of Swiss and Norwegian students reporting being bullied or bullying others at different places in and around school

	To/from school	*Playground*	*Classroom*	*Corridors*	*Toilets*
Victims' reports:					
• Switzerland	35.6	33.4	34.4	19.9	2.7
• Norway	35.3	58.8	31.7	19.0	11.0
Bullies' reports:					
• Switzerland	31.4	35.6	35.8	19.0	2.2
• Norway	27.9	56.5	36.4	14.5	3.7

criteria and giving access to both high school and vocational training), and Gymnasien (schools with high requirements). One of the questions very often asked about bullying is whether high competition could promote bullying (see Olweus, 1993). Given the selection procedures practised in the Swiss education system, one might expect the track with the highest requirements to promote competition. The data for the Swiss students in the seventh through ninth grades belonging to the three types of schools described above were compared. The results are presented in Table 15.4.

As to all three types of bullying, students from the school track with the highest requirements reported being bullied less and bullying others less than their peers from the two other tracks. Students from the lowest track yielded the highest percentages. Physical bullying was almost absent from the highest track, but interestingly, verbal and indirect bullying were also lower than in the other tracks. That is, students from the highest school track did not compensate for their lack of physical aggression through other aggressive practices.

Conclusion

The offices that answered our informal enquiry clearly indicated that bullying was present in the minds of school professionals and counsellors. The results from the recent Swiss–Norwegian survey support their observations and concerns. Bullying in all its three main forms is part of the daily life of children and adolescents in Switzerland, to approximately the same extent as in other countries. Contrary to some myths about competition and school selection the major problems seem to occur in the school type without any requirements for entry. Since the selection takes place approximately after the sixth grade, one may ask first whether victimised and bullying students are already less competent in their earlier school years, and therefore do not manage to enter the tracks with higher requirements; second, if there may be some bias in the counselling they get by the end of primary school (they may be oriented towards lower tracks because of their behaviour); or third,

Table 15.4 Percentages of Swiss students in the seventh through ninth grades reporting being bullied or bullying others according to school type; level 1 corresponds to schools without any particular requirements, level 2 to schools with certain requirements, and level 3 to schools with high requirements

	Bullied by peers			*Bullying their peers*		
	Level 1	*Level 2*	*Level 3*	*Level 1*	*Level 2*	*Level 3*
Physically	5.5	2.0	0.4	5.0	2.4	0.0
Verbally	10.9	8.5	5.6	10.1	10.5	6.0
Indirectly	8.0	5.7	2.7	5.1	4.8	3.8

if the different school types offer diverse opportunities to act in antisocial ways and therefore engender variations in the occurrence of bully/victim problems. Independent of the direction of the relationship between bullying and school type, it is clear that the primary school level and the lowest track at secondary level I are the places to start with when resources do not suffice for everything. In addition, the figures reported here suggest that there is no need to wait until a bullying situation has become very serious in order to intervene. Swiss students report 'enough' bullying to justify the implementation of prevention programmes.

As additional information regarding Swiss authorities' concerns about and work against violence, it should be noted that a research programme of the Swiss National Science Foundation on 'Violence in daily life and organised crime' (see Wyss, 1997) was recently begun. Twenty-one projects have been funded and two projects on bullying are currently being conducted. One of these is taking place in kindergartens (under the leadership of Françoise Alsaker) and includes the implementation and evaluation of a prevention programme.

Acknowledgements

The survey among Swiss and Norwegian adolescents was funded by grants from the Swiss National Science Foundation (Grant No. 4033–035779) to August Flammer, W. Felder, W. Herzog, F. D. Alsaker and A. Grob, and from the Norwegian Research Council (Grant No. 104030/330) to Françoise D. Alsaker. We wish to thank Ursula Peter who translated the section on Switzerland and the survey among educational institutions from German into English. We also thank August Flammer for valuable comments on an earlier draft of the chapter.

References

Alsaker, F. D. and Flammer, A. (in press) Cross-national research in adolescent psychology. In F. D. Alsaker and A. Flammer (eds) *The adolescent experience in twelve nations. European and American adolescents in the nineties*. Hillsdale, NJ: Lawrence Erlbaum.

Brechbühl, H., Brünggel, H., Iseli, D., Joray, M. and Mathys, R. (1996) *Ein Handbuch zum Umgang mit Gewalt in der Schule* [A manual on coping with violence at school]. Report. Praxisforschung: Erziehungsberatung 2502 Biel, Switzerland.

Bundesamt für Statistik (1992) *Bildungsmosaik Schweiz* [Education mosaic Switzerland]. Report 353. Bundesamt für Statistik, Bern.

Guggenbühl, A. (1992) Krisenintervention bei aggressiven Schulklassen [Crisis intervention in aggressive school classes]. *Schweizerische Lehrerinnen- und Lehrerzeitung*, 23, 6–10.

Mülli, C. (1992) *Physische Gewalt an der Oberstufe* [Physical violence in high school]. Unpublished manuscript. Rorschach: Lehrerseminar.

Olweus, D. (1991) Bully/victim problems among school children: Basic facts and effects of a school based intervention program. In D. Pepler and K. Rubin (eds) *The development and treatment of childhood aggression* (pp. 411–448). Hillsdale, NJ: Lawrence Erlbaum.

Olweus, D. (1993) *Bullying at school. What we know and what we can do*. Oxford: Blackwell.

O'Moore, A. and Hillery, B. (1989) Bullying in Dublin schools. *The Irish Journal of Psychology*, 10, 426–441.

Perry, D. G., Williard, J. C. and Perry, L. C. (1990) Peers' perceptions of the consequences that victimized children provide aggressors. *Child Development*, 61, 1310–1325.

Whitney, I. and Smith, P. K. (1993) A survey of the nature and extent of bullying in junior/middle and secondary school. *Educational Research*, 35, 3–25.

Woringer, V. (1994) *Etude prospective sur les mauvais traitements* [Prospective study on maltreatment]. Unpublished Report. Lausanne, Service médical des écoles.

Wyss, E. (ed.) (1997) *Gewalt im Alltag und organisierte Kriminalität* [Violence in daily life and organised crime]. Bulletin no. 1. Schweizerischer Nationalfonds, Bern, Switzerland.

16 Poland

Andrzej Janowski

Overview

The phenomenon of bullying has not previously been treated as a major issue in Polish schools. It was only the rapid escalation of crime in general, and juvenile crime in particular, that has over the past few years drawn attention to bullying at school. The police and media report growing juvenile crime, increased cruelty and failure to identify motives that would be understandable to adults.

There is little research into the causes of bullying. The public puts the blame on television, deteriorating family relationships, the tendency of the young to form gangs, and the general confusion which that part of society feels in the circumstances of system transformations. One can hope that the recent sudden realization of the threat of bullying will trigger off research, followed by action plans to control the phenomenon.

Country summary

Poland is situated in central eastern Europe. Its territory totals 312,683 square kilometres and it has a population of 38.7 million. In the west, Poland borders Germany; in the south, the Czech and Slovak Republics; in the north, the Baltic Sea and part of Russia; and in the east, the states created after the disintegration of the Soviet Union (Lithuania, Belarus and the Ukraine).

Most of the country is low lying. In the south there are the country's only two mountain chains. The climate is moderate. Poland's capital is Warsaw. About 35 per cent of the population live in the agricultural areas, and the rest in cities. There are three highly urbanized and industrialized regions which are inhabited by over 20 per cent of the population.

Poland is exceptionally uniform from a nationality point of view. The small minority groups (German, Ukrainian, Belarussian, Lithuanian and Slovakian) do not account for more than about 2.5 to 5 per cent of the entire population. The predominant religion is Catholicism.

School summary

The Polish system of education consists of the following levels: kindergarten, primary school, secondary school, and higher school.

Primary school lasts for eight years and is common and compulsory for everybody. A child starts school in the year of his or her seventh birthday and continues to completion of primary education, but not past the age of 17. Primary school attendance is almost 100 per cent.

Primary curricula are uniform for the whole country. Grade O is a special phenomenon in the Polish system. It is compulsory for 6-year-olds and exists either as the highest class in kindergarten or as the lowest one in primary school.

There are twenty periods per week in Grade 1, 21 in Grades 2 and 3, 25 in Grade 4, 27 to 28 in Grade 5, 28 to 29 in Grade 6, 27 to 29 in Grade 7, and 28 to 30 in Grade 8. The average grade size is 23 students, depending mainly on the location of the school. In the cities grades tend to be larger, while in the countryside their sizes are smaller.

About 97 per cent of students who complete primary education proceed to post-primary schools. These comprise general secondary schools (four years), vocational *lycées* and technical schools (four or five years), and basic vocational schools (three years). In 1995–1996, 32 per cent of primary school graduates entered general secondary education, 31 per cent vocational *lycées* and technical schools, and 34 per cent the basic vocational schools.

From the first year of general secondary school students may choose the following streams: humanities, classical, mathematics/physics, biology/chemistry, pedagogical, and general. The average grade size is 29. There are 28 to 30 class periods per week. Students must study two foreign languages.

In 1989, it became legal for private schools to be created. In 1996–1997, about 1 per cent of primary, 2.4 per cent of vocational and 4.3 per cent of general secondary school students attended private schools. Most private schools are non-profit organizations and are attended mainly by children of highly educated parents.

Some 22 per cent of 19-year-olds completing secondary school continued their education in higher schools or the so-called two- or three-year post-secondary schools not categorized under higher education.

Bullying in schools: how is the term defined, and what terms are used?

The Polish language has no exact equivalent of 'bullying'. To convey the accurate meaning of the word, one has to talk about 'acts of aggression', 'violence' or 'oppression' perpetrated by schoolchildren against their school mates. The uncertainty as to which Polish word is the best equivalent of bullying shows in the translations of foreign publications. For example, in a recently published collective work, 'Aggression among children and youth: A psychoeducational perspective' (Fraczek and Pufal-Struzik, 1996), Poland's top expert on bullying, psychology professor Adam Fraczek, included a translation of Dan Olweus' paper 'Bullying at school: Research findings and an effective intervention program'. While the Polish title of the paper reads 'Aggression at school', the list of contents features it as 'Violence at school'. In general, Polish publications and research projects on bullying usually use the words 'aggression' or 'violence'.

For the purpose of this chapter, 'bullying' will cover all kinds of physical or verbal aggression as well as intentional or thoughtless harming, ridiculing, humiliating and name-calling of peers and younger children.

What has been the history of interest in this topic?

For many years the public took no major interest in the issue of bullying. The few cases that made it to public awareness were treated as sporadic incidents of no relevance for the overall picture of interpersonal relations in Polish schools.

Bullying from the present-day perspective

The last few years have seen social phenomena which have shed new light on the issue of bullying. These are:

- A rapid rise in juvenile crime rates, reflected in the three-fold increase between the years 1985 to 1986 and 1995 to 1996. Juvenile offenders were responsible for 26 cases of homicide in 1995 and 36 in 1996, compared to three to four cases annually ten years earlier. In 1996, children aged under 13 committed 3575 offences (Mirska, 1997); the police caught 57,000 juvenile delinquents, double the number ten years before.

> Heinous crimes are increasingly the doing of juveniles. They are becoming more and more brutal. The age of children implicated in crime is going down, with more and more 13-year-olds getting involved in assaults, burglaries, extortions, rapes, theft and even forgery and fencing. A juvenile delinquent is typically 13–16 years old, in the same grade for the second time, with a record of running away from home. He will usually work in a team – this ensures his anonymity and increases aggressiveness. . . . Students of the last grades of the primary school often choose to rob younger children, and more and more frequently help themselves with gas weapons, knives, knuckle-dusters and the like.
>
> (Stasik, 1997)

During 1997, public opinion has been shaken every few weeks by descriptions of comprehension-defying events: two girls aged 14 killed their girlfriend, two boys tried to hang another boy (for fun?), a university student was killed by casually encountered vocational school students, a boy killed a 12-year-old because he 'was hanging around', and so on. In April and May 1997, these issues received an unusual amount of coverage in several of the most influential Polish magazines. It seems that after a long period of overlooking the escalating problem, the public has suddenly realized its scope and its danger to public order.

- In April 1997, a student of one of Warsaw's secondary schools committed suicide. Prior to this, he wrote a letter accusing a teacher of driving him to doing so through his behaviour. Irrespective of the true reasons, the story created a stir. The students of the school supported the view that the teacher was responsible, and organized mourning and protest marches under the slogan 'We want teachers, not bullies'. 'In 1996 as many as 63 individuals under 20 committed suicide due to failure at school' (Filas, 1997; Pietkiewicz, 1997).
- Irrespective of what the young do, the last few years have seen a growing belief that public safety is deteriorating. Crime in general, not only juvenile, is on the rise. Detection rates are considered very low. Various political forces and social organizations are making increasingly vocal demands for public safety improvement.
- Football club fans are also becoming increasingly aggressive. In 1996, the fighting started by teenage spectators resulted in a number of casualties, including deaths, as well as vandalized facilities. The game itself does not matter any more – the pseudo-fans get together mainly for the purpose of having a fight with the police and feel proud of and honoured by their resulting bruises and injuries.
- Recent years saw also the growing brutality of political demonstrations. A special role in these demonstrations is played by groups of young people, mostly students of higher and secondary schools. While these groups call themselves right, left or national, an onlooker has the impression that the political motivation is just a convenient excuse and justification for starting clashes and scuffles. Brawls are fuelled by the hope that if you do something spectacular it will be shown on television, and ideological or political justifications for such activities are all the easier to build for the language of hatred used by some of the adult politicians.

All of the above can be summed up by saying that the behaviour of young people is rapidly gaining in brutality and that, by all indications, bullying is also becoming an urgent issue.

What are the reasons for the rise of bullying?

General social reasons

There is a lack of a comprehensive and exhaustive study on why the negative phenomena outlined above are intensifying. The stories that have been appearing in magazines usually mention the following issues:

- The system-transforming process, initiated in Poland in 1989, has brought about a number of effects, one of them being the increased feeling of insecurity about the future among some Poles. Under the old system, there was no official unemployment – it was the state's duty to provide jobs. These were therefore easy to find, and while the pay was meagre, security of employment was guaranteed. Large industrial enterprises maintained a number of economically non-viable positions, but the average employee was not bothered by this hidden unemployment. The transformation of the system meant the rationalization of employment, but also the collapse of many unprofitable enterprises and consequently unemployment. This proved particularly painful for the elderly, for people with poorer educational backgrounds, for those reluctant to learn new skills and for those unaccustomed to relying on their own resourcefulness, especially former workers of the giant state farms. Some of the unemployed seem to be tempted by organized crime as an easy way of improving their financial condition. This attitude is watched by children and youth, who sometimes follow their example.
- The transformation of the system has also produced a considerable social diversity, with some getting rich quickly and others getting poor equally quickly. This is creating a great deal of tension in a society which has traditionally espoused the value of egalitarianism. A clear social policy has not yet been developed to tackle the emerging areas of poverty. It is, however, recognized that a high proportion of children at school are undernourished, and the tension caused by the differences in consumption and life-styles is probably more acute among schoolchildren than among adults.
- All of the above are often accompanied by a sense of confusion, the inability to come up with a clear definition of what is happening in Poland or to understand where this country, freed from the dictates of the Soviet Union in 1989 and now building and managing its realities, is going. Even the well educated find it difficult to define the situation of themselves and of their country. No wonder, then, that this is a problem for simple people, especially if they bear the costs of the transformation. The low standards of political leaders and elites have also discouraged many from treating their behaviours as beacons, and the popular feeling is that politicians care only about themselves. Very strong for many years, the Catholic church has, for many reasons, somewhat fallen in public esteem, and there is an evident lack of a recognized authority.
- There has been a considerable drop in the effectiveness of the police force, a pillar of the pre-1989 political system of the state. When it was being transformed into a police force of a democratic country, many of the long-serving policemen feared being accused of unjustified use of

force. This fear has affected the performance of the police and has made the criminals feel exempt from punishment. The impunity of criminals is accompanied by the helplessness of the public. The latter complain of low crime detection rates and mild punishments, and this helplessness is reflected in organizing no-violence marches and exhorting politicians to address safety issues. Leaflets distributed in one of the cities encouraged the lynching of criminals.

- The system transformation also involves the opening of borders. Besides the clear advantages, open borders facilitate the mobility of organized gangs, of fighting with foreign and local mafia, new forms of crime, increased numbers of illegal aliens, including children and youth, beggary, and so on.
- The changes of the last few years brought a major breakthrough in terms of openness and 'calling a spade a spade'. While there must have been some areas of poverty and children going hungry before 1989, the censorship made sure that these issues would not be revealed to the public. Now things are totally different, so much so that there is in fact a trend to overstate the inadequacies of social conditions.
- The overall improvement of the openness of public life has helped the public become aware of such phenomena as violence in families, sexual abuse of children, maltreatment of women, etc. No one can say, though, which of these pathologies have just appeared and which have been present for a long time but were either concealed or rejected by the public consciousness.
- The last few years have seen a rapid growth of the availability of films, with mushrooming satellite and cable television networks and video rentals targeted chiefly at young people. Particularly popular are films rich in scenes of violence. As video rentals are virtually uncontrolled, a young person spending hundreds and thousands of hours in front of a television set can treat such films as manuals of criminal behaviour. Sociological research confirms that it is television and VCRs that some adults blame as the main cause of the growing brutality of life in Poland.

Reasons related to educational establishments

Writers about aggression among young people point to a number of unfavourable phenomena related to schools:

- The social diversity produced by the system transformation finds an interesting manifestation in the aspirations and lives of school graduates. Under 'real socialism', as the pre-1989 era was commonly known, the majority of primary school leavers would continue their education in three-year vocational schools that trained workers in narrow skills specific to the needs of the local plants. In fact, these schools were blind alleys of the educational system, for their graduates were not eligible to enter universities. After 1989, many plants that previously needed the skilled workforce went bankrupt or restructured themselves and started looking for totally different sets of skills, such as computer literacy, languages, etc. Graduates of vocational schools thus lost a chance to work and faced unemployment as the only realistic prospect.

Nowadays, 70 per cent of vocational school graduates cannot find any work (Filas *et al.*, 1997). They see the future as dangerous and devoid of opportunity – a perception in stark contrast with those young people for whom parents had earlier decided, and could afford, to invest in broad general education, languages, etc. Some young people thus see their future as hopeless, while others treat the new circumstances as an opportunity and challenge. The failures are driven by a sense of hopelessness and frustration to aggression and a search for scapegoats.

- An interesting phenomenon appeared in the Polish army in the 1980s, later to spread to the realm of education. Conscription at the time embraced a very large number of young men and the service period was very long. The military units evolved a special style of behaviour whereby seniors made their lives easier at the expense of junior soldiers. While modelled on the informal prison subculture, it was in the army that such behaviour became widespread. Known in Poland as the 'fala', it consists of soldiers in the last year of service subjugating recruits to performing all kinds of services. This would not matter if it had stayed limited to boot-polishing for the seniors, but it did not. Junior soldiers were blackmailed and beaten in order to perform exhausting physical exercises, provide humiliating services, including sex, and so on. The whole situation was surrounded by an aura of a 'truly manly initiation', with the beaten and humiliated recruit cherishing the hope that one day he would be senior and it would be his turn to dominate his juniors.

The military authorities long ignored the problem. Suicides by recruits were explained by various reasons but not the 'fala'. The public suspected that officers welcomed the phenomenon, as the terror practised by senior soldiers enforced some kind of order in the barracks. These days the 'fala' is said to be milder than ten years ago, what with the smaller army and shorter service, but is instead affecting a large number of schools, especially three-year vocational ones. Descriptions are known of several cases of harassment of schoolchildren by their older colleagues – some have become part of the local, informal school lore. This is the second life or the 'hidden curriculum' typical of totalitarian, unbearable organizations. The symptoms of this second life are not at all trivial: this is a painful experience that may damage health and invariably inflicts feelings of debasement and humiliation. Examples include having one's head put in a toilet bowl and being forced to eat the larvae of worms from rotting fruit (Filas *et al.*, 1997). Students who spontaneously and readily think up and use torture against their school mates will develop a durable tendency to bully after a few cases, and will often feel beyond any punishment. Unlike the military, teachers seem not to approve of such things happening in their schools, but some have little idea of what is going on among students while others feel helpless and do not know how to cope with it.

- This situation is further aggravated by the serious problems that schools have experienced over the past few years in performing their broadly understood educational function. For dozens of years of existence of what was referred to as socialist education, the authorities spoke about the schools' 'ideological and educational impact'. Since ideological education in the understanding of the then educational authorities, that is, political indoctrination, is gone from the agenda, many teachers also reject the upbringing aspect, saying that their main responsibility in the new reality is to impart knowledge rather than bring up their pupils, which is the domain of the family. This is compounded by the paucity of educational finances, inflicted by the government's decision to cut spending on extra-curricular activities in the first years of the system transformation, and never revoked despite a considerable improvement in the state's finances.
- Teachers are not particularly concerned about bullying among children and youth. It is rarely discussed during the special lessons that all class teachers have at their disposal. Similarly, there are no accounts of religious instructors addressing the subject of bullying in their lessons. Some observers feel that teachers are frustrated and hate school as much as their students.
- While Poland has never really had an established tradition of school sports, the past few years have seen a further dwindling of interest in intramural and extramural sports activities and facilities. This has further reduced the opportunities of a healthy venting of excessive energy through organized team activities and has paved the way for acts of hooliganism.
- A major educational role has always been played by youth and children's organizations. Some, for instance, scouting, can boast a long and proud tradition. Despite the state's supervision, this and some other organizations in a country of 'real socialism' did enjoy certain public recognition and shaped the attitudes of a series of generations. Nowadays some of these organizations have disappeared, others are torn apart by inner quarrels, and the new ones lack vigour. Some, supervised by reasonable adults and potentially educationally useful, have little impact.
- Given such conditions, there is a notable growth of informal groups belonging to the young subculture. Sometimes manipulated by adults affected by the nationalistic ideology, they attract young people through patriotic and nationalist slogans (Podgorska, 1997). Their leaders exploit the idealism of youth in founding groups which can be described as squads to fight the hostile subculture groups as well as any other people whose life-styles earn them the name of 'rubbish'. Although not large in number,

the nationalistic fighting squads are worrying because of their growing trend. In some towns they are the only outlet for students and graduates of vocational schools who are frustrated by the prospect of unemployment. These groups have a long record of beatings and riots and have even caused a few deaths.

- One also hears more and more often about satanic groups and religious as well as quasi-religious sects drawing in young people. 'The need to set up gangs is an expression of a child's dream of a community where children can be children, one that ensures a minimum level of risk, criticism and comparison of achievement. Children who join gangs express their rebellion against their weak position at home, at school and in the world' (Filas, 1997).

Educational studies on bullying

While all I have written so far about the mounting wave of crime and aggression in my country is not tantamount to a description of what is called 'bullying in schools', it does show that bullying is a fact, that it is developing, and that soon we are likely to witness media debates on 'what is going wrong in Polish schools and why aggressive behaviours are becoming increasingly common'. For the time being, though, educational researchers seem to have the least to say on the issue. There are no studies that examine bullying in a wider perspective, probably because until very recently researchers still did not consider it to be a particularly important issue.

In 1995, the Institute for Educational Research published a booklet entitled 'Aggression of children and youth: Causes, symptoms, therapy – a selective bibliography for 1974–1994'. Compiled and prefaced by Grazyna Klimowicz (Klimowicz, 1995), the booklet shows that 156 books and 120 articles on aggression of children and youth have been published in Poland in the last twenty years. Bullying, however, is a topic that few have pursued. The list of publications features plenty of translations, new editions of old papers and a considerable number of general educational and psychological work that is but loosely related to violence in school. Some topics have now become obsolete.

The years 1995 to 1997 have, however, seen a few publications of the latest research findings. In 1995, Maria Dabrowska-Bak's study 'Violence at school: A study of oppressive education' came out (Dabrowska-Bak, 1995). The main objective of the study was to identify the extent and scope of the use of violence in teacher–student relationships. In August 1993, a group of about 1000 preselected students of secondary schools in the city of Poznan were asked to complete a questionnaire. The answers showed that over half of the students, more from vocational than general secondary schools, had had a negative school experience. The author believes that in-school relationships have deteriorated in the 1990s compared with the 1980s. Students' accounts of the student–student relationships, a by-product of the research, indicate a frequent use of physical aggression, sometimes combined with stealing money or valuables from other students. The 'fala' phenomenon finds its most frequent expression in the beating of junior students. Physical violence occurs more frequently among students of vocational than general secondary schools. The teacher–student violence results in the anti-educating rather than educating influence of school. The author is convinced that the rising crime in society at large fuels violence in schools, and the growing brutality of teacher–student relationships encourages the brutality of student–student relationships. Dabrowska-Bak (1995) makes this appeal in the conclusion of her book: 'It is imperative that sound educational relationships between teachers and students are restored' (p. 68).

In another study, Grazyna Milkowska-Olejniczak (1996) asked nearly 300 headteachers of different types of schools in several regions of the country to complete a questionnaire on violence at school. Almost all the headteachers wrote about student aggression, expressed in similar ways in all schools, with the exception of damaging property which occurs in bigger rather than smaller schools. Aggressive behaviour is becoming increasingly common among the younger schoolchildren. The headteachers say that teachers fail to cope with student aggression. They also say that aggression is not caused by the school and that teachers do not perceive their behaviour as cause for aggression. 'Most of the respondents disagree that the school and teachers cause student aggression' (p. 192). The headteachers indicate three causes of aggression: the media, especially television and video; bad influence of peer groups; and dysfunctional families. Teachers feel helpless in the face of aggression and do not understand how it originates, nor know how to tackle aggressive individuals. Despite all this, 'the vast majority of the headteachers do not perceive aggression as a problem that would need to be addressed with urgency ... they do not see the need to take action in their schools' (p. 192).

Some other studies of aggression and violence (e.g. Stoklosa, 1996) mention what I have already indicated here: the trend to blame the family for the aggressiveness of children at school. Some researchers (e.g. Krezel, 1996) stress that students prefer not to tell their teachers that they are victims of their peers' aggression.

All the studies mentioned here give only outlines of the issue and their findings do not allow for generalization. The data presently available are limited and local and usually acquired in an indirect way. They tell us more about the attitudes of headteachers and teachers to schoolchildren's aggressiveness than about bullying as such. Nothing is known about bullying of, and among, girls. Indeed, focused research is needed to show the exact scale of the problem. Given the awakening of public interest and concern, I would think that such research will soon be conducted, especially now that the climate is favourable. Like many other social phenomena, the image of education and schools under 'real socialism' was also based on somewhat idyllic assumptions, and it is only in recent years that the studies of teacher–student relationships have started using the categories of pressure, symbolic violence, fighting and strategy. School pressure was finally treated as an actual or potential fact of life.

To sum up these fragmented pieces of information, I would say that:

- boys who do worse at school tend to be more aggressive towards better students
- the poor tend to be aggressive towards the rich
- aggression is often triggered off by the divisions into believers and non-believers and into Catholics (the predominant denomination of Polish youth) and other denominations
- aggression often occurs between people from cities and people from rural areas.

Counteracting initiatives

Few organized activities have so far been undertaken to counteract the rise of bullying in schools. As I have sought to point out, there is not much awareness of bullying. Although bullied children can report what has happened to class teachers, they will usually have little trust in them, and can be severely punished by their peers for doing so. Every kuratorium (the regional educational board) has a students' ombudsman to whom any issues may be referred. Although the ombudsman is usually a trustworthy teacher of vast experience, he is too distant from an average student's perspective. Moreover, it is not easy to be an ombudsman as one is likely to come into conflict with the teacher community. Young people may still ring the special help number, but it is not so simple to do this given Poland's limited telephone network.

Teachers are not trained to cope with bullying either during initial or in-service training. This may soon change for the better however, for one of the universities has recently designed a therapeutic programme for under-age bullies staying in re-socialization institutions and for their victims (Bartkowicz, 1996). Another programme that has recently been developed addresses the prevention of school bullying and is modelled on Olweus' initiatives (Kolodziejczyk, 1996). No data are available as yet as to how widely the two programmes are used.

References

Bartkowicz, Z. (1996) *Pomoc terapeutyczna nieletnim agresorom i ofiarom agresji w zakladach resocjalizacyjnych.* Lublin.

Dabrowska-Bak, M. (1995) *Przemoc w szkole; analiza wychowania opresyjnego.* Poznań.

Filas, A., Janecki, S. and Szczesny, J. (1997) Szkola frustracji. *Wprost*, 4 May.

Fraczek, A. and Pufal-Struzik, I. (eds) (1996) *Agresja wsród dzieci i mlodzieży; perspektywa psychoedukacyjna.* Kielce.

Klimowicz, G. (ed.) (1995) *Agresja dzieci i mlodzieży. Przyczyny – objawy – terapia. Bibliografia selekcyjna za lata 1974–1994*. Warszawa.
Kolodziejczyk, A. (1996) Agresja w szkole; programy, zapobieganie i przeciwdzialanie agresji w środowisku szkolnym. In K. Ostrowska and J. Tatarowicz (eds) *Zanim w szkole bedzie zle. . . . Profilaktyka zagrożeń. Poradnik dla nauczycieli*. Warszawa.
Krezel M. (1996) Wybrane przejawy zachowań agresywnych wśród mlodzieży szkolnej. In A. Fraczek and I. Pufal-Struzik (eds) *Agresja wśród dzieci i mlodzieży; perspektywa psychoedukacyina*. Kielce.
Milkowska-Olejniczak, G. (1996) Kto rzadzi w polskiej szkole? – czyli o agresji dzieci i mlodzieży w sytuacjach szkolnych. In M. Dudzikowa (ed.) *Nauczyciel – uczeń*. Krakow.
Mirska, D. (1997) Zabójcze dzieciaki. *Uroda*, 5, May.
Pietkiewicz, B. (1997) Śmierc na wolnym rynku. *Polityka*, 17.
Podgorska, J. (1997) Toruń dla Polakow. *Polityka*, 17.
Stasik, D. (1997) Dlaczego dzieci zabijaja. *Gazeta Wyborcza*, 94.
Stoklosa, B. (1996) Przejawy zachowań agresywnych i ich uwarunkowania u dzieci ze szkol wiejskich w opinii nauczycieli wychowania poczatkowego. In A. Fraczek and I. Pufal-Struzik (eds) *Agresja wśród dzieci i mlodzieży; perspektywa psychoedukacyjna*. Kielce.

Further reading

Dudzikowa, M. (ed.) (1996) *Nauczyciel – uczen. Miedzy przemoca a dialogiem: obszary napieć i typy interakcji*. Kraków.
Karkowska, M. and Czarnecka, W. (1994) *Przemoc w szkole*. Kraków.
Kawula S. and Machel H. (1995) *Podkultury mlodziezowe w środowisku szkolnym i pozaszkolnym*. Toruń.
Muszyńska, E. (1997) *Swoboda, przymus i przemoc w relacjach dziecko – dorosly*. Poznań.
Ostrowska, K. and Tatarowicz, J. (1996) (ed.) *Zanim w szkole bedzie zle. . . . Profilaktyka zagrożeń. Poradnik dla nauczycieli*. Warszawa.
Pietrzak, H. (1992) *Agresja indywidualna i zbiorowa w sytuacji napieć i konfliktów spolecznych*. Rzeszów.
Tabaczynska, A. (ed.) (1993) *Sytuacja dzieci i mlodzieży w Polsce – raport*. Warszawa.

Part II

North America

17 United States

Tracy W. Harachi, Richard F. Catalano and J. David Hawkins

Overview

There appears to be no one standard definition of bullying either in the popular or research literature within the US. Generally speaking, it appears that bullying is interpreted as both direct, physical aggression, as well as indirect behavior such as verbal threats. Bullying has generally been referred to as a childhood occurrence and has been depicted in a range of popular literature and media, including children's books, newspapers, and television talk shows. Although the literature and media have focused specifically on the topic of bullying, bullying has not received widespread attention in educational programming in the US or in the scientific literature. There have been limited studies conducted to examine the incidence and prevalence of bullying behavior and/or victimization. Studies have reported estimates ranging from 10 percent of third through sixth graders reporting being chronically bullied by peers, to 29 percent of middle school students reporting engaging in bullying behavior in the past 30 days. In another study of middle and high school students, 75 percent reported being bullied by peers at some point over the course of their schooling. These wide-ranging estimates reflect, in part, the varying definitions, age groups and self-reporting by victims or bully perpetrators. Other research examining characteristics of bullies is encompassed within a broader focus on aggressive behavior, particularly research examining the etiology of proactive bullying aggression. Much of this latter research has been conducted utilizing contrived playgroup methodology. Further, most of the examination to date has focused on direct forms of bullying, with indirect forms of bullying and relational aggression studied less often. Studies have also focused on victimization, including characteristics of victims and the development of chronic victims. A critical next step to be taken is to develop a common definition of bullying and use it to conduct research to provide comparable data on the incidence and prevalence of bullying in the US. Additionally, research is needed to increase our understanding of the familial, school, and other contextual factors that predict either bullying or victimization, as well as those conditions that moderate the effects or reduce the likelihood of bullying occurring. These findings should be utilized in developing prevention and intervention programs that are specific to the issue of bullying.

Country demographics

Based on data from the 1990 census, the 1995 estimated total population of the US was 263,034,000 (including Armed Forces personnel abroad). Eighty-three percent of the population is Caucasian, 12.6 percent black, 0.9 percent American Indian and 3.5 percent Asian/Pacific Islander. Based on the 1990 census total, 75.2 percent of the population resided in urban areas and 24.8 percent in rural areas. Regions with the largest percentage population growth between 1990 and 1995 were the south (+43 percent) and midwest (+13 percent) while there were population decreases in the west (–34 percent) and in the northeast (–22 percent). The median household income was $32,264 in 1994. The incidence of families below the poverty level was 13.3 percent, and 22.1 percent for individuals.

System of education

There are three types of schools: public, private, and federal. Public schools are established and operated by local educational authorities under guidelines of the respective state's office of superintendent of public instruction and federal legislation. Federal schools include overseas schools operated by the Department of Defense. Private schools must provide programs for students that meet the guidelines mandated by the state and federal authorities. Approximately 32 percent of private schools have a religious affiliation with the Catholic church (Office of Educational Research and Improvement, 1995).

The school year set by federal authorities comprises 180 days. States have the authority to determine the ages for compulsory school attendance; consequently this varies by state and ranges from 5 to 8 years of age to 15 to 18 years of age. Schooling may begin at the pre-kindergarten level which is non-compulsory. The elementary school grade levels begin at kindergarten (typically age 5) and range to grades 5 or 6. There is some overlap in grade range at the next level, junior high or middle school, which may include grades 5 through 9. Some schools combine elementary and middle school and include kindergarten to grade 8. Senior high school may either be three years or four years ranging from grades 9 or 10 through 12. Finally, some schools combine junior and senior high and include grades 7 through 12.

Enrollment in primary and secondary schools peaked in 1971 and gradually decreased annually from 1971 until 1984. From 1985 through 1994 there has been a small increase in overall enrollment reflecting a moderate increase in the primary grades. Enrollment in public school grades from kindergarten through eighth grade rose from 27 million in 1985 to 32.3 million in 1995 (Office of Educational Research and Improvement, 1995). It is estimated that public school enrollment in the elementary grades will grow by 9 percent from 1994 to 2000 and 12 percent growth at the secondary level. Approximately 11 percent of the eligible elementary and secondary students attend private school, totaling 5.7 million in 1995. This proportion has changed little in the past decade. Another trend is the increased attendance among 3- to 4-year-olds in pre-kindergarten. In 1984, 36 percent of the children of these ages attended school while 48 percent attended in 1994.

In 1992, the total number of institutions was 85,393. The average enrollment of a public elementary school is 468 and 695 for a public secondary school. The student to teacher ratio was 16.9 to 1 in 1995. The average number of students per class in elementary school is 24 and 26 for secondary classes.

Definitions of bullying

There appears to be no one standard definition of bullying either in the popular or research literature. Many articles on this topic refer to the work conducted by Olweus, and make a general reference to the definition he has used in his research. Few, however, include a specific definition that clarifies two key elements which are part of Olweus' definition: (1) that bullying behavior occurs repeatedly over time, and (2) that there is a power imbalance between the bully and the victim. Some literature clearly specifies that bullies are a subset of aggressive children who seem to derive satisfaction from harming others, physically or psychologically, while other references use the term bullying as synonymous with aggressive behavior. Generally speaking, it appears that bullying is interpreted as both direct, physical aggression, as well as indirect behavior such as verbal threats. Bullying is generally referred to as a childhood occurrence; however, increasingly the term is being used to refer to adult behavior as well. For example, the term has been used to describe adult interactions in social groups characterized by differential power relationships such as within corporate organizations.

An effort has been made by Hazler and colleagues (1997) to construct a list of characteristics of bullies and victims to assist in early identification of potential problem students. They surveyed fourteen experts from the US, England and Australia and asked them to evaluate a list of 70 characteristics in terms of their ability to identify bullies or victims. As a result of the expert feedback, a list of nineteen characteristics of a bully and nineteen characteristics of a victim was constructed. An inherent implication with this typology is that individuals would fit into one category or the other. This may be problematic given that research has shown that a proportion of bullies are also victims. Additionally, there is empirical evidence demonstrating that bullies and victims are heterogeneous groups, for example, some bullies are rejected by their peers while others are not, hence separate profiles for bullies or victims may be overly simplistic.

Historical interest as a social problem and media attention

The 1955 novel by William Golding, *Lord of the flies*, is an example of the portrayal of bullying in popular fiction. There are numerous children's and adolescent stories with themes about bullies, and victims. Newspapers have contained articles reporting incidents of bullying, including child suicides that resulted from bullying, profiles of bullies, or suggestions to schools and parents on how to address the issue. US newspapers have also contained a number of articles highlighting the problem of bullying in Japan, particularly those incidents which have resulted in suicides. Surprisingly, few of these articles on Japanese bullying drew parallels to the situation in the US. Popular television talk shows such as Donahue (1994) have discussed the topic of bullying, emphasizing the prevalent nature of the problem. The World Wide Web (WWW) contains home pages from such entities as *Good Housekeeping Magazine* and a local news station column (*Ask Dr. Brenda Wade*) that provide tips and information on "taming your child's bully," or "bully proofing your school." The WWW also provides access to other home pages from the United Kingdom and Australia which are specific to bullying and include child helplines (see Kidscape and Kids Helpline). There is no comparable national entity or similar effort in the US. The professional or practice literature has had an increased interest in the topic of bullying in the past few years. For example, a recent issue (1996) of *Reclaiming Children and Youth: Journal of Emotional and Behavioral Problems* was devoted to bullying and includes an article by Olweus, and one on victimization by Hodges and Perry. Other articles include a description of a comprehensive program for "bully proofing your school" that is available from a US developer, a program for antisocial youth, and alternatives to school suspension.

While the media and literature have focused specifically on the topic of bullying, bullying has not received widespread attention in educational programming or in the scientific literature as a specific problem issue to address. More often, bullying is subsumed within broader issues such as school safety, or violence in schools. For example, different national surveys have been conducted that assess school safety, perceptions of school violence, and reports of being threatened or injured (see for example, National Institute of Education, 1978; US Department of Health and Human Services, 1978). These surveys provide an insight into the incidence of violent behavior in high schools, but may be less informative on the specific issue of bullying. For example, these statistics do not assess the repetitive nature of the violence or whether there is a power imbalance between the aggressor and the victim. In addition, the National Education Goals Panel in 1993 stated as one of six educational goals, "by the year 2000, every school in America will be free of drugs and violence and will offer a disciplined environment conducive to learning." While school violence has traditionally been defined as acts of assault, weapon carrying, and theft, the act of bullying was included in their definition.

In 1984, the National School Safety Center (NSSC) was created by Presidential mandate through a partnership with the US Department of Justice's Office of Juvenile Justice and Delinquency Prevention and US Department of Education. NSSC was charged to serve as a clearing-house for school safety information, technical assistance, and programs. Within NSSC's broad focus, it has disseminated information on the topic of bullying. In May 1987, the first Schoolyard Bullying Practicum conference was sponsored by the National School Safety Center to examine strategies to handle the perceived escalating problem of bullying. The conference took place after a tragic suicide occurred in 1987 in Missouri involving a 12-year-old victim of bullying who brought a pistol to school and mortally shot himself as well as another student. A number of researchers and practitioners were brought together to propose ways to develop a comprehensive national awareness campaign. A number of key points to be communicated to educators, students and communities were recommended. In 1988, the NSSC produced an eighteen-minute educational documentary entitled *Set Straight on Bullies* which received several awards. It was followed by a book published in 1989 under the same title. The latter contains an overview of the problem and recommended solutions, as well as sample student and adult surveys modeled after questionnaire items developed by Olweus. The NSSC news journal *School Safety* has also published a number of articles relating to school bullying dating from 1987 to the present. These topics range from "bully proofing your school: a comprehensive approach," to "sample student survey on bullying in school." Additionally, NSSC has published a resource paper, "School bullying and victimization" (1995).

In the past decade there has been legal activity specific to bullying which has resulted in articles in the local media and an issue of NSSC Newsjournal entitled "Victims can sue bullies, schools." A judicial ruling permits the parents of California schoolchildren to sue the school district if their children are threatened or injured. Cases have appeared in several superior courts on the basis that "safe, secure, and peaceful schools are constitutionally mandated." In 1989, the California Court of Appeals overturned a decision that school districts may be held monetarily liable for campus violence under California's Victims' Bill of Right. The appellate judges determined that the initiative's "safe schools" provision simply "declares a general right without specifying any rules for its enforcement." An appeal of the decision of the California Supreme Court was denied, but the state law still allows students to sue school systems for negligence (Greenbaum *et al.*, 1987). In another California case, attorneys alleged that the bullying behavior inflicted on a sixth grade girl constituted sexual harassment and failure of the school to stop it was a violation by the school of Title IX of the federal Education Amendments of 1972 (*Los Angeles Times*, October 2, 1994). Members of the US Supreme Court have stated that "the serious challenge of restoring a safe school environment has begun to reshape the law" (Greenbaum, 1987), citing that schools have an obligation to protect pupils from mistreatment by other children.

While this type of legal activity suggests increased attention on the topic of bullying, there has yet to be widespread adoption of bullying prevention and intervention as a specific social issue that requires federal and state funding. The National Youth Victimization Prevention Study (Finkelhor and Dziuba-Leatherman, 1994, 1995) asked about the child's experience with child abuse and victimization prevention programs. Overall, 67 percent of the children reported having received a school-based abuse or victimization prevention program at some time, 37 percent within the past year. The most frequently reported topic was reporting or telling an adult about abuse (95 percent). The least frequently covered although still prevalent topic was the problem of bullies (63 percent). There did not appear to be regional, racial, or class differences in exposure. Children attending private, non-parochial schools were less likely to have received a program than children in public or parochial schools. Children were also asked to remember concrete instances in which the program information had proved useful to them. Forty percent said it had specifically helped them and cited examples. Children who reported attending a bullying prevention program were more likely to say they had made use of the program knowledge.

Research related to bullying

This section begins with details of studies that have been conducted to examine the frequency of bullying in the US. This is followed by a description of related studies that have examined characteristics of bullies and those of victims, as well as the development of chronic victimization. Finally, studies that have examined factors associated with bullying are described.

There has been limited research conducted in the US to examine the incidence and prevalence of bullying among school-aged children that adheres to a definition of bullying which includes elements of power imbalance and repetitiveness. Large-scale studies with national, representative samples have contained related items such as frequency of threatening or injuring another student with a weapon on school property in the past year. While such items certainly assess aggressive behavior, they do not specifically address these critical components of bullying.

The National Youth Victimization Prevention Study (Finkelhor and Dziuba-Leatherman, 1994, 1995) interviewed a representative sample of 2000 US children (ages 10 to 16) and their caretakers about the children's possible victimization. The sample was selected using a multistage area probability/random digit dialing strategy and had a participation rate of 88 percent of the adults and 82 percent of the eligible children. The phone interview asked several screening questions about victimization, including non-family and family assault, kidnapping, sexual abuse/assault, violence to genitals and corporal punishment. More extensive questions were asked of two episodes with a priority given to sexual victimization and to victimization occurring in the past year. This method probably resulted in undercounting non-sexual, less severe, and more temporally remote victimization. The non-family assault screening questions were: "Sometimes kids get hassled by other kids or older kids, who are being bullies or picking on them for some reason. Has anyone – in school, after school, at parties, or somewhere else – picked a fight with you or tried to beat you up?" and "Has anyone ever ganged up on you, you know, when a group of kids tried to hurt you or take something from you?" Non-family assaults were the most numerous type of victimization (32.5 percent of the sample). Boys were over three times more likely than girls to have experienced a non-family assault in the previous year, and the majority of these incidents were committed by known perpetrators under the age of 18. The majority of the children stated they had reported the non-family assault incidents (74 percent) to someone.

A few studies have collected data from students in late elementary through high school to examine the frequency of specific bullying behavior and/or victimization. In a study involving a sample of 165 third through sixth grade students attending a university school serving a middle-class community, 10 percent reported being chronically abused by peers (Perry, Kusel and Perry, 1988). Victimization was assessed by three items regarding how often the child was picked on, hit or pushed or called names by other students. This reported rate of frequency appeared to be relatively stable over a three-month test–retest period. Girls appeared to be at risk of victimization about as much as boys. Age did not appear to decrease risk although verbal abuse was more likely than physical aggression in the later grades. In another study which was part of an evaluation for a violence prevention program, 558 (41 percent of those eligible) middle school students from a midwestern metropolitan area were surveyed at baseline (Bosworth, Espelage, DuBay, Dahlberg and Daytner, 1996). Twenty-nine percent of the students reported engaging in high amounts of bullying behavior in the past 30 days. Bullying was assessed by a scale formed of four items involving teasing, name-calling, and threats of physical harm. Finally, Hazler, Hoover and Oliver (1991) surveyed 207 students in grades 7 to 12 from interested classrooms in the midwest. Approximately 75 percent of the students reported being bullied by their peers (81 percent of males, 72 percent of females) at some time over the course of their schooling (Hazler, Hoover and Oliver, 1991; Hoover, Oliver and Hazler, 1992).

The longitudinal study conducted by Eron, Huesmann and colleagues (1987) is frequently cited in the practice and popular literature as evidence of the long-term consequences of childhood bullying. In their study, an entire population of third-grade students from a semi-rural county in New York State were enrolled as subjects (n = 870, modal age of 8 years). Peer nominations were used to identify a sub-sample of highly aggressive students. An example item included naming students who pushed or shoved children. At the 22-year follow-up, they found that these highly aggressive children had about a one in four chance of having a criminal record by age 30 compared with other children who have a one in twenty chance (1987). It is of note that these children are frequently referred to in the literature as "young bullies" and the study findings are framed as long-term consequences of bullying, though the items on the peer nomination index are more reflective of a broader definition of aggression.

There are distinct bodies of research examining characteristics of bullies and those of victims. The research examining bullies is encompassed within a broader focus on aggressive behavior. Research examining aggressive behavior has categorized aggression into a reactive form and a pro-active form. The latter has been further delineated into pro-active instrumental aggression, in which the aim appears to be a nonsocial outcome such as object acquisition, and pro-active bullying aggression, in which the aim is clearly to intimidate and dominate a peer, and comes closest to the definition of direct bullying in the literature. Dodge (1991) suggests that the origins and development of pro-active aggression probably differ from those of reactive aggression. The experiences which lead to pro-active aggression are likely ones that enhance the child's repertoire of aggressive tactics, limit the child's repertoire of competent non-aggressive tactics and promote the child's evaluation of outcomes of aggressive behavior in positive ways.

In addition, social information-processing mechanism studies have examined cognitive mechanisms implicated in these different forms of aggressive behaviors. Dodge and Coie (1987) found that errors in intention-cue detection and hostile attributional biases are not related to pro-active aggression; but favorable evaluations of the outcomes of aggression were associated with pro-active aggression. In another study, Crick and Dodge (1996) examined social information-processing patterns and found that pro-active aggressive children evaluated verbally and physically aggressive acts in significantly more positive ways than did non-pro-actively aggressive children. Pro-active aggressive children were less likely than other children to endorse relationship-enhancing goals during social interaction. Rather, they were more likely to prefer goals that were instrumental in nature and relatively self-enhancing. These results have implications regarding intervention strategies focused on pro-active aggressive children which includes direct bullies. Strategies which focus on enhancing a bully's or pro-active aggressive child's repertoire of competent, non-aggressive alternatives, as well as reducing their favorable evaluation of an aggressive response, may be more appropriate. In addition, these strategies should address the greater importance which pro-active aggressive children place on instrumental versus relational social goals.

The findings which suggest that pro-active aggressive children are less likely than other children to endorse relationship-enhancing goals during social interaction raise an interesting question related to gender differences in the expression of aggression. Girls have generally been viewed as being less involved as bullies, partly due to their exhibiting less direct physical bullying behavior than boys. Girls are more likely to engage in indirect forms of bullying such as social exclusion, ostracism, the spreading of malicious gossip, and scapegoating (Ross, 1996). Aggressive behavior most characteristic of girls tends to focus on damaging or manipulating peers' relationships, often described as relational aggression (Crick and Grotpeter, 1995). Crick and Grotpeter state that one reason that girls are more likely to use relational aggression, rather than overt aggression, is because relationally aggressive behaviors damage social goals that are particularly important to girls. These differences in expression of aggressive behavior through either direct or indirect bullying reflect a gender preference for relationship-enhancing goals during social interaction.

Relational aggression is by no means expressed only by girls. Crick, Casas and Mosher (1997) report that relationally aggressive behaviors appear in the repertoires of both girls and boys at preschool age, and children at this age show an ability to distinguish between relational and overt aggression. In Crick and Grotpeter's studies (1995, 1996), relational aggression was associated with maladjustment as assessed by ratings on depression, loneliness, and social isolation. Both girls and boys who rated high on relational aggression were more likely to be rejected by their peers or nominated among the controversial group. Further investigation is needed among both girls and boys to examine whether choice of direct or indirect bullying is related to preference for social or instrumental goals.

Many of the studies examining characteristics of bullies as well as victims utilize contrived playgroup methodology. Unacquainted children are brought together in playgroups and observations made of their social interactions. Coie, Dodge, Terry and Wright (1991) formed 23 playgroups in order to examine various aspects of aggressive behavior. The groups were formed based on the classroom sociometric status of a sample of African-American boys in first and third grades. Each group included two average-status boys, two rejected boys, one popular boy, and one neglected boy. Groups were brought together for 45-minute free play sessions over five consecutive days. Aggressive bullying behavior was the most common form (49 percent) of aggressive interaction. Most aggressive bullying and instrumental aggressive episodes involved only a single aggressive act. Similar to the results reported in Dodge, Coie, Pettit, and Price (1990), bullying seemed to have more negative social significance for the third grade boys than for the first graders. Bullying may serve a more adaptive function for young boys as they begin to relate in a new peer group than for older boys who have had greater experience in establishing themselves socially with peers. In the first grade, aggressive boys were more often the target of bullying than non-aggressive boys, whereas the reverse was true among third graders. Price and Dodge (1989) examined the social evolution of pro-active aggressive boys in kindergarten and first grade. Peers did not necessarily dislike boys who were pro-actively aggressive. The correlations varied slightly across age groups, with the older boys having a slightly more negative evaluation of pro-active aggression. Some positive evaluation from Dodge and Coie (1987) found that among third graders the pro-active aggressors were disliked by peers, and viewed as more disruptive to the peer group, but they were also viewed as having the strongest leadership qualities and best sense of humor. Dodge, Coie, Pettit and Price (1990) demonstrate that in the younger group, bullying and overt persuasion attempts were displayed at high rates by popular boys. Young peers apparently like some boys who bully, as long as those boys also engage in co-operative play and leadership. By the third grade, bullying behavior is less tolerated, and boys rated as popular by the newly acquainted group members are leaders who refrain from bullying and coercion. This raises two questions. First, do first grade bullies learn to refrain from using bullying as a way to exert leadership by third grade? Second, do the consequences of bullying on peer ratings change over time?

In another playgroup study, Dodge, Price, Coie and Christopoulos (1990) classified peer dyads into the following categories: (1) mutually aggressive; (2) asymmetric (only one aggressor); (3) low conflict; (4) unstable; and (5) low interaction. Pro-active aggression, including both instrumental and bullying aggression, was most likely to occur in asymmetric dyads (82 percent). This finding is compatible with the definition of bullying which emphasizes an imbalance of power among the involved parties. The aggressive members of the asymmetric dyads displayed significantly less parallel imitative play than did their partners and less parallel imitative play than any member of any other dyad.

Turning to studies of victims of bullying, work in this area has focused on characteristics of victims and the development of chronic victimization. The contrived playgroup procedure has also been utilized to examine the behavioral patterns leading to chronic victimization by peers. Victimization of a child is likely when two conditions co-occur: (1) the child exhibits behaviors that attract and reinforce aggressors, and (2) the child's social ties encourage and condone aggression. In an early study by Patterson (1967), frequently victimized preschoolers were ones who reinforced their attackers by acquiescing to their demands. Other cross-sectional data show that non-aggressive victims typically display a pervasively submissive behavioral style (Perry, Williard and Perry, 1990). Some victimized children also display "externalizing argumentativeness" which may serve to irritate and provoke other children, especially bullies (Perry, Kusel and Perry, 1988; Perry, Perry and Kennedy, 1992). Schwartz, Dodge and Coie (1993) hypothesize three stages in the development of chronic victimization by peers: (1) during initial encounters with peers, the eventual victim submits to non-aggressive persuasion attempts and acts of pro-active (instrumental and bullying) aggression by peers; (2) this submissive behavioral pattern serves to reinforce victimizing behavior by peers, leading peers to increase the rate and severity of their coercive behavior toward victims; and (3) the social behavior of the victim changes in response to high rates of victimization. They tested their hypotheses with data from 30 playgroups of unacquainted African-American boys aged 6 or 8 years old. Each playgroup met for 45 minutes on five consecutive days. Thirteen boys were identified in post-coding as being chronically victimized and non-aggressive. The patterns they found were congruent with their hypotheses. The sub-sample of chronically victimized boys displayed a behavioral pattern that was non-assertive and socially incompetent. This pervasively submissive behavior occurred in the first two sessions, and by the third session there were marked individual differences in victimization by peers, suggesting that non-assertive immature behaviors increased the likelihood that a boy will be selected for victimization by his peers.

An early study conducted by Perry, Kusel and Perry (1988) is frequently cited for its contributions on examining profiles of victims. Ten percent of the children in the sample of 165 third through sixth graders attending a university school serving a middle-class community were characterized as extreme or chronic victims. Perry, Williard and Perry (1990) have suggested that in the early stages of group formation, children direct aggressive behavior at a variety of targets, and as they learn the reactions of their peers their pool of victims becomes increasingly smaller and their choice of victims more consistent. Perry, Kusel and Perry (1988) found similar victim profiles as Olweus (1978), who used the terms "high-aggressive" and "low-aggressive" victims. These heterogeneous categories were further delineated by Perry into the following categories: victimized/rejected, aggressive/rejected, and victimized/aggressive/rejected.

Kochenderfer and Ladd (1996) provide results examining students during the kindergarten year and categorized them as non-victims, fall-only victims, spring-only victims, or stable victims over both time periods. Students were recruited from three school systems in the midwest. Victimization was broadly defined and not specific to bullying. Children were considered victims if they reported scores that averaged above the scale's midpoint suggesting a persistent targeting of aggression. Using this criterion, 20.5 percent of the 200 sample were classified as being victims in either fall or spring. The correlations between time points was low in magnitude ($r = .24$) with 8.5 percent of the children being rated as stable victims at both time points. This study also provides evidence of peer victimization as a precursor of some school adjustment problems at a very early age and suggests that there may be delayed effects from victimization.

Hodges and Perry (1997) found that social risk moderates the relation of behavioral risk to victimization by peers. Data were collected from a sample of 119 boys and 110 girls in grades 3 through 7. As predicted, behavior problems (internalizing problems, externalizing problems, and physical weakness) were more strongly related to victimization when children had few friends, had friends who were incapable of fulfilling a protective function (i.e. were physically weak, characterized by internalizing problems), or were rejected by peers, than when children with behavioral problems had more friends, had friends capable of defending them, or were better liked by their peers. Their results suggest that behavioral risk variables depend on social context.

Results from two studies suggest that peers devalue victims, and hence place less negative value on their victimization. In Troy and Sroufe's (1987) study of 175 fourth through seventh grade students, peers not only expected many rewarding outcomes and few negative outcomes for attacking victimized children, but they also cognitively exaggerated the importance of prevailing over victimized children and cognitively minimized the potentially harmful and punitive consequences of such action. Perry, Williard and Perry (1990) had children in similar grades imagine acts of aggression against victims and non-victims and then state how much the respondents would care about hurting the victims. Hurting the victims caused significantly less upset than hurting the non-victims. Hence, the identity of a potential target is a major discriminator affecting the cognitions that promote or discourage aggression.

While there are multiple studies that have examined other risk factors than individual characteristics of the child associated with the development and maintenance of aggression, few such studies have used a definition of aggression that differentiates bullying aggression from reactive aggression. Strassberg, Dodge, Pettit and Bates (1994) hypothesized bullying aggression to be acquired or learned through violent punishment practices as the child comes to hold positive evaluations for the victimization of others. Their study involved 273 children and their parents recruited randomly at kindergarten (70 percent of those contacted at spring registration agreed to be contacted in the subsequent fall). Following the fall parental interviews and assessment, direct observations were made of children's aggressive behaviors towards peers and categorized as reactive, instrumental or bullying aggression. The latter was defined as an unprovoked attack on a peer. Mothers' and fathers' punishment practices were categorized as nonuse of physical punishment, spankers, and violent. Specific to bullying aggression, only boys who were spanked by fathers, compared to those who did not receive physical punishment, were ones that displayed high rates of bullying aggression. Although the article did not provide specific behavior rates for comparison, children whose parents used violent punishment enacted bullying aggression more frequently than did spanked children. Results from a study conducted by Espelage, Bosworth, Karageorge and Daytner (1996) found a greater proportion of high-level bullying students who reported being physically punished (slapped, spanked, or hit) for wrongdoing (15 percent), in comparison to 7 percent of the moderate bullies and 4 percent of the non-bullies. Their findings also suggest consequences of bullying in an association between bullying and gang involvement with 34 percent of the high bully group reporting friends involved with gangs, in comparison to 19 percent of the moderate group and 5 percent of the non-bullying group.

Less research has been conducted to assess the perception of children in terms of responses to intervening when observing a bullying incident. In Hoover, Oliver and Hazler's (1992) study of middle and high school students, 60 percent of the students who reported being victimized over the course of their schooling reported that school personnel responded poorly.

Initiatives and interventions

There has not been any national or other large-scale initiative taken by any organization that is specific to bullying. The National School Safety Center is clearly an organization that comes closest to providing a clearing-house of resources and information on the topic of bullying, though the overall mandate of the organization is much broader. Despite the lack of broad programmatic attention to the issue, there are a variety of materials and resources on the subject available to parents and/or lay persons and those focused more for professionals, particularly school personnel. These range from information packets and videos, to handbooks on how to implement a school-wide intervention modeled after Olweus' program. Perhaps given the lack of centralized focus, adoption, usage and/or implementation of these resources becomes very individualized even within school districts.

We could find no evaluations of programs that specifically address bullying prevention or intervention in the US research literature. The programs that are listed as resources to address bullying typically have been developed to address broadly defined aggressive behavior, e.g. cognitive behavioral skills training, and do not target only bullying. These programs include skills training, conflict resolution, friendship groups, counseling, student watch programs, and peer helpers.

Future directions

A critical future step to further our understanding of bullying behavior within the US is to develop or agree upon a common definition of bullying and to specify clearly what behaviors are being included in the term. This includes distinguishing bullies from other aggressive children, as well as distinguishing victims of bullies from victims of other forms of aggression. This critical step must be taken before other research is conducted to provide comparable data on the incidence and prevalence of bullying in the US. While several individual precursors of direct physical bullying have been explored in the literature, only a few studies have examined familial, school or other contextual factors that predict either bullying or victimization. More work needs to be done in this area. Further, much of the examination to date has focused on direct forms of bullying, and less is known about indirect forms of bullying, including its prevalence, associated factors and conditions that moderate the effects or reduce the likelihood of it occurring. Much of the work completed to date on direct forms of bullying provides important information that could be used to develop effective interventions. In particular, the information-processing studies suggest that positive evaluation of outcomes of direct bullying and hostile attributions are characteristics of bullies. Direct bullies also appear to place little value on relationship-enhancing goals during social interaction. The findings related to victims also have implications for intervention design. Stable victims are more likely to develop when they acquiesce to demands by bullies. These findings should be utilized in developing prevention and intervention programs for bullying. More investigation is required about the developmentally changing role of bullying and victimization in establishing popularity and leadership. The findings from several studies suggest that bullying behavior may have positive as well as negative results for the bully in terms of social relationships, particularly when the bully is young. Chronic victims appear to play some role in classroom and playgroup dynamics that is associated with valuing bullying behavior. As they become more stable victims, they become less valued members of the social group and bullying of these stable victims may be less socially disapproved. Finally, further examination of the gender differences in bullying behavior and the role of social relationship goals in producing these differences should be explored.

References

Bosworth, K., Espelage, D., DuBay, T., Dahlberg, L. L. and Daytner, G. (1996) Using multimedia to teach conflict-resolution skills to young adolescents. *American Journal of Preventive Medicine*, 12, 65–74.

Coie, J. D., Dodge, K. A., Terry, R. and Wright, V. (1991) The role of aggression in peer relations: An analysis of aggression episodes in boys' play groups. *Child Development*, 62, 812–826.

Crick, N. R., Casas, J. F. and Mosher, M. (1997) Relational and overt aggression in preschool. *Developmental Psychology*, 33, 579–588.

Crick, N. R. and Dodge, K. A. (1996) Social information-processing mechanisms in reactive and pro-active aggression. *Child Development*, 67, 993–1002.

Crick, N. R. and Grotpeter, J. K. (1995) Relational aggression, gender, and social-psychological adjustment. *Child Development*, 66, 710–722.

Crick, N. R. and Grotpeter, J. K. (1996) Children's treatment by peers: Victims of relational and overt aggression. *Development and Psychopathology*, 8, 367–380.

Dodge, K. A. (1991) The structure and function of reactive and pro-active aggression. In D. J. Pepler and K. H. Rubin (eds) *The development and treatment of childhood aggression* (pp. 201–218). Hillsdale, NJ: Lawrence Erlbaum Associates.

Dodge, K. A. and Coie, J. D. (1987) Social-information processing factors in reactive and pro-active aggression in children's peer groups. *Journal of Personality and Social Psychology*, 53, 1146–1158.

Dodge, K. A., Coie, J. D., Pettit, G. S. and Price, J. M. (1990) Peer status and aggression in boys' groups: Developmental and contextual analyses. *Child Development*, 61, 1289–1309.

Dodge, K. A., Price, J. M., Coie, J. D. and Christopoulos, C. (1990) On the development of aggressive dyadic relationships in boys' peer groups. *Human Development*, 33, 260–270.

Donahue, P. (1994) Twelve-year-old sues school for allowing sexual harassment. Transcript #4109, the Phil Donahue Show, 28 October, New York.

Eron, L. D., Huesmann, L. R., Dubow, E., Romanoff, R. and Yarmel, P. W. (1987) Aggression and its correlates over 22 years. In D. H. Crowell, I. M. Evans and C. R. O'Donnell (eds) *Childhood aggression and violence* (pp. 249–262). New York: Plenum Publishing Corporation.

Espelage, D., Bosworth, K., Karageorge, K. and Daytner, G. (1996) Family/Environment and Bullying Behaviors: Interrelationships and Treatment Implications. Paper presented at the annual meeting of the American Psychological Association, Toronto, Canada, August.
Finkelhor, D. and Dziuba-Leatherman, J. (1994) Children as victims of violence: A national survey. *Pediatrics*, 94, 413–420.
Finkelhor, D. and Dziuba-Leatherman, J. (1995) Victimization prevention programs: A national survey of children's exposure and reactions. *Child Abuse and Neglect*, 19, 129–139.
Golding, W. (1955) *Lord of the flies*. New York: Capricorn.
Greenbaum, S. (1987) What can we do about schoolyard bullying? *Principal*, 67, 21–24.
Hazler, R. J., Carney, J. V., Green, S., Powell, R. and Jolly, L. S. (1997) Areas of expert agreement on identification of school bullies and victims. *School Psychology International*, 18, 3–12.
Hazler, R. J., Hoover, J. H. and Oliver, R. (1991) Student perceptions of victimization in schools. *Journal of Humanistic Education and Development*, 29, 143–150.
Hazler, R. J., Hoover, J. H. and Oliver, R. (1992) What kids say about bullying. *The Executive Educator*, 14, 20–22.
Hodges, E. V. E. and Perry, D. G. (1996) Victims of peer abuse: An overview. *Reclaiming Children and Youth: Journal of Emotional and Behavioral Problems*, 5, 23–28.
Hodges, E. V. E. and Perry, D. G. (1997) Individual risk and social risk as interacting determinants of victimization in the peer group. *Developmental Psychology*, 33, 1032–1039.
Hoover, J. H. and Hazler, R. J. (1991) Bullies and victims. *Elementary School Guidance and Counseling*, 25, 212–219.
Hoover, J. H., Oliver, R. and Hazler, R. J. (1992) Bullying: Perceptions of adolescent victims in the midwestern USA. *School Psychology International*, 13, 5–16.
Kochenderfer, B. J. and Ladd, G. W. (1996) Peer victimization: Cause or consequence of school maladjustment? *Child Development*, 67, 1305–1317.
National Education Goals Panel (1993) *The National Education Goals Report: Volume One*. Washington, DC: US Government Printing Office.
National Institute of Education, US Department of Health, Education and Welfare, Violent Schools – Safe Schools (1978) *The Safe School Study Report to Congress*. Washington, DC: Government Printing Office.
National School Safety Center (NSSC) (1988) *Set straight on bullies*. Westlake Village, CA.
NSSC (1995) *School bullying and victimization*. Westlake Village, CA: Resource Paper.
Office of Educational Research and Improvement (1995) *Digest of education statistics*. US Department of Education, NCES 95–029.
Olweus, D. (1978) *Aggression in the schools: Bullies and whipping boys*. New York: Wiley.
Olweus, D. (1996) Bully/victim problems at school: Facts and effective intervention. *Reclaiming Children and Youth: Journal of Emotional and Behavioral Problems*, 5, 15–22.
Patterson, G. R. (1967) Selective responsiveness to social reinforcers and deviant behavior in children. *Psychological Record*, 17, 369–378.
Perry, D. G., Kusel, S. J. and Perry, L. C. (1988) Victims of peer aggression. *Developmental Psychology*, 24, 807–814.

Perry, D. G., Perry, L. C. and Kennedy, E. (1992) Conflict and the development of antisocial behavior. In C. U. Shantz and W. W. Hartup (eds) *Conflict in child and adolescent development* (pp. 301–329). New York: Cambridge University Press.

Perry, D. G., Williard, J. C. and Perry, L. C. (1990) Peers' perceptions of the consequences that victimized children provide aggressors. *Child Development*, 61, 1310–1325.

Price, J. M. and Dodge, K. A. (1989) Reactive and pro-active aggression in childhood: Relations to peer status and social context dimensions. *Journal of Abnormal Child Psychology*, 17, 455–471.

Putting Bullies Out of Business (1996). *Reclaiming Children and Youth*, 5 (1).

Ross, D. M. (1996) *Childhood bullying and teasing: What school personnel, other professionals, and parents can do.* Alexandria, VA: American Counseling Association.

School Safety (fall 1996) *Bullying – prevention requires adult leadership*. National School Safety Center Newsjournal.

Schwartz, D., Dodge, K. A. and Coie, J. D. (1993) The emergence of chronic peer victimization in boys' play groups. *Child Development*, 64, 1755–1772.

Strassberg, Z., Dodge, K. A., Pettit, G. S. and Bates, J. E. (1994) Spanking in the home and children's subsequent aggression toward kindergarten peers. *Development and Psychopathology*, 6, 445–461.

Troy, M. and Sroufe, L. A. (1987) Victimization among preschoolers: Role of attachment relationship history. *Journal of the American Academy of Child and Adolescent Psychiatry*, 26, 166–172.

US Bureau of the Census (1994) *Current population reports*. Washington, DC: US Department of Commerce, Economics and Statistics Administration.

US Department of Health and Human Services, Centers for Disease Control and Prevention, National Center for Chronic Disease, Prevention and Health Promotion, Division of Adolescent and School Health (1993) *The Youth Risk Behavior Surveillance System.*

Further reading

Batsche, G. M. and Knoff, H. M. (1994) Bullies and their victims: Understanding a pervasive problem in the schools. *School Psychology Review*, 23, 165–174.

Crick, N. R. (1996) The role of overt aggression, relational aggression, and prosocial behavior in the prediction of children's future social adjustment. *Child Development*, 67, 2317–2327.

Crick, N. R., Bigbee, M. A. and Howes, C. (1996) Gender differences in children's normative beliefs about aggression: How do I hurt thee? Let me count the ways. *Child Development*, 67, 1003–1014.

Crick, N. R. and Dodge, K. A. (1994) A review and reformation of social information-processing mechanisms in children's social adjustment. *Psychological Bulletin*, 115, 74–101.

DeRosier, M. E., Cillessen, A. H. N., Coie, J. D. and Dodge, K. A. (1994) Group social context and children's aggressive behavior. *Child Development*, 65, 1068–1079.

Hazler, R. J. (1996a) *Breaking the cycle of violence: Interventions for bullying and victimization.* Washington, DC: Accelerated Development.

Hazler, R. J. (1996b) Bystanders: An overlooked factor in peer on peer abuse. *The Journal of the Professional Counselor*, 11, 11–21.

Hoover, J. H. and Oliver, R. (1996) *The bullying prevention handbook: A guide for principals, teachers, and counselors*. Bloomington, IN: National Educational Service.
Oliver, R., Hoover, J. H. and Hazler, R. (1994) The perceived roles of bullying in small-town midwestern schools. *Journal of Counseling and Development*, 72, 416–420.
Stephens, R. D. (1995) *School bullying and victimization*. National School Safety Center, Resource Paper.

18 Canada

Tracy W. Harachi, Richard F. Catalano and J. David Hawkins

Overview

In Canada, bullying appears to be broadly defined as direct, physical aggression as well as indirect behaviour, though no one standard definition seems to prevail. The popular literature and media depict bullying as behaviour that involves both boys and girls and is a childhood and adolescent occurrence. Limited research has been conducted within Canada focused on bullying. Of the two studies that have examined the incidence of bullying among elementary and middle school students, one reported 28 per cent of the students being bullied and the other 21 per cent. Other research has been conducted using naturalistic observations of bullying episodes among elementary school-aged children in the classroom and on the playground; these findings illuminate the role of peers in bullying episodes and opportunities for intervention. More research is needed on the epidemiology of this problem across Canada, as well as examining the familial, school and contextual predictors of bullying behaviour and victimization. In addition, given the high prevalence rates reported at least in urban schools, continued research examining the effectiveness of prevention and intervention programmes with adequate comparison groups is suggested.

Country demographics

The total population of Canada was 27,296,859 based on data from the 1991 Census. Fifty-nine per cent of the population is of single origin European descent, 4.3 per cent Asian, 1.7 per cent American-Indian, 0.8 per cent black, 5.4 per cent other single origin and 28.9 per cent other multiple origin. Of the 1991 total, 76.6 per cent of the population resided in urban areas and 23.4 per cent in rural areas. Provinces with the smallest population growth were Quebec and Manitoba with less than half of the national rate (1.2 per cent). In contrast, British Columbia had the largest increase (2.6 per cent) in population. The median household income was $39,013 in 1991. The incidence of families below the poverty level was 13.2 per cent and 36 per cent for individuals.

System of education

There are four types of schools: (1) public, (2) private, (3) federal and (4) schools for the handicapped (limited to special facilities and training for the blind and deaf). Public schools are established and operated by local educational authorities according to the public school act of the province. Also included in the public school category are Protestant and Roman Catholic separate schools, and schools operated in Canada by the Department of National Defense within the framework of the public school system. Federal schools include overseas schools operated by the Department of Defense and Indian schools operated by the Indian and Northern Affairs Department. Private schools are commonly known as independent schools in most provinces outside of Quebec. These schools must provide programmes for students that meet the provincial goals of basic education. Approximately half of the private schools have a religious affiliation, while two-thirds of public schools are non-sectarian. An exception is Quebec, where almost all public schools are sectarian and nearly all private schools do not report whether or not they are sectarian.

Provincial authorities determine a number of the basic policies regarding education. For example, the age for compulsory school attendance and length of school year are determined individually by each province. The range for compulsory education varies across provinces from age 5 or 6 to 16 depending on whether kindergarten is compulsory. Although kindergarten is not required, it is offered and many students enrol. For example, approximately 95 per cent of eligible students enrol in kindergarten in Alberta where it is not compulsory. Elementary schools, also called primary schools, include kindergarten and grades 1 through 6. There is some overlap in grade range at the next level, junior high or middle school, which may include grades 6 through 9. Senior high school includes grades 10 through 12. In addition, some schools may be called secondary schools and be configured to include all of the upper grades, 7 through 12. Some unique provincial conditions include Quebec which has no grade 12, and Ontario which has a secondary system with grade 13.

Total public and private elementary/secondary school student enrolments decreased between 1971 and 1985 (Education Statistics Review, 1995). However, the trend began to reverse and reached a total of 5.3 million students in 1993–1994. This total remains substantially below the high of 5.8 million attained in 1970–1971. Approximately 5 per cent of all elementary and secondary students attend private schools. Overall, private school enrolment has risen fairly steadily since 1971. Though pre-elementary school is not compulsory, enrolment has shown a general upward trend since 1978, increasing by approximately one-third to total 490,800 in 1993.

In 1992, the total number of institutions was 15,950, of which 12,441 were elementary schools and 3509 secondary. Most public schools range between 200 and 1000 students in capacity. The typical capacity for private schools is much smaller; for example, most private schools especially those outside of Quebec offer both primary and secondary grades, yet typically have fewer than 100 students. The student to teacher ratio at the national level was 15.7 to 1 in 1993.

Definitions of bullying

There appears to be no one standard definition of bullying in the popular or research literature. Most give no reference nor include a specific definition. However, a limited amount of research has been conducted specifically on bullying and utilized the definition of Olweus. More broadly the definition of bullying utilized in Canada includes direct, physical aggression, as well as indirect behaviour such as teasing, and involves both boys and girls. It appears to be generally referred to as a childhood occurrence.

Historical interest as a social problem and media attention

There are numerous articles about bullies and bullying in the popular literature. Newspaper articles, home-maker magazines and publications targeting parents of school-aged children contain discussions on bullying, and suggestions on how parents and schools can address the issue.

Despite the apparent visibility in the media, bullying has not received widespread attention in educational programming or in the scientific literature as a specific problem issue to address. Rather, broader issues such as school safety and violence in schools have garnered more co-ordinated support. For example, school boards within particular provinces have adopted policies and programming related to school safety. In addition, organizations such as the British Columbia Teachers Federation or Principals and Vice Principals Association have placed violence prevention initiatives on their agenda. An exception is the Toronto Board of Education which has specifically targeted bullying as an issue towards which resources have been directed.

Research related to bullying

A major contributor has been Dr Debra J. Pepler at the LaMarch Centre for Research on Violence and Conflict Resolution at York University. The Centre is mandated to support, conduct and disseminate the results of research on violence and conflict resolution. The Centre sponsored a conference entitled 'Putting the Brakes on Violence' (August 1996), along with the North York Board of Education.

A descriptive study was conducted in 1991 by Pepler and colleagues at the request of the Toronto Board of Education. The study involved a survey of students, staff and parents from a random sample of elementary schools. The survey component was based closely on items utilized by studies in Scandinavia (Olweus, 1989). It was administered to 211 children (105 boys, 106 girls) in

14 classrooms from grades 4 to 6 and grade 8 (ages 8 to 14), their teachers and parents. In addition, qualitative data were collected from classroom discussions involving 457 students from kindergarten to grade 8. Students in the classroom were read a story about bullying at school, which was followed by a class discussion and/or role-play activity related to bullying. There follow selected findings from the study (see Ziegler and Rosenstein-Manner (1991) for a complete report).

Based on the qualitative data, all students understood the concept of bullying. While only a few kindergarten children used the word bullying, most understood what it was, but assumed the referent was only physical aggression. By grades 1 to 3, students knew the meaning of the term and applied it to the situation in the story, including the non-physical aspect of bullying like verbal taunting. By grades 5 to 6, children had a broader definition which included threatening and exclusion. In general, students expressed strong disapproval of bullying. For primary grade students, bullies were seen as bad kids who liked to fight, wanted to get other students to do their homework, or tried to take something from other students. By grades 4 to 8, bullies were seen not just as students who were physically bigger, but students who wanted power, who were perhaps victims themselves or were jealous of those who do well. Students in these later grades said that some kids were picked on a lot because they were scared and would not report or tell on the bully, did not fight back or were new students at the school. Cultural differences were also mentioned as a factor in being bullied, and by the eighth grade, students said there was definitely racist bullying. Students felt that both boys and girls could be bullies, but that boys were more often bullies.

The results of the survey component of the study suggest that almost half of the children responding experienced bullying at school. This ranged from 28 per cent who reported being bullied once or twice, 12 per cent now and then and 8 per cent on a weekly or more basis. Twenty-four per cent of the students identified themselves as bullies and reported having bullied at least once or twice during the term, while another 15 per cent reported more frequent bullying. Overall, the highest percentage of self-identified bullies was among the 11- to 12-year-olds. Three-quarters of all bullies are boys which corresponds with 23 per cent of the boys in the sample. Only 8 per cent of the girls in the sample self-identified as a bully. Of the self-identified bullies (n = 32), 28 per cent also reported being victims. Of the students who reported being victimized, 30 per cent reported being bullied by a group of boys, 28 per cent by an individual boy and 5 per cent by an individual girl. According to victims, bullies were usually in the same grade and class (60 per cent). According to the students, the playground is the most common setting for bullying (87 per cent), but other settings are also common venues. Many more students reported the occurrence of bullying in closely adult-supervised settings such as the classroom (50 per cent) than in some unsupervised ones, such as the streets surrounding the schools (35 per cent).

In general, responses by parents and teachers greatly underestimated the frequency of bullying behaviour when compared with student responses. For example, only 27 per cent of the parents reported that their student had experienced bullying at some time compared with 48 per cent of the students' self-report. Conversely, teachers reported a lower percentage of children in their classroom being bullied at least once a week, 49 per cent, as opposed to 59 per cent reported by the students.

Qualitative data from class discussions indicated that the younger primary grade students thought that adults should intervene more. By grade 6, the general reaction was that bullying behaviour could not be prevented, but students made recommendations of strategies like not being alone and avoiding bullies. However, by grade 8, students thought the school should work with bullies and that the focus of intervening should be on bullies rather than on victims.

The survey results suggest that children and adults agree that the best thing a student can do about being bullied is to tell a parent or teacher. About half the students say they tell their teachers and close to two-thirds tell parents when they are bullied, but many who are frequently victimized do not seek adult help. Teachers reported that many students come to them for help. Almost three-quarters of teachers say they usually intervene if they see bullying going on; only a quarter of students, however, perceived that teachers typically do so. Many students and most staff say that children do sometimes intervene to stop bullying. Fighting back was not a popular alternative among most child respondents. More boys than girls endorsed fighting back, as did a higher proportion of bullies than other children. Thirty-three per cent of the students stated that they did nothing in response to bullying, but thought they should do something. Most students reported bullying as being very unpleasant, and either tried to help the victim or would have liked to be able to help. About a quarter of the students did not want to be involved in intervening and about 90 per cent reported that bullying was distressing.

In summary, results of the Toronto study suggest a frequency of bullying behaviour that is higher than that reported in Scandinavia. According to Norwegian data, 9 per cent report being bullied now and then or more frequently (Olweus, 1991) in contrast to 20 per cent in these data. These rates appear more similar to those reported for British 13- and 15-year-olds (21–27 per cent) (Boulton and Underwood, 1992; Stephenson and Smith, 1989; Whitney and Smith, 1993).

Another descriptive study was conducted in Calgary by Bentley and Li (1995), who assessed 379 4th to 6th graders (ages 8 to 12) using the Bully/Victim Questionnaire (Olweus, 1989) and Belief Measures (Slaby and Guerra, 1988). The definition of bullying was based on that used by Olweus (1989), and Smith (1991). Results showed that 21.3 per cent of the subjects were bullied and 11.6 per cent bullied others. Victims were bullied by both peers and older children. Verbal abuse was the most common form of bullying and the playground was the most common location. There was no significant association between gender and direct or indirect bullying. Bullies tended to be in the older grades and were mainly boys. Bullies were more likely than victims, or students who were neither bullies nor victims, to endorse aggression-supporting beliefs. Many of the victims (35.1 per cent) reported that teachers almost never intervene or try to stop it when a child is being bullied, whereas only 11.7 per cent of all other students in the sample felt this way. When asked how often other students try to stop bullying at school, many of the victims (40.3 per cent) and other students in the sample (32.5 per cent) reported that peers almost never intervene. In terms of reporting victimization, students were more apt to tell someone at home rather than their teacher whether they were a victim, bully or other student. Of those who reported telling a teacher about being bullied, 68 per cent felt that telling a teacher did help their situation and 32 per cent reported it did not help.

In addition to survey research, Pepler and Craig have also conducted naturalistic observations of bullying episodes on playgrounds to examine the roles of peers and the potential processes within the peer group as they impact on bullying. Participants were 6- to 12-year-olds attending urban schools in Toronto (see Craig and Pepler, 1995a; Pepler and Craig, 1995). Target children were those rated as aggressive and non-aggressive by their teacher. Each target child wore a small remote microphone and pocket-sized transmitter, which picked up the target child's speech as well as those around him or her; they were aware of being videotaped. They were instructed to play as they would normally. Observers recorded bully, victim, other peers and staff behaviour. Selected results of these observations include the following:

- Peers were involved in some capacity in 85 per cent of the bullying episodes.
- In 81 per cent of the episodes, peers reinforced the bullying.
- Peers were more respectful and friendly towards the bullies than the victims.
- Peers were active participants in 48 per cent of the episodes. In two-thirds of these episodes, only one peer was involved. In general, involved peers tended to be male.
- Thirty per cent of the peers took pleasure in the bullying, 46 per cent were neutral, 24 per cent reported being uncomfortable.
- Peers intervened in only 13 per cent of the episodes in which they were present and these interventions were often in a socially inappropriate manner.
- Staff were present in only 17 per cent of the overall observed bullying episodes and intervened in 23 per cent of these episodes.

In addition, a comparison of naturalistic observations on the playground and in the classroom was conducted in an urban, lower middle-class elementary school in Toronto with grades 1 to 6 (Pepler *et al.*, in press). The sample comprised students rated by their teacher as aggressive or non-aggressive who were subsequently observed in a bullying episode. Results include:

- There was a higher frequency of bullying in the playground (4.5 episodes per hour) compared to the classroom (2.4 episodes per hour).
- Mean duration of bullying episodes was 33.6 seconds (s.d. = 63.5 seconds) with a range from 2 to 448 on the playground; the mean in the classroom was 26 seconds (s.d. = 35.4 seconds) with a range from 2 to 227 seconds.
- Direct bullying was more prevalent on the playground and indirect bullying in the classroom.
- The majority of the episodes in both contexts involved verbal bullying (42 per cent in the playground and 53 per cent in the classroom).
- Non-aggressive children were more likely to bully in the playground, whereas aggressive children were more likely to bully in the classroom.
- Episodes with male bullies were likely to involve male victims in either context; however, only about half of the episodes involving female bullies had female victims.
- Reinforcement of bullying, assessed by peer involvement, and peer or teacher intervention, was relatively equivalent in the playground and in the classroom.
- There was no difference across context in proportion of episodes with peers present and in the rate of peer and teacher intervention.

The Montreal Longitudinal Study of Disruptive Boys has been conducted by Dr Richard E. Tremblay since 1984 (Tremblay *et al.*, 1992). The study was planned both to investigate the development of boys at risk of antisocial behaviour and to experimentally evaluate the effects of a preventive effort. One set of analyses reported in Pulkkinen and Tremblay (1992) compared a profile and outcomes of boys termed 'bullies'. Boys from the Montreal sample were compared to boys from the Jyvaskyla (Finland) Longitudinal Study of Social Development who had a cluster of behaviours including high scores on aggression, non-pro-sociality and hyperactivity and low scores on anxiety and inattentiveness. This profile or cluster of behaviours appeared similar to the personality pattern defined by Olweus (1978), justifying the term 'bullies'. Assessments occurred at ages 8, 14 and 26 for the Finnish sample and at 6 and 10 to 11 for the Montreal sample. In the later Montreal sample, those boys clustered under the bully profile showed less stability of behaviour pattern over the four-year period than the overall stability of aggressive behaviour patterns versus non-aggressive patterns. Of those classed at time 1 as bullies, only 12 per cent were again classed at time 2 (n = 5). Bullies in the Canadian sample identified by teacher report at age 6 also had higher self-reported delinquency in middle childhood than other clusters of boys including those identified as anxious, passive, inattentive, nervous, uncontrolled and normal.

Initiatives and interventions

There have been no nation- or province-wide initiatives taken by any organizations that are specific to bullying. At the local level, the Toronto Board of Education provides an example of a local educational authority specifically targeting the issue of bullying and co-ordinating of resources. In addition to publishing a research bulletin on the topic, *Bullying at School: Toronto in an International Context* (Ziegler and Rosenstein-Manner, 1991), the Board produced a booklet on bullying and a film to raise sensitivity and concern for the problem of bullying.

Toronto is also the site of a whole-school intervention effort. The Toronto Anti-Bullying Intervention was a pilot study implemented in four elementary schools (Charach *et al.*, 1995; Pepler *et al.*, 1993, 1994) and modelled after the Norwegian programme (Olweus, 1987). Its goals are to increase awareness of and knowledge about the problem, actively involve teachers and parents in planning and implementation, develop clear rules against bullying behaviour and support and protect victims. Three of the schools were kindergarten grade 8 and one was a middle school, grades 7 to 8. All schools were selected because of their interest in the problem and willingness to collaborate. Each school had two team leaders who were school staff trained in the summer of 1991. Implementation at each school varied somewhat; however, all schools introduced three critical elements: staff training, codes of behaviour, and improved playground supervision.

Self-administered questionnaires were given in October and May of the first year and completed by 898 students (Pepler *et al.*, 1993) and utilized the same questionnaire as in the previous descriptive study (Ziegler and Rosenstein-Manner, 1991). A second study compared 1052 students at baseline and 1041 at eighteen-month follow-up (Pepler *et al.*, 1994). Students below grade 3 were excluded given the reading level of the questionnaire, unless the third graders were part of a multi-age 3/4 classroom. The reference period for bullying was since the beginning of the term, approximately two months. In addition, team leaders from each of the schools were interviewed and 78 (74 per cent) teachers completed the Classroom Activities Questionnaire.

The preliminary assessment of six-month data indicated a 30 per cent reduction in reported incidents of bullying when children were asked, 'How many times have you been bullied in the last five days?' (see Pepler *et al.*, 1993). Fewer children reported spending time alone at recess and at lunch following the intervention. There was, however, no significant change in children's reports of the prevalence of bullying in the last two months, racial bullying, peer intervention, or in discussions about bullying with adults. Children reported significantly less adult intervention in the spring than in the fall. Fewer children reported being uncomfortable observing bullying in the spring than in the fall.

Results of the eighteen-month follow-up indicated some unfavourable and some favourable changes in students' reports of bullying. There was a significant increase in the number of students who reported bullying. At pre-test, 16 per cent of the students reported bullying once or more in the past five days while 21 per cent reported bullying at post-test. This increase was also reported with a longer time period (over the past term or approximately two months) with 7 per cent of the students reporting that they bullied more than once or twice at pre-test and 9 per cent at post-test. More students reported racial bullying at post-test (5 per cent versus 9 per cent) and more students reported spending the recess alone (14 per cent versus 20 per cent). There was, however, a significant decrease in the number of students who reported thinking about joining in a bullying episode (18 per cent versus 15 per cent). There was not a corresponding increase in the proportion of children who reported feeling uncomfortable watching bullying. In terms of victimization, the number of students who reported being bullied in the past five days fell from 28 per cent at pre-test to 23 per cent at post-test. There was a non-significant increase in reported victimization over the previous term. The frequency with which peers intervened did not change over time. However, there was a significant increase in students' report of teacher intervention. At pre-test, 47 per cent of the students reported that teachers sometimes or always stopped bullying. This proportion increased to 55 per cent at post-test. There was also a significant increase in whether teachers talked to bullies about their bullying behaviour. Among bullies, 42 per cent reported being talked to about their bullying behaviour at pre-test and 50 per cent at post-test. There was no change in the number of students reporting that their parents had talked to them about their bullying or victimization.

We identified several areas that suggest further focus and attention. There continued to be a marked discrepancy between teachers' and students' reports of intervention. First, although victimization had declined in the recent period, rates appeared similar over a longer period of time and rates of racial bullying increased. Second, the percentage of bullies increased. The increase in bullying occurred despite reports of teachers talking about and stopping bullying more frequently as reported by students. We believe that greater emphasis should be given to the integrated nature of the whole-school intervention for implementation to be successful. More steps need to be taken to facilitate consistent and cohesive communication and action across all parties, including students, school staff and parents. In addition, greater emphasis on peer intervention is suggested. Results also suggest a need to bolster efforts to involve parents whose behaviour appeared to be unaffected by the present level of implementation. However, the lack of a control group does not allow definitive conclusions to any of these questions since these changes cannot be compared to normal developmental growth or decline of bullying or victimization. For example, although the percentage of bullies increased, this increase may be below that normally occurring during this stage of children's development. Without a control or comparison group against which to judge these changes, it is unclear what conclusions may be drawn regarding the effects of the intervention.

Future directions

Much of the Canadian literature has utilized a common definition of bullying. The rates of bullying appear to be higher than reported in other countries where a similar definition has been used. However, the study of bullying in Canada has been confined to a few investigators examining bullying mostly in urban contexts. More research is needed on the epidemiology of this problem across Canada. While several studies have examined the individual predictors of bullying and victimization, more research is needed to examine the familial, school and contextual predictors of these behaviour patterns. The results of observation studies of bullies and victims are enlightening. There appears to be much reinforcement of bullying by peers despite survey reports which indicate that a vast majority of children are disturbed by bullying behaviour. This highlights a potential social desirability bias of questionnaires and suggests that future survey work should be informed by these observational studies. The descriptive studies suggest that intervention is needed to reduce the prevalence of bullying. There is a misperception of the extent of the problem by parents. This suggests that children who are bullied do not report these experiences to their parents. In addition, students report that teachers and students do not intervene in many cases to stop bullying behaviour. If bullying behaviour is to be curtailed, these data suggest that teachers need better training to identify bullying incidents and to respond appropriately after identification of bullying. Furthermore, given the high prevalence rates reported at least in urban schools, studies of the effectiveness of prevention and intervention programmes with adequate comparison groups are needed.

References

Annual Report of Statistics Canada (1991) *Statistics Canada*. Ottawa: Statistics Canada, 93–315; 93–340.

Bentley, K. M. and Li, A. K. F. (1995) Bully and victim problems in elementary schools and students' beliefs about aggression. *Canadian Journal of School Psychology*, 11, 153–165.

Boulton, M. J. and Underwood, K. (1992) Bully/victim problems among middle school children. *British Journal of Educational Psychology*, 62, 73–87.

Charach, A., Pepler, D., and Ziegler, S. (1995) Bullying at school: A Canadian perspective. *Education Canada*, spring, 12–18.

Craig, W. M. and Pepler, D. J. (1995a) Peer processes in bullying and victimization: An observational study. *Exceptional Education Canada*, 5, 81–95.

Craig, W. M. and Pepler, D. J. (1995b) Understanding bullying at school: What can we do about it? In S. Miller, J. Brodine and T. Miller (eds) *Safe by design:*

Building interpersonal relationships (pp. 205–230). Seattle, WA: Committee for Children.

Education Statistics Review (1995) *Education in Canada*. Ontario: Ministry of Industry.

Olweus, D. (1978) *Aggression in the schools*. Washington, DC: Hemisphere.

Olweus, D. (1987) Schoolyard bullying: Grounds for intervention. *School Safety*, 6, 4–11.

Olweus, D. (1989) Questionnaire for students (junior and senior versions). Unpublished manuscript. University of Bergen, Norway.

Olweus, D. (1991) Bully/victim problems among school children: Basic facts and effects of a school-based intervention program. In D. J. Pepler and K. H. Rubin (eds) *The development and treatment of childhood aggression* (pp. 411–448). Hillsdale, NJ: Erlbaum.

Pepler, D. J. and Craig, W. M. (1995) A peek behind the fence: Naturalistic observations of aggressive children with remote audiovisual recording. *Developmental Psychology*, 31, 548–553.

Pepler, D. J., Craig, W. M. and Atlas, R. (in press) Observations of bullying on the playground and in the classroom. *Canadian Journal of School Psychology*.

Pepler, D., Craig, W., Ziegler, S. and Charach, A. (1993) A school-based anti-bullying intervention: Preliminary evaluation. In D. Tattum (ed.) *Understanding and managing bullying* (pp. 76–91). Oxford: Heinemann Books.

Pepler, D. J., Craig, W. M., Ziegler, S. and Charach, A. (1994) An evaluation of an anti-bullying intervention in Toronto schools. *Canadian Journal of Community Mental Health*, 13, 95–110.

Pulkkinen, L. and Tremblay, R. E. (1992) Patterns of boys' social adjustment in two cultures and at different ages: A longitudinal perspective. *International Journal of Behavioral Development*, 15, 527–553.

Slaby, R. G. and Guerra, N. G. (1988) Cognitive mediators of aggression in adolescent offenders: 1. Assessment. *Developmental Psychology*, 24, 580–588.

Smith, P. K. (1991) The silent nightmare: Bullying and victimization in school peer groups. *Bulletin of the British Psychological Society*, 4, 243–248.

Stephenson, P. and Smith, D. (1989) Bullying in the junior school. In D. P. Tattum and D. A. Lane (eds) *Bullying in schools* (pp. 45–57). Stoke-on-Trent, UK: Trentham Books.

Tremblay, R. E., Vitaro, F., Bertrand, L., LeBlanc, M., Beauchesne, H., Boileau, H. and David, L. (1992) Parent and child training to prevent early onset of delinquency: The Montreal longitudinal-experimental study. In J. McCord and R. E. Tremblay (eds) *Preventing antisocial behavior: Interventions from birth through adolescence* (pp. 117–138). New York: Guilford Press.

Whitney, I. and Smith, P. K. (1993) A survey of the nature and extent of bullying in junior/middle and secondary schools. *Educational Research*, 35, 3–25.

Ziegler, S. and Rosenstein-Manner, M. (1991) *Bullying at school: Toronto in an international context*. Toronto Board of Education, #196R.

Part III

Pacific Rim

19 Japan

Yohji Morita, Haruo Soeda,
Kumiko Soeda and Mitsuru Taki

Country summary

Demographics

Based on 1995 census data, the estimated total population of Japan was 125,569,000; the population density was 336.8 persons per square kilometre. The proportion of the population aged over 65 years has rapidly increased and accounted for 14.1 per cent of the total population in 1994. A baby boom has also occurred, and the proportion of the population between 0 and 14 years old accounted for 16.3 per cent (20,415,000 persons). The number of children born to one female in her lifetime was 1.50 on average in 1994.

There are 47 prefectures in Japan; as of October 1995, there were 3246 municipalities within these prefectures. There are eleven municipalities with populations of over one million people, and the proportion of the population of these amounted to 20.1 per cent of the total population in 1995.

System of education

Major characteristics of each of the different types of institution of formal education are presented below.

1 *Kindergartens*: Non-compulsory schools which cater for preschool children aged 3 or over.
2 *Compulsory education*: Elementary schools and lower secondary schools. All children who have reached the age of 6 are required to attend a six-year elementary school within their attendance district. The elementary school is intended to provide children between the ages of 6 and 12 with a general primary education. After having completed the elementary school course, all children are required to go on to a three-year lower secondary school in their attendance district. The lower secondary school aims to provide children between the ages of 12 and 15 with a general secondary education.

Most elementary and lower secondary schools are public schools, which are established by municipalities and operated by local boards of education under national guidelines and legislation. Curricula of elementary and lower secondary schools are based on the Course of Study issued by the Ministry of Education, Science and Culture (referred to as the 'Monbusho' in Japan). Textbooks used in these schools are authorized by the Monbusho, adopted by local boards of education, and distributed free to all children.

3 *Upper secondary schools*: Non-compulsory schools which are intended to provide lower secondary school graduates with general, specialized, and comprehensive courses. About two-thirds of upper secondary schools are public schools which are run by prefectural governments; the rest are private schools.

Most public and private upper secondary schools select students on the basis of both of the entrance examinations given by local boards of education or upper secondary schools and the school recommendation prepared by the lower secondary schools. The advancement rate to upper secondary schools was 96.8 per cent in 1997.

The curriculum of upper secondary schools is based on the Course of Study, and textbooks used are authorized by the Monbusho.

4 *Higher education*: Major institutions of higher education are universities (mostly four-year courses, and six-year courses for medicine, dentistry and veterinary medicine) and junior colleges (two- or three-year courses). These schools require the completion of upper secondary schooling or its equivalent for admission. The advancement rate to universities or junior colleges was 47.3 per cent in 1997.

Size of classes and schools

There were 24,376 elementary schools, 11,257 lower secondary schools and 5496 upper secondary schools in 1997. An average elementary school contained 341 pupils in 1995, and an average lower secondary school contained 398 students.

The national government establishes various standards for each school level. In kindergartens, elementary and lower secondary schools, classes, in principle, should comprise students of the same grade. In special cases, however, several different grades may attend the same class. There were 6909 multi-graded classes as compared with 282,974 single-graded classes in elementary schools in 1997, and 238 and 127,307, respectively, in lower secondary schools. Most of the multi-graded classes are in rural areas.

The maximum number of students per class in local public elementary and lower secondary schools is prescribed by law, and the present limit is 40 students per class. The average number of pupils per class in elementary schools was 27.8 in 1997, and that of lower secondary schools was 33.2.

Definition and problematization of *Ijime* (Japanese bullying)

Definitions of Ijime

The counterpart of bullying in Japanese vocabulary is 'ijime'. 'Ijime' has been utilized in daily life for many years. One handy Japanese–English dictionary lists translations of '*Ijime*-ru', a verbal form of 'ijime', as follows: ill-treat; treat someone harshly; be hard on someone; be cruel to; tease; annoy; bully. But problems of *Ijime* in schools, as described below, drew the attention of researchers and this necessitated its academic definition. Several definitions have attempted to describe this problematic phenomenon in schools. Among these, the one most often cited in various research papers, governmental documents and general books on *Ijime* is by Morita (1985):

> A type of aggressive behavior by which someone who holds a dominant position in a group-interaction process, by intentional or collective acts, causes mental and/or physical suffering to another inside a group.

This definition of *Ijime* appears to be similar to those in Europe (e.g. Olweus, 1972, 1993b; Whitney and Smith, 1993). But special attention should be given in translating 'ijime' into 'bullying' or vice versa. There will be further discussion on this point in the final section of this chapter; for the time being, readers are encouraged to keep in mind that Morita's definition of *Ijime* includes the phrases 'who holds a dominant position in a group-interaction process', that the word 'mental' comes *before* 'physical', and that the words 'inside a group' are included.

Shocking cases of Ijime covered sensationally in the media

We describe below two *Ijime* cases which shocked Japanese society through their sensational coverage by journalists. They made people aware of the deeply rooted problems of *Ijime* in school. Note that they are chosen here *not* because they are typical *Ijime* but because they are so sensationalized as to ensure that most Japanese people will remember them.

The Funeral Play Case in Tokyo

In December 1986, a 13-year-old boy committed suicide in Tokyo. His suicide note claimed that *Ijime* led him to his death. His class mates had given him *Ijime* both mentally and physically. On one occasion, they treated him as if he was dead and staged a mock funeral for him in the classroom. Even some of the teachers joined in the play and wrote messages of condolence with students: 'Goodbye and have a peaceful sleep.' The victim wrote that it was hell on earth for him.

In March 1991, the Tokyo District Court passed judgment on the case, based only on its recognition of the aggressors' violent physical actions, but excluding the mental *Ijime* as in the mock funeral. It handled the case as a usual one of school violence, rather than one of *Ijime*. The newspapers commented that this was in practice a defeat for the victim's parents, and they later appealed to the High Court against the District Court ruling.

In May 1994, this district decision was overturned by the Tokyo High Court whose decision was never appealed to the Supreme Court. The High Court recognized the existence of mental *Ijime* by his class mates as a cause of the victim's suicide and ordered Tokyo Metropolitan, Nakano Ward, and the parents of two of the aggressors, to pay 11,500,000 yen for the damage. This precedent-setting sentence is the first judicial recognition and definition of mental *Ijime* in history.

The Suicide Note with Aggressors' Names Case in Aichi

In November 1994, a 13-year-old male student committed suicide in Aichi Prefecture as a result of suffering *Ijime*. His suicide note said that several of his friends had often threatened him in an attempt to get large amounts of money. They hit and kicked him many times, and pushed his face into the river when he did not give them money. The sum of money they robbed him of, over a period of more than two years, was more than one million yen, approximately US $8000. His suicide note listed the names of the four boys who made *Ijime* on him. It was discovered later that seven other boys were also involved in this *Ijime* as aggressors. One news-show anchorman commented that this was not mere *Ijime* but a genuine crime. There is no doubt it was a crime but the fact that the victim and the aggressors were reported to be 'close friends' made this case even more tragic. They would often go around with each other as a group. The victim's father became aware that his son sustained injuries while with the group and told him to avoid them, but the victim rejected this advice, pretending he had no problem. As a matter of course, the aggressors pretended that the group, including the victim, were involved in friendly horseplay, particularly in the presence of authority figures.

Despite warnings by some scholars and teachers that *Ijime* was a persistent problem deeply embedded in children's peer culture and relations in schools, and often invisible to adults, most Japanese people believed the problem had been 'solved' in the 1980s. This case of suicide ironically proved the existence of the underlying problem of *Ijime* and made people aware of the need for effective action against it.

The 1970s and early 1980s – the 'prehistorical' period

In the late 1970s, secondary school teachers devoted all their energies to 'Kounai Bouryoku' or school violence. This included violence between students, against teachers, and vandalism. Though most of the attention of teachers, parents, students, administrators and journalists was drawn to school violence, a small number of teachers had already 'discovered' a new type of problematic behaviour, at the latest by the end of the 1970s. They called it 'ijime' or 'yowaimono ijime'. It is true that actions labelled 'ijime' or 'yowaimono ijime' were not rare in Japanese daily life, but they warned that this was different from the commonly and traditionally perceived type. They claimed that it had characteristics such as 'numbers', 'duration' and 'cunning'; such traits turned out to be identical to those of *Ijime* in the 1980s and the 1990s.

But the harshness and cruelty of school violence was so severe and so overt that these 'discoveries' about *Ijime* were neglected in most cases. Most people believed *Ijime* was less physical and accordingly less problematic than school violence.

The media never missed a chance to criticize teachers and schools for the occurrence of school violence. Government, the police, educational administrators, teachers, parents and students made every effort to prevent school violence. Actions taken in those days included monitoring in the playground, making strict school rules, co-operative action between teachers and parents, and between teachers and the police. It is significant that many of these intervention programmes are very similar to those dealing with bullying in Europe. This similarity may be explained by the fact that the word 'bullying' in Europe more often refers to physical bullying, which in those days was perceived as school violence in Japan.

These prevention/intervention programmes functioned effectively in a sense and, in the early 1980s, the occurrence of school violence gradually decreased, though some people claimed that such behaviour had just been submerged; but at least the atmosphere in schools became quiet again. As if educators could afford to deal with another problem, they began to notice the deeply rooted evilness of *Ijime*, though this recognition was very slow to dawn until 1984.

The mid- and late 1980s – focusing on the social problem

Ironically, this recognition among educators of *Ijime* problems was followed by a tragic chain of suicides. In 1984 seven pupils in elementary and lower secondary schools and in 1985 nine students committed suicide, reportedly because of being victims of *Ijime*. Reporters began to focus on *Ijime* in school. They usually reported cases in ways heavily biased on the side of the victims and criticized teachers and educational administrators. Cases of suicide by victims of *Ijime* were not only handled by news programmes but by television chat shows and popular shows which feature human interest stories rather than taking an objective approach. *Ijime* became one of the biggest social problems featured through mass media in the mid-1980s.

The Monbusho attempted to address the problem of *Ijime*. In 1983, the Informal Gathering on Recent Problematic Behaviour in School (*Saikin no gakkou ni okeru mondaikoudou ni kansuru kondankai*), constituted by the Monbusho, suggested measures to combat school violence and delinquency. *Ijime* was mentioned in several paragraphs of the report. In 1984, the Monbusho published a teachers' manual on *Ijime* in elementary school, *Problems on guidance concerned with relationships among children* (*Jidou no yuujinkankei wo meguru shidoujou no shomondai*).

In 1985, the Ministry of Justice issued a notification to encourage positive measures against *Ijime*. The Monbusho added the item on *Ijime* to the 'Annual fact-find on problem behaviour in school', which was the questionnaire survey to the local board of education begun in 1982. In April 1985, the Monbusho convened a Meeting on Problematic Behaviour of Children (*Jido seito no mondai koudou ni kansuru kento kaigi*), which released an urgent suggestion, *Appeals for a solution to the* Ijime *problem* (*Ijime no mondai no kaiketsu no tame no apiiru*) in June. Even prime ministers mentioned *Ijime* in their speeches to Parliament: Prime Minister Nakasone in October 1985 and Prime Minister Kaifu in January 1986. In the meantime, most local school boards of education began to cope with *Ijime* problems as one of their priority issues.

In spite of these efforts, people's anxiety and distrust of schools culminated in the aforementioned Funeral Play Case in Tokyo. More than a hundred books on *Ijime* were published and many articles were written for journals aimed at teachers. Teachers had taken every thinkable action against the occurrence of *Ijime*.

In 1987, based on the statistics of 'Annual fact-find on problem behaviour in school', the Monbusho announced that the number of *Ijime* occurrences and of schools involved in *Ijime* problems had decreased sharply; only 52,610 cases in 12,222 schools in 1986, and 35,067 cases in 8506 schools in 1987, compared with 155,066 cases in 21,899 schools in 1985. People's concerns about *Ijime*, together with the attention from journalists, rapidly declined. However, it should be noted that *Ijime* problems did not go away but simply disappeared from public view.

These statistics of the 'Annual fact-find on problem behaviour in school' are an accumulation of data originally compiled by local boards of education based on reports by teachers. The data reported represent those cases that teachers could recognize; however, it does not indicate the concrete number of cases of *Ijime* which children actually suffered. Since *Ijime* is often concealed from teachers, and considering their unwillingness to report cases, information provided by teachers is likely to underestimate its prevalence (Farrington, 1993; Morita, 1987, 1991, 1996; Morita and Kiyonaga, 1986; O'Moore and Hillery, 1991).

Morita and his research group conducted a survey on *Ijime* in Tokyo and Osaka in 1984. They applied a self-report, anonymous questionnaire to a representative sample of 1718 fifth- and eighth-grade schoolchildren. There is a remarkable variation in the results between their study and the statistics provided by the Monbusho in 1985. The rate of *Ijime* occurrence in the total sample is 11.3 per cent in Morita's research, whereas the Monbusho's statistics show no more than 0.88 per cent (Monbusho, 1994; Morita, 1985). Morita *et al.* conducted a second survey on bullying in 1988. Their study shows that the decline of *Ijime* is not remarkable and the rate of decrease for those four years is only by 27.4 points (Morita, 1996). Taki (1992) carried out a longitudinal survey from 1985 to 1987, based on Morita (1985), and provided substantial evidence to support Morita's hypotheses concerning the occurrence of *Ijime*.

Based on the survey in 1984 and their successive researches, which were the pioneer studies that provided the standard definition of bullying in Japan, Morita (1985) indicated a more realistic occurrence rate of *Ijime*, and suggested hypotheses about the structure of *Ijime* behaviour; in particular, the four-tiered structural theory of *Ijime*.

In the late 1980s, dozens of papers and quantitative research studies were published in an attempt to analyse *Ijime* problems. Most Japanese researchers and laypeople paid no attention to foreign studies. This explains why many Japanese believed *Ijime* was a problem uniquely rooted in Japanese culture and tradition. One of the few exceptions was Hirano (1991), who carried out a quantitative survey using Olweus' translated questionnaire. It was not until the 1990s that European bullying studies began to be referred to by Japanese researchers.

The 1990s – a new phase

The data from the 'Annual fact-find on problem behaviour in school' in the 1992 school year showed a slight increase in *Ijime*. In 1993, several suicide cases were reported on television and in the newspapers. Some of these suicides were said to have occurred as a result of victimization or *Ijime*. This was the beginning of a second round of *Ijime*, following an incubation period in the late 1980s. The Tokyo High Court's recognition of mental *Ijime*, through the Funeral Play Case mentioned above, accelerated the second period of *Ijime*.

In July 1994, the Researchers' Conference Regarding Problematic Behaviour Among Children (*Jidou seito no mondaikoudou tou ni kansuru chousa kenkyuu kyouryokusha kaigi*) was constituted by the Monbusho. Incessant reports on *Ijime* prompted the Conference to call an Emergency Meeting for Measures against *Ijime* (*Ijime taisaku kinkyu kaigi*); this released an *Urgent appeal* in December 1994 and submitted to the Monbusho a report entitled *The measures to be taken for seeking a solution to the problem of* Ijime (*Ijime no mondai no kaikestu no tameni toumen torubeki housaku ni tsuite*) in March 1995.

Ten cases of suicide by pupils were reported between November 1994 and November 1995, including The Suicide Note with Aggressors' Names Case in Aichi mentioned above. In 1995 alone, 57,000 cases of *Ijime* were reported in elementary schools, lower and upper secondary schools and special education schools. *Ijime* became a social problem once more, the mass media reporting cases of *Ijime* every day.

In December 1994 and January 1995, the Conference conducted a major survey by questioning about 20,000 children, guardians (parents) and teachers regarding bullying behaviour among children (see below for a summary of its results). In August 1996, the Conference submitted to the Monbusho a survey-based report, *On comprehensive measures regarding the problem of* Ijime (*Ijime no mondai ni kansuru sougoutekina torikumi ni tsuite*). The report reconfirmed the five fundamental factors regarding the problem of *Ijime*, one of which is a strong recognition of the idea that 'It is never, ever tolerated for one person to inflict *Ijime* on another.' The Monbusho also directed the local boards of education and schools to re-examine the effectiveness of measures taken against *Ijime*. The number of counsellors sent as reinforcement to schools totalled about 150 in 1995, about 500 in 1996, and about 1000 in 1997. In June 1996, the Monbusho also held the International Symposium on the Problem of Bullying, in Tokyo and Ōsaka, with the help of the National Institute for Educational Research.

Many researchers, teachers and so-called educational commentators have now published books and articles on *Ijime*. Some blamed 'examination hell' for creating *Ijime*, and others attributed the problem to too strict control of bureaucracy over school education, hoisting the national flag in school, competitive society, Japanese groupism, the so-called homogeneous society, lack of moral education, teachers' inability to understand students, television programmes filled with violence and sex, computer games, nuclear families, a baby boom, and so on. These researchers and commentators are very fluent in criticizing would-be causes and in drawing up convenient figures, but few seem to be successful in proving that they are the real causes. Many books and articles claim that bullying happens only in Japan. They tend to describe foreign countries as being free from any problems, in some cases based on false data or invalid comparisons, as pointed out in Soeda (1996).

The International Symposium on the Problem of Bullying held in Tokyo and Osaka gave an awareness that 'we are not alone'. Information on bullying and its prevention/intervention programmes has begun to be exchanged across countries. This exchange will produce valuable clues to common aspects of bullying and *Ijime* and those characteristics unique to *Ijime*. Findings through these analyses, in turn, will give various suggestions for solution or reduction of bullying/*Ijime* victimization.

Findings in the latest national survey available

A national survey on *Ijime* (1994–1995), also known as the Monbusho survey, was administered by the Researchers' Conference Regarding Problematic Behaviour Among Children mentioned above. A nationwide sample of the following population was drawn from students in elementary, lower secondary and upper secondary schools (N = 9420); their teachers (N = 557); and their guardians (parents) (N = 9420).

Main findings on children

Experience of being victims of Ijime (since the beginning of the April 1994 school year)

The number of students who 'currently are victims' or 'were victims in the year but are not now victims' is as follows: elementary schools (ES) 21.9 per cent; lower secondary schools (LSS) 13.2 per cent; upper secondary schools (USS) 3.9 per cent.

Experience of being aggressors of Ijime (since the beginning of the April 1994 school year)

The number of students who 'currently are aggressors' or 'were aggressors in the year but are not now aggressors' is as follows: ES 25.5 per cent; LSS 20.3 per cent; USS 6.1 per cent.

Frequency of Ijime (since the beginning of the April 1994 school year)

The number of the victims who suffer from *Ijime* 'more than once a week' is as follows: ES 60.4 per cent; LSS 71.2 per cent; USS 74.8 per cent.

Types of Ijime

Verbal (e.g. teasing, verbal threats) and indirect (e.g. exclusion from social groups, ignoring) forms were much more frequent than physical *Ijime* (e.g. hitting, kicking) across three school levels of students: 42.3 per cent of the victims' replies mentioned verbal *Ijime* and 56.6 per cent received indirect *Ijime*, while 22.7 per cent received physical *Ijime* (multiple answer). Exclusion and ignoring appear much more frequently among girls (cross-level average 58.3 per cent of the victims) than among boys (23.6 per cent).

Individual or group Ijime

The number of victims given *Ijime* by 'two or three aggressors' is as follows: ES 50.0 per cent; LSS 45.2 per cent; USS 47.6 per cent. The number of those given *Ijime* by 'from four to nine aggressors' is: ES 22.8 per cent; LSS 27.5 per cent; USS 24.3 per cent.

Are victims 'good friends' of the aggressors?

Some 23.6 per cent of the ES aggressors described their victims as 'close friends', as did 20.7 per cent of the LSS aggressors, and 17.2 per cent of the USS aggressors. The rate of aggressors who described their connections with the victims as 'regular relationships' was: 36.2 per cent in ES; 37.0 per cent in LSS; 39.3 per cent in USS. The rate of aggressors who said they were 'on bad terms with' their victims was: 17.6 per cent in ES; 14.2 per cent in LSS; 13.5 per cent in USS.

When does Ijime usually take place?

On average, 64.7 per cent of the victims at the three school levels reported that *Ijime* took place during 'class break', followed by 'after school' (20.7 per cent) and 'on the way to school or home' (19.0 per cent).

Reactions of the victims to aggressors

Victims were asked what they usually did when they experienced *Ijime*: 40.9 per cent said 'they told the aggressors to stop *Ijime*' and 27.4 per cent reported that 'they kept quiet and let the aggressors do as they liked'. There is a clear indication that 'telling the aggressors to stop' decreases with age (ES 47.1 per cent; LSS 38.4 per cent; USS 31.1 per cent). The number of victims who said they would 'tell teachers' is: ES 29.2 per cent; LSS 18.9 per cent; USS 7.8 per cent, and the number responding that they would 'tell guardians (parents)' is: ES 26.3 per cent; LSS 20.2 per cent; USS 13.6 per cent.

Can aggressors become the victims of Ijime?

The 53.7 per cent of ES children who 'are currently aggressors' also experienced being victimized within the year. More surprisingly, 15.5 per cent of the current aggressors answered that they are currently being victimized as well. (This figure, 15.5 per cent, is included in the 53.7 per cent mentioned above.) Counterparts of these rates in LSS are respectively 27.4 per cent and 5.0 per cent; those in USS are 23.5 per cent and 6.2 per cent.

How did aggressors feel after Ijime actions?

On this question, 41.1 per cent of the aggressors reported that 'they felt bad' after inflicting *Ijime*, and 29.3 per cent of them reported that 'they felt sorry for their victims'; however, 22.1 per cent felt that their victims 'deserved *Ijime*', 17.7 per cent felt 'sprightliness', and 15.3 per cent felt that '*Ijime* was fun'. The number of aggressors who feel regret for inflicting *Ijime* tends to decrease with age, while the number of those who 'enjoy inflicting *Ijime*' increases with age.

Main findings on teachers

Do pupils tell teachers about Ijime incidents?

Some 22.5 per cent of the victims at the three school levels said they had reported *Ijime* incidents to their teachers (ES 28.3 per cent; LSS 26.5

per cent; USS 12.6 per cent). On the other hand, 42.9 per cent of victims reported that teachers had no knowledge of the incidents (ES 30.8 per cent; LSS 38.6 per cent; USS 59.2 per cent).

What were the main reasons that pupils did not tell their teachers about Ijime incidents?

Among elementary students, the main reason is 'fear of retaliation by aggressors' (46.0 per cent). Lower secondary school students pointed to 'fear of retaliation' as the main reason (34.3 per cent), followed by 'doubt that teachers would be able to solve the problem' (31.1 per cent). Upper secondary school students' main reason is that 'the *Ijime* is their own problem, but not the teacher's affair' (29.5 per cent), followed by 'the doubt that teachers would be able to solve the problem' (26.1 per cent).

What happened after the teacher's intervention in Ijime?

The numbers of the victims who reported 'The teacher's intervention in *Ijime* stopped the *Ijime*' are: ES 47.6 per cent; LSS 43.9 per cent; USS 37.3 per cent.

Main findings on parents

Did parents know that their children had been given Ijime?

Among the guardians (parents) of the victims, 50.6 per cent replied that their children had not been victimized (guardians of ES children, 45.5 per cent; guardians of LSS children, 48.6 per cent; guardians of USS children, 57.8 per cent).

How did they learn about their children being victimized?

Across the three school levels, 67.4 per cent of parents of victims heard about these incidents from their victimized children (ES 74.3 per cent, LSS 65.7 per cent, and USS 62.2 per cent). On the other hand, 33.2 per cent of them learned about their children being victimized through witnessing some behavioral changes in their children (ES 34.7 per cent, LSS 36.9 per cent, and USS 27.9 per cent).

Why did parents not tell teachers about their victimized children?

The main reason pointed out by guardians (parents) was that '*Ijime* is not a problem sufficiently important to tell teachers about it' (52.3 per cent).

Did guardians (parents) know about their children being aggressors?

The numbers of the guardians (parents) who did not learn about their children being aggressors were as follows: ES 78.1 per cent; LSS 74.0 per cent; USS 71.9 per cent.

How did parents learn about their children being aggressors?

The most frequent source from which guardians (parents) might learn about their children being aggressors is that 'they heard about these incidents from their own children' (ES 28.5 per cent; LSS 31.8 per cent; USS 26.1 per cent). Among the guardians (parents) of elementary school and lower secondary school bullying children, the second most frequent source is 'the teachers of their children' who told them about their own children (ES 20.8 per cent; LSS 24.0 per cent).

Is *Ijime* identical to bullying?

As mentioned above, the definition of *Ijime* is similar to that of bullying in Europe. Let us compare the one by Morita (1985) and the one presented by Roland (1989) as a common definition in Scandinavia.

> A type of aggressive behavior by which someone who holds a dominant position in a group-interaction process, by intentional or collective acts, causes mental and/or physical suffering to another inside a group.
>
> (Morita, 1985)

> Bullying is longstanding violence, physical or psychological, conducted by an individual or a group and directed against an individual who is not able to defend himself in the actual situation.
>
> (Roland, 1989: 21)

Most Japanese find common features between bullying and *Ijime*: name-calling, teasing, exclusion, mobbing, and so on. Such instances seem enough for us to believe that *Ijime* is identical to bullying. There are, however, some differences between the two words, which will be discussed in the final section.

Bullying is not only a problem for boys

> *Bullying is not only a problem for boys.*

We often find that the above statement or similar is used in headings in European books on bullying. The use of this phrase indicates that many people do usually perceive bullying as a boys' problem. But it is true that we can find bullying behaviour in both boys and girls, and it is the same with *Ijime*. On the contrary, in Japan people will say:

> *Ijime is not only a problem for girls.*

The word 'ijime' is mostly used for 'feminine' attitudes and actions but it is not used for masculinity. The Japanese word 'ijime' does not usually mean 'abstract' violence, but if several boys hit one boy in order to obtain money, most Japanese would not call it *Ijime*. If they hit one or more boys for insulting them, most Japanese think of it as *Ijime*. Girls' *Ijime* in Japan is more frequent than girls' bullying in other countries; and its frequency is equivalent to or even higher than that of boys' *Ijime* in Japan. Most types of *Ijime* involve ignoring or exclusion; i.e. behaving as if the victim did not exist or was invisible.

European researchers have concluded through a survey that bullying against boys is more 'physical' or 'direct' and that bullying against girls is more 'verbal' or 'indirect'. The same tendency may be observed with *Ijime* in Japan. European researchers have also pointed out that the occurrence of bullying against boys ('physical' and/or 'direct') is more frequent than that against girls ('verbal' and/or 'indirect'). But this is *not* true of *Ijime* in Japan. Many Japanese surveys show the occurrence of *Ijime* to be more frequent among girls than among boys.

Table 19.1 shows data of first grade boys and girls of lower secondary schools in 1985 from Taki's (1992) longitudinal survey in Japan. The results indicate that:

- Aggressors are more numerous among girls than among boys.
- Victims are also more numerous among girls than boys, if we exclude threatening and blackmailing from *Ijime*.

The Japanese have no consensus on whether to include threatening and blackmailing under the heading of *Ijime*. This is why the Japanese word 'ijime' has a less violent meaning, and why *Ijime* is considered as a post-school violence problem.

In the classroom or in the playground? From older children or from class mates?

One typical intervention against bullying in Europe is monitoring in playgrounds. As mentioned above, this was one of the measures carried out to reduce school violence in Japan. This decrease in school violence was followed by the turbulence of *Ijime* in the mid-1980s. For this reason, most Japanese teachers do not believe that such actions can easily solve the *Ijime* problem.

European data and research find that bullies are often older children, while victims are younger. Does this mean that older children bully pupils younger

Table 19.1 The rate of victims and bullies by sex and by type

	Kept out, ignored	*Harassed, teased*	*Hit or kicked in fun*	*Threatened, blackmailed*	*Total*
Boy victims	3.7	5.2	2.2	5.2	12.7
Girl victims	6.2	2.8	1.5	0.7	8.3
Boy bullies	4.5	5.2	2.2	2.2	6.7
Girl bullies	10.3	2.1	1.4	0.7	12.4

than themselves? On this point, Japanese *Ijime* is different from bullying. In Japan, aggressors and victims are often class mates; if not, they are in most cases in the same grade (see Table 19.2).

Remember that the most common form of *Ijime* among both boys and girls is exclusion or ignoring. This kind of *Ijime* will be more effective if the victim and the aggressors belong to the same group, and generally takes place in a classroom or in a club activity (for instance, extra-curricular activity in sports or the arts).

'A friend yesterday is an enemy today.' This headline, ironically changed from the old Japanese proverb 'An enemy yesterday is a friend today' appeared in a newspaper article reporting the *Ijime* survey of the Monbusho. *Ijime* frequently occurred between members of the same group, such as a class or a club. Findings in the Monbusho survey show that more than 20 per cent of the aggressors are 'close friend(s)' of the victim. This makes the occurrence of *Ijime* more covert and causes teachers and parents to mistakenly believe that the victim and the aggressors are just playing for fun even if some activities 'seem' to be *Ijime*. This ironic tragedy does not end here. Few children would step in to save a class mate from being victimized. The Monbusho survey (1996) indicates that 47.2 per cent of students report that they would rather avoid being involved in *Ijime* affairs which they witness. They might watch the *Ijime* or pretend that nothing has happened for fear they themselves might in turn become new targets. In the worst cases, class mates of the victim take part in giving others *Ijime* in order to defend themselves and avoid being on the wrong side of the aggressors (Morita and Kiyonaga, 1986). It is as if being an aggressor functions as a loyalty test.

Table 19.2 The proportion of victims and bullies in the same class or grade by sex and by type

	Kept out, ignored	*Harassed, teased*	*Hit or kicked in fun*	*Threatened, blackmailed*
Boy victims	100.0	85.7	66.6	71.5
Girl victims	77.8	75.0	50.0	0.0
Boy bullies	100.0	85.7	100.0	66.7
Girl bullies	100.0	100.0	100.0	0.0

Within this atmosphere, the victim feels total isolation. This chain of reactions occurs in a closed group. This may be said to be one of the characteristics of *Ijime*.

References

Hirano, K. (1991) Towards reducing bullying in schools [*Ijime* mondai kaiketu no tameni]. *The Bulletin of Bunkyo University*, vol. 25.

Monbusho [Ministry of Education] (1994) *Seito Shidojo no shomondai no Genjo to Monbusho no Shisaku ni tsuie* [The present situation of issues concerning student tutelage and measures by the Ministry of Education]. Tokyo: Ministry of Education.

Morita, Y. (ed.) (1985) *Sociological study on the structure of bullying group* [*Ijime shuudan no kouzo ni kansuru shakaigakuteki kenkyu*]. Department of Sociology, Osaka City University.

Morita, Y. (1987) Ehimeken Kyushoku Noyaku Konnyu Jiken Hodo no Kigo wo Yomu: Ijime Ron Saikou [Understanding the 'significance' of news stories about chemical impurities in school lunch, in Ehime prefecture: controversies on bullying]. *Shonen Hodou* (Osaka, Shonen Hodo Kyokai), no. 377, pp. 20–28.

Morita, Y. (1991) *Futoko Gensho no Shakaigaku* [Sociology of 'non-attendance' phenomenon in schools]. Tokyo: Gakubunsha.

Morita, Y. (1996) Bullying as a contemporary behavior problem in the context of increasing 'societal privatization' in Japan. *Prospects: Quarterly Review of Comparative Education*. UNESCO: International Bureau of Education, 26, 311–329.

Morita, Y. (1997) Privatisierung in der japanischen Gesellschaft und die Strukt ur von Schikane an Schulen. In G. Foljanty-Jost and D. Rossner (eds) *Gewalt unter Jugendlichen in Deutschland und Japan: Ursachen und Bekämpfung* (pp. 85–99). Baden-Baden: Nomos Verlags.

Morita, Y. and Kiyonaga, K. (1986) *Ijime: Kyoshitsu no Yamai* [Bullying: The ailing classroom]. Tokyo: Kaneko Syobo.

Morita, Y. and Ohsako, T. (1997) National bullying survey in Japan, 1994–95: An international perspective. Paper presented at the Eighth Conference of Developmental Psychology, Rennes, France.

Olweus, D. (1972) Personality and aggression. In Cole, J.K. and Jensen, D.D. (eds), *Nebraska Symposium on Motivation*. Lincoln, NB: University of Nebraska Press.

Olweus, D. (1993) *Bullying at school: What we know and what we can do*. Oxford: Blackwell.

O'Moore, M. and Hillery, B. (1991) What do teachers need to know? In M. Elliott (ed.) *Bullying: A practical guide to coping for schools*. Harlow: Longman.

Roland, E. (1989) Bullying: The Scandinavian research tradition. In Tattum, D.P. and Lane, D.A. (eds) *Bullying in schools*. Stoke-on-Trent: Trentham Books.

Soeda, H. (1996) Reconsideration of statements that bullying is unique in Japan (Jinbun-Kenkyu 48–9). Faculty of Letters, Osaka City University.

Taki, M. (1992) The empirical study on the occurrence of *Ijime* behavior [*Ijime* koui no hassei youin ni kansuru jisshouteki kenkyu]. *Journal of Educational Sociology*, 50.

Whitney, I. and Smith, P.K. (1993) A survey of the nature and extent of bully/victim problems in junior/middle and secondary schools. *Educational Research*, 35, 3–25.

20 Australia

Ken Rigby and Phillip T. Slee

Introduction

Since the early days of its convict settlement by the European colonists in the late eighteenth century, Australia has prided itself on its desire for social justice and its championing of the underdog. It has not always lived up to these ideals. For instance, policies directed towards maintaining a 'White Australia', and the non-incorporation of the indigenous people of Australia in an equal partnership with other Australians, for many years badly tarnished its image. But running through much of Australian life there has always been, and still is, a powerful desire for a community that is accepting of all people and an unyielding abhorrence of tyranny and oppression towards those who might be seen as 'outsiders'. Nowhere is this more evident than in the contemporary movement in Australian schools to abolish the evil practice of bullying.

As is the case in many other countries, the catalyst for action in Australia to stop bullying in schools came from Europe in the late 1980s. The prime influence was that of Professor Dan Olweus, whose theoretical and above all practical and effective work in reducing bullying in Norwegian schools became increasingly well known from 1988 onwards. Again, as in other countries, the injustice of domestic violence against women was at this time gaining increasing recognition. This sensitised many Australians to the prevalence of oppressive behaviour in their own community. While it could not be said that Australia was actually becoming more violent, it had become increasingly accepted in the 1990s that violence as a way of life was totally unacceptable, even in the form of verbal abuse of others. In 1994 an influential Australian government publication, *Sticks and stones: A report on violence in schools* (Commonwealth of Australia, 1994), sought to provide leadership in a nationwide movement to end violence, including bullying, between schoolchildren.

Bullying is widely regarded in Australia as a particularly unacceptable form of violence or aggression. By its nature it is unjust. Bullying is oppression directed by more powerful persons or by a group of persons against individuals who cannot adequately defend themselves. This is not to say that Australians typically find all forms of aggressive behaviour unacceptable. Popular sport is often marked by rough play, as in Australian Rules football; Australians have excelled in boxing tournaments. If the so-called 'little Aussie battler' can turn the tables on his or her oppressor, no matter how, there will be many to stand and cheer. But the miserable practice of bullying, particularly in its more malign form, when stronger individuals or groups set out to hurt or intimidate an individual without any justification at all and then go on to enjoy their petty triumph: this is something that will not be tolerated.

Country demographics

Australia is an island continent; much of the interior is hot, dry desert, and most settlements are on the coast, especially in the south, southeast and east of the country. Australia's population is now (1998) approximately 18.5 million. A large majority (77 per cent) of the people were born in Australia. Of these, about 3.4 million are second generation Australians. Of those born outside Australia, the majority (2.4 million) were Europeans, principally from the United Kingdom and Ireland, followed by Italy, the former Yugoslavia, Greece, Germany, The Netherlands and Poland. Immigrants from Asia total about 770,000, most of whom are from China, Vietnam and Korea. Approaching 600,000 other immigrants are from Oceania, principally New Zealand, and the Middle East and North Africa. The original indigenous population of Australia comprises 350,000 people. Given such a diversity of background and origin of its people, Australia is commonly regarded as having a multicultural community.

Social relations between Australians are notably egalitarian, and there is little of the 'class distinction' evident in some European countries. Nevertheless, there are wide variations in personal income with substantial numbers of people on low wages or unemployed (nationally the unemployment rate is currently just under 10 per cent). At the same time, social services which ameliorate the worst effects of poverty are well developed by world standards. The predominant family type is a couple with dependent children (40.85 per cent), followed by a couple only (33.9 per cent), and one-parent family (9.4 per cent).

The provision of schooling in Australia

Schooling for children in Australia is provided mainly by government schools run by state or territory authorities of which there are eight: namely, New South Wales, Victoria, Tasmania, Australian Capital Territory, South Australia, Western Australia, Queensland and Northern Territory. A substantial minority of the schools (26 per cent) are non-government, most of which have a religious affiliation, the most common being Roman Catholic (see Australian Bureau of Statistics, 1996). Students normally first attend primary school at age 5 and subsequently transfer to a secondary school at age 12 or

13. Attendance is compulsory until students are age 15; more than half of them, however, continue their schooling until they are at least 17 years old. Most schooling is co-educational, although in the non-government sector single-sex schools are much more common. There are some variations between states and territories in the way schooling is structured; for example, the transfer to secondary schools occurs in Year 7 in Victoria when children are on average 12 years old; whereas in South Australia the transfer occurs a year later (in Year 8) when children are 13 years old. This particular variation has implications for the observed incidence of bullying for Australian children, as will be discussed below.

Bullying in Australian schools

Reports from abroad in the 1980s and early 1990s from such researchers as Olweus (1991) in Scandinavia and Smith and Thompson (1991) in England suggested that bullying was prevalent in all schools. Some Australian school principals chose not to believe it: surely not in our schools, they said. Before long, however, Australian-based research had confirmed their worst fears. In 1991 Rigby and Slee published the first Australian report on the incidence of bullying among children (N = 685) between 6 and 16 years in a sample of South Australian schools. Estimates differed according to the judgements of informants and the criteria adopted. Estimates of schoolchildren surveying other children in their class suggested that about 10 per cent were 'picked on a lot'. Self-reports of being personally bullied by other children 'pretty often' provided a figure of 13 per cent of girls and 17 per cent of boys.

More recent studies have shown that our initial estimate from self-reports that about one child in six or seven is being bullied in Australian schools with quite unacceptable frequency, that is on a weekly basis or more often, was in fact reasonably accurate. Between 1993 and 1996 data were collected from 60 Australian schools using the Peer Relations Questionnaire (PRQ) (Rigby and Slee, 1993a). Results were pooled from schools sampled in each of the Australian states. The ages of the students ranged from 8 to 18 years. Estimates of the incidence of bullying were made on the basis of self-reports of 15,152 boys with a mean age of 13.83 years and a standard deviation of 1.95 years, and 10,247 girls with a mean age of 13.60 years and a standard deviation of 2.02 years. (Details of the main results of the national survey are given in Rigby, 1997a.)

In seeking information from the students about being bullied by peers, care was taken to differentiate between fighting or quarrelling between children of about equal strength or power and 'bullying', which respondents were told involved an imbalance of power, with the bully or group of bullies being in some way more powerful than the victim. In addition, it was made clear that bullying could take many forms, physical and verbal, and might include being repeatedly and deliberately excluded by others. Care was also taken to ensure that responses were made anonymously. Under these

Table 20.1 Incidence of victimisation according to age; students reporting being bullied 'at least once a week' in co-educational schools

Age	*Boys*			*Girls*		
	Schools	*%*	*Students*	*Schools*	*%*	*Students*
8	7	50.0	110	7	35.3	116
9	10	30.3	185	11	31.1	212
10	12	25.4	232	12	28.4	271
11	26	22.6	336	25	23.2	388
12	42	27.8	1193	42	22.1	1055
13	39	25.5	1807	40	20.9	1658
14	36	22.7	1675	35	13.2	1600
15	33	16.6	1510	32	12.2	1390
16	31	11.8	906	31	9.9	878
17	24	10.6	462	23	7.0	474
18	19	7.5	80	17	14.5	69

conditions, 20.7 per cent of boys and 15.7 per cent of girls reported being bullied at least once a week.

The incidence of reported bullying was strongly influenced by age, as the results in Table 20.1 drawn from a sample of co-educational schools clearly shows.

The results from single-sex schools followed a similar pattern, with reported bullying generally declining with age. The results were obtained from a pooling of data gathered in different Australian states, which provide secondary schooling beginning at different year and age levels. When schools in the two systems are compared, it is evident that there is a significant increase in bullying when children move from primary to secondary school in Australia, regardless of the stage in a student's life when the transfer occurs: at 12 years for children in some states and at 13 years for students in others (see Rigby, 1996c).

The forms of reported bullying vary widely in frequency and are also affected by age and gender (see Table 20.2). Clearly, verbal forms of bullying are the most common, especially name-calling; physical bullying is the least common and its incidence declines with age. The main gender difference is that girls are more inclined to employ indirect methods of bullying, such as exclusion; boys are more likely to use direct physical means (see also Owens, 1996; Owens and MacMullin, 1995; Tulloch, 1995). However, boys and girls are alike in indicating that they are slightly more likely to experience bullying from individual students compared with bullying by a group of students. There were some expected differences regarding the gender of the bully. Girls were equally likely to report being bullied by boys and girls, whereas boys reported being bullied almost exclusively by boys. In a study conducted among second year high school students in New South Wales, it was reported that girls were much more likely to report being bullied by boys than reports by

Table 20.2 Percentages of schoolchildren reporting being bullied by peers in different ways, according to gender and age group

		8–12 Years			*13–18 Years*		
		Never	*Sometimes*	*Often*	*Never*	*Sometimes*	*Often*
Being teased	Boys	50.1	38.0	11.9	52.6	38.8	8.6
	Girls	52.6	38.8	8.6	58.1	33.5	8.4
Hurtful names	Boys	49.7	36.4	13.9	56.0	33.1	10.8
	Girls	49.6	38.4	12.0	56.7	33.2	10.1
Left out	Boys	65.9	26.9	7.3	75.7	18.8	5.5
	Girls	58.7	32.3	9.0	69.0	24.4	6.6
Threatened	Boys	71.5	22.7	5.8	74.4	19.8	5.9
	Girls	84.9	12.6	2.5	87.8	9.7	2.5
Hit/kicked	Boys	63.5	28.5	8.0	72.4	21.3	6.3
	Girls	77.2	18.9	3.9	88.5	9.3	2.2
Total	Boys		3320			10,657	
N	Girls		2587			6973	

boys indicated (Tulloch, 1995). Sexual harassment is an aspect of bullying evident in Australian schools, but as yet its incidence has not been reliably assessed.

It is generally acknowledged that a particularly pernicious aspect of bullying is its continuity over time, with some children being bullied by the same individual or group for long periods. Most of the bullying reported by the Australian students was of relatively short duration, not more than a week or so. However, among students aged 16 to 18 years who had been bullied at some time, some 13 per cent (the same percentage for boys and girls) indicated that the bullying had continued for a year or more.

How Australian students respond to bullying

As one might expect, responses to being bullied varied widely. A large proportion (about 55 per cent of boys and 40 per cent of girls) reported that they were 'not really bothered' by it. However, among those bullied more frequently, that is at least weekly, the proportions reporting that they were not bothered by it dropped to about 30 per cent of boys and 20 per cent of girls. We may reasonably assume that some students wished to deny being affected by it. At the same time, some children appeared to be more resilient than others: older children were much less likely than younger children to report being upset. By and large boys were more likely to say that being bullied made them feel angry; girls were more likely to say that bullying made them feel 'mostly sad and depressed' (Rigby, 1995c). A substantial proportion of students (about 30 per cent of boys and 45 per cent of girls) reported that they felt 'worse about themselves' after being bullied.

Some students (6 per cent of boys and 9 per cent of girls) reported staying at home to avoid being bullied. More commonly however, students told someone that they were being bullied, usually a friend or friends: girls (over 75 per cent) told more often than boys (60 per cent). Teachers were relatively rarely told – about one in three had informed a teacher; telling a teacher occurred much more often when students were attending primary school. Parents, especially mothers, were informed by about half the students who had been bullied; again, girls were more commonly the informants. Did telling someone help? Among older children, it was more likely that things would stay the same than get better; and for about 8 per cent things got worse. Telling someone more often than not improved the situation for younger children (under 13 years), especially for girls. These results suggest that many older boys are reluctant to inform because they do not have much confidence in the outcome.

Safety in Australian schools

In the light of the results given thus far, can we say that Australian schools are safe places for children? Clearly the answer depends on how we define 'safety'. Generally speaking, in contrast to the American culture, violent and life-threatening situations are rare in Australian schools (Martin, 1994). But if we mean by 'safe' being free from the threat of being bullied by peers, we must accept that for the most vulnerable children, schools are not such safe places. Judgements about safety from bullying appear to depend on the individual's own sense of vulnerability, as shown in Table 20.3.

Table 20.3 Schoolchildren's judgements of the safety of their school for young people who find it hard to defend themselves, according to gender, age group and frequency of being bullied (percentages)

		Never bullied		*Bullied less than once a week*		*Bullied once a week or more*	
Age in years		*8–12*	*13–18*	*8–12*	*13–18*	*8–12*	*13–18*
Yes it is safe	Boys	28.2	24.0	18.8	12.2	11.0	8.5
	Girls	31.3	20.0	18.4	9.1	16.7	7.3
Usually safe	Boys	63.8	64.1	71.3	69.7	63.6	58.1
	Girls	61.8	68.9	73.0	73.9	63.5	64.3
Hardly ever safe	Boys	6.4	8.7	8.9	14.7	19.2	22.6
	Girls	5.5	9.4	7.1	15.7	16.5	22.9
Never safe	Boys	1.5	3.2	1.1	3.5	6.3	10.9
	Girls	1.4	1.7	1.5	1.4	3.3	5.5
Total N	Boys	1445	6294	1214	3011	911	2221
	Girls	1316	4654	792	1851	636	972

Among those who are bullied at least once a week approximately one in three children saw their school as 'never or hardly ever' a safe place for children who find it hard to defend themselves. Contrast this estimate with the one given by children who say they are never bullied; these children think that about one in ten are always or almost always under threat. Yet even among these seemingly invulnerable students, over 70 per cent of them imply by their answers that one cannot say unequivocally that their school is a safe place for those who find it hard to defend themselves.

Health consequences of bullying

In a study conducted by Rigby and Slee in 1993, high school students provided reports of the extent to which they had been victimised by their peers and also completed a standardised measure of their mental and physical health, the General Health Questionnaire of Goldberg and Williams (1988). The results indicated that students who were more frequently bullied (at least once a week) were much more likely than others to suffer poorer health (Rigby, 1994c; see also Table 20.4).

Table 20.4 Percentages of secondary schoolchildren indicating worse than usual health in relation to their status as victims (V) or non-victims (NV) of peer bullying at school (Boys, N = 377; Girls, N = 400)

	Boys		*Girls*	
	V	*NV*	*V*	*NV*
General illness				
• Not in good health	25	13	42	22
• Felt ill	34	18	47	26
Somatic complaints				
• Hot or cold spells	20	10	43	19
Anxiety				
• Lost sleep over worry	27	15	57	31
• Constant strain	29	16	56	28
• Panicky without reason	17	4	40	15
Social dysfunction				
• Not keeping occupied	16	7	26	9
• Not enjoying activities	22	7	26	13
Depression				
• Feeling worthless	21	8	34	20
• Life not worth living	23	11	40	16
Suicidal				
• Wishing one were dead	23	12	40	21
• Recurring idea of taking own life	23	11	32	15

Suicide

In a number of countries, including Norway, England and Japan, there have been media reports of children committing suicide allegedly following episodes of severe bullying. Because the reasons for suicide are multiply determined and difficult to establish through case studies, it has been difficult to evaluate these reports. However, recent work in Australia has shed further light on the question. In a series of three studies undertaken in Adelaide, South Australia, indications of suicidal ideation and attempts at self-harm have been found to be significantly associated with self-reports and peer reports providing evidence of being bullied by peers and also bullying others (Rigby and Slee, in press).

Long-term effects

Recent research in Australia has added substantially to results from earlier longitudinal studies conducted in Norway (Olweus, 1992, 1993) and Farrington (1993) which suggested that the loss of self-esteem due to victimisation at school is sustained into adult years, and school bullies are more likely than others to engage subsequently in acts of delinquency and violence. In 1994 a retrospective study conducted by Dietz and Rigby confirmed that low self-esteem and the tendency to be depressed were typical of adults who reported being frequently bullied at school (Dietz, 1994). In 1997 Rigby and Slee completed a three-year longitudinal study of Australian adolescent schoolchildren from which it was concluded that both male and female students who reported a relatively high incidence of physical health complaints in their final two years at high school had been victimised by their peers more frequently during the first two years at the school. Among girls only, significant effects were also found in relation to mental health (Rigby, 1998).

The link between peer abuse and other forms of antisocial behaviour

There is some suggestive evidence from Australian studies that the involvement of schoolchildren in bully/victim problems is related to other forms of antisocial behaviour. In a study by Rigby and Cox (1996) it was found that young adolescents identified as bullies at school were more likely than others to be absent from school, scrawl graffiti, shoplift and get into trouble with the police. The experience of repeatedly being a victim of peer abuse may also have unfortunate effects on subsequent antisocial behaviour. In a study of attitudes of teenage students in the Australian state of Victoria towards wife abuse, it was found that boys who were more frequently victimised by their peers at school were more likely than others to support actions by husbands in abusing their wives (Rigby, Whish and Black, 1994).

Causes of bullying

Personality characteristics

Some Australian research has focused on possible causative factors. Whether personality characteristics have the status of causative influences is controversial. However, it is clear that bullying behaviour is associated with low levels of empathy, as indicated by relatively high scores on the P factor in Eysenck's Personality Inventory (see Slee and Rigby, 1993). Students who were identified as bullies were also found to be generally uncooperative in many areas of life, a characteristic they shared with students who were regularly victimised (Rigby, Cox and Black, 1997). Another factor identified as associated with students being bullied more than most others is extreme introversion (Slee and Rigby, 1993).

Family factors

Family and parent characteristics evidently play a part in predisposing some students to bully others. Extensive research into the family background of Australian children involved in bully/victim problems showed that self-reported male bullies came more frequently than others from dysfunctional families in which there was relatively little sense of love, support or belonging. Girl bullies too tended to come from similarly dysfunctional families, as did girl victims (Rigby, 1993, 1994b). Among Australian adolescents, the rate of involvement in bully/victim incidents has been shown to be significantly higher than average among students identified by means of the Parental Bonding Instrument (Parker, Tupling and Brown, 1979) as frequently being criticised by their parents and strictly controlled by them (Rigby, Slee and Cunningham, in press).

School ethos

Wide variations between schools in Australia suggest that specific kinds of school environments may greatly encourage bullying. In one study in South Australia conducted by Rigby and Slee, a high and a low bullying school were found to differ significantly in the extent to which students held attitudes conducive to bullying, with students in the low bullying school on average showing less admiration for bullies and more support for children who were victimised (Rigby, 1997b).

Dealing with bullying

No comprehensive survey has yet been conducted in Australia to determine what proportion of schools are taking action to specifically target bullying in their school community. There can be no doubt, however, that the proportion is increasing and that a diversity of approaches is being employed. This trend has been strengthened by the growing availability of resources to counter bullying in schools. In 1996 the Australian Council for Educational Research supplied fifteen such resources in the form of books, packages and videos. Of these, four were produced in Australia. Workshops and conferences attended by school counsellors and teachers to address the problem of school bullying in Australia have become increasingly common. Many Australian schools have conducted surveys of the incidence and nature of bullying in their schools, for example, using the Peer Relations Questionnaire (Rigby and Slee, 1993b). Some schools have devised their own surveys. Their purpose has been largely to raise awareness of the problem as a preliminary step to employing a whole-school approach to counter bullying. But not only do these studies help to assess the situation in a school – and often act to convince sceptical teachers that there *is* a problem – they also enable schools to discover what degree of support they can expect from members of the school community and especially students. From applications of the Peer Relations Questionnaire, approximately half of the students between ages 8 and 12 indicated that they could personally use help to stop being bullied; older students are generally less concerned about receiving such help than younger ones, but even among these, some one-third report that they too could use help. Readiness to participate in class discussions about the problem of bullying varies according to age and gender, as Figure 20.1 shows.

It appears that constructive discussion in Australian classrooms may be relatively easy to facilitate among younger students and students in later years of secondary schools, more especially girls (see Rigby and Slee, 1993c). Nevertheless, even among students in their early teens, one can usually be confident that about one-third of the students will be eager to take part in relevant classroom discussions; a further one-third at that age appear to be 'on the fence' in this regard. Talking with students in groups about bullying and seeking collaborative solutions presents a challenge to which increasing numbers of teachers and students are responding.

Generally, schools in Australia where steps have been taken to counter bullying have adopted a so-called whole-school approach in which a general anti-bullying policy is written with the active collaboration of teachers, students and parents, and a plan formulated and implemented to prevent bullying (see Hyndman and Thorsborne, 1994; Rigby, 1995b, 1996c; Slee, 1996a and b). Should prevention fail, steps taken to deal with cases of peer bullying often differ between schools. Broadly, the approaches of schools to counter bullying can be categorised as moralistic (the assertion of school values that are inimical to bullying); legalistic (the imposition of punishments, sanctions or 'consequences' for children who bully others); and humanistic (counselling or talking with students in an attempt to change their behaviour). In some Australian schools, so-called no blame approaches have been used for working with bullies, especially the method of shared concern (Pikas, 1989) and, with younger children, the 'no blame approach'

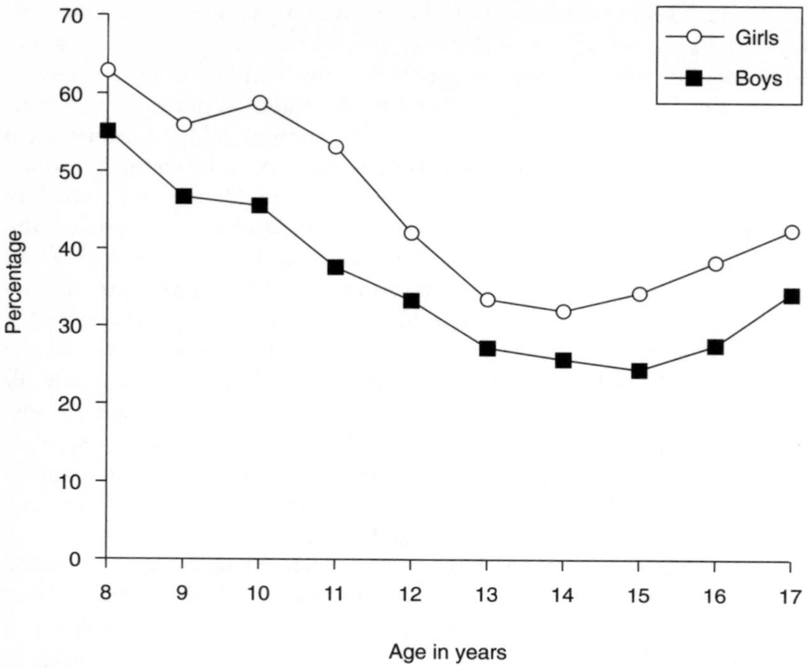

Figure 20.1 Percentages of students reporting a readiness to talk about the problem of bullying at school with other students in class, according to age. Taken from samples of 15,418 boys and 10,476 girls.

of Maines and Robinson (1992). Some schools employ a combination of these approaches. (For a review of these approaches as applied in Australia, see Rigby, 1994a, 1996a, b and c.)

Other contributions to countering bullying in Australia are evident in the work of the peer support movement which provides training for members of school communities to assist in creating a school ethos in which bullying is unlikely to occur. Kids Helpline in Australia provides counselling services for children who phone in with their problems, many of which are concerned with bullying. Safety houses have been created throughout Australia to which children can go on the way to and from school if they feel threatened. Although the impetus for peer mediation has come from the United States (see Bodine, Crawford and Shrumpf, 1994; Johnson and Johnson, 1991), in many Australian schools, especially in New South Wales, training is being provided for students who wish to assist their peers in providing peaceful resolutions in conflict situations. Useful curriculum or teaching material and other resources to counter bullying in schools have been provided by several Australian practitioner/researchers, including Forsey (1994), Fuller and King

(1995), Jenkin (1996) and Slee (1996a and b). Advice to Australian parents to help their child to avoid being bullied at school has been provided by Berne (1996) and by Griffiths (1995).

Social skills training has been viewed by some as helpful in preventing peer abuse, more especially for students who find it difficult to assert themselves and are for that reason easily bullied (see Bates, 1992; Rigby and Sharp, 1993). Some schools run special group training sessions in assertiveness to which frequently victimised children are invited. For extreme cases of bullying the use of community accountability conferences has been advocated and trialed in Australia (see Hyndman and Thorsborne, 1994; Moore, 1993). At these meetings bullies may be invited to hear what their victims and others think about them, and may be persuaded to accept responsibility for the distress they have caused. Finally, in Australia the media have played an important part in continually raising and discussing the issue of bullying, sometimes sensationalising it or providing simplistic solutions, but also in some cases providing useful information and helpful comment.

Evaluation

We are now moving into a phase in which interest is centring on what forms of intervention actually work in reducing bullying. As yet, in Australia carefully conducted evaluations are sparse and often reveal difficulties in drawing firm conclusions. For example, in 1996 in one secondary school in Victoria where a planned intervention took place, there was a large and statistically significant increase in students reporting to the teaching staff that they were being bullied, combined with an overall increase in students reporting through anonymous questionnaires that they were being bullied. It seemed probable that the increase was in part due to increased sensitivity among students as to what constituted bullying.

One of the few systematic and documented attempts to demonstrate the efficacy of interventions to reduce bullying was reported by Slee (1996a and b). His programme involves the implementation of a package known as the 'P.E.A.C.E. Pack', which includes guidance for schools on how to raise awareness in the school community regarding salient issues and to develop relevant policy; how to work with children in classrooms so as to gain their support; how to counsel children and work with parents; and how to evaluate interventions. To date, results have been supportive of the use of the Pack with reports of reductions in bullying of at least 25 per cent in schools where it has been used; and associated increases in reported student safety, awareness of whom to talk to about bullying, and student knowledge of how to stop bullying (Slee, 1996a and b).

Further evaluations of intervention methods are needed in which alternative methods are compared and the particular components of programmes are clearly differentiated. A critical overview of such methods has been provided in publications by Rigby (1994d, 1996c).

Conclusion

It is clear that there has been much development in both research and practice in the 1990s relating to bullying in Australian schools. Many of the newer ideas and methods for countering bullying in schools mentioned in this chapter are currently being presented, and related training provided in seminars and workshops for teachers and counsellors throughout Australia. The ACER has taken an important lead in this activity. Australian-produced instructional videos and packages based on Australian research and aimed at improving practice are now available for schools (see, for example, Rigby and Slee, 1992; Slee, 1996a). Much remains to be done, however. For example, departments of education in universities in which teachers are trained have sometimes been slow to recognise the need for skilling in this area. More research is still needed, especially action research in which practitioner/researchers engage in collaborative problem solving with schools that are concerned about bullying – and carefully evaluate and publicise what has been done.

References

Australian Bureau of Statistics (1996) Schools, Australia. Commonwealth of Australia: Australian Government Publishing Service.

Bates, B. (1992) *Living safely: A guide for children to keep safe using self-protection and awareness*. Adelaide: Bill Bates.

Berne, S. (1996) *Bully-proof your child*. Melbourne: Lothian.

Bodine, R.J., Crawford, D.K. and Shrumpf, F. (1994) *Creating a peaceable school*. Champaign, Ill.: Research Press.

Commonwealth of Australia (1994) *Sticks and stones: A report on violence in schools*. Canberra: Australian Publishing Service.

Dietz, B. (1994) Effects on subsequent heterosexual shyness and depression of peer victimization at school. Paper presented at the International Conference on Children's Peer Relations. Institute of Social Research: University of South Australia, Adelaide.

Farrington, D.P. (1993) Understanding and preventing bullying. In M. Tonry and N. Morris (eds) *Crime and justice*, Vol. 17. Chicago: University of Chicago Press.

Forsey, C. (1994) *Hands off! The anti-violence guide to developing positive relationships*. Melbourne: West Education Centre Inc., DEET.

Fuller, A. and King, V. (1995) *Stop bullying!* Melbourne: Mental Health Foundation of Victoria.

Goldberg, D. and Williams, P. (1988) *A user's guide to the General Health Questionnaire*. Windsor, Berks: NFER-Nelson.

Griffiths, C. (1995) Cowering behind the bushes. In R. Browne and R. Fletcher (eds) *Boys in schools* (pp. 8–24). Sydney: Finch Publishing.

Hyndman, M. and Thorsborne, M. (1994) Taking action on bullying: Whole school multi-stage approaches to intervention and protection. In K. Oxenberry, K. Rigby and P.T. Slee (eds) *Children's peer relations*. Conference Proceedings. Adelaide: Institute of Social Research, University of South Australia.

Jenkin, J. (1996) *Resolving violence through education*. Camberwell: Australian Council for Educational Research.

Johnson, D.W. and Johnson, R. (1991) *Teaching students to be peacemakers*. Edin, MN: Interaction Book Co.

Maines, B. and Robinson, G. (1992) *The no blame approach*. Bristol: Lame Duck Publishing.

Martin, R. (1994) Violence in Australian schools. *Criminology Australia*, 16–19.

Moore, D. (1993) Shame, forgiveness and juvenile justice. *Criminal Justice Ethics*, 12, 3–25.

Olweus, D. (1991) Bully/victim problems among schoolchildren: Basic facts and effects of a school-based intervention program. In D. Pepler and K.H. Rubin (eds) *The development and treatment of childhood aggression*. Hillsdale, NJ: Erlbaum.

Olweus, D. (1992) Victimisation by peers: Antecedents and long term outcomes. In K.H. Rubin and J.B. Asendorf (eds) *Social withdrawal, inhibition and shyness in children*. Hillsdale, NJ: Erlbaum.

Olweus, D. (1993) *Bullying at school*. Oxford: Blackwell.

Owens, D. (1996) Sticks and stones and sugar and spice: Girls' and boys' aggression in schools. *Australian Journal of Guidance and Counselling*, 6, 45–55.

Owens, D. and MacMullin, C.E. (1995) Gender differences in aggression in children and adolescents in South Australian schools. *International Journal of Adolescence and Youth*, 6, 21–35.

Parker, G., Tupling, H. and Brown, L.B. (1979) A parental bonding instrument. *British Journal of Medical Psychology*, 52, 1–10.

Pikas, A. (1989) The common concern method for the treatment of mobbing. In E. Roland and E. Munthe (eds) *School bullying: An international perspective*. London: David Fulton.

Rigby, K. (1993) Schoolchildren's perceptions of their families and parents as a function of peer relations. *Journal of Genetic Psychology*, 154, 501–514.

Rigby, K. (1994a) School bullies. *Independent Teacher*, 10, 8–9.

Rigby, K. (1994b) Psychosocial functioning in families of Australian adolescent schoolchildren involved in bully/victim problems. *Journal of Family Therapy*, 16, 173–187.

Rigby, K. (1994c) Family influence, peer-relations and health effects among school children. In K. Oxenberry, K. Rigby and P.T. Slee (eds) *Children's peer relations*. Conference Proceedings. Adelaide: The Institute of Social Research, University of South Australia, pp. 294–304.

Rigby, K. (1994d) An evaluation of strategies and methods for addressing problems of peer abuse in schools. In M. Tainsh and J. Izard (eds) *Widening horizons: New challenges, directions and achievements* (pp. 1–11). Melbourne: The Australian Council for Educational Research Ltd.

Rigby, K. (1995a) *New thinking about bullying in schools*. Independent Education. Sydney: New South Wales Education Union, July, pp. 3–6.

Rigby, K. (1995b) *What schools can do about bullying*. The Professional Reading Guide for Educational Administrators, 17, No. 1, November.

Rigby, K. (1995c) Peer victimisation and gender among Australian schoolchildren. Paper presented at the IVth European Congress of Psychology, Athens, July.

Rigby, K. (1996a) What should we do about school bullies? *Australian Journal of Counselling and Guidance*, 6, 71–76.

Rigby, K. (1996b) Preventing peer-victimisation in schools. In C. Sumner, M. Israel, M. O'Connell and R. Sarre (eds) *International victimology* (pp. 303–311). Selected papers from the Eighth International Symposium (held in Adelaide, 1994). Canberra: Australian Institute of Criminology.

Rigby, K. (1996c) *Bullying in schools – and what to do about* it. Melbourne: ACER.

Rigby, K. (1996d) Peer victimisation and the structure of primary and secondary schooling. *Primary Focus*, 10, 4–5.

Rigby, K. (1997a) Attitudes and beliefs of Australian schoolchildren regarding bullying in schools. *Irish Journal of Psychology*, 18, 202–220.

Rigby, K. (1997b) What children tell us about bullying in schools. *Children Australia*, 22, 28–34.

Rigby, K. (1998) Peer relations at school and the health of adolescents. *Youth Studies Australia*, 17, 13–17.

Rigby, K. and Cox, I.K. (1996) The contributions of bullying at school and low self-esteem to acts of delinquency among Australian teenagers. *Personality and Individual Differences*, 21, 609–612.

Rigby, K., Cox, I.K. and Black, G. (1997) Cooperativeness and bully/victim problems among Australian schoolchildren. *Journal of Social Psychology*, 137a, 357–369.

Rigby, K. and Sharp, S. (1993) Cultivating the art of self-defence among victimized children. *International Journal of Protective Behaviours*, 1, 24–27.

Rigby, K. and Slee, P.T. (1991) Bullying among Australian schoolchildren: Reported behaviour and attitudes to victims. *Journal of Social Psychology*, 131, 615–627.

Rigby, K. and Slee, P.T. (1992) *Bullying in schools: The video*. Institute of Social Research, University of South Australia. Distributed by the Australian Council for Educational Research, Camberwell, Melbourne.

Rigby, K. and Slee, P.T. (1993a) Dimensions of interpersonal relating among Australian schoolchildren and their implications for psychological well-being. *Journal of Social Psychology*, 133, 33–42.

Rigby, K. and Slee, P.T. (1993b) *Peer relations questionnaire*. Adelaide: University of South Australia.

Rigby, K. and Slee, P.T. (1993c) Children's attitudes towards victims. In D. P. Tattum (ed.) *Understanding and managing bullying* (pp. 119–135). London: Heinemann Books.

Rigby, K. and Slee, P.T. (in press) Suicidal ideation among adolescent schoolchildren, involvement in bully/victim problems and perceived low social support. *Suicide and Life-threatening Behavior*.

Rigby, K., Slee, P.T. and Cunningham, R. (in press) Effects of parenting on the peer relations of Australian adolescents. *Journal of Social Psychology*.

Rigby, K., Whish, A. and Black, G. (1994) Implications of schoolchildren's peer relations for wife abuse in Australia. *Criminology Australia* (August), 8–12.

Slee, P.T. (1995) Peer victimisation and its relationship to depression among Australian primary school children. *Personality and Individual Differences*, 18, 57–62.

Slee, P.T. (1996a) *The P.E.A.C.E. Pack: A programme for reducing bullying in schools*. Adelaide: Flinders University.

Slee, P.T. (1996b) The P.E.A.C.E. Pack: A programme for reducing bullying in our schools. *Australian Journal of Guidance and Counselling*, 6, 63–69.

Slee, P.T. and Rigby, K. (1993) The relationship of Eysenck's personality factors and self-esteem to bully/victim behaviour in Australian school boys. *Personality and Individual Differences*, 14, 371–373.

Smith, P.K. and Thompson, D. (eds) (1991) *Practical approaches to bullying*. London: David Fulton.

Tulloch, M. (1995) Gender differences in bullying experiences and attitudes to social relationships in high school students. *Australian Journal of Education*, 39, 279–293.

21 Aotearoa/New Zealand

Keith Sullivan

Introduction

The following article entitled 'Fear and loathing at lunchtime' (Catherall, 1994) appeared in a Wellington newspaper:

> Six year old 'Peter' was picked up and thrown off an adventure playground a fortnight ago by two 12-year-old bullies at a suburban primary school. The young boy who used to love school now dreams up any excuse to stay away. It wasn't till 'Peter' complained of a sore back while in the bath that his parents finally wrung it out of him that he had been bullied.
>
> 'He said a couple of 12-year-olds had picked him up by his hands and feet and chucked him off some play equipment. Then they held him down and sat on him and pulled his arms behind his head', his father says. The bullying has apparently ceased but 'Peter' is terrified of the boys and doesn't want to go back to school.
>
> 'I'm angry that those big boys are picking on younger kids. The school promotes itself as a safe area from 9 am to 3 pm and it must take responsibility for those kids', says his dad.
>
> After hearing that his son had been tormented, he spoke to his teacher who told him the boys 'wouldn't have done that'. That night, Peter's father heard that three other boys had been bullied by the same offenders. He contacted their parents and the next day they confronted the principal who said he would pull the boys out of the playground during the school breaks. 'But I went back later that afternoon and nothing had been done. The deputy principal said it was just "rough play"', Peter's father says.
>
> He then wrote to the school board of trustees but he hasn't heard back. He says he has been 'duck shoved', his son's learning is in jeopardy and the school admits it has a problem with violence. He suggests a roster of extra teachers to patrol the playground at lunchtime, confront the offenders and help the victims. The school principal says that the incident has been investigated by the board of trustees but he cannot

discuss the outcome. He says bullying exists in every school. The staff and board were taking steps to address violence by having 'time out' spots for disobedient and violent children, getting children to class on time, and reviewing the school suspension policy.

Although newspaper reports can sensationalise incidents and present just one perspective to the exclusion of others, I decided to use this article to introduce this chapter on bullying in New Zealand schools as it both tells a true story and raises important issues that have emerged during the course of my research. They are as follows:

1 *Having a policy isn't enough; you must have effective practice*. Although in this case the school promoted itself as a safe place, what existed in theory did not exist in practice. Not only were 'Peter' and several other boys bullied, but also nothing was done about it, and the school was unable to come up with an acceptable solution. If a school cannot effectively protect its pupils in a preventive fashion or at least deal properly with a bullying incident when it occurs, then good intentions become empty rhetoric.
2 *Parents and communities need to be part of the solution, not part of the problem*. Rather than listening to 'Peter's' father, the school treated him as a trouble-maker who they hoped would go away if enough doors were closed on him. I would argue that such treatment is both unprofessional and in the long run counter-productive for the school.
3 *If an anti-bullying policy is to be effective, it must be clearly stated and fully endorsed by the school*. At 'Peter's' school there appeared to be both internal confusion and contradiction between staff members and no clear guidelines for dealing effectively with bullying incidents:

   (a) One teacher's response was that the boys accused of bullying were innocent of these accusations.
   (b) After 'Peter's' father brought in the parents of three other children who had been bullied by these two boys, the principal said that the perpetrators would be removed from the playground during breaktime.
   (c) Upon returning to the school at breaktime, 'Peter's' father found that not only had this not been done but that the deputy principal had re-framed the bullying behaviour as just 'rough play'.

   These factors seem to indicate internal confusion and the lack of school 'ownership' of a cohesive anti-bullying policy.
4 *Schools must take responsibility for any incidents and seek to find appropriate solutions*. A statement of defence was made by the principal citing school policies for dealing with disobedient or aggressive behaviour and stating that all schools have a bullying problem. This avoids dealing with the problem at hand, and by closing ranks the school is, in effect, trying to bully the father of the bullied child.

It may be asked whether this scenario is typical of New Zealand. There are certainly some schools which fit this description and some which do not. I would argue, however, that acknowledgement of the presence of bullying may be a difficult step for a school to take. The reform of educational administration in New Zealand has created a quasi-free market of education. Traditional zoning was abolished, which means that parents are not restricted to their local area but can apply to the school of their choice. Funding is directly related to the size of the student enrolment, and schools are in competition for pupils. No school wants bad publicity and bullying attracts such publicity. This may account, at least in part, for the muddled reaction of the staff at 'Peter's' school to accusations of bullying and requests for action and accountability.

A short while ago, another newspaper article reported that a school, which is located in a middle-class Wellington suburb, had a bullying problem. This problem was brought to public attention because an Education Review Office (ERO) report on the school mentioned the school's adoption of an anti-bullying programme. Although the principal was acting with responsibility and forethought in adopting such a programme, he subsequently had to do a lot of work to counter the bad publicity the school received as a result of the newspaper report.

The public has to accept that bullying is endemic and not an indicator of a 'bad' school, and schools have to learn how to handle bullying and to find ways of reconciling criticism with accountability and competition. When blame is attributed, some schools will naturally 'close ranks' and become entrenched in a defensive position. It would be better for all parties, both in the short and long term, if strategies are developed and solutions found by working through the problems together: ideally, a whole-school approach includes a school's community.

In order to go beyond these illustrative examples and explore the issue of anti-bullying initiatives in New Zealand, I have posed four questions that I will answer in order to provide an overview of 'the state of the art'. They are as follows:

- What is the public perception of bullying in New Zealand schools?
- What is the extent and nature of school bullying?
- What programmes have we developed and how effective are they?
- What are our future directions?

First, however, is a section on the country itself, and the school system.

Aotearoa/New Zealand: the country

New Zealand is a small island nation (with two main islands, the North and the South, and a number of smaller islands) in the Southwest Pacific at the southern tip of the triangle that makes up Polynesia. Aotearoa, meaning 'land of the long white cloud', is New Zealand's Maori name. New Zealand has 3.6 million people, the majority (79 per cent) being of European origin and British descent (referred to as Pakeha). The indigenous Maori population make up 13 per cent of the population, 5 per cent are of Pacific Island Polynesian descent (also referred to as Pacific Nations peoples and comprised of people from Samoa, Tonga, Nuie, Fiji – whose people are described as being physically Melanesian and culturally Polynesian – and Tokelau) and 3 per cent are Asian. English and Maori are New Zealand's two official languages. The Maori and Pacific Nations populations are younger (concentrated in the 5 to 29 age range) than their Pakeha counterparts; 20 per cent of the school population are Maori and 7 per cent are Pacific Island Polynesian.

In recent years there has been a Maori renaissance, central to which has been the development of an alternative but state-funded schooling system for, by and in Maori, which includes early childhood *kohanga reo* (language nests), *kura kaupapa Maori* (Maori language and culture schools) and *whare wananga* (Maori tertiary institutions/universities). There have also been language nests developed in Pacific Nations languages (most notably in Samoan and Cook Island Maori). Accompanying this resurgence of Maori and Pacific Nations culture, there has been a growing sense of a distinct and vibrant identity among Pakeha New Zealanders. For all New Zealanders this has meant a re-evaluation of their identities and an emerging sense of being a multi-ethnic Asia-Pacific nation rather than a pale European reflection in the South Seas.

The Aotearoa/New Zealand school system

New Zealand provides free education in its 2667 state primary and secondary schools. School is compulsory between the ages of 6 and 16, and most children start school on their fifth birthday.

New Zealand schools are perhaps somewhat distinct in that the potential for parental influence and control is greater than in most other countries. This can be linked to recent educational reform. Starting in the mid-1980s and continuing up to the present, the New Zealand public sector has undergone a process of extensive administrative reform aimed at making government departments and public institutions more efficient, effective and accountable for their spending of public money. Competition and the devolution of decision making and responsibility have been encouraged in the public service and free market practices have replaced notions of social responsibility and collegiality. In the context of education, budgetary and individual school policy decisions that were formerly made centrally, regionally or at local school board level (excluding teachers' salaries) can now be made in the individual schools (see Sullivan, 1994, 1997, 1998a, for a discussion of the implications of this).

School governance now centres on the board of trustees (BOT), most members of which are elected from and by the parents of the pupils. Besides the five elected parent members, one of whom will be chairperson, *ex-officio* members include the principal, a teacher representative (and a pupil representative for secondary schools) and up to three co-opted members from the community. The BOT's job is essentially one of management and in this role its members can not only identify issues of importance for the school, but they also have the power to ensure that appropriate policies and programmes are developed, effectively resourced, implemented and evaluated. (As an example, intercultural bullying may be a problem; an issue that needs exploration in Aotearoa/New Zealand is the interface between bullying and racism; see Sullivan (1999) for an overview of this issue.)

What is the public perception of bullying in New Zealand schools?

School bullying comes up recurrently in the news media and reflects society's concerns with the larger issue of law and order. Schools are a microcosm of the world to come, so there is felt to be a need to intervene and put things right at an early stage. Although a recent newspaper article (see Boland, 1996) focused on the varied nature of bullying among both boys and girls, bullying in New Zealand is still largely conceived as the stereotypical beating up and tormenting of a physically frail but intelligent and socially isolated boy (read 'nerd') (or of a much younger boy as in the initial illustration) by a physically superior but cowardly thug. Other recent reports of bullying conform to the stereotype. One newspaper article revealed that at a prestigious boys' school in Christchurch, the upper school boys, in true British public school fashion, had been systematically bullying chosen victims and that the school had turned a blind eye (see Long, 1996). Similarly, two well-respected Maori boys' schools were criticised for not dealing with the extensive boy-to-boy bullying that was taking place there. Most recently (August 1997) an Invercargill coroner attributed the suicide of a male secondary school student largely to bullying.

In a country where for many boys the crowning glory is to become an All Black (i.e. to play rugby for New Zealand), there is a sense that standing up to bullies or at least enduring bullying stoically is an appropriate response. The message is that a victim needs to be staunch and fight back or 'take it like a man'.

While physical boy-to-boy bullying is serious, there are other types of bullying that occur in every school: it happens to girls and can be perpetrated by girls; or it can be between the sexes; it can be both physical and psychological; and it can be racist. This message is only just starting to be heard.

What is the extent and nature of school bullying?

In the Office of the Commissioner for Children study, *Children's experience of violence at school* (Lind and Maxwell, 1996), the authors focus not only on bullying *per se*, but also on other forms of violence and intimidation, including general physical violence and sexual and emotional abuse. They also elicited information in relation to other traumatic life events such as accidents, illnesses, death, separation, loss and loneliness in order to provide a wide frame of reference. Their study provides several interesting findings.

The research found that from a sample of 259 form 1 and form 2 students in relation to physical assault in the school, 49 per cent of respondents reported having been punched, kicked, beaten or hit by children; 23 per cent reported having been in a physical fight; and 5 per cent reported having been hurt or threatened with a weapon. In relation to what the authors term direct experience of emotional abuse, the authors reported that 70 per cent of respondents had had tales told on them, and were subjected to catty gossip or rumours; 67 per cent reported having been threatened, frightened or called names; 54 per cent reported having been ganged up on, left out or not spoken to; and 14 per cent reported having been treated unfairly or bullied by adults.

In relation to witnessing violence or abuse, 64 per cent of respondents reported having watched people being threatened, frightened or called names; 62 per cent watched people being ganged up on, left out or not spoken to; 53 per cent reported watching someone being 'punched, kicked, beaten up'; 51 per cent reported having watched a physical fight; and 4 per cent reported having watched someone being hurt/threatened with a weapon.

Several other interesting findings were reported:

1 That 'when children were asked about the worst experience they ever had, the death of a person close to them was most often mentioned but physical or emotional bullying by other children came second' (p. 5).
2 That when bullying is placed in the context of other acts of violence, the authors report that '90% of the incidents of emotional abuse and most of the physical violence between children occurs at schools'.
3 The authors suggest that in relation to the 14 per cent of children who report being treated unfairly or bullied by an adult, that adult is most likely to have been a teacher and that the teacher may not have been aware of the effect of their actions or words (in other words, they were ignorant of what pupils interpret as bullying).
4 The authors say it is commonly assumed that the most extreme forms of bullying in New Zealand schools occurs in low-socio-economic status (SES) schools and in the large Polynesian areas of South Auckland and Porirua. The study indicates that contrary to this popular and racist impression, bullying occurs to the same extent in country and urban schools and in low-SES and high-SES areas to similar degrees and is of a similar nature although there are some variations.

Lind and Maxwell make the following general conclusions (1996: 4):

> Bullying is occurring at all schools. It is the experience of most of the children no matter how capable, popular and well-adjusted they are. Most children, either individually or in a group, become involved in carrying out some type of bullying at some time. Bullying is part of a school climate and not a response to the characteristics of the victim and the school area. Changes in the amount of bullying are not, therefore, going to come about simply from changing the behaviour of a few. Change will only occur through changing the atmosphere of the whole school.
>
> The effects of watching other children being bullied also need to be recognised. Children vicariously respond to what they see. They may feel for the victim and learn to fear those who bully. But they may also respond to the bully and imitate the inappropriate actions they have taken.

These results must be treated with caution as the survey that was carried out involved participants 'opting in'. The authors state that they wrote to all parents of potential participants, and only 23 per cent agreed to their children taking part, 4 per cent did not and 73 per cent did not reply. The authors rightly concluded that their results are not therefore representative and cannot be taken to indicate incidence and prevalence in the schools, although they can suggest patterns.

What programmes have we developed and how effective are they?

As a response to school bullying, three major anti-bullying programmes have emerged in recent years: the New Zealand Police's Kia Kaha, the Foundation for Peace Studies Aotearoa/New Zealand Cool Schools Peer Mediation Programme and the Special Education Services' Eliminating Violence – Managing Anger programme.

Other support in the anti-bullying area has come from the Commissioner for Children and the New Zealand School Trustees Association (NZSTA) (the School Trustees Association is the influential national organisation that has emerged to represent the interests of school boards of trustees). The NZSTA set up a taskforce in 1993 to examine school violence. It then disseminated its findings (Taskforce on Solutions to Violence in Schools, 1993) and made suggestions with a series of short publications known as the *Healthy Schools* newsletters. The Office of the Commissioner for Children which publishes a regular newsletter to address issues in the area of children's rights has focused on school bullying and has commissioned a study on school violence. It has also brought overseas experts to New Zealand to provide seminars around the country for educators (Delwyn and Eve Tattum from the Countering Bullying Unit, Cardiff; and Michael Gruner of the Violence in Schools: Prevention and Countermeasures Programme, Department of School Support Services, Hamburg).

The following will examine the three major anti-bullying programmes.

Kia Kaha

In the past six years the New Zealand Police have developed pro-active policies of community involvement and crime prevention. As part of their law-related education initiative, they have developed the highly successful Keeping Ourselves Safe programme, designed for young children; a drug prevention programme for teenagers, the DARE programme; and an anti-bullying programme, Kia Kaha.

Kia Kaha is a resource kit for students, teachers and parents to combat bullying in schools. It was designed for children in the standard 3 to form 4 age range (around 8 to 14 years old). Kia Kaha means 'to be strong' in Maori. The programme was released to schools in 1992 free of charge. The services of a police education officer to help set up the programme were also made available. The kit is attractively designed and includes a booklet which describes the programme and how to put it in place, a video of typical bullying scenarios and some possible solutions, and pamphlets that can be distributed to parents.

Two postgraduate studies of Kia Kaha (Cleary, 1993; Phelps, 1995) suggest that the programme has proved to be useful for reducing bullying. Cleary's study concludes that 'The Kia Kaha programme, implemented and taught carefully and supported by a school-wide commitment, resulted in a marked decrease in intimidation' (p. 9). However, a more recent study (Bell, 1997) suggests that Kia Kaha is ready for a major overhaul.

The strengths and weaknesses of Kia Kaha

I have recently completed an evaluation of Kia Kaha (Sullivan, 1998b, 1998c). While it is important to acknowledge the efforts of the New Zealand Police for their initiatives in developing and supporting safe structures and processes for young people, much has changed since 1992 and international studies of bullying have become more refined.

Kia Kaha has created a useful and logical structure for tackling bullying. It provides an eight-step process designed to be the basis of a holistic approach that includes the community as well as teachers and pupils, and a plan of action for what to do in a bullying situation (stop, think, consider the options, act, follow up). It also provides a well-scripted and attractively presented video which depicts some typical bullying situations and a range of activities. It gives examples of both physical and psychological bullying and focuses on scenarios that are both girl based and boy based. It is also culturally inclusive, as the actors in the video are both Maori and Pakeha and the concept of Kia Kaha is Maori.

A major criticism is that although it offers solutions for victims, bullies and bystanders, it is largely focused on victims learning to stand up for themselves. This may be an unrealistic stance, for as Australian bullying expert Ken Rigby (1996) has observed, many bullies like a good fight and are not cowards (as the Kia Kaha video suggests) and do not always back down. Precipitating a physical fight is a very questionable strategy. Other programmes such as the 'No Blame' approach in England do not place the onus on the victim as this can be seen as double victimisation (Robinson and Maines, 1997). Recent international scholarship has increased our understanding of the underlying issues and suggested practical solutions for dealing with bullying (for instance, Cowie and Sharp, 1996; Olweus, 1993; Rigby, 1996; Robinson and Maines, 1997; Sharp and Smith, 1994; Slee, 1997; Smith and Sharp, 1994). An update of the Kia Kaha programme incorporating recent thinking would be very beneficial. In Sullivan (1998b) the following provisional recommendations were made:

- Kia Kaha was an appropriate response to a challenge in 1992. Before redesigning Kia Kaha an investigation of the many new responses that have been developed internationally is appropriate.
- If a programme is developed, it should be offered completely or not at all, so that a whole-school implementation is possible.
- The new Kia Kaha should develop a better understanding of the range of anti-bullying techniques with a wider range of solutions, involving a whole-school approach. The programme should be based on a series of strategies which are adaptable to any given situation.
- A revised Kia Kaha should change its emphasis from placing the onus on the victim to giving at least equal responsibility to the bully and the bystanders. The idea of being assertive, of standing up for oneself, as suggested in the Kia Kaha programme, is theoretically laudable. However, to do this in a situation of crisis such as the boy-bullying scenarios in the video is inappropriate, as in real life this could result in an escalation of the bullying or serious injury. In the instance of girl bullying as described in the Kia Kaha video, on the other hand, the assertiveness of the girl in a physically non-threatening situation is an effective way of handling a situation that was not likely to escalate physically.
- If a new video is developed, the bicultural and New Zealand-based focus should be retained. Children should be used rather than adult actors.
- The scenarios presented could be reused as the basis for group discussion and as a way of raising awareness and finding solutions. However, the solutions currently presented are not always useful or practical and should be replaced.
- Bullying is not humorous or trivial and should not appear to be made so in any of the kit materials.

- Within the kit there should be some materials to aid in training teachers to deal with bullying and in supporting the implementation of the programme. Positive contact may be made with parents and community members from New Zealand's various ethnic groups by sending out letters about the kit in appropriate languages.

The Cool Schools Peer Mediation Programme

The Cool Schools Peer Mediation Programme (usually just referred to as Cool Schools) was developed by the Foundation for Peace Studies Aotearoa/ New Zealand. Its main originator, Yvonne Duncan, developed a simple form of mediation to resolve conflicts in her primary school classes in 1984. The story goes that there was a subsequent boom in popularity for the game of marbles, and apparently the conflicts that arose over the game were such that the school threatened to ban it. The children, who had learned mediation skills in the classroom from Yvonne, decided to use these skills to sort out these playground conflicts, which they did successfully.

Central to the Cool Schools approach is 'the belief that if you raise children's awareness and understanding of what conflict is about and teach them skills they can implement themselves it is the most effective way of changing behaviour' (personal communication from Yvonne Duncan, 5 December 1996).

Since that time Duncan and her colleagues have thought through the issues and have created a training package in playground peer mediation that they market in schools. Initially the programme was designed to train individual teachers who would then take this training back to the school and provide training for other teachers and pupils. This has been replaced by an approach where the school gets the training first- rather than second- or third-hand.

> 'There is nothing wrong with conflict', one eleven-year-old explained to me, 'It's what we do with it, how we handle it'. 'And the same for anger', piped up another. As the young people explain it, it is 'cool' to resist violent confrontation and settle disputes in a non-violent way.
>
> (Cool Schools, 1994: 24)

There has been much demand for the Cool Schools training programme. Duncan and Stanners (1996) reported that evaluations from 48 schools showed very positive responses to the programme. Cool Schools was initially developed for primary and intermediate schools (ages 5 to 12) but due to its success, the Foundation has recently developed a programme for secondary schools.

Benefits that are reported to have come out of the project are as follows:

1 students develop an appreciation of conflict as something that can be handled positively and learned from;
2 disputes between students are permanently settled in 80–85 per cent of cases;
3 students become equipped with valuable skills for handling conflict both within and outside of school;
4 a much improved and more co-operative school atmosphere develops;
5 there are fewer incidents of students involved in 'troublesome' behaviour beyond the school gates and a general increase in students' self-esteem;
6 teachers are more able to leave students to find suitable solutions to their problems, thus freeing teachers from a good deal of time-consuming dispute settlement and disciplinary action;
7 students are provided with an excellent resource for dealing with future conflicts in life (Foundation for Peace Studies, 1994: 3–4).

The Radford Group (1996) (a consultancy group) carried out a study of the programme with the objective being 'to understand the benefits and gaps in the services currently being delivered by The Foundation for Peace Studies to schools in New Zealand' (p. 3). In the study, ten personal interviews were used to identify areas of importance and a questionnaire was developed from this. One hundred and eighty-eight telephone interviews of principals or nominated staff were undertaken and this provided the raw data for their results. In relation to the Cool Schools programme, their key findings were as follows:

- Cool Schools was the most mentioned effective means of dealing with conflict and violence by a substantial margin.
- People familiar with the Cool Schools programme were almost unanimous in rating it as effective.
- There was a high agreement that the Cool Schools programme had many positive features (Radford Group, 1996: 3).

Although supportive of the Cool Schools approach, the Radford Group's findings are generalised and of limited use since their primary purpose was to look at the Foundation's programmes rather than to evaluate them outside of that context. Similarly, results of evaluations run by programme initiators can provide useful information about what works and what does not, but cannot be considered as objective research findings. A neutral evaluation of the programme should provide useful and neutral information to the Cool Schools programme.

Eliminating Violence – Managing Anger

The Eliminating Violence programme has been praised in many quarters as being New Zealand's most effective and extensive anti-bullying initiative. It was developed at Auckland's Manakau North Special Education Service and has been adopted by schools throughout the country. Its intention is to support teachers, students, parents and the community in working together to create a safe school environment. A special feature of the programme is that before working with a school and community they must commit themselves to working together on the project's objectives for a year; that is, they must decide to own it. The programme is concerned not only with bullying but also with violence in all its forms.

Under New Zealand's current system of free market competition and devolution of funding to schools, those wishing to use the Eliminating Violence programme must pay for it. This is seen as problematic in that middle-class schools with funding shortfalls can raise extra money more easily than lower SES schools, particularly those in high Polynesian areas such as South Auckland, where such programmes could potentially produce the most benefit. In 1995, the Crime Prevention Unit agreed to support the implementation of the programme by providing funding in six such schools on condition that the Ministry of Education ran an evaluation of the programme. This was agreed to and the evaluation was contracted to a team of researchers at Auckland University's Education Department. These findings are reported in Moore *et al.*, 1997.

The programme's stated objectives are to:

1 Heighten awareness of the pervasiveness and impact of violence in school and community.
2 Teach parents, teachers and students the principles underlying the effective management of violence at a number of levels, e.g. individual, group, systems and community.
3 Teach students and others how to overcome their own and others' anger and to channel such anger positively.
4 Enskill parents, teachers and students in pro-social alternatives to violent behaviours.
5 Help teachers to provide an environment where students feel safe, welcome and respected at school (Moore *et al.*, 1997: 26).

The programme is conducted in the following six phases over a twelve-month period:

- One two-day course for the school staff.
- Constitution of a school management group and development of school policy.
- Staff in-service training sessions comprising three sessions of two hours each (developed from needs-based analysis).
- Three parent training sessions comprising two hours each.
- Child training sessions (pro-social skills training).
- Individual case work with identified children, review and planned steps.

With an underlying ownership philosophy, the programme operates on a cascade principle; that is, the staff of the school are introduced to the programme in the initial stages and are then involved in developing the next phase of the programme which includes the participation of selected parents, members of the community and pupils.

In evaluating the programme, the researchers' primary research question was, 'Does the Eliminating Violence from Schools programme reduce the levels of violence in schools?' Their purpose, in effect, was to evaluate the programme's effectiveness in terms of the stated objectives. Information was generated using an adapted bullying questionnaire (Olweus, 1984, cited in Moore *et al.*, 1997), an attitudes to violence scale (developed by the research team), incident reports, classroom and playground observations, and teacher and parent interviews. The evaluations took place in three schools in the Greater Auckland area. A distinct characteristic of the schools was that they all had very high Pacific Island Polynesian and Maori populations and small Pakeha populations; one was considered a high risk school and another a moderate risk school.

There were many useful insights and recommendations that came from the evaluation but only a brief summary can be given here. The evaluation reported that 'the results clearly indicate that the Eliminating Violence from Schools programme has been associated with a reduction in both the level and the severity of violence, and additionally, lower tolerance to violent behaviour at all three schools' (Moore *et al.*, 1997: 2). In terms of the programme's stated objectives, the researchers found the following positive results:

1 The teachers and students have gained an increased awareness of violence and a clearer understanding of the principles underlying the management of violence, particularly at the group and systems level.
2 Teachers have generally been able to provide an environment where students feel safer and more welcome at school.
3 Additional benefits have been observed in the school in terms of improved staff relations and cohesiveness, increasingly consistent approaches to discipline, and an increased feeling among staff members that the control or elimination of violence is not an insurmountable problem.

They also made the following criticisms:

1 The programme has been less successful in teaching students specific skills at the individual level for the management of their own and others' anger and in the development of pro-social alternatives to violent behaviour.
2 Although the involvement of parents and community is considered vital both by the programme's developers and by the parents and teachers interviewed, there is little evidence of any impact on parents or community.

3 The integrity of the programme has been limited both with respect to the difference between the designed programme and that delivered and to the amount of time expended at each school.

The researchers reported several limitations to their evaluation. These were that two of the schools were undergoing major changes at the time of the evaluation, and other programmes were running concurrently in some of the case study schools (assertive discipline, peer counselling). Further to this, the schools were treated as three individual case studies and although changes over the course of the study could be described, causal assertions in relation to the programme's effectiveness could not be determined. They also pointed out that the voluntary nature of the participation could have biased external validity.

Conclusions

With Kia Kaha, final recommendations have been worked on and were presented to the New Zealand Police in March 1998. In relation to Cool Schools, although research has been done its evaluative value is limited, as the scale of the research was small. In the case of the Eliminating Violence – Managing Violence programme, the evaluation clearly identifies both the major successes of the programme and the areas that need improvement. This is very useful, in that identifying the weak spots is the first step towards fine-tuning what is an excellent response to school bullying.

What are our future directions?

Although New Zealand is a small nation, the effort that has been put into dealing with school bullying is substantial. However, instead of there being a concerted effort to combat bullying in schools, current government policies encourage competition, devolution and a market mentality in education. This means that programmes such as Cool Schools and Eliminating Violence must compete for customers (read 'schools') in an educational free market, and central funds are not available for such things as a national anti-bullying campaign.

Teachers expressed fears to me that rather than making bullying initiatives an integral part of school processes, schools may choose to adopt a bullying programme one year, but then, having 'done bullying', put it off for the next few years in favour of, for instance, a truancy programme. Another concern is that schools have come to rely on fund-raising by parents to get 'the extras'. While the Ministry of Education has developed a formula which tops up the funding of schools which are 'at risk', this is not a solution or even appropriate in the running of a national education system.

Some of the general conclusions to the Eliminating Violence evaluation provide a useful reference point for possible future directions of anti-bullying initiatives in New Zealand. The need for a whole-school approach to anti-bullying programmes, in which schools have a clear anti-bullying policy and take responsibility for finding solutions, is now universally accepted as appropriate. However, in this particular programme, ensuring effective community involvement was difficult, particularly where it was most needed. There was a major problem in that the programmes were developed by Pakeha but for this research were implemented in schools that had large Maori and Pacific Island populations and where the cultural expectations of the pupils and the community were at odds with the programme implementers. The question of whether current anti-bullying programmes address the needs of all ethnic groups must therefore be raised. The issues are clearly complex, and the availability of international as well as local scholarship, research and programme development is crucial, both in challenging policy and in the process of implementation, of turning policy into practice.

References

Bell, L.M. (1997) Teachers' and principals' perspectives on the Kia Kaha programme: A resource kit about bullying for students, teachers and parents. Unpublished M.Ed. thesis, University of Otago.

Boland, Mary Jane (1996) Hard lessons. *The Dominion*, 18 April.

Catherall, S. (1994) Fear and loathing at lunchtime. *The Dominion*, 12 October.

Cleary, M. (1993) *Countering intimidation through school-wide intervention*. ASTU Research Project, Palmerston North Teachers College.

Cool Schools (1994) *Towards non-violent conflict resolution*. Broadsheet.

Cowie, H. and Sharp, S. (eds) (1996) *Peer counselling: A time to listen*. London: David Fulton.

Duncan, Y. and Stanners, M. (1996) Secondary peer mediation (Draft). Auckland: Foundation for Peace Studies, Aotearoa/New Zealand.

Foundation for Peace Studies, Aotearoa/New Zealand (1994) *Cool schools peer mediation programme: Training manual* (2nd edn). Auckland.

Law Related Education Programme (1992) *Kia Kaha*. Wellington: New Zealand Police.

Lind, J. and Maxwell, G. (1996) *Children's experience of violence at school*. Wellington: Office of the Commissioner for Children.

Long, J. (1996) Bully boys face an enfeebled isolation. *The Press*, 19 January.

Moore, D., Adair, V., Lysaght, K. and Kruiswijk, J. (1997) Eliminating violence from schools evaluation project (Final Report, April). Auckland: Auckland Uniservices Limited, University of Auckland.

Olweus, D. (1993) *Bullying in schools: What we know and what we can do*. Oxford: Blackwell.

Phelps, K. (1995) Kia Kaha research: Does the kit prevent bullying? Research Study as part of B.Ed. degree, Otago University, Dunedin.

Radford Group (1996) *The Foundation for Peace Studies: A summary of quantitative research*. Auckland.

Rigby, K. (1996) *Bullying in schools and what to do about it*. Melbourne: ACER.

Robinson, G. and Maines, B. (1997) *Crying for help: The 'No Blame Approach' to bullying*. Bristol: Lucky Duck Publishing.

Sharp, S. and Smith, P.K. (eds) (1994) *Tackling bullying in your schools: A practical handbook for teachers*. London: Routledge.

Slee, P. (1997) *The P.E.A.C.E. Pack: Reducing bullying in our schools* (2nd edn). Adelaide: School of Education, Flinders University.

Smith, P.K. and Sharp, S. (eds) (1994) *School bullying: Insights and perspectives*. London: Routledge.

Sullivan, K. (1994) The impact of educational reform on teachers' professional ideologies. *New Zealand Journal of Educational Studies*, 29, 1–16.

Sullivan, K. (1997) They've opened Pandora's box: Educational reform, the New Right and teachers' ideologies. In Olssen, M. and Morris-Matthews, K. (eds) *Education policy in New Zealand: the 1990s and beyond*. Palmerston North: Dunmore Press.

Sullivan, K. (1998a) The great New Zealand educational experiment and the issue of teachers as professionals. In Sullivan, K. (ed.) *Education and change in the Pacific Rim: Meeting the challenges*. Wallingford: Triangle Books/Oxford Studies in Comparative Education, Vol. 7, No. 1.

Sullivan, K. (1998b) 'The David and Goliath routine can backfire – tread carefully': A focus-group evaluation of the Kia Kaha anti-bullying kit. *New Zealand Annual Review of Education*, 7.

Sullivan, K. (1998c) *An evaluation of the New Zealand Police's Kia Kaha programme – a resource kit about bullying*. Wellington: New Zealand Police.

Sullivan, K. (1999) Racist bullying: Creating understanding and strategies for teachers. In Leicester, M., Modgil, S. and Modgil, C. (eds) *Values, culture and education*, Series One, Vol. Two. Institutional Issues. London: Cassell.

Taskforce on Solutions to Violence in Schools (1993) Report of the New Zealand School Trustees Association: Taskforce on Solutions to Violence. Wellington: NZSTA.

Tattum, D.P. and Herbert, G. (eds) (1993) *Countering bullying*. Stoke-on-Trent: Trentham Books.

Part IV

The developing world

22 The developing world

Toshio Ohsako

Introduction

This chapter is designed to highlight some of the main issues on school violence/bullying in several developing countries. The researchers in the developing countries concerned share with their counterparts in industrialised countries an awareness of the importance of the issue of bullying and school violence, particularly its impact on schooling and society in general. However, the amount of information available on this subject in these countries is relatively scarce, in particular the research information on bullying. The methods employed by these countries to analyse the subject do not rely so much on the quantitative analysis of data, as is the case of some industrialising countries whose studies appear in the preceding chapters of this book. One also has to be careful not to generalise the findings and observations of the current studies to the school violence and bullying issues of all other developing countries. Given these limitations of the study, I will attempt to synthesise the main findings reported from the studies conducted in a number of developing countries, and to highlight some critical issues of bullying in school faced by young people in the light of the sociocultural realities and backgrounds of their countries.

Secondly, attempts were made to compare some issues of violence prevalent in developing countries with those reported by researchers from industrialised countries. However, being faced with a relatively modest amount of existing research information on the part of developing countries, I have found it particularly difficult to undertake quantitative comparison of the bullying/school violence issues between the two groups of countries. I have had to rely heavily on the interview data, expert observations and critical incidence analysis reported by the researchers. By doing so, I have tried to draw some tentative conclusions and to pose questions concerning bullying/school violence between the two groups. I am also convinced of the need for further enquiry in order to achieve a better understanding of the common factors and variations of bullying in school violence issues. Such enquiry may be effectively pursued if one takes into consideration the different socio-economic or sociocultural backgrounds and different developmental stages of both industrialised and developing countries.

The information dealt with in this chapter has been derived mainly from a series of comparative studies initiated by UNESCO International Bureau of Education (IBE, Geneva). The studies were carried out during 1995 and 1996 in Ethiopia, Jordan, Malaysia, Malawi, Palestine, South Africa and in six Latin American countries (Brazil, Colombia, El Salvador, Guatemala, Nicaragua and Peru). The studies from Cambodia and Sierra Leone were commissioned by the Graduate Institute of Development Studies of the University of Geneva.

Case analyses

Palestine and South Africa: a cross-fire of poverty and political violence

The studies in some developing regions strike us by their focus on an intensive scenario of violence whose experiences are unknown in the majority of industrialised countries. Palestine and South Africa provide protocol examples of such cases. Young people living in Palestine and South Africa are experiencing a dual blow of poverty and political violence, both at school, in the family and in society. The following studies conducted by Sylvie Mansour (France) in Palestine in 1996 and by Fraser *et al.* (1996) in South Africa provide us with protocol examples of such a case.

Palestine

The life of young Palestinian people is, according to Mansour, constantly affected and threatened by the combination of political violence and poverty. For example, her study conducted in 1993 on a group of 2797 children aged between 8 and 15 years in different refugee camps in the Gaza Strip, Gaza City and other villages in the Strip show that a high percentage of the children were exposed to tear-gas (92.5 per cent), beaten by soldiers (42 per cent), exposed to night raids on their homes (85 per cent), and detention (19 per cent).

Mansour points out serious negative effects of the 'political socialisation' of children. Take, for an example, the child's play. The Palestinian child, she observes, often engages him or herself in 'militant games' depicting, instead of 'cowboys and Indians', a play between 'Israelis and Palestinians'. Concern was expressed that such play tends to facilitate in the mind of the child a simple dichotomisation of the world between us as a victim who needs to fight back and the other as an aggressor.

Mansour also reports a high level of corporal punishment inflicted upon Palestinian children by teachers and parents. Teachers are frustrated and stressed by extremely overcrowded classes, the lack of appropriate educational materials and textbooks, low salaries, no promotion prospects, etc. The Palestinian children are also unhappy, humiliated and overwhelmed by the feeling of failure and despair at school. The level of tension to which the

Palestinian family is subject has risen, due to social violence, frustration and an insecure social environment. This tendency, on the contrary, increased the use of corporal punishment by parents and guardians. A study conducted by the Palestinian Centre Against Violence on a sample of 1000 parents and guardians of children indicates that 66 per cent of the city-dwellers used violence, for those living in camps (69 per cent) a high rate of physical violence. More and more Palestinian children are also deprived of their father's presence, due to his travelling a considerable distance to work or to his being imprisoned. The loss or absence of a father figure hinders the moral and disciplinary development of children, which places children at risk of engaging in violent acts and acting in a tyrannical manner towards parents (particularly towards mothers) and teachers.

The Palestinian study also reports a heavy educational loss due to the prolonged political violence. An International Workshop on Educational Destruction and Reconstruction in Disrupted Societies, jointly organised by the University of Geneva and the UNESCO International Bureau of Education (15–16 May 1997), bears witness to the negative impact of the political situation in Palestine. Dr Said Assaf, a participant from the Ministry of Education of Palestinian National Authority, pointed out the following: low economic status of schools; textbook censorship including the exclusion of the word 'Palestine' from the textbooks; lack of opportunities for teacher training; school closures; research in school forbidden; low academic achievement; strikes and demonstrations by students; large class sizes; behavioural problems of students; closure of higher education institutions and deportation and harassment of university professors and foreign teachers; and substantially lower salaries for Palestinian teachers. Mansour further notes that school textbooks of Egyptian and Jordanian origin, whose contents are linked to the history, culture or geography of Palestine, are banned.

Mansour however insists that a cure for the violence-ridden community of Palestinian children is possible if all the psychological, material and family factors which breed unfavourable grounds conducive to violent behaviour are tackled and eliminated with great care. Such tasks inevitably require concerted efforts on the part of society, institutions, the media, the family and individuals. However, these efforts may not lead to truly fruitful results without the guarantee of lasting peace in the region.

Assaf agrees with Mansour that fully-fledged educational improvement of Palestinian children cannot be fully pursued without peace in the region. However, he thinks that the efforts to improve the educational process should be continued, particularly the attempts of the Palestinian National Authority to establish better educational policies, to reinforce the teacher training system, to increase school counsellors and activities, better provision of special education, community–parents–teacher collaborative activities, creation of a common curriculum for all Palestinian children, and research and educational information activities including the information management system, designed to strengthen demographic and economic data collection in Palestine.

South Africa

Now let us turn to South Africa. While the occupied territory has been a major concern for Palestinian children since 1967, the apartheid history of South Africa traces back to as early as the sixteenth century. According to Fraser *et al.* (1996) who conducted a study in this country over several generations, children have suffered from racial discrimination and denial of democratic rights and continue to suffer from violence. For them, life without violence is a utopia and violence has long been perceived as an unavoidable daily event, as well as an indispensable and sometimes the only means to struggle for and achieve a non-discriminatory and democratic society. The living conditions and housing, unemployment, poor sanitary conditions, poor school facilities, low income and segregation have also contributed to the high rate of violence among the children of South Africa.

A survey on South African teachers' opinions on violence in education conducted by Fraser *et al.* (1996) in the provinces of Gauteng, Free State and KwaZulu-Natal reveals serious cases of student violence including burning down classrooms, pupils attacking teachers and principals, pupils setting fire to teachers' cars, and students attacking taxi drivers in order to steal their cars. South Africa's rate of 141 reported rapes per 100,000 females is almost double the US rate for 1995 of 72 rapes per 100,000 females, according to law reinforcement statistics from both countries. Child rapes account for 38 per cent of South Africa's total rape case load (*Washington Post*, 15 February 1997). As is the case for Palestinian children, South African children are also subject to a high rate of corporal punishment. Racial discrimination in employment makes children in South Africa question the value of schooling and training – this fact seems to substantially influence their level of motivation and academic achievement.

Summary

In summary, children simultaneously suffering from poverty and political violence in developing countries tend to face a risk of cultivating a view of the world which is quite different from their counterparts in industrialised countries. In such developing countries, the lives of children and young people centre around violence while simultaneously their educational, occupational and social opportunities are extremely restricted by poverty and poor living conditions. In industrialised countries, physical violence is a phenomenon more or less restricted to certain areas (e.g. congested urban cities, high unemployment areas) and groups (e.g. delinquent and gang groups) and violence is also considered as improper or, in some serious cases, criminal behaviour. Violent behaviour of children living under the cross-fire of political violence and poverty is not necessarily to be condemned or punished – violence often becomes part of life itself and also a means to overcome poverty in order to survive. That is why children from developing countries are sometimes ready to fight violence with violence and to use violent means to protect themselves and avenge violence. These children live in a 'culture of violence', and their view of the world is shaped by it. This fact is tragic and extremely dangerous.

Secondly, children risk the development of simplified, stereotyped or dichotomised notions of people – the world consists of people who are either 'enemies' or supporters, victims or aggressors, in-groups or out-groups. This rigid categorisation of people hinders the child from developing an open, flexible and positive personality, which often forms a base for his or her ability to compromise, negotiate and communicate for a peaceful solution to problems or conflict resolution.

Thirdly, living in the world of poverty and political violence, children often have no choice but to develop a pessimistic and insecure concept of the world, their life and future. Poverty threatens their survival and deprives them of constructive life alternatives, cultural and social activities. Too much thought and effort is devoted to the protection from immediate danger of violence and retaliation for violence and, due to this fact, it is difficult under such a stressful and hostile atmosphere for children to develop a long-term perspective of life or to aspire for and think about the future.

Ethiopia

Ethiopia is the third most populous country (approximately 50,000,000) in Africa, after Nigeria and Egypt. The country's population is young: 48 per cent are below 15 years of age.

An Ethiopian study (Terefe and Mengistu, 1996) using a sample of three junior secondary and five senior secondary schools in innermost cities around Addis Ababa reported 240 incidences of violence – 30 cases per school. Although, given the relatively small sample size of this study, one must be careful not to generalise this study to other schools outside of Addis Ababa, it revealed the following interesting results:

- Girls and younger children are the main victims of violence – Terefe and Mengistu attribute this to the fact that girls 'have no endurance to resist the males and boys in physical confrontations' and that the smaller children are punished by older students for their 'failure of obedience and conformity' to older children's demands. It is interesting to note that the French study in this book, on the contrary, reports that girls tend less often to be bullies and bullying victims. However, studies from industrialised countries show generally that girls more than boys tend to be the victims of sexual harassment and crimes.
- Bullying and snatching objects (books, bags, etc.) are the most frequently occurring forms of violence, followed by physical violence (hitting, kicking, etc.). Attempts of rape at school are frequent among students, particularly among senior high school students (20 per cent of the total

violence counted). This high rate of rape attempts at school is probably surprising to people living in industrialised countries, who usually observe that rape is more or less a crime committed by male adults outside of schools.
- A study in eight schools around Addis Ababa revealed that teachers and headmasters feel a high to medium level of impact of violence upon the teaching–learning processes, school rules and regulations and students' psychological well-being. Nearly 90 per cent of students reported that they have either repeated classes or dropped out of school due to violence. Violence often leads to physical injuries and death of students.
- As regards the causes of violence, the Ethiopian study indicates that the break-up of families, poor living conditions (insufficient food, clothing, etc.), media violence, inadequate educational expenditure which is responsible for unmanageably large classes, poor school transportation means and school facilities and untrained school personnel, are probably responsible.

The study ends by recommending the following anti-violence measures:

- the establishment of clear school regulations and codes of conduct;
- school–student–parent–community co-operation in anti-violence campaigns and programmes;
- improvement of teacher–student relationship, i.e. more positive and communicative;
- all learning institutions (schools, community learning centres, youth clubs, the media, churches, mosques, etc.) should teach the attitude of tolerance and encourage student counselling.

Malawi

Malawi is classified by the UN as one of the least developed countries; it is located in southeast Africa, and is bordered by Zambia, Mozambique and Tanzania. The total population is estimated at 11.5 million. The percentage of the population under 15 years is 47.3 per cent.

Alarmed by the rapid deterioration of discipline in Malawi's secondary schools, the Ministry of Education commissioned a study on this issue in 1996, which produced a report 'Secondary school discipline study' written by J.B. Kuthemba Mwale *et al.* of the Centre for Educational Research and Training.

This study, through interviews with students, school personnel, parents and educational policy makers, investigated: the types of discipline problems including bullying, physical violence and vandalism; the occurrence of discipline problems in three school settings – government schools, grant-aided schools and private schools; the perceived causes of discipline problems; the impact of discipline problems; and the actions taken by institutions and the Ministry of Education.

Some results of the study are very interesting. It revealed a range of frequently occurring violent behaviour in Malawi – physical violence, bullying, use of vulgar and rude language, rioting, vandalism, and sexual abuse. The study found that boys' schools, whether governmental, grant aided or private, witnessed the widest category of discipline problems including bullying and violence. In co-education schools, despite the above-mentioned different settings, gender conflict was almost non-existent. In private co-education schools, according to the study, there were relatively few discipline problems, such as bullying, teasing, the use of vulgar language, and physical violence. Private girls' schools did not have a single case of vandalism.

In 1994 Malawi went through a political transition from a one-party system to a multi-party government. Given the reality of newly emerged political pluralism in Malawi, the interview data collected from the school personnel, parents, secondary schoolchildren and politicians revealed that the discipline problems of young students in Malawi is a result of 'gross misunderstanding, misconception and gross abuse of the terms democracy, human rights and freedom'. The study also claims that schoolchildren are not receiving adequate civic education on the implications of political pluralism – the idea that 'when exercising one's freedom and individual rights, people must not violate the freedoms and rights of others or of institutions'. The study also points to the fact that most schools in Malawi lack basic teaching and learning materials which seriously hinders the learning process. Under these circumstances, students are frustrated and not motivated to sustain their learning. Consequently, according to the Malawi study, this lack of a positive learning environment renders students more vulnerable to conflicts and temptations of violent behaviour.

The Malawi discipline study revealed the impact of problems at both individual and school level. At individual level impacts are pain inflicted by punishment, rejection by school mates, parents and teachers, loss of self-confidence and self-esteem as a result of being labelled and treated as a problematic student, and the loss of prestige of being a secondary school student (being a student at this level is still a prestigious status in Malawi).

Schools suffer from loss and damage to their property and facilities which is a further blow to the economy of schools and to the education budget of the country. Classroom activities are disturbed and teachers have to spend a considerable amount of time in disciplining students instead of teaching. With disrupted classrooms, schools also find it very difficult to maintain an appropriate level of academic performance of students and their skills training which is so essential to the national development of Malawi. The social image of the school also suffers due to loss of confidence in the school as a credible institution for learning and training.

Malawi's secondary schools take three types of actions against disciplinary problems including bullying and violence. The first is 'rustication', applied to minor offences; this brings the parents or guardian of a student together to examine the case and to assist in counselling the student. The second method is suspension, which is applied to more serious cases such as drunkenness, bullying, rioting and vandalism. The third method, exclusion, is a most severe form of punishment applied to students who are uncontrollable and have repeated serious discipline problems. The study concludes that all forms of intervention including the above-mentioned three methods fail unless the roots of the problem are identified and treated.

Jordan

Jordan is a country whose future depends heavily on its large young population (42.5 per cent of which is below age 15). Seventy per cent of the population live in the urban areas and the remaining 30 per cent occupy the rural areas and the Badia. Moslems comprise 92 per cent of the population and Christians 8 per cent.

A study conducted by Zougan Obiedat (1996), of the Jordanian Ministry of Education, indicates that students' aggressive behaviour such as rioting, assaulting teachers, bullying and using sharp tools has increased in the past five years. His Royal Highness Prince Hassan himself declared that violence in schools reflects teachers' 'weak acquaintance with the proper methods to handle students' affairs and to maintain discipline in classrooms' (Seminar on School Violence, Amman, September 1996).

Obiedat, who studied the documents of the school discipline boards during 1995 and 1996, found that rioting in school (376 cases: 29 per cent) is the most frequent form of violent behaviour, followed by bullying (317 cases: 24 per cent). Using vulgar language towards class mates and teachers is increasing (196 cases: 15 per cent, and 145 cases: 11 per cent, respectively). Out of the total 1309 violent behaviours recorded, boys committed 1092 cases (83 per cent).

Obiedat reports negative impacts of violence in schools, such as a substantial amount of time spent on disciplining and observing violent children by teachers and other school personnel, severe punishment leading to reporting to police authorities, and disturbing the school atmosphere, weakening school discipline and learning, and transferring acts of violence from school to society.

The Jordanian studies suggest the following preventive and intervention methods at schools: reinforcement of counselling programmes and increasing numbers of school counsellors; holding training courses in violence management for teachers and other school personnel; strengthening schools' relations and co-operative links with communities to deal with violence at the school; designing university research to implement a comprehensive study on violence; anti-violence campaigns involving parents, students, teachers, the media and social bodies; clarification of behavioural codes and reinforcement of school disciplinary regulations; development of anti-violence, pro-tolerance, and co-operative and communicative school curricula and of conflict-resolution and peaceful negotiation strategies and programmes; holding a conference on school violence with a view to coping with the issue; and declaring a school year free of violence.

Malaysia

Malaysia is a multi-ethnic nation with a population of nineteen million consisting of three main groups: the Malays, Chinese and Indians, and several indigenous groups such as the Ibans, Kadazans, Kenyahs, Bidayuhs and Muruts. The national language is Bashasa (Malay language). Islam is the official religion, but there is complete freedom of worship.

According to Rahimah and Norani, authors of the Malaysian study (1997), bullying and violence in school steadily increased in the 1980s and 1990s. Consequently, since 1984, schools have been required to submit to the District Education Office (DEO) a report entitled 'School Discipline Student Report'.

The Malay word *dera* (abusive punishment) has been used in this country to mean bullying. The 1993 criminal offences record of the Student School Discipline Report indicate that there were 516 cases (0.02 per cent of the total students enrolled) and 560 cases (0.06 per cent) among primary and secondary school students, respectively. However, Rahimah and Norami argue that if acts of extortion and threatening behaviour by students are considered as bullying, this statistic jumps to 4712 cases (0.17 per cent) and 6950 (0.46 per cent), respectively. Furthermore, violent acts and other acts relating to violence – fighting with teachers and prefects, extortion, bullying, sexual harassment, threatening students – amount to 5290 cases (0.20 per cent of the total students enrolled) at the primary level and 8658 cases (0.59 per cent) at the secondary level.

The DEO reports and studies carried out by the Ministry of Education show that school discipline problems including bullying and violence predominate in the urban poor and working-class groups. Recent surveys also indicate that school and class absenteeism is highest among those students with disciplinary problems.

As regards the causes of disciplinary problems, low socioeconomic status, peer influence, lack of parental guidance and religious instruction, and a shortage of schools and teachers have been considered to be contributing factors. In particular, Malaysian society still strongly believes that much of the responsibility for the disciplinary problems of children lies largely with parents and family. Strong family ties and values, sound moral and religious teachings and consistent care and supervision of parents are considered to be crucial factors in curbing disciplinary problems of young people in this country.

At school, the improvement in the school environment has been increasingly recognised as a contributing factor in combating school violence, in addition to learning problems and low self-esteem of students. Schools have recently found it useful to link up with out-of-school agencies, such as police, welfare departments, parents and NGOs in dealing and coping with the disciplinary problems of students. Police officers conducting workshops or giving talks to schoolteachers and students on topics of discipline are current innovations in curbing bullying and school violence in Malaysia.

Cambodia

While the focus of most of the industrialised countries in this book is on violence occurring within school settings, a study prepared by Pich Sophoan (1997) on Cambodia presents one of the worst scenarios of political violence in human history. Civil wars and armed conflicts among different political groups which have continued for more than 25 years have resulted in almost total destruction of the educational system and resources in Cambodia.

At the end of the Khmer Rouge regime in 1997, according to Sophoan, the whole Cambodian educational system was in a state of collapse. At that time, Cambodia needed to restart educating 724,058 enrolled students in 2481 primary schools and with 13,619 teachers. Substantial governmental education funds have been diverted to finance its civil wars, and school buildings have disappeared or been badly damaged. Only some 87 of the 1009 teachers in higher education prior to the Khmer Rouge period survived. There are still two land mines in the ground for every Cambodian child, and children still experience daily the effects of war and violence – the loss and disabilities of family members among other misfortunes due to land mines and armed conflict. Cambodia has 150,000 physically handicapped people due to wars – the largest number in the world. The illiteracy rate is 50 per cent. The school repeat rate is quite high, particularly among secondary school students – 16,000 students are repeating the final grade of secondary school for the third time.

Despite the devastating effects of wars on education, the newly elected government in 1993 has been struggling to reconstruct and renew the educational system and schools, in co-operation with external bilateral and multilateral donor agencies, United Nations Agencies and non-governmental organisations. The priority educational activities and projects focus on teacher training, ideology-free textbooks and teaching, peace and civic education, quality basic education for all, environmental education, and rural and agricultural education. The reconstruction of Cambodia cannot be pursued without basic education for the eradication of illiteracy, and technical and vocational education to create skilled labour forces and other needed qualities of human resources, for which the government has pledged to devote 15 per cent of the annual national budget by the year 2000 (10.7 per cent in 1996).

Sierra Leone

Civil war broke out in Sierra Leone in 1991 and, following a military *coup* in 1992, internationally observed elections in 1992 ended military rule to establish a democratic civilian government.

Although the preceding studies are predominantly concerned with the negative effects of wars, armed conflicts and violence on educational systems, practices and teaching and learning, a study prepared by Cream Wright (1997) takes an interesting view, considering education both as an 'unintended accomplice' of the civil war and as an instrument for the reconstruction of education.

Access to education and the quality of education often fall short when the promises of more schools or the establishment of new schools are based more upon election manifestos of politicians than upon careful educational planning. Sierra Leone's elitist education, mingled with a narrow academic curriculum, has created a large number of drop-outs and 'forgotten aspirants' who are frustrated losers within the school system. These young 'forgotten aspirants' play a role as combatants on both sides of the rebel war in Sierra Leone. The frustration manifested by forgotten aspirants takes a form of disillusion among those young learners who have successfully completed their schooling when job creation lags behind outputs of university and school graduates. They realise that society's promises are unfulfilled and education is no longer a guarantee of a good job, or a successful career.

Wright further argues that education in Sierra Leone has produced 'clever conformists' rather than 'daring innovators'. People tend to be judged or valued more by their qualifications rather than by their actual job performance. The counterbalance to this situation is the emergence of a culture of 'youthful irreverence', which encourages forgotten aspirants to rebel against authority, resulting in social violence.

Commenting on the impact of civil war on education in Sierra Leone, Wright points out several major consequences. The civil wars, as a result of vandalising and destroying schools, created a significant proportion of displaced pupils and teachers, which has made it difficult to ascertain basic enrolment and to maintain general school activities. The Revolutionary United Front (RUF) movements abducted some staff members and students (many joined the RUF of their own free will) who were medical doctors, engineers and ex-teachers and ex-students and were otherwise useful human resources in the past.

Civil wars gave many young people reasons to take a new look at educational philosophy and goals. Forgotten aspirants and 'youthful irreverence' have been given a new sense of worthiness and accomplishment; this experience compensated for what they could not otherwise achieve through the process of schooling. Under the military government, these youngsters hold important and decision-making positions. The former young civil war fighters have also brought positive consequences by prioritising education and training, demanding 'free education', and the educational practices favouring and rewarding a wider range of abilities, skills, knowledge and talents for national development. More efficient relocation of educational institutions, absorption of displaced pupils into existing schools, and opening new schools for displaced pupils and refugees, UNICEF's demobilisation of child combatants and its detraumatisation of Children Affected by War (CAW) to minimise the negative effects of civil wars on children are some examples of practical activities that Sierra Leone has already launched in the post-civil war period.

Latin American countries – Brazil, Colombia, El Salvador, Guatemala, Nicaragua and Peru

The direct penetration of drug-trafficking in school is a rare issue in most industrialised countries. Although what Eloisa Guimaraes (1996) reports from Brazilian cities around Rio de Janeiro cannot be applied to Brazilian schools in general, it does provide us with a worst case scenario of schools being seized by drug-traffickers and consequently being used as a battleground for fights between different drug-traffickers and gangs, and also as a place for drug-traffickers to organise action to control the school personnel in order to expand their business through blackmailing, threats, and physical violence and intimidation. This is an example of schools being directly threatened and destroyed by gangs, and failure on the part of the legal reinforcement sector to control and punish drug-trafficking puts the most sacred place of human learning and growth – the school – at the mercy of a criminal act. One cannot expect this kind of problem to be solved by the school alone. I recommend that community-based violence intervention programmes are probably effective, linking police and police information systems, schools, anti-violence agencies and other bodies. Concerted efforts for anti-crime and anti-violence campaigns and measures are also needed. As a matter of urgency, the strict law reinforcement and security measures for all types of crime may be the first priority in these cities, followed by post-crisis social and educational remedial and preventive actions against violent crimes.

Liliana Mayora Salas of the Centre for Research and Information in Education (CIDE), Chile, investigated violence and aggression in Colombia, El Salvador, Guatemala, Nicaragua and Peru (1997). These five Latin American countries altogether have a population of approximately 80 million people. Per capita income ranges from US$830 (Nicaragua) to US$1470 (Peru). These countries were selected for study because they are particularly known to have school violence problems. Poverty, unemployment of young people, illiteracy, malnutrition of children, social marginality, congested living quarters, and poor sanitary conditions are constant problems, making the lives of people in these countries difficult and miserable. The misery and poverty of the country has had a serious negative impact on the lives and education of children and young people.

The problems associated with the violence committed by children and the violence directed towards children in this region, according to Salas (1997), cannot be tackled without understanding their economic, political, cultural and social backgrounds. What triggers the violence of children needs to be understood in relation to how socially unfavourable and adverse conditions affect and frustrate young people, how much educational options and occupational choice young people have, and the psychological impact of sociopolitical instability and the violence-permeated society, and moreover, the hardened and troubled attitudes of adults due to economic hardships, which, on the other hand, often put them in a difficult situation when it comes to dealing with or understanding the problems of violence among children and young people living in these troubled countries.

Poor academic performance is one of the causes of drop-out or school repeating in industrialised countries, but poverty pushes children out of school at an early age in order to earn an income for the survival of the family and also to pursue family responsibilities in Latin American developing countries. Once children are pushed out of school, they often turn into so-called 'street' children, and in some cases they join 'maras' (gangs), and some children start establishing themselves as traffickers of drugs. These out-of-school children often becomes gang members themselves or the victims of gangs, and violence is one of the most effective and readily available instruments to expand their power and territory.

The Colombian situation reveals that the stress and frustration created by a heavy family workload both inside and outside the family tends to lead to less time dedicated to childcare by parents, marital and familial problems and physical punishment directed towards children. Children tend to carry over the negative effects of these problems to their schools.

In the same country, corporal punishment delivered by teachers is a pedagogic tradition and a common practice. In a survey conducted in 1988, 62.8 out of every 100,000 children declared that they are beaten with sticks, rulers, electric cords, shoe heels, etc. The study points to the negative effects of corporal punishment on learning (low self-esteem, lack of interest in schooling, depression and sadness, etc.).

Another frequently reported violence issue in the five Latin American countries is the maltreatment and abuse of children both within and outside the family, which is considered as violence directed towards children. The maltreatment and abuse of children goes beyond the level of corporal punishment and covers child prostitution, sexual abuse, forced drug-trafficking, child kidnapping and murder. An El Salvador study which investigated the causes of maltreatment of children attributes the high frequency of child maltreatment to social conditions (poverty, unemployment, etc.), cultural factors (e.g. parents' belief that children are their property), personal situation (family problems, marital problems, sexual abuse in family, etc.) and legal conditions (lack of legislative and legal measures to protect children).

Guatemala reports very high rates of malnutrition in children, poverty, unemployment and illiteracy and social marginalisation. Frustration is a major problem in this country, originating in unfavourable economic and living conditions. Together with frustration, children frequently experience rigid pedagogical discipline, poor classroom environments and a lack of trained teachers, and Guatemalan schoolchildren manifest various types of violence.

Nicaragua has not yet recovered from its long-lasting wars and armed conflicts. The negative effects of war, inflation, a high rate of unemployment, etc. are affecting children's schooling and lives. Children witness kidnaps, murder, massacre, rape, and are affected both physically and psychologically. The limited educational opportunities, poverty and a high level of unemployment among young people are contributing to the formation of gangs, early drop-out from school, and young people's frequent resort to violence as a means to solve problems.

Peruvian society is, according to Salas (1997), characterised by political violence. Political violence is caused by subversive groups who use arms to control and take over the schools and community in order to indoctrinate their members. As power is a very salient means to establish order and security, children tend to develop a combatant and militant mentality which facilitates the use of violent means to solve various problems.

In summary, the Latin American studies appeal to the need to link the issue of school violence to the economic, cultural and political conditions of the region, in order to fully understand the violence issue there. Street children who become the victims of traffickers are often drug addicts and are exploited and abused. They need to be integrated in order to gain a better education and to become responsible citizens. A concerted effort by the government, schools, the community and the family is required to solve violence problems of children and young people.

Conclusions

In analysing the issue of violence in developing countries, we may draw the following conclusions:

- It seems that, despite a high rate of incidences of violence, major efforts to include explicit violence management policies into the official agenda of education and social policies have yet to be made in developing countries. The establishment of such policies and guidelines can substantially facilitate the implementation of practical work of violence management and prevention at school and community levels.
- Research on bullying and violence is relatively scarce in developing countries, particularly that of a comparative, analytical and quantitative nature. The relative shortage of research information on violence in these countries should not be mistaken for a lack of such problems in these countries. In cases where there is a cross-fire of poverty and

political violence in developing countries, the problem of violence is grave – violence becomes a justifiable means to counter violence, thus creating a vicious circle of violence among young people.

- One cannot expect that a high research priority will be assigned to the issue of violence when the national resources allocated to research are scarce. Under these circumstances, violence research in developing countries must be linked to national development programmes and activities. Rather than pursuing research exclusively dealing with bullying and school violence in developing countries, efforts should be made to integrate this research into priority areas, such as health, food, and technical and vocational training. The Malaysian study (Rahimah and Norani, 1997) points out that in Malaysia, a total of 54 studies was done on discipline, but none categorically examine bullying or incorporate the word 'bullying'. Developing countries generally find research a rather expensive enterprise; if they do decide to conduct it, they prefer to carry out research of a comprehensive and applied nature (or action research), addressed widely to policies, planning and practices. Malawi's case bears witness to this fact – its study attempted to examine bullying and school violence issues within a general framework of school discipline. Research planning and strategies which help to reduce the economic burden of developing countries must be taken fully into consideration.
- Despite the fact that the researchers of the above-mentioned studies were asked to report on both bullying and violence by giving them a general definition of bullying ('brimades' in French and 'intimidacion' in Spanish, for example), they tended not to draw a clear distinction between these two concepts. The term 'bullying' seems to be a less familiar concept than the term 'violence' for researchers in these countries. There is a need for more communication between researchers in industrialised countries and their counterparts in developing countries to discuss and clarify this conceptual issue.
- The studies in developing countries generally insist that violence issues cannot be understood or tackled sufficiently without examining wider socioeconomic, political and cultural contexts and issues, such as civil wars, ethnic violence, poverty, poor health conditions, and under-equipped or congested classes. The issues of violence in schools as reported in Cambodia, Sierra Leone and South Africa are closely interlinked with their post-civil war nation building and human resource developmental tasks. Naturally, the studies in these countries focus more on those socioeconomic factors, rather than on the variables associated with the family, the teacher, peer relations, the personality and attitudes of a student, and the school environment, which are more often the popular targets of investigation by researchers in industrialised countries. It is also fairly clear that violence research in industrialised countries tends to pay more attention to both victims and aggressors, whereas studies in developing

countries seem to be preoccupied by the negative effects or consequences of wars and civil strife, wrong political systems or policies, or poverty and underdevelopment – in other words, their concern is primarily the victimisation of individuals by the system and politics.

- The experiences of some industrialised countries (e.g. Japan, Norway, USA), where a high rate of violence is committed by young people, bear witness to the fact that mere economic affluence of a nation does not guarantee violence-free children and people. Why do wealthy societies as well as poor ones produce violent children? This fact seems to caution us that eradication of poverty is not a sufficient condition for the solution to violence. It seems that the quality of violence management, whether in economically affluent nations or in poor ones, is a key factor. However, if the quality of violence management is guaranteed, countries with more financial and material resources have an advantage over poor ones, as they can offer more options, services and support systems for the development of peace-loving individuals.
- Finally, in order for the researchers of industrialised and developing nations to understand each other better, both groups need to examine a wide spectrum of violence research variables, covering not only methodological and statistical issues but also widely encompassing the historical, cultural and political background variables associated with research on school violence.

Acknowledgements

I wish to thank the International Bureau of Education (IBE, Geneva) and Dr Dan Chimwenje (Director, Malawi Institute for Education) for their co-operation and assistance towards the preparation and finalisation of this chapter.

References

Fraser, W.J., Meier, C., Potter, C.S., Sekgobela, E. and Poore, A. (1996) Reflections on the causes of violence in South African Schools. *Prospects*, XXVI(2), June (Open file: Violence in the school. Guest editor: T. Ohsako).

Guimaraes, E. (1996). The school under siege: The relationship between urban environment and the education system in Rio de Janeiro. *Prospects*, XXVI(2), June (Open file: Violence in the school. Guest editor: T. Ohsako).

Kuthemba Mwale, J.B., Hauya, R. and Tizifa, J. (1996) *Secondary school discipline study*. Centre for Educational Research and Training, University of Malawi.

Mansour, S. (1996) The intifada generation in the schoolroom. *Prospects*, XXVI(2) June (Open file: Violence in the school. Guest editor: T. Ohsako).

Obiedat, Zougan (1996) *Bullying/violence at the school in Jordan*. Geneva: IBE.

Rahimah, Hajii Ahmad and Norani, Mohd. Salleh (1997) *State-of-the-art report on bullying/school violence in Malaysia*. Geneva: IBE.

Salas, L.M. (1997) *State-of-the-art report on violence and aggression in the schools of Colombia, El Salvador, Guatemala, Nicaragua and Peru*. Geneva: IBE.

Sophoan, P. (1997) *Educational destruction and reconstruction in disrupted states: Cambodia*. A commissioned paper by the Graduate Institute of Developmental Studies (University of Geneva) for a workshop, 'Educational Destruction and Reconstruction in Disrupted Societies'. Geneva: IBE.

Terefe, D. and Mengistu, D. (1996) *Violence in schools: a baseline study in and around some Addis Ababa schools*. Geneva: IBE.

Wright, C. (1997) *Educational destruction and reconstruction in disrupted societies: Reflections on the case of Sierra Leone*. A commissioned paper by the Graduate Institute of Developmental Studies (University of Geneva) for a workshop, 'Educational Destruction and Reconstruction in Disrupted Societies'. Geneva: IBE.

Name index

Subject index